D1592675

Memoirs, Official and Personal

MEMOIRS, OFFICIAL AND PERSONAL

Thomas L. McKenney

Introduction by Herman J. Viola

A BISON BOOK

UNIVERSITY OF NEBRASKA PRESS · LINCOLN

Library of Congress Catalog Card Number 72-94789
International Standard Book Number 0-8032-5776-7
Manufactured in the United States of America

First Bison Book printing: December 1973
Most recent printing shown by first digit below:
1 2 3 4 5 6 7 8 9 10

The text of the Bison Book edition is reproduced from Volume I of the second edition of Memoirs, Official and Personal; with sketches of Travels among the Northern and Southern Indians; Embracing a War Excursion and Descriptions of Scenes along the Western Borders *published in 1846 by Paine and Burgess, New York.*

CONTENTS

INTRODUCTION

Thomas Loraine McKenney is one of the most significant yet least known figures in the history of the American Indian. For fourteen years, between 1816 and 1830, he administered the nation's Indian affairs, first as superintendent of Indian trade and then as head of the Office of Indian Affairs. Not only did McKenney pioneer the study of North American ethnology, establishing in his office a remarkable collection of books, manuscripts, artifacts, and paintings, which he called his "archives of the American Indian," he was also the major architect of two government programs that had tremendous impact on the native Americans in this period: reform and removal. Largely through his efforts Congress in 1819 passed the Indian Civilization Act, which provided ten thousand dollars annually for the support of schools in the Indian country, and in 1830 it passed the Indian Removal Act, which provided for the resettlement of eastern tribes west of the Mississippi River. Although one historian has characterized McKenney as a vacillating, self-seeking opportunist who used the Indians as his steppingstones to political prominence, this interpretation is not supported by the evidence. True, some of McKenney's actions, particularly with respect to the Indian removal program, leave him open to criticism, but overall he appears to have been a man of honor and integrity, more idealistic than practical, who did his best to maintain a balance between national desires and national honor by just treatment of the Indians.[1]

Born March 21, 1785, into a staunch Quaker family, McKenney grew to be tall, slender, and rather handsome, with blue eyes, prematurely gray hair, and a sharply hooked nose. His nose and gray hair gave him a striking appearance. The Indians called him White Eagle; and sometimes, because of his strong features and military bearing—he liked to be called Colonel—they confused him with Andrew Jackson. McKenney's friends referred to him as the White Hawk, because he never retreated from a fight.[2]

Little is known of McKenney's private life. At age twenty-one he married Editha Gleaves, "an exemplary and truly estimable lady," by whom he fathered two children: a daughter, Maria, who died in infancy, and a wastrel son, William. In 1809 McKenney moved his family from Maryland's Eastern Shore to Georgetown, then a bustling port city, where he opened a dry goods store. He spent several uneventful years as a storekeeper and then, when the War of 1812 broke out, rallied to the colors. He participated in the Battle of Bladensburg, witnessed the burning of Washington, which, he later wrote, "wrung my soul," and then marched to the defense of Baltimore.[3] After the war he briefly resumed his mercantile career, this time as the partner of Joseph C. Hall,

1. Dorothy Ann Dondore, "Thomas Loraine McKenney," in Allen Johnson and Dumas Malone, eds., *Dictionary of American Biography*, 20 vols. (New York, 1928–36), 12:89. For a comprehensive study of McKenney, see Herman J. Viola, *Thomas L. McKenney* (Chicago, forthcoming).

2. Thomas L. McKenney, *Memoirs, Official and Personal; with Sketches of Travels among the Northern and Southern Indians,* 2 vols. in 1 (New York, 1846), 1:156; J. Hall Bready to John Bell, March 4, 1841, Secretary of War, Letters Received, M-1841, Records of the Office of the Secretary of War, Record Group 107, National Archives (henceforth cited as RG, with the appropriate number, NA).

3. [Thomas L. McKenney], *A Narrative of the Battle of Bladensburg in a Letter*

who owned a store on Pennsylvania Avenue. The partnership's only redeeming feature appears to have been that through it McKenney befriended President James Madison, who on April 2, 1816, offered him the recently vacated position of superintendent of Indian trade. Although McKenney later admitted having had no knowledge of the details of the position beforehand, he accepted the appointment "with great pleasure."[4]

Perhaps McKenney should not have been so eager, for the factory system, as the network of government-owned trading houses for the Indians was known, was in a state of decline.[5] Established by Congress in 1795, the factories were to provide the Indians with quality merchandise in a fair exchange for their furs. No profit was anticipated except a sum sufficient to maintain the system's $300,000 trade fund. In spite of its humanitarian overtones, the primary purpose of the factories was to wean the Indians away from foreign influence. The War of 1812, however, besides virtually ending the Indian menace to national security, almost ended the system as well. Of the ten factories in operation when hostilities began, the British and their Indian allies forced the abandonment of two, destroyed three, and caused an estimated $43,369.61 worth of damage. The bankrupt condition of the factory system, coupled with renewed American interest in the fur trade following the war, led to public clamor against government participation in the

to Henry Banning, Esq., by an Officer of Gen. Smith's Staff (n.p., 1814), pp. 9, 14.

4. William H. Crawford to Thomas L. McKenney, April 2, 1816, Secretary of War, Letters Sent, RG 107, NA; McKenney to Crawford, April 12, 1816, Secretary of War, Letters Received, ibid.

5. Published material on the factory system is sparse. Most satisfactory is chapter 4, "The Factory System," in Edgar Bruce Wesley, *Guarding the Frontier: A Study in Frontier Defense from 1815 to 1825* (Minneapolis, 1935). Ora Brooks Peake, *A History of the United States Indian Factory System, 1795–1822* (Denver, 1954) is the only published full-length treatment of the subject, but it is an extremely unreliable account.

realm of private enterprise. Then, in 1819, a devastating depression hit the country, making Congress extremely economy conscious. Especially vulnerable was the factory system, which not only was failing to maintain its capital endowment but was going deeper into debt each passing year.[6]

McKenney, however, came to view the factories as more than tools to win Indian loyalty; he viewed them as a means to introduce the tribes to civilization. Thus, in the face of rising opposition, he worked not only to save the factories but also to expand the system. He wanted Congress to raise the trade fund to $500,000. With the increased appropriation he planned to increase the number of factories from eight to sixteen; he wanted to open a second Office of Indian Trade in St. Louis, correctly believing his Georgetown office too remote for effective supervision of the distant factories he planned to establish; and he wished to purchase a steamboat to reduce the system's transportation costs. At the same time he attacked the private fur interests, led by John Jacob Astor's powerful American Fur Company, who were lobbying so effectively for abolition of the factory system. McKenney wanted, ideally, a monopoly of the fur trade for the factories. He would have been satisfied with stricter licensing laws which could screen undesirable fur traders from the business; he wanted effective legislation against the use of whiskey in the fur trade, a commodity he prohibited his factors from using but which was a basic tool of the private traders; and, above all, he wanted Congress to require private traders to operate from fixed locations like the factors, instead of allowing them to roam at will through the Indian country. Congress ignored his wishes. Instead, on May 6, 1822, it abolished the factory system; McKenney's career as superintendent

6. Wesley, *Guarding the Frontier,* pp. 33–34, 44, 52.

of Indian trade was terminated a month later.[7]

No matter. McKenney had already charted his "future course." He was not out of office a week before he was circulating the prospectus of the *Washington Republican and Congressional Examiner,* a semiweekly newspaper he founded to support John C. Calhoun's bid for the 1824 presidential nomination. Although the secretary of war insisted that "my name must not be used in connection with the paper," Calhoun was instrumental in starting it, had a hand in drafting the prospectus and soliciting subscribers, and furnished McKenney with "reflections" which the editor was to bring out in his own words.[8]

The *Washington Republican* had a short and turbulent history. It lost money and did little for either Calhoun's image or candidacy. McKenney, however, found the newspaper very useful. He had left office under fire, and the controversy over his handling of the trade continued long after the system's official end. What caused the most concern was the system's heavy financial loss. By May 25, 1824, two years after the close of the factories, the government had recovered only $38,178 of the $300,000 invested in the system.[9] At best only half the capital investment was ever recovered. That any money could have been lost in the fur trade seemed

7. McKenney to John C. Calhoun, August 19, 1818, Office of Indian Trade, Letters Sent, vol. E, pp. 141–43, Records of the Bureau of Indian Affairs, RG 75, NA; *U.S. Statutes at Large,* 3:683.

8. McKenney to Lewis Cass, June 14, 1822, Michigan Superintendency, Letters Received, RG 75, NA; the prospectus is reprinted in the first issue of the paper (*Washington Republican and Congressional Examiner,* August 7, 1822). For Calhoun's help with the newspaper, see William M. Meigs, *Life of John Caldwell Calhoun,* 2 vols. (New York, 1917), 1:294; see also D. L. Corbitt, "John C. Calhoun and the Presidential Campaign of 1824," *North Carolina Historical Review* 12 (January 1935):29n.

9. *American State Papers: Indian Affairs,* 2 vols. (Washington, D.C., 1832–34), 2:513.

inconceivable at a time when private fur companies were reaping large profits. To many in Congress and others around the country, the explanation seemed obvious: the superintendent and his factors had enriched themselves at public expense. This suspicion was so rife that Congress had not even allowed McKenney and his factors to liquidate the factory operations, appointing in their places "active, intelligent gentlemen of unexceptionable character, and suitable qualifications, for that purpose."[10] It was anticipated that these men would uncover evidence of fraud, graft, and theft which McKenney and his factors would otherwise have been able to conceal.

Criticism of McKenney eventually reached such proportions that the House Committee on Indian Affairs in February, 1823, launched a two-week investigation into his administration of the factory system. The committee examined the account books and other records of the Office of Indian Trade; it questioned fur traders, Indian agents, and other authorities on the fur trade; and it interrogated McKenney. The results, announced March 1, completely cleared the ex-superintendent. The investigators concluded that "the conductors of the Indian trade, were generally men of integrity and honor; not deficient in talent or enterprise, or any of the requisite qualifications for discharging the duties of their respective stations. And how it does happen, [that] the government should not now be able to realize a sum equal to the original stock, appears to be inexplicable."[11]

Meanwhile, the *Washington Republican* was serving McKenney to good advantage. He used the newspaper to refute all insinuations, accusations, and charges against his handling of the Indian trade; he printed copious extracts from letters, reports, and official documents to show that he was the victim of circumstances and had

10. *House Doc.*, 17 cong., 2 sess., no. 104 (serial 82), p. 1.

11. Ibid., p. 3.

been neither negligent nor dishonest; and he published the texts of congressional debates on the factory system as well as the testimony and findings of the investigation.[12] Perhaps, then, it is more than coincidence that he resigned as editor on May 31, 1823, only three months after the investigation ended.

McKenney did not remain unemployed for long. Calhoun rewarded his able lieutenant by placing him in charge of the Office of Indian Affairs, a bureau the secretary of war established without legislative sanction in March, 1824. Despite the obvious favoritism, McKenney was a good choice and he served capably until the autumn of 1830, when he was dismissed from the public service during President Andrew Jackson's general house cleaning.

In taking the new post, McKenney accepted a responsibility of major proportions. He handled annually up to one million dollars in appropriated funds; he supervised the activities of twenty Indian agents, twenty-seven subagents, three territorial governors who served ex officio as superintendents of Indian affairs, another superintendent at St. Louis, plus additional personnel who brought the total number to nearly one hundred people; and he watched over an expanding school system in the Indian country with a working capital of over one hundred thousand dollars, mostly from private sources.[13]

Nevertheless, in the space of six years, he turned the amorphous Indian section of the War Department into a cohesive, centralized unit, an accomplishment that was preserved by two major pieces of legislation. The act of July 9, 1832, gave the president power to appoint a

12. See, for example, *Washington Republican and Congressional Examiner,* September 7, 18, and 28, 1822; November 16, 1822; March 22, 1823.

13. For a full discussion of McKenney's years as superintendent of Indian affairs, see Herman J. Viola, "Thomas L. McKenney and the Administration of Indian Affairs, 1824-30" (Ph.D. diss., Indiana University, 1970).

"Commissioner of Indian Affairs, who shall . . . have the direction and management of all Indian affairs, and all matters arising out of Indian relations, and shall have a salary of three thousand dollars per annum." The act of June 30, 1834, recognized McKenney's organizational achievements by providing the legal foundation for a fully integrated agency system.[14]

Even in his new position, however, controversy surrounded McKenney. In 1826 he and Governor Lewis Cass of Michigan Territory journeyed to Fond du Lac, at the western tip of Lake Superior, where they negotiated a treaty with the Chippewa Indians. The following year the two commissioners went to Green Bay, in present-day Wisconsin, where they negotiated a treaty with the Menominee Indians. From Green Bay McKenney returned to Washington by way of the Chickasaw, Choctaw, and Creek Indian agencies, where he met with leaders of the southern tribes to persuade them to at least visit the area across the Mississippi proposed for their future home. But McKenney had scarcely returned from his second trip when Jacksonians in Congress accused him of having engaged in political activities during his travels. They charged McKenney specifically with having distributed "coffin" handbills and other anti-Jackson campaign literature.[15]

McKenney managed to weather that crisis, only to become involved in one more serious. This time it was a minor scandal that implicated Sam Houston and Secretary of War John H. Eaton, both very close friends of President Jackson. As part of the removal program, it was anticipated that the government would let a contract

14. *U. S. Statutes at Large,* 4:564, 735–38.

15. See, for instance, the "Address of Thomas R. Moore to His Constituents," June 27, 1828, printed in the *Louisville Public Advertiser,* July 19, 1828; McKenney responded to his critics in a letter to "a Friend," May 15, 1828, which appeared in various local newspapers, including the *Alexandria Gazette,* May 22, 1828, and the *Washington National Intelligencer,* May 31, 1828.

for feeding the eighty thousand or so Indians that would be moved across the Mississippi River. The Indians were to be fed not only enroute but also for their first year in the West, which meant the contract would be worth millions. McKenney claims Houston offered him a bribe to ensure he got the rations contract. When McKenney refused to cooperate, Houston threatened him with dismissal from office. Since his dismissal came only six months later, McKenney held Houston responsible. McKenney claimed that by blocking Houston's efforts to obtain the contract, "I was *marked* as one of Gl Jackson's '*enemies.*' His motto was—'I reward my friends, and *punish* my enemies.' *His* enemies were all those who dared to have any conscience, or will, that did not square with his own. . . . I know of no case of conflict between us, except this ration case, and no cause for my removal, if it be not that."[16]

McKenney left office a bitter and impoverished man. The following spring he opened an Indian Emporium in New York City for the sale of goods used in the fur trade, but the venture was unsuccessful. The remainder of the decade he devoted to writing and politics. With Judge James Hall of Cincinnati, Ohio, he published between 1836 and 1844 the monumental *History of the Indian Tribes of North America.* Any profits the authors anticipated, however, were erased by the Panic of 1837, which left few who could muster the $120 purchase price for the three-volume work. McKenney's political activities were equally fruitless.[17] In 1836 and again four years

16. "Rations to Emigrating Indians," July 5, 1832, *House Doc.,* 22 cong., 1 sess., no. 502 (serial 228), p. 1; much of the information in the House report appears in McKenney's *Memoirs,* 1:206–22. McKenney to Walter Forward, November 3, 1841, Simon Gratz Collection, Historical Society of Pennsylvania, Philadelphia.

17. McKenney in March, 1831, sent out a circular announcing his "New York Indian Emporium"; a copy is in the Papers of Henry Rowe Schoolcraft, Manuscript Division, Library of Congress, Washington, D.C. McKenney to Forward, November 3, 1841, Gratz Collection.

later, he worked zealously for the Whig party in its efforts to unseat the Democrats; at his own expense he stumped the states of Delaware, New Jersey, and Pennsylvania, and when William Henry Harrison swept to victory in 1840, McKenney wanted and expected only one reward—his return to the Indian Office. But he did not get the appointment. He said Harrison promised it to him but died before he could make it official. His claim, however, is refuted by a presidential aide who, shortly after the inauguration, confided: "McKenney *won't* do for anything but a subordinate station with limited definite powers." An attempt to get President John Tyler to appoint McKenney to the Indian Office also proved futile.[18]

McKenney was stunned. For ten years he had hungered for the defeat of the Jacksonians and restoration to the office he created. Now it was denied him. Scandalmongers, he rationalized, must have resurrected the lies about his mismanagement of Indian affairs. "Some insidious enemy started the insinuation that I had made improper use of the public money, and had left the [Indian] Department *rich.* And anon, another no less designing whisperer, charged me with being *embarrassed in my pecuniary affairs, therefore, not to be trusted,*" he confided to Walter Forward, congressman from New York. The colonel was convinced that he had been the victim of a smear campaign and reacted in typical fashion—he attacked. "I must reverse the order of *defences,* & bring forth *the charges,*" he explained to Forward. "I fear *no* enquiry. I challenge it. But I do fear the secret, designing, wily enemy."[19]

18. Charles MacAlester to Charles S. Todd, March 19, 1841, William Henry Harrison Papers, Box 1805-41, Benjamin Harrison Collection, Manuscript Division, Library of Congress; Barbour to John Tyler, April 6, 1841, Secretary of War, Letters Received, RG 107, NA.

19. McKenney to Forward, November 3, 1841, Gratz Collection.

McKenney sent a thirteen-page letter to cabinet officers, members of Congress, and friends. "I mean that you shall know me," he affirmed, launching into a personal and poignant description of his early life and years in public office. While superintendent of Indian trade, he swore, "I never employed, or derived a dollar's benefit—*not a cent*—more, or less, directly, or indirectly, in the passage through my hands of the millions that did pass, tho' I might not only have relieved my embarrassments, brought on me, by my friends. . . . but enriched myself, without the loss of a dollar to the Government." He had accepted Calhoun's call to organize the Bureau of Indian Affairs "*upon the express condition* that I should receive the pay of an Auditor—viz: 3,000$," which he had never received. "The omission . . . *embarrassed me. I feel it to this hour.*" To compound the injustices against him, he was thrown out of office for thwarting Houston's illegal attempt to get the rations contract. "I had, like Bellisarious, faithfully given my time to the public service, and like him was rewarded by having my eyes torn out."

Since then, McKenney continued, "I never . . . relaxed my efforts, thro' the presses of the Country, as a volunteer, to break down a party that had broken down the Country. Success, at last, crowned our cause." With Harrison's triumph there had been an outcry of public opinion "calling for my restoration to the head of the Indian Department," he claimed. "I have yet to see the first man who did not expect my instant recall—and I have seen thousands, and from every State, & Territory of the Union. The Indians rejoiced in the prospect of once more having me to preside over their affairs." But all this fell like water upon the sand because he was poor. "My pecuniary circumstances are such as to make the income of the Indian Commissioners pay, desireable," he admitted, "but I can, with God's blessing live with[out] it."

One of the autobiographical letters went to the secretary of war. "Rumor has for some time past been sending in the direction of my ears, charges implicating my official integrity," McKenney explained in his covering note. "Feeling the sting of these flying rumors, as any sensitive soul would, I determined to address [this] letter . . . . You will, I am sure, appreciate my motive. It is vindicatory, wholly—and the poorest of the free, are respected in the exercise of this privilege."[20] Whatever McKenney's motive, it did not work and he remained unemployed.

Having failed in business, writing, and politics, McKenney next tried public speaking, and for the next several years he lectured on Indian affairs in various cities and towns along the eastern seaboard from Maine to Maryland. His purpose, he claimed, was "to awaken in the public mind an interest in behalf of the Indian race, and their destiny; to give impetus to public opinion in regard to what ought to be done, and done speedily, for their welfare; and when that opinion should be fully formed, bring it to bear on Congress, in connection with a plan for the preservation and well-being of the remnants of this hapless people."[21]

McKenney's lecture series consisted of two discourses he normally delivered on consecutive evenings. The first lecture, in which he relied heavily on the published works of Antoine Du Pratz, John Ledyard, and others for much of his material, traced the origins and early history of the American Indians.[22] They were descendants, McKenney believed, of Tartars who migrated across the Bering Strait. "In what numbers they came, or how long they continued to cross over, we know nothing." As the Tar-

20. McKenney to John C. Spencer, November 3, 1841, ibid.

21. McKenney, *Memoirs,* 2:v.

22. The discourses form volume 2 of McKenney's *Memoirs.* The following quotations are from that volume.

tars spread across this continent they met a superior civilization, either Mexican or Peruvian, which they overwhelmed and destroyed. All that remains to prove its existence are the mounds that dot the North American landscape. "Few things are more certain," McKenney insisted, "than that this country was inhabited by a race, prior to the coming into it of those from whom the present race of Indians are descended . . . and that *that* race was advanced in civilization and the arts, *especially in the art of fortification*." The Tartars could not have built the mounds—"the result of skill so consummate and labor so immense"—because present-day Indians had no oral tradition of their having done so and because "their intellectual acquirements were as low as they are recorded to have been among any people on the face of the earth. They had no letters, and no learning." Even as late as the discovery of America, McKenney continued, "I presume there was scarcely an Indian on the continent, who could comprehend an abstract idea; and at this day, the process is neither common nor easy."

In his second discourse McKenney waxed eloquent about the unhappy history of relations between Indians and white men. He highlighted his story with personal experiences; he punctuated it with melodrama and rhetoric. "Was it the purpose of the merciful God to introduce one race of men upon this continent, though they were destined to make the wilderness blossom as the rose, and to ornament it with all that was refined in the civilized, and adorn it with all that is captivating in the Christian state, at the mighty cost of annihilation of another?" he asked. "NEVER! NEVER!" Americans had a Christian obligation to preserve and reform the Indian. "Physically, intellectually, and morally, he is, in all respects, like ourselves; and there is no difference between us, save only in the color, and in our superior advantages." Others had tried to help the Indians, but their plans were incomplete and ill conceived. No one, moreover, had tried to reform and civilize them as a race.

McKenney proposed to change all this. Why not establish an Indian Territory, "giving to the Indians the same fee-simple title to the soil, and the same privileges . . . that are enjoyed by the citizens of Iowa, and that were possessed by the citizens of Michigan and other Territories, when occupying a territorial relation to the Union?" The removal program in effect had already created such a territory. More than one hundred thousand Indians now occupied a strategic block of land west of the states of Missouri and Arkansas. Perhaps it seemed unwise, in retrospect, to have congregated so many Indians in such a small area. Should they organize, "a war more costly, and more bloody, will ensue, than any that has ever yet been inflicted upon this country. Philip, and Pontiac, and Tecumthé, and Osceola, have read us lessons on the capacity of Indians to revenge themselves; but never in all their history did they occupy a position so formidable as that which is now held by their successors." This misfortune would never occur if the Indians were made citizens of the United States. Moreover, "a new and hitherto unfelt impulse would be at once given to all the higher and nobler elements of their nature," McKenney promised, "which could not fail of raising them in a very short time, *as a race,* upon the same platform with ourselves. Our destiny, in a word, would be their destiny."

The plan was not new. When in office McKenney had viewed it as a second phase of the Indian removal program; and, in fact, a bill calling for the establishment of "the Western Territory" was introduced in the House in 1834 but met severe opposition and was not acted upon.[23] Its failure also meant the failure of the

23. Francis Paul Prucha, *American Indian Policy in the Formative Years: The Indian Trade and Intercourse Acts, 1790–1834* (Cambridge, 1962), pp. 272–73.

humanitarian philosophy behind removal. McKenney knew this, but the idea was good and he continued to advocate it. Perhaps he hoped a sympathetic administration would return him to office to implement the program.

In 1844 McKenney temporarily quit the lecture circuit to write his memoirs. He sequestered himself on the Maine coast near Cape Cottage and by early February, 1845, had completed a rough draft, which he sent for criticism to Jared Sparks, editor of the *North American Review* and an old friend. "I send the confused mass—confused in the order of arrangement, & in its execution," McKenney wrote February 27. "I know it is a tax; but you have a heart that knows how to excuse each trespass. Deal freely—& frankly with every thing. Tell me like a Brother what to lop off, & what to add. As soon as your convenience will admit, please return all, with notes & suggestions &c on bits of paper in pencil. That you have *amended*—or in any way *endorsed* the thing, shall remain between us," he promised.[24]

After a week McKenney asked about the manuscript. "Do not suppose this little message is designed to prompt you," he lied. "It is intended, only, to say, that as I *design* leaving Boston tomorrow, it would be gratifying to be able to take my *bantlings* home with me; but if your time has been so occupied, as to prevent your inspection of the (*very sad* I fear) condition of the papers, why then only hold on." Sparks could leave the edited manuscript with the proprietor of the Fremont House, who would gladly forward it. "I know & feel, the tax levied upon you by me, is a heavy one."[25]

Sparks returned the manuscript in early summer and by autumn McKenney had struck a bargain with Paine

24. McKenney to Jared Sparks, February 27, 1845, Papers of Jared Sparks, Houghton Library, Harvard University, Cambridge, Mass.

25. McKenney to Sparks, March 5, 1845, ibid.

and Burgess of New York City for its publication. "I am here, & shall be here, in re-adjusting (till I finish it) the work, upon the basis you recommend," he wrote when thanking Sparks for his "practical, & Judicious" suggestions. "I shall follow you out, in all the particulars—approving, as I do, the whole of them. What is loose, or careless, or written in haste, I will try and correct, & amend. When the work is finished, I will have the pleasure of sending you a copy."[26]

The memoirs, which appeared in late summer, 1846, are actually two separate volumes bound together. Volume one, entitled *Memoirs, Official and Personal; with Sketches of Travels among the Northern and Southern Indians; Embracing a War Excursion, and Description of Scenes along the Western Borders,* is more official than personal, and at first glance it is disappointing, for McKenney made no mention of his family, private life, or activities following his dismissal from office. Roughly half of the 284 pages he devoted to his tour of 1827, drawing on notes he took during his travels among the northern and southern tribes. McKenney originally had hoped to use the material in a companion volume to *Sketches of a Tour to the Lakes, of the Character and Customs of the Chippeway Indians; and of Incidents Connected with the Treaty of Fond du Lac,* which he published in 1827, following his first trip into the Indian country.[27] *Sketches* enjoyed only limited success, however, so McKenney never completed his publication plans. The rest of volume one, except for anecdotes and asides, such as his description of the Battle of Bladensburg and the attack on Washington during the War of 1812, is a defense of his public career in which McKenney repeats the grievances and injustices he outlined in his autobiographical letter of 1841. Much

26. McKenney to Sparks, November 3, 1845, ibid.

27. Herman J. Viola, introduction, *Sketches of a Tour to the Lakes,* by Thomas L. McKenney (Barre, Mass., 1972).

of this text comes from letters, reports, and other official records of the Office of Indian Trade and Bureau of Indian Affairs, which McKenney altered slightly to fit his narrative. A fifty-five-page appendix consists entirely of documents that support statements in the text.

The second volume is far less important than the first and was not included in this new edition. Entitled *On the Origin, History, Character, and the Wrongs and Rights of the Indians, with a Plan for the Preservation and Happiness of the Remnants of That Persecuted Race,* it is little more than an expansion of his discourses, which, McKenney admits in the preface, he based heavily on published works. "It not having been in my view, at the time of preparing these Discourses, to publish them, I was not particular in making, always, quotation marks, or marks of reference to authors whom I consulted; and it sometimes happened, when their language was better than mine, I employed it." McKenney had no reason to be sensitive on this point, he believed, because other writers had taken similar liberties with his own published material.

Although written some twenty years after the events discussed, the memoirs are surprisingly accurate. Often it is possible to compare printed letters or documents with the originals; except for minor differences, they are identical. Not everything, of course, can be taken as gospel. As John Quincy Adams once remarked, McKenney tended "to magnify his office." The likable colonel may have rubbed elbows with the Washington elite but it is unlikely he moved in their inner circles as he would like his readers to think. McKenney also colored his role in controversial issues. He may not have carried anti-Jackson literature on his 1827 tour but he admitted doing so on his trip to Fond du Lac the year before. As he confidentially informed Cass at the time, "I shall have some materials, I hope, that the public would not refuse to *con,* & especially as I mean not to frighten it with the *bulk,* but only invite it by the nature of the subjects, & the manner of managing them."[28]

Whatever its weaknesses, however, the *Memoirs* provide valuable insights into the workings of federal Indian policy in the first quarter of the nineteenth century. Jared Sparks, who reviewed the work in the October, 1846, issue of the *North American Review,* went even further. "It is the tribute," he wrote, "of a sincere philanthropist to a cause which he has given not fair words alone, but the substantial efforts and costly sacrifice of many years."[29]

Not everyone, even then, concurred in Sparks's kind assessment of the work. Publication of the *Memoirs* sparked a brisk and angry pamphlet war between McKenney and Kosciuszko Armstrong, son of General James Armstrong who was secretary of war when the British burned Washington. According to McKenney, the attack succeeded because of Armstrong's inadequate preparations. McKenney never considered the secretary of war a traitor, although others at the time thought so. His mistake had been the lack of foresight to realize the nation's capital might be a target of the invaders. The popular outcry following the assault forced Armstrong's resignation and led to the appointment of James Monroe in his place.

Kosciuszko Armstrong replied in a twenty-page *Review of T. L. McKenney's Narrative of the Causes Which, in 1814, led to General Armstrong's Resignation of the War Office.* "Imagination and memory are so blended in our author," the son charged, "that it is impossible to say where the operations of the one cease, or of the other begin." The pamphleteer, who claimed to be writing a

28. McKenney to Cass, February 10, 1826, Michigan Superintendency, Letters Received, RG 75, NA.

29. *North American Review* 63 (October 1846): 481.

biography of his father, accused McKenney of having been part of a conspiracy to get Monroe appointed secretary of war. Armstrong admitted he could present no evidence "*directly*" contradicting McKenney's tales, since all the principals but the author were dead. Nevertheless, he proposed "to furnish a chain of evidence sufficiently strong to support the inference, that the witness has misrepresented what passed, and that the opinions which he assumes to have heard, are such as could not have been expressed," especially the inference that General Armstrong had been a traitor. "Treason! why, the foul suspicion was never breathed in any circle of honest men; and the admission that . . . [McKenney] heard it, is a damning proof of the filthiness of his associations at that period."[30]

McKenney, ready as usual to enter a controversy, responded immediately. A card entitled *An Opening Reply to Kosciusko Armstrong's Pamphlet* and dated December 18, 1846, asked readers to withhold judgment until McKenney could "communicate with witnesses at Washington, and elsewhere, by whom I promise to prove my narrative *true*." His *Reply to Kosciusko Armstrong's Assault upon Col. McKenney's Narrative of the Causes That Led to General Armstrong's Resignation of the Office of Secretary of War in 1814* appeared the following February. The twenty-eight-page pamphlet vindicated McKenney, who had found five witnesses to verify the accuracy of his statements. "How far my 'narrative' can be, with justice, tortured into an 'attack' upon General Armstrong, is referred . . . to the decision of the public."[31]

Armstrong remained unconvinced. A month later he

30. Kosciuszko Armstrong, *Review of T. L. McKenney's Narrative of the Causes Which, in 1814, Led to General Armstrong's Resignation of the War Office* (New York, 1846), pp. 9, 6, 19.

31. Thomas L. McKenney, *Reply to Kosciusko Armstrong's Assault upon Col. McKenney's Narrative . . .* (New York, 1847), p. 4.

published an *Examination of Thomas L. McKenney's Reply to the Review of His Narrative, &c.,* the final shot in the exchange. Armstrong congratulated the ex-superintendent of Indian affairs "on having at last discovered the propriety of supporting his statement of facts, by evidence, derived from other and more respectable sources" but refused to change his opinion of McKenney or his book.[32] The twenty-page pamphlet, although sprinkled with extracts from letters evidently gathered for the biography that never appeared, did little to damage McKenney's reputation or to change the verdict of history on the incompetence of General Armstrong. In fact, the exchange seems to have served only one useful purpose. It prompted Paine and Burgess to print a second edition of McKenney's *Memoirs.*

Actually, Armstrong's charges angered McKenney more than his rather mild reply would indicate. "I do not know whether you saw Kos. Armstrong's pamphlet," he wrote Sparks in March, 1847, "but if you did, you saw the most malignant work that has issued from the press for a long time—the coarsest, & most personally abusive. I believe I am the only writer that ever ventured to screen his Father from the effect of the imputations that were so universally cast upon him—and for which the son undertook to denounce &, I may say, blackguard me." In return, McKenney continued, "I treated him mildly—but saught to take myself, & my book out of the categories in which he saught to involve both: That is I saught to prove my narrative, *true.*" Although McKenney had not yet seen the second pamphlet, he was not worried. A mutual acquaintance thought it was only for circulation among Armstrong's friends "—to break the force of his fall, with them." McKenney was not so sanguine about his *Memoirs,* however. "It has been *profitless*

32. Kosciuszko Armstrong, *Examination of Thomas L. McKenney's Reply to the Review of His Narrative, &c.* (New York, 1847), p. 3.

so far," he complained.[33]

Profit may not have been McKenney's only concern. Convinced that lies and lack of knowledge about his accomplishments had kept him from office in 1841, he probably hoped the *Memoirs* would refurbish his public image, silence his critics, and pave the way for a restoration to office. If this was his intent, it failed. In 1848 Zachary Taylor, another Whig, was elected to the presidency. Despite the *Memoirs* and a renewed attempt to arouse public support in his behalf, McKenney failed to receive an appointment.[34]

Following the latest in what had become an endless series of disappointments, McKenney faded into obscurity. Death found him at age seventy-three in a Brooklyn boarding house on February 20, 1859. Although his passing received little notice, McKenney years earlier had provided his own epitaph. "The Office I was sent from is my monument—its records, its inscriptions, I stand or fall by them." It is a monument that has endured to this day.[35]

HERMAN J. VIOLA

National Anthropological Archives
Smithsonian Institution

33. McKenney to Sparks, March 9, 1847, Sparks Papers.

34. McKenney to Bishop Whittingham, May 7, 1849, Duke University Library, Durham, N.C.

35. Certificate of death, Municipal Archives and Records Center, New York, N.Y.; McKenney to John McLean, January 29, 1831, Papers of John McLean, Manuscript Division, Library of Congress.

Preface to Volume I

PREFACE TO VOL. I.

No traveller expects, when he sets out upon a journey, to meet only with smooth roads, cultivated fields, lovely gardens, wide-spread and magnificent scenery, a clear sky, and, at every stopping-place, inns filled with comforts, but goes forth prepared to have all these diversified with rugged roads, desolate fields, weedy and odorless gardens, lowering skies, and the inconveniences and discomforts of road-side accommodations. I cannot promise in my book more than is contained in the combined volumes of art and nature.

Should any one, on opening this volume with the intention of reading it, expect to find *everything* in it captivating, or even agreeable, he will find himself mistaken. A good deal of the contents will, I fear, prove to the general reader wholly uninteresting; but this portion of the work may not be so regarded, by kind, and generous, and sympathizing friends. I have reference to those parts that are wholly personal to myself. I would gladly omit them, if, with justice to myself, or to those who cherish an interest in my reputation and destiny, as also to those who bear my name, and who are connected with me by the ties of consanguinity, I could do so.

Apart from these personal references, may I not hope that the reader will be repaid for the time spent in following me? And especially do I trust, that much may be found to interest, when, having got fairly in among the scenes of nature—vast—wild—boundless—I shall attempt a reflex of them; and when the incidents and events, which, in my journeyings, I have witnessed, are attempted to be portrayed, in which the RED MAN of the forest is the chief actor, and wherein will be seen his habits, his principles, his occupations, and whatever attaches to him in his wilderness home.

But, even at the hazard of offending some—and really I shall not write a word with any such intention—I have concluded to cast these MEMOIRS upon the patronage, and kind indulgence of an enlightened and liberal public.

T. L. M'K.

Cape Cottage, February, 1845.

Dedication of Volume I

DEDICATION OF VOL. I.

To Mrs. James Madison.

Madam—There is such a thing as the memory of the heart. It is kept fresh and odorous by being cherished. Mine for your illustrious husband can never die. I delight in the contemplation of his purity—his patriotism—his statesmanship—and in his polished and beautiful writings. All these, and more, adorn his name, like gems, which time, instead of dimming, is every day making brighter and more glorious.

My first call to the performance of civil duties, in connection with the government, and to the discharge of a highly responsible trust, was from James Madison. I am proud of the honour of the confidence of such a man, and shall cherish, to my last hour, a grateful sense of it.

Your fame, madam, is so delicately and beautifully mingled with his, as to become identified with it. Such a blending I have never witnessed, in anything, except in the rainbow. In ease, and in dignity, in purity and patriotism, in the admiration and affection of millions, in the glory shed upon the highest place in the republic—all these, in the view of your countrymen, you shared, and continue to share, with him. If his is the column that sustains the capitol, yours, madam, is the cap that ornaments it.

Entertaining such views, and cherishing such feelings, how could I do else than ask the privilege, and covet the honor, of dedicating these memoirs to you? The offering I know is a poor one: I wish it were more worthy of your acceptance; but it is an offering of the heart, and your permission, so kindly granted, to dedicate them to you, forms another link of friendship in the chain that binds me to you, and to the memory of JAMES MADISON.

THOMAS L. M'KENNEY.

Cape Cottage, February, 1845.

CONTENTS OF VOL. I.

CHAPTER I.

PUBLIC OFFICE—ITS DUTIES, DIFFICULTIES AND DANGERS.

CHAPTER II.

IMPROVEMENT, MORAL AND INTELLECTUAL, OF THE INDIANS. PRESIDENT MONROE. ANECDOTES ILLUSTRATING HIS CHARACTER.

CHAPTER III.

THE BUREAU OF INDIAN AFFAIRS. COMMISSIONS TO TREAT WITH THE INDIANS. VOYAGE ON THE LAKES. GREEN BAY. BUTTE DE MORTS.

CHAPTER IV.

INCIDENTS OF THE COUNCIL AT LE PETIT BUTTE DE MORTS.

CHAPTER V.

EXPEDITION AGAINST THE WINNEBAGOES. SURRENDER, RECEPTION, AND APPEARANCE OF "RED-BIRD."

CHAPTER VI.

PASSAGE DOWN THE OUISCONSIN AND MISSISSIPPI RIVERS.

CHAPTER VII.

SOJOURN AT ST. LOUIS. PASSAGE DOWN THE MISSISSIPPI. HARD JOURNEY FROM MEMPHIS TO CHICKASAW BLUFFS.

CHAPTER VIII.

INCIDENTS OF TRAVEL FROM THE CHICKASAW BLUFFS, THROUGH THE CHOCTAW COUNTRY TO TUSCALOOSA—THENCE, THROUGH THE CREEK COUNTRY, HOME.

CHAPTER IX.

RETURN TO WASHINGTON. CHANGE OF ADMINISTRATION. POLITICAL EXCITEMENT. CORRUPTION AND FAVORITISM IN HIGH PLACES.

CHAPTER X.

PLANS FOR IMPROVING THE CONDITION OF THE INDIANS. HINDRANCES IN THE WAY OF THEIR EXECUTION.

CHAPTER XI.

ABOMINABLE ABUSE OF POWER IN OUR RELATIONS WITH THE INDIANS.

Memoirs, Official and Personal

MEMOIRS.

CHAPTER I.

PUBLIC OFFICE—ITS DUTIES, DIFFICULTIES AND DANGERS.

First appointment to office—System of government trade with the Indians—Trading companies and individuals—Contrast between the two systems—American Fur Company—John Jacob Astor—Missouri Fur Company—Difficulty of supplying the factories during the war—Unsuitable stock on hand at its close—Loss in disposing of it—Satisfaction of the Indians on receiving the new supplies—Clerks in the office—Miles, the trusty messenger—Inestimable value of competent and faithful clerks—Folly and wickedness of proscription—Transfer of the property of the Indian trade establishment—Increase of the capital—Assailed by Mr. Benton—The reply—Mr. Monroe's opinion—Payment of Indian annuities—Caution in keeping the accounts—Charged with defalcation—Mysterious disappearance of vouchers—Duplicates produced—Accounts settled—Charges of defalcation reiterated—Rules adopted in purchasing articles for the Indians—Anonymous charges of favoritism—Discomforts of office—Accounts kept open.

I OWE my first connection with our Indian relations, and the first civil trust conferred upon me, to the confidence of PRESIDENT MADISON, who, unsolicited by myself, and, so far as I know, by any one for me, honored me, on the 2d April, 1816, with the commission of "Superintendent of the United States Indian Trade with the Indian Tribes." I had been informed, a few days previous, of the intention of President Madison to call me to the discharge of the duties of this office, but had never spoken to him on the subject, nor he to me. My commission* was brought to me by Hon. William Jones, Secretary of the Navy.

The plan of a United States government trade with the Indians dates as far back as the year 1796. The system was one of pure humanity, embracing a supply of the wants of the Indians without reference to profit; and receiving, in exchange from them, their furs and peltries, at fair prices; the law governing this trade contemplating nothing more than the preservation of the capital employed in it. The convenience of the Indians was consulted in the establishment of factories along the border, and at such distances from each other, as to approximate upon the one hand, as near to the hunting grounds of the Indians as was convenient; upon the other, with the readiest access to them by water, or otherwise, for the transportation of the annual supplies. Suitable and competent persons, as factors, clerks, and interpreters, were appointed to carry on this trade.

There were in operation, at the same time, two other systems of trade with this people. One of these was conducted by individuals, the other by companies. The contrast between these and the government trade, will not

---

* (COPY.)

THE PRESIDENT OF THE UNITED STATES OF AMERICA—

To all who shall see these presents, Greeting:

KNOW YE, That reposing special trust and confidence in the integrity, ability, and diligence of Thomas L. McKenney, of the District of Columbia, I do appoint him superintendent of Indian trade, and do authorize and empower him to execute and fulfil the duties of that office, according to law; and to have and to hold the said office, with all the powers, privileges and emoluments to the same of right appertaining, unto him the said Thomas L. McKenney, during the pleasure of the President of the United States, for the time being.

Given under my hand at Washington, this second day of April, in the year of our Lord one thousand eight hundred and sixteen, and in the fortieth year of the Independence of the United States.

JAMES MADISON.

By command of the President of the United States of America.

WM. H. CRAWFORD, *Secretary of War.*

fail to strike the most casual reader. The leading features of the government trade were protection and justice, based in humanity. Its tendencies were kind and merciful. The bane of the Indian was wholly excluded from the United States trade; not a drop of brandy, rum, or whiskey, being permitted to pass through the factories. Not a cent of profit was contemplated, as has been stated. With no other system but this, or others in harmony with it, the Indians would have been protected, and blessed, and preserved. Many of the bloody strifes with one another, and of wars between tribes and bands, and the probability is, the greater portion of these border difficulties between the Indians and our people, would never have been heard of; whilst the Indians, preserved from the double action upon them of these wars, and the consuming effects of the "fire-water," would have retained their native strength and dignity, and not wasted away and perished, as they have done.

I can conceive of no contrast more decided than that which marked the United States' treatment of these exposed people, and that which characterized the traffic carried on with them by private individuals, and companies. To sum it up in few words, the first was a shield to protect, and a fountain to sustain, and refresh, and bless the Indians; the last two operated to place them amidst the unobstructed, full, and unmitigated blaze of a consuming avarice! No profits were sought by the government—nothing but gains were contemplated by the traders. No consuming, and strife, and war-kindling agencies, were employed by the first, to attract and lure the unhappy victim; no laws could be enacted by Congress, and no regulations framed, of adequate force or vigilance, to prevent the employment, by the traders, of these lures, and of this bane. No one who has not witnessed it, can conceive the sacrifices an Indian will make for whiskey; how far he will travel, laden with the returns of his winter's hunts; how little he foresees, or regards the consequences to himself, or any body else, of his indulgence in this fatal poison. The awaking from his delirious dream, and finding his furs and peltries gone, and in their places a few worthless articles, unsuited in quality or quantity to screen himself and his family from the winter's cold, may distress him, and kindle his revenge, for the time being, but it is forgotten whenever a new occasion happens in which he can indulge in the same excess! Of all men, an Indian is the most improvident, and furnishes the most painful example of a reckless disregard to the impoverishing and life-consuming effects of intemperance.

Many fortunes have been made in the trade with the Indians. The company that has flourished most, and become most enriched by it, is the "American Fur Company," at the head of which, for many years, as owner and manager, was JOHN JACOB ASTOR. This sagacious and wonderful man pushed this trade wherever the beaver, the otter, or the muskrat, could be found in sufficient quantity to authorize the adventure, until the range east of the Rocky Mountains becoming too limited for his enterprise, he doubled the Cape, and felt his way up the Columbia river, opening a trade with the natives of that far-off region. Next in enterprise and success, was the "Missouri Fur Company," whose operations were, and are yet, conducted by the sagacious CHOUTOU'S. It was to make the range of this company's operations wider, and secure to it, mainly, the unobstructed way to a monopoly of the trade within the limits of its range, that the United States system was, by act of Congress, broken down.

In the discharge of my trust, I found it necessary, almost from year to year, in my annual reports, to refer to the manner in which these companies carried on their operations; protesting against the use of whiskey, and urging the adoption of more rigid regulations to prevent its being carried into the Indian country. For this was the charm, and the trading house at which the poor

Indian was most certain of meeting with this beverage, was sure of his custom. It was not so much a competition in blankets, and strouds, and calicoes, and beaver-traps, and other articles that were necessary for the trade, or their prices, as in whiskey. My reports were not regarded in the light of very friendly interpositions, and from these it was quite natural for the feelings they occasioned to glance off, and become personal. The consequence was, I was not in favor either with the private trade, or with the more formidable power concentred in the companies.

I shall take occasion, in the sequel, to refer again to the breaking down of the United States trade; and to a part, at least, of the means employed to accomplish it.

My immediate predecessor, General John Mason, a man of talents and integrity, had found it difficult during the war to procure suitable supplies, except in part, for the trade. Mackinac blankets, and strouding, two indispensable articles, were wholly beyond his reach; made so by the war with Great Britain, on the one hand, and the infant state of our manufactures, on the other. For blankets, resort was had to a sort of cloth made of wool, united, without weaving, after the manner in which hats are made. It was these or none. These, with numerous other articles, as little adapted to the comfort of the Indians, were purchased and forwarded, and as little in accordance with their wants and tastes. But nothing better in the then condition of the country, could be done.

I found, on entering upon the duties of this trust, a large portion of the capital absorbed in these unsuitable supplies, and the factories laboring under their weight. On the return of peace, the markets resumed their former ability to supply the demand, and were prepared, when I took charge of the department, to respond to my calls. But to make way for the new and appropriate supplies, it was necessary for me to get rid of the old and unsuitable;

when I ordered the old stock to be got rid of, regardless of loss. It was customary to pack the supplies in water-proof tierces. In making up the outfit the first year of my superintendency, the quantity of goods required for it was so large, that the tierces required for their transportation were found, on being measured, to extend in length over one mile and a quarter.

The loss on the old stock was very great, and made, of course, a corresponding inroad upon the capital, and this required the adoption of a new scale of advances upon the articles sent, as also another for the regulation of the prices allowed the Indians for their furs and peltries. This scale was so graduated as to run through more than one season—thus making the annual advance to bear easy upon the Indians. The prices of furs, &c., owing to the re-opening of our commercial relations after the war, having increased, enabled the government to allow an increase upon them—so that the Indians felt very little of the advance which had been put upon the goods.

Great satisfaction was expressed by these poor fellows, in being able once more to provide for themselves and families the substantial woven and almost weather-proof Mackinac blanket, and the almost water-proof and enduring strouding. I received letters from Governor Cass, whose office of governor of Michigan made him *ex-officio* superintendent of the Indians of that Territory, as also from General William Clark, who was superintendent of Indian affairs for Missouri, conveying their high satisfaction at this new influx of the right sort of articles—and assuring me that no such supplies, either in fitness or cheapness, had ever before found their way into their superintendencies.

I owed this success mainly to others. I was assisted by clerks whose integrity and experience made them of great value, as well to the public as to myself; and I can never forget the obligations I was placed under, for zealous co-operations, and honesty of purpose, of my chief clerk, Jere W. Bronaugh; my book-keeper, Mr. Rich, and my copying clerk, Mead Fitzhugh—nor should I be doing justice to my feelings, were I to omit to name Miles, my trusty messenger. Miles was honest, and he was faithful to his humble trust. He had a horror, somehow, of Indians. Miles was bald—and Fitzhugh, being given to mischief, had almost persuaded him that he had, in some far-back period of his life, been scalped by Indians; and sometimes, when the business of the day was over, I would, in passing, hear Fitzhugh urging upon Miles, this almost questionless fact; when the artless creature would raise his hand, place it well back, and then draw it over his forehead, and with a shake of his head, say—"No, no—Mr. Fitzhugh; no, no"—at the same time his looks betraying his own suspicions, if no more, that such *might* have been the case. One little anecdote may serve to show how the artlessness of Miles was blended with his fears, and how these were set off by his want of a better knowledge of his mother tongue.

I was in the warehouse, during the packing season, overlooking this operation—the operation, I mean, of separating and dividing articles, so as to make up the assortments and quantities, which were destined to Chicago, on the North; to Fort Osage, in the West, and the Chickasaw Bluffs, in the South, and, in all, eight factories—when Miles coming up to me in a great flurry, with hat in hand, said—"Sir, there are eighteen *hostile* Indians at the office—please come up, sir, directly." Nonsense, Miles, I replied, hostile Indians—it cannot be so. "'Pon honor," said Miles, giving a most knowing shake of his head, "it is true, for they are every one on horseback!"

No one who has not experienced it can know how strong the ties become between the head of a department and his clerks, provided there is mutual zeal, and a corresponding intelligence, to carry on the business entrusted to each, in his sphere. And then the experience acquired after a long service in the various departments of the government, is of incalculable value, not to the government only, but to all having business with it. To dismiss from office, in those days, without cause—and there could be no cause for turning an incumbent out of office except *incompetency, neglect of duty, or dishonesty*—and especially the dismissal of a bureau officer or clerk, for any other than one or all of these causes, would have been deemed an outrage, no less against the public interests, than the party proscribed. Hence, competency, zeal, and honesty, being the characteristics of the clerks I found in the office of Indian trade, when I succeeded to its management, it no more occurred to me to turn them out, than it did to cut their throats. We met, and continued each to perform his appropriate duties, until death deprived me of the services of Mr. Rich, and the abolition of the office, by act of Congress, of further use for the services of the rest. We parted as we had met—*friends.*

The act abolishing the United States Indian trade establishment, which was passed May 6, 1822, provided for the appointment of an agent to wind up the concern. George Graham, Esq., a most estimable citizen, was selected for this duty. When I succeeded General Mason, the entire property, in merchandise and cash, &c., was invoiced, and the amount credited to him, and charged to me. So, in like manner, when Mr. Graham succeeded me, all the merchandise and cash, &c., was charged to Mr. Graham, and credited to me. I gave back over thirty thousand dollars to Mr. Graham, more than I had received of General Mason—everything being charged, both ways, at cost. But this was, perhaps, as much the result of accident, as of forecast or good management; for the law having contemplated no more than the preservation of the capital, if the business had been wound up immediately after the sacrifice that had been made on the sale of the unsuitable articles which have been referred to; or after one of those seasons which occasionally occurred, when the worms obtained the mastery, and the fragments of their ravages, not being worth the cost of transportation to market, were thrown into the lake or the Mississippi, the balance, even to a greater amount, might have been found on the other side of the ledger. In this case, a fruitful theme would doubtless have been furnished, in which both my competency and integrity would have been assailed. As it was—although I had, in my reports, urged the passage of laws for the protection of the system from the inroads made upon it by the whiskey traffic of traders, or, if Congress should not see fit to pass such laws, then that the system had better be abolished—I was assailed by Hon. Thomas H. Benton, of the United States Senate, with such severity and bitterness, as indicated a purpose not to abolish the factory system, only, but to demolish my humble self along with it. It was quite natural, perhaps, that Mr. Benton should kindle up into an uncommon zeal, and make war with extra energy upon whatever connected itself with the United States factory system, seeing that the Missouri Fur Company had much at stake in the result, and he was the legitimate organ of the individuals' composing it. That gentleman's speech, in the Senate, on his proposition to abolish the government trade, being marked with special rancor towards myself, personally, I felt called upon to reply to him, which I did, through the National Intelligencer. (See Appendix, A.)

When President Monroe read Mr. Benton's speech, he said to a friend who communicated the fact to me, "I am made unhappy by this attack of Colonel Benton upon Colonel McKenney." On reading my answer, he said to the same person, "I am relieved. Colonel McKenney has completely vindicated himself. He is what I always believed him to be. My confidence in him is unimpaired." Besides the large disbursements made, annually, in the purchase of supplies for the trade, it was made my duty, also, to disburse the sums due to the various Indian tribes, on account of the annuities due them; nearly the whole of which, in those days, were paid, not in money, of which they were very certain to be robbed, but in useful articles of merchandise. This duty added very much to my labors and responsibility. I saw my position, appreciated its delicacy, and prepared against any possible contingency. One of my rules was, never to fill up and number a check for money, but to have this done by either my book-keeper or chief clerk, whose duty it was made to hand the check to me, in company with the invoice, or whatever expenditure it was intended to pay, with the *attest* of the examining clerk, that the sum, and all the details, were correct, when I *signed the check*. Another was, to keep separate my public and private accounts, and never, under any emergency, to touch, either for my own use, or the use of my friends, a cent of the public money. In not a single case were these rules departed from. Another was, to take triplicate vouchers, in all cases; one set for the Treasury Department, one for my office proper, and the third for a safety vault. This latter precaution saved me from utter ruin, as the sequel will show.

I took up a paper, one morning, and read, in substance, what follows :—"*Whenever Colonel McKenney's accounts shall be settled, he will be found a defaulter to the amount of one hundred and twenty thousand dollars!*" I called up my chief clerk, Mr. Bronaugh, and showing him the paper, asked what it could mean. He did not know. Have not the quarterly returns been sent in? I asked. "Yes, sir." Who took them? "Mr. Rich, always, except on one occasion, when he being sick, I took them myself." I lost no time in going to the Auditor's office, taking Mr. Bronaugh with me. To the inquiry, of the auditor—Are my accounts settled, sir? I was referred to his clerk. Of him I received for answer, "They are, sir, so far as they can be." I soon learned *the obstacle* to be "*the absence of vouchers!*" I called for the returns, in which they were alleged to be missing. They were presented, when, sure enough, they were unaccompanied, in great part, by vouchers! Whereupon Mr. Bronaugh said, "These returns were made up by myself; and I am ready to swear, that when I brought them to this office, there was not omitted *a single voucher.*" I saw the ties had been severed, and the whole package bore marks of mutilation; so without troubling the clerk with further inquiries, I directed Mr. Bronaugh to take up the package, which he did.

I immediately made known the affair to the Secretary of War, telling him that I had, yet, duplicate vouchers. He rang his bell, sent his messenger for the auditor, who, on appearing, was requested to put his entire force on my accounts, and keep it there, until they were settled. I furnished duplicates, but did not feel at liberty to allow them to pass out of my clerk's hands, except as they should be admitted and entered. The remainder were brought away and taken back, from time to time, till all was settled, when this one hundred and twenty thousand dollars of alleged defalcation had no basis to rest upon, either in whole, or in part, and the books of the auditor so demonstrated it. And yet, as the rancor of the press—of which this was only the premonitory symptom—began to break forth, this assault upon my official integrity was kept going, whenever, and wherever, the party charging it thought there could be any political capital made out of it. I can never know, nor can any body ever know, the extent of the mischief which this aspersion produced, upon both my name and my circumstances. I was met by it everywhere; and in many instances could see confidence in me giving way before its withering tendencies.

Quite a formal disinterring of the charge was made as recently as 1840; and, pending the canvass which resulted in the election of General Harrison to the Presidency, I was put to the trouble to exhibit the original document which testified that all my public accounts, as well those relating to the trade, as to the annuities, were settled, showing a balance in my favor. I shall insert this document in the sequel.

But I was subjected to other, and scarcely less injurious attacks. The amount of supplies which I purchased, annually, was great. My rule in regard to purchasing was a fixed one. It was, to give as wide a range as I could to the demand, its nature, and variety; and to produce all the competition I could, I gave samples of the kinds of articles which were required in the Indian trade—even, for the purpose of making them portable, to the cutting of guns in two. But I made no commitment to purchase of any one, except on the following conditions: *First*, that the importations should be in time. *Second*, that the quality and fitness of the article should be entirely acceptable; and *Third*, that the prices should be as low as like articles could be elsewhere commanded. All this I knew involved contingences, on the part of the merchant, but these were often encountered. It rarely happened that any single importer ordered *all* the varieties, but all were ordered; and the general result was, a market well stocked with articles, which, but for this policy, would have furnished very few of them, for the reason that almost all kinds of goods suited to the Indian trade, are wholly different from goods required by civilized communities. And this superior market was in the District of Columbia, where more suitable goods could be at all times had, than could be found in any of the cities of the Union. The mercantile principle, "that wherever a demand exists, *there* will be found a corresponding ability to supply it," was never more fully illustrated and established.

But I could not deal with every body. There were merchants, some of whom went to Europe, expressly for the purpose, who, by a closer attention, and a more active observation of the nature of the supplies wanted, the time when wanted, and the value of the articles, would be better qualified to supply the demand, than were others who were less vigilant, and less intelligent. The consequence was, that anonymous letters were addressed to the committee of Indian affairs, of the House of Representatives, charging me with partiality, and with making purchases of favorites, to the exclusion of persons who were prepared to sell to the public better, more suitable, and cheaper goods. I was summoned to appear before the committee. An investigation, in due form, was made. The parties named by the anonymous prosecutors, were summoned before the committee, and questioned under the solemnities of an oath. With what success I escaped from this searching ordeal, the reader may see by referring to Appendix. (B.)

A useful lesson may be drawn from these facts—a lesson that may teach the numerous aspirants for public office, that there are not only duties to be performed, when the goal of their ambition is reached, but that priceless pearl, "*a good name*," is constantly in danger of being torn from them, no matter how cautious they may be, how honest, or how capable, or how devoted to the duties of the trust which they seek to encounter. Few men, somebody has said, bring out of office the same good character they took into it.

It is not only the personal suffering which an assault upon one's good name causes, but a suffering coming from the sympathy of friends which combines with it, as well as the effects which are not unfrequently seen to desolate one's property. I was made to endure all these. Nor does the charge, like the destructive flash, exhaust itself in the explosion. If it did, it could be better borne, as well as endured with less suffering. A man's virtues may be heralded, and the remembrance of them soon dies; but affix to his name and character a charge, of no matter what sort, involving his *reputation*, and it never dies! What if I did exhibit to thousands, and publish in the press, the utter falsity of the imputation that I was a government defaulter, as charged upon me in the manner stated; did that wipe out the stain which the annunciation implicating me in that charge, had affixed to my character? As I have said, it was revived and circulated from the time it was made, till 1840, and its flickerings have not ceased to blaze up even to this day. About the time of my dismissal, by command of President Jackson, from my office, as Chief of the Bureau of Indian Affairs, in August, 1830, the implication had new vigor imparted to it by the refusal to close my public accounts, which, being kept open, gave sanction to the assertion that all had not been right in my public disbursements, or in my accountability for the same. Four years, from 1829 to 1833, was this state of things continued; when, at last, all the injury that could be done me, arising out the story of *unsettled accounts*, having been endured, an order was given to settle them. They were settled. How that settlement resulted, will be shown hereafter. It has always been a source of consolation to me, that this settlement was not made by officers connected with the political party of my preference—but by those who occupied towards me relations of a totally different sort. There have been periods in the history of this government when political feelings were not permitted to mingle with official accountability and duty; and when the moral sense of an accounting officer of one political party would not permit him to overlay, or blur, or delay the settlement of the accounts of a disbursing officer, because his political preferences did not happen to run in the same direction with his own. But this was before political intolerance was tolerated; and before that "Hydra," as "Party" had been so characteristically denominated by General Jackson, had so severed the ties of a national brotherhood, and gathered round it its "*friends*," as to exclude from any participation in the government, if not the greater, yet a large portion of the purest patriotism, and most renowned wisdom and intelligence of the country. A *ban* was literally put upon it.

CHAPTER II.

IMPROVEMENT, MORAL AND INTELLECTUAL, OF THE INDIANS. PRESIDENT MONROE—ANECDOTES ILLUSTRATING HIS CHARACTER.

Fourth of July address—Subsequent reflections—Wrongs of the Indian—Correspondence with Mr. and Mrs. Gambold—The Cherokees—Their reluctance to intercourse with the Whites—Capacity for improvement—Plan for elevating their condition—Appropriation by Congress for this purpose—Effects of this plan—David Brown's letter—Progress of civilization among the Cherokees—Commission annulled—Re-appointed—Fourth Auditor Treasury, *almost*—Mr. Monroe's scruples—His sensitiveness to reproach—Interview with him just before his death—Charged with undermining General Armstrong—Facts in the case—The British forces in the Chesapeake—Affair of Bladensburg—General Armstrong vindicated—Mr. Monroe's personal efforts and sacrifices in 1814—The General Post-Office—Mr. M'Lean's appointment—What led to it.

It was during my superintendency of the United States Indian Trade Department, that my feelings became first interested for the welfare of the Indians. I had delivered a Fourth of July address to the citizens of Washington and Georgetown, in a beautiful grove on the heights of the latter, when, on reaching my home that evening, my thoughts became occupied with the condition and prospects of the Indians. I had been talking of liberty and independence, of the glory of our institutions, the grandeur of our system, and of our future destiny, and of the sacrifices of blood and treasure that had been made to secure all these—but had not thought of those to whose country we had succeeded, and who had been driven by our injustice and cruelty from river to river, and from forest to forest, until not only they had become lost to our sight, but even their memorials, along nearly the whole of the Atlantic border, were also consigned to oblivion, except where the plough turned up their stone axes and arrow points. No remains were left of their villages, or the ashes of their council fires, both having long since become mingled with the warrior's bones, and the bows and arrows of the hunter. I had been engaged in sending to survivors upon the western border articles of both taste and necessity, but as yet no great plan, alike worthy of this noble race, and of this great nation, had been devised for the preservation and happiness of the former.

The next day a newspaper fell into my hand, in which was a letter from the Reverend John Gambold, dated, "*Spring Place, Cherokee Country.*" This good man was a Moravian and a missionary. From this letter I learned something of his hopes and prospects in regard to the condition of the Cherokees. I immediately opened a correspondence with him, as also with his "help-mate"—for she was truly such—which continued with both of them till their death. This estimable lady, well known at Bethlehem, in Pennsylvania, as "*Sister Kliest,*" had separated herself from her charge, as directress of the Bethlehem academy, to unite her destiny with the good Mr. Gambold, and assist him in his missionary labors, among, at that time, an almost benighted people, no longer as "Sister Kliest," but as "*Anna R. Gambold.*" I cannot resist the inclination to make the reader better acquainted with these estimable people. They may be seen in the light of their own goodness in a few extracts from their letters to me, which may be found in the Appendix. (C.)

Such was the dread of the Cherokees of the approach of the white man, that Mr. Gambold, who enjoyed their confidence in a greater degree than any white man then living, could not prevail upon them to allow a road to be opened through a part of their country, although it was indispensable to their own convenience, in their travel to and from places of trade and barter, and to the means of a more comfortable living. They were not to learn for the first time the tender mercies of the white man, and, therefore, feared that the opening a way for their own accommodation, might be to open one, also, for his advances, and for afflictions for themselves that had never failed to accompany him. They preferred their own present lot, rather, than by this attempt to improve it, to involve themselves in this much dreaded contingency.

I did not doubt then, nor do I now, the capacity of the Indian for the highest attainments in civilization, in the arts and religion,* but I was satisfied that no adequate plan had ever been adopted for this great reformation. Proof enough, however, had been elicited by the labors of good men, to satisfy me that the Indian was, in his intellectual and moral structure, *our equal.* I therefore sought to introduce a system adequate alike in its extent and elements, and in the means to sustain it, for the promotion of the future happiness of his race. This I knew could be accomplished, only, by act of Congress. Having witnessed a feeling in several of the churches, as also in associations for alleviating the distresses of the Indians, I determined to give effect to it, if I could, in the only way in which, as I believed, it could be made successfully, and permanently useful.

A period had now arrived—I believe it was in the year 1817 or 1818, I forget which—that appeared to me to be propitious for the making of the experiment. There was general tranquillity among the Indians, as well as the

* Notwithstanding the hardness of the destiny of the Cherokees—the oppressions that have been heaped upon them; the contrivances resorted to, even in high places, for the purpose of retarding their advances in letters and learning, and to deprive them of the privileges resulting from an organized government of their own; it is my firm belief that, in proportion to population, there are more Cherokees who read, either the English or their own tongue, the latter by means of an alphabet invented by one of themselves, than can be found among the whites in any of the States of the Union.

kindest dispositions towards them in the executive. No exciting onsets were being made to dislodge them from their homes, or to jostle them in their possessions, or alarm and distract them in the enjoyment of them. Besides, there were now several missionary stations already in operation, though on a small scale, all of them furnishing proof that a plan commensurate to the object, would reform and save, and bless this long neglected, and down-trodden people. I was convinced that if a general expression of the popular will could be made to Congress, by the instrumentality of memorials, backed by committees to present them in person, the great design would be accomplished. I accordingly addressed circulars to as many of the corresponding secretaries of associations for meliorating the condition of the Indians, as were known to me, as also to such other Christian people as I thought it likely would co-operate in this work of mercy, recommending a general action in as many states as could be reached, and that memorials should be sent from each, borne by committees of their most honored men to Washington, and presented simultaneously to Congress; the committees urging in person, upon their respective representatives, their prompt and zealous attention to the prayer of the petitioners.

The recommendation was adopted, and carried out to the letter. The result was, a prompt action by Congress upon the subject, and an annual appropriation made of ten thousand dollars, "for the civilization of the Indian tribes adjoining the frontier settlements." Regulations were issued by the War Department (Mr. Calhoun being Secretary) for the carrying of this act into effect. Upon these, a system was put in operation, the beneficial effects of which, upon the condition and happiness of the Indians, were felt from Lake Superior, to the Chattahoochee, in Georgia. Everywhere the schools flourished, and when I left the department in 1830, there were over *eighteen hundred*

Indian children in these schools, deriving instruction, and making as rapid advances in the various incipient branches of learning, in agriculture, and the mechanic arts, as are made in any part of the United States by the children of the whites. Everywhere, the day seemed to have come, when "the wilderness was to blossom as the rose." But let a son of the forest, a youth, and over whose mind had rested, but a few years previous, the mantle of paganism and ignorance, tell of this change in the condition, and hopes, and prospects of his hitherto benighted people. The writer was David Brown, of the Cherokee nation; and his communication (extracts from which I subjoin) was made to the editor of the Family Visiter, at Richmond, Virginia, and bears date Willstown, Cherokee Nation, September 2d, 1825.

"In my last letter from Creek path to you, I stated that there was some probability of my returning to Arkansas, &c., &c., and referred to the improved condition of the Cherokees on this side of the Mississippi, in a moral, intellectual, and religious point of view, &c.; to the slow progress I make in translating the New Testament, in consequence of the non-existence of a dictionary, or complete grammar, in Cherokee—and to the philological researches of one in the nation, whose system of education had met with universal approbation, &c. Allow me, dear sir, now, the pleasure to fulfil the promise I made you, that I would pick up and send you what I had omitted. Recently I have been travelling a good deal in the nation, in order to regain my impaired health. My Heavenly Sovereign permitting, I expect to return to Arkansas in the month of October next. I have made a hasty translation of the four Gospels, which will require a close criticism. On my arrival at Dwight, I shall pursue the delightful work; and I hope the day is not far distant, when the Cherokees, my brethren and kindred, according to the flesh, shall read the words of eternal life, in their own tongue. I will here give you a faint picture of the Cherokee nation and its inhabitants. In the meantime, however, it must be borne in mind, that it is the mass and common people that form the character of a nation, and not officers of government, nor the lowest grade of peasantry.

"The Cherokee nation, you know, is in about thirty-five degrees north latitude; bounded on the north and west by the State of Tennessee, on the south by Alabama, and on the east by Georgia and North Carolina. This country is well watered; abundant springs of pure water are found in every part. A range of majestic and lofty mountains stretch themselves across the nation. The northern part of the nation is hilly and mountainous. In the southern and western parts, there are extensive and fertile plains, covered partly with tall trees, through which beautiful streams of water glide. These plains furnish immense pasturage, and numberless herds of cattle are dispersed over them. Horses are plenty, and are used for servile purposes. Numerous flocks of sheep, goats, and swine, cover the valleys and hills. On Tennessee, Ustanala, and Canasagi rivers, Cherokee commerce floats. The climate is delicious and healthy; the winters are mild. The spring clothes the ground with its richest scenery. Cherokee flowers, of exquisite beauty and variegated hues, meet and fascinate the eye in every direction. In the plains and valleys, the soil is generally rich; producing Indian corn, cotton, tobacco, wheat, oats, indigo, sweet and Irish potatoes. The natives carry on considerable trade with the adjoining States; and some of them export cotton in boats down the Tennessee, to the Mississippi, and down that river to New Orleans. Apple and peach orchards are quite common, and gardens are cultivated, and much attention paid to them.

"Butter and cheese are seen on Cherokee tables. There are many public roads in the nation, and houses of entertainment kept by natives. Numerous and flourishing villages are seen in every section of the country. Cotton and woollen cloths are manufactured here. Blankets, of various dimensions, manufactured by Cherokee hands, are very common. Almost every family in the nation grows cotton for its own consumption. Industry and commercial enterprise are extending themselves in every part. Nearly all the merchants in the nation are native Cherokees. Agricultural pursuits, (the most solid foundation of our national prosperity,) engage the chief attention of the people. Different branches in mechanics are pursued. The population is rapidly increasing. In the year 1819, an estimate was made of all Cherokees. Those on the west, were estimated at 5,000, and those on the east of the Mississippi, at 10,000 souls. The census of this division of the Cherokees has again been taken within the current year, and the returns are thus made—native citizens, 13,563; white men married in the nation, 147; white women married in the nation, 73; African slaves, 1,277. If this summary of Cherokee population from the census is correct, to say nothing of those of foreign extract, we find that, in six years, the increase has been 3,563 souls. If we judge the future by the past, to what number will the Cherokee population swell in 1858?*

"White men in the nation enjoy all the immunities and privileges of the Cherokee people, except that they are not eligible to public offices. In the above computation of the

* Alas! it was not given to this gifted youth to foresee that a day was coming, and was even then near at hand, when the plough-share of sectional and political power would turn up and turn over all these visions; and that when a just appreciation of the Cherokees of their own advances in the mechanics and the arts, and religion, caused them to cling closer and closer to their beautiful country, and to refuse to sell or exchange it, a device would be resorted to, by which, without their consent, they would be forced to cross the Mississippi, pursued by those elements of distraction which such flagrant injustice and high-handed oppression combined to create. I need not say that I refer here to the miscalled *treaty* of New Euchota.

present year, you perceive that there are some African slaves among us. They have been, from time to time, brought in and sold by white men. They are, however, generally well treated, and they much prefer living in the nation, to a residence in the United States. There is hardly any intermixture of Cherokee and African blood. The presumption is, that the Cherokees will, at no distant day, co-operate with the humane efforts of those who are liberating and sending this proscribed race to the land of their fathers. National pride, patriotism, and a spirit of independence, mark the Cherokee character.

"The Christian religion is the religion of the nation. Presbyterians, Methodists, Baptists, and Moravians, are the most numerous sects. Some of the most influential characters are members of the church, and live consistently with their professions. The whole nation is penetrated with gratitude for the aid it has received from the United States government, and from different religious societies. Schools are increasing every year; learning is encouraged and rewarded. The young class acquire the English, and those of more mature age, the Cherokee system of learning. The female character is elevated, and duly respected. Indolence is discountenanced. Our native language, in its philosophy, genius and symphony, is inferior to few, if any, in the world. Our relations with all nations, savage or civilized, are of the most friendly character. We are out of debt, and our public revenue is in a flourishing condition. Besides the amount arising from imports, a perpetual annuity is due from the United States, in consideration of lands ceded in former periods. Our system of government, founded on republican principles, by which justice is equally distributed, secures the respect of the people. Newtown, pleasantly situated in the centre of the nation, and at the junction of Canasagi and Gusuwati, two beautiful streams, is the seat of government. The legislative power is vested in what is denominated, in native dialect, Tsalagi Tinilawigi, consisting of a national committee and council. Members of both branches are chosen by and from the people, for a limited period. In Newtown, a printing-press is soon to be established; also a national library and a museum. Immense concourses of the people frequent the seat of government when *Tsalagi Tinilawigi* is in session, which takes place once a year."

The first regular school established among the Cherokees, was in the year 1817—(incipient steps had been taken, however, before that)—so that all this culture, and this converting the waste into a garden, was the product of the labor of only about eight years. It was during my superintendency of the government trade with the Indians, and, as I have before stated, in 1818 or 1819, that I addressed the circular before referred to, to the corresponding secretaries and others friendly to the cause of the Indians, and to their rescue from the sad condition in which they were everywhere known to be; and in 1819, the act of Congress was passed, appropriating the annual sum of $10,000 for their benefit. It was in the same year that an act was passed by Congress, annulling the power of the President to appoint the officers for the trade department, *without the consent of the Senate.* On the passage of this act, which I interpreted as annulling my own commission, as also the commissions of the factors and clerks, &c., I waited on President Monroe, and told him that, in my view of it, my powers were annulled, as were those, also, of all others connected with the department; and that I had suspended all further action until his pleasure could be known. "Go on, sir," said this good man and pure patriot, "and furnish me with a list of the names of those connected with the service, and I will place it at once before the Senate." I did so, omitting my own. The Senate's action being had upon the nominations, it resulted in confirming the entire list, with myself as principal.* The system was continued, as I have stated, until 1822, when it was abolished.

In 1823, I think it was, I write from memory, Colonel Freeman, then fourth auditor of the Treasury, died. Mr. Calhoun, being then Secretary of War, asked me if I would accept the office made vacant by the Colonel's death. I assented—when leaving me in his office, he went over to see Mr. Monroe, the President, and ascertain his pleasure on the subject. Mr. Calhoun soon returned, telling me the President very cordially assented—but had scarcely finished the sentence, when the President's messenger came in, saying to Mr. Calhoun that the President would be glad to see him. He left me, requesting me to remain until his return; and being gone some half hour, he came back, saying, in substance, "It is very strange! The President, I think, is singularly scrupulous. He recognized you just now with great pleasure as Colonel Freeman's successor; and then sent for me to say he could not nominate you—giving as his reason, that you had been active and useful in defending his administration, and if, with the knowledge the public had of this fact, he should appoint you to office,

---

* JAMES MONROE, PRESIDENT OF THE UNITED STATES of AMERICA—

To all who shall see these presents, Greeting:

KNOW YE, That reposing special trust and confidence in the integrity, diligence and discretion of Thomas L. McKenney, of the District of Columbia, I have nominated, and by and with the advice and consent of the Senate, do appoint him Superintendent of Indian Trade, Georgetown, District of Columbia, and do authorize and empower him to execute and fulfil the duties of that office according to law: And to have and to hold the said office, with all the rights and emoluments thereunto legally appertaining, unto him, the said Thomas L. McKenney, during the pleasure of the President of the United States, for the time being.

In testimony whereof, I have caused these letters to be made patent, and the seal of the United States to be hereunto affixed. Given under my hand [SEAL] at the City of Washington, the twentieth day of April, in the year of our Lord one thousand eight hundred and eighteen, and of the Independence of the United States of America, the forty-second.

[Signed,] JAMES MONROE.

By the President. JOHN Q. ADAMS, *Secretary of State.*

it might be interpreted as a compensation to you, out of the public money, for those services." He went on to say that Mr. Monroe was anxious for my appointment to some suitable office in the government, provided a situation could be found that would not devolve upon him the duty, for the reasons stated, of conferring it upon me.

I introduce this little anecdote to show how *sensitive* was this good man, and how constantly alive to his fame; and also, that it may serve as a contrast to the practice which was destined in a few short years to take the place of it—of an exactly opposite character.

Another anecdote illustrative of this sensibility in Mr. Monroe to his reputation. It is known that his entire devotion to the public service, left him but little time to attend to his private affairs. He became embarrassed—greatly so; but was perhaps never more so, than during the term of his Presidency. He owned, by bequest, I believe, a valuable estate in Virginia—known as the Albemarle estate. It was his great object, if possible, to save this, and pass it down to his descendants. But the pressing nature of his finances forced from him, at last, a reluctant offer of this property for sale. Some time after the appearance of the advertisement, he was waited upon by a gentleman, who said to him—"Sir, I am just from Virginia, and from your estate in Albemarle. My object in going there, was to examine it, with a view to its purchase. I have done this, and have also learned from your agent your terms. I am here to say, that I am ready, when you shall have made out the title deeds, to pay you the stipulated price."

Mr. Monroe replied, "Colonel O——, I cannot sell that estate to you. My necessities, I know, are great; and these, alone, prompted me to advertise that property for sale—but———" Colonel O—— interrupting him, asked, with surprise, "Why not sell to me?"—For no other reason than one—and that is, you were a contractor during the war; and you received your contracts from me as Secretary of War. You were faithful, I know, and fulfilled your trust like an honest man, and made money. And now were I to sell you my estate, I might incur the suspicion of having, by these contracts, purposely placed it in your power to buy it." All remonstrance on the part of Colonel O—— proved vain. Mr. Monroe held to his first decision, preferring to bear the weight of heavy embarrassments, to the liability of incurring the suspicion that he had converted his trust, as Secretary of War, into an instrument of pecuniary gain and personal emolument.

Such instances of purity in public life are refreshing. They will appear to the reader of the present day, perhaps, as fable; and the patriotic Monroe may, probably, be considered, when contemplated through the medium of modern times, as fastidious.

I must crave the reader's indulgence while I make one more reference to this tried patriot, and good man.

During the late war with Great Britain, or the greater part of it, as is known to every body, Mr. Monroe was Secretary of State, and General Armstrong Secretary of War; it is known, also, that soon after the capture of Washington, and the conflagration of its capitol, General Armstrong was superseded in the office of Secretary of War by Mr. Monroe. It was soon whispered, that this change had been produced by the *undermining agency of Mr. Monroe.* Whence the rumor came, or by whom it was originated, no one knew. But it remained a source of deep disquiet to harrass Mr. Monroe to the hour of his death.

I can never forget, when, being in New York during his last illness, I called, and within only a few days of his death, at Mr. Gouverneur's—his son-in-law—to see him. He was greatly emaciated, and his cough was so oppressive to him, as to make even the ordinary intercourse, under such circumstances, painful to the visiter. I had but just seated myself, when he began—"Colonel McKen ney, your call is welcome to me. I am glad to see you. I have something to say to you, and hope you will allow me time. You see I am very feeble, and can say but little at a time, owing to this cough." He then proceeded to state, in substance, that it was among his most cherished wishes to leave to his descendants a spotless reputation; that he had but little else left for them. "There is one thing," he continued, "which you must know something of. I want to talk to you about it, and to get your knowledge of the case, embodied in a written form. I have reason for believing that General Armstrong indulges the belief that I was instrumental in causing his removal from the office of Secretary of War. I know I had no agency whatever in producing that result, but the general opinion being that he is writing a book, he may, if he really believes in the truth of this implication, so state it; and I may be regarded by posterity in that most unenviable light in which such a record would place me. Pray tell me all you know about the circumstances that led to that change—to his removal, I mean, or separation from the War Department." I gave him the following reply:—

My intercourse was frequent with General Armstrong, beginning with the arrival of the British forces in the Chesapeake. It was made my duty, from time to time, to report to him the arrival of troops, and their wants, in equipments, &c., &c. He appeared to me to doubt the intentions of the enemy to invade the capital; and under the influence of this belief, in which I had no doubt he was sincere, I found some difficulty in procuring the necessary arms and equipments, &c., for troops as they came in. After Commodore Barney had been forced to blow up his flotilla in the Patuxet, and our troops being at the battalion Old Fields, and I had come in as a vidette, having rode along the enemy's flanks, for over a mile, and picking up, on my return to camp, two British deserters, whom I brought in with me, I found on horseback, in our camp, President Madison, General Armstrong, and two or three other persons, to whom, in presence of the Commanding General, I stated the position of the enemy, and what appeared to be their numbers, and gave it as my opinion that they would be at our encampment before daylight next morning. To which General Armstrong replied, "They can have no such intention. They are foraging, I suppose; and if an attack is meditated by them upon any place, it is Annapolis." The deserters were then interrogated, chiefly by President Madison. But they knew not who commanded them; knew nothing of their destination, and as little of their numbers. I then asked them to look at our force, and say whether theirs was equal to it. They did so, and with a smile, said—"We think it is."

The President and party then rode off on the way to Washington; and I was ordered to make another reconnoitre, which I did, when, as you know, sir, for I found you on your roan horse, observing the enemy, who was still advancing upon us, we continued to observe them, till they halted—began to *bivouac*, sling their kettles, &c., &c., when I returned to battalion Old Fields, (you taking the road to Bladensburg) to report all this, and to say they were within a mile of us. Whereupon my commanding officer, General Smith, ordered formed a line of battle, Commodore Barney's artillery being in advance of our main line, and near the wood that intervened between the two armies. The line being formed, I was ordered to go in quest of General Winder, General Smith remarking, "I do not feel at liberty to take the responsibility of the fight, if the commander-in-chief of the forces can be had to give direction to it." Putting spurs to my horse, I lost not a moment in reaching what I had learned was the position of General Winder. I met him about eight miles from our encampment, delivered the message with which I was charged, when, putting spurs to his horse, we galloped back to camp together. Riding round the field, and observing the line of battle, he remarked, "It is all well arranged, but the manifest object of the enemy is, to attack us in the night. We have not the material for a night fight." Whereupon he gave orders to take up the line of march; cross the eastern branch bridge, and occupy the heights beyond. We did so. This was the evening of the 23d of August. The next day, the affair of Bladensburg occurred. The result is known to every body.

The enemy's next movement was upon Baltimore. Our forces were ordered to march for the defence of that city. We had not proceeded far, before a rumor reached us that the citizens of Washington and Georgetown did not feel safe, from causes of a domestic nature—when General Smith's command was ordered to repair to the city, and encamp on Windmill Hill. Meantime, the British shipping were in the Potomac. Alexandria had been captured and sacked. Apprehensions being entertained that they might ascend the Potomac in their boats, for the purpose of destroying the cannon foundry, &c., batteries were thrown up on the shore of the Potomac, at the foot of Windmill Hill. While engaged in this duty, General Armstrong, of whom we had heard nothing after the evening of the interview at the Old Fields, rode on the ground. The impression had become universal, that, as Secretary of War, he had neglected to prepare the necessary defences; and that to this neglect, the capitol had been desecrated, and the glory of our arms tarnished. Indeed, many went further, openly and loudly. Charles Carroll, of Bellevue, the moment General Armstrong rode upon the ground, met him, and denounced him, openly and vehemently, as the cause of all the disasters that had befallen the city—when, with one impulse, the officers said to General Smith, "There, sir, are our swords; we will not employ them, if General Armstrong is to command us, in his capacity of Secretary of

War; but we will obey the orders of any other member of the Cabinet." At the same moment, the men at the batteries threw down their spades, avowing a like resolve.

General Smith called me to him, saying, "You see the state of things; I have just ordered Major Williams to report it to the President. Do you accompany him. Say to the President, that under the orders of any other member of the Cabinet, what can be done, will be done." We rode off in haste, and overtook President Madison, Richard Rush, (I believe,) and a third person, on F. Street, in Washington, on horseback—the government having been again organized at Washington. The message delivered to President Madison, was in accordance with the above, to the letter—the last sentence—"*But under any other member of the Cabinet, the most cheerful duty will be rendered.*" The answer by the President was, "Say to General Smith, *the contingency*, (namely, that of any future orders being given by General Armstrong,) *shall not happen.*" A short time only had elapsed before it was known that General Armstrong had ceased to be Secretary of War, and that you had succeeded him. We learned, and I remember we confided in the source whence we derived our information, that President Madison suggested to General Armstrong, in view of the state of things, as narrated, whether it might not be proper for him to suspend his functions as war minister, over the District of Columbia, but to exercise them elsewhere. To which the general was said to have answered, "he would be Secretary of War over the whole, or none." Mr. Madison receiving this as an inadmissible alternative, told him so, when General Armstrong ceased to be Secretary of War. "This," said Mr. Monroe, "is all I want. It exonerates me from the charge of having undermined General Armstrong, by any agency of mine. So far as the facts were made known to me at the time, you state them correctly; and the rest I have had from other sources since, and they corroborate what you say." I promised to write out the narrative, as he had requested, and did so. Mr. Monroe died a few days after this interview, and with him, the demand for a forthcoming of the facts. But I promised to shield him under such forms as might be in my power, from the charge; and in incorporating the narrative here, I only make good that promise. The charge of traitor, which was lavishly employed against General Armstrong, I never believed. His whole fault lay in a total absence of faith in the intention of the British to attack Washington. And, indeed, the act struck every military mind then, as it does now, as one of the most unexampled temerity. An incursion, such as was made into a country densely peopled, without artillery or cavalry, exposing both flank and rear to the capacity of such a city as Baltimore, was one of that kind of onsets which secures success only by the general apathy arising out of the belief that nothing so desperate would be attempted.

Another fact or two, illustrative of President Monroe's patriotism. No darker period in the history of our country is known, save only that which marked occasional epochs of the revolution, than was that of the year 1814. Not only was the money, the sinew of war, in time of war, all gone, but with it also had departed the credit of the nation. The stock of the government, as well as its issues of every other sort, was held in little more estimation than would have been so much blank paper; and yet the war was to be prosecuted! The banks having advanced all they could advance, could come in aid of the government no further. There was not even money enough to buy fuel to keep the cadets at West Point from perishing, when resort was had, by them, to every old building and out-house, to fence rails, and shrubs and roots, until Governor Tompkins threw in five hundred dollars' worth of wood, which was met by the cadets on its way to the Point, and borne to their quarters on their shoulders.

It was at this dismal period that Mr. Monroe assumed the duties of the Department of War. He was advised against the undertaking, and the downfall of his prospects was predicted by his friends, who importuned him not to hazard his own ruin, by engaging in duties which must end in his overthrow. "It is when such dark prospects shroud the hopes of the people, that the country has the stronger claims upon her sons," replied the patriot Monroe; "that which you urge upon me as a reason for declining to contribute my mite towards the rescue, is conclusive in determining me to come to it. The day of my country's adversity is that on which my best energies are more freely at her service." With these views, and these feelings, he assumed the arduous duties of the War Department.

There was mind enough, with all the appropriate qualities, and zeal enough for the right management of this arm of the nation's defence; and there was justice on the side of the republic, and a consequent just reliance upon Heaven—but there was no money! Applications were made in all directions; appeals to the patriotism of the people were heralded in all directions, and the most imploring calls uttered to come to the rescue. But the arm of the nation was paralyzed. There was no more money, and confidence was gone! It was in this dark crisis that Mr. Monroe went in person to the Bank of Columbia, and made an appeal. Government securities were freely offered, and at great sacrifices, but in vain; when he looked the cashier, William Whann, in the face, and throwing into his countenance all that was imploring and impressive, he said, "Mr. Whann, have you confidence in my *honor?* Will you accept a pledge of that, backed by all my private fortune, that this sum, now so indispensable to the wants of the government, shall be made good? I pledge them!" Mr. Whann repaired to the directors' room, and with a heart full of solicitude, reported all that had passed, when the amount wanted was placed at the disposal of the government. It was that very amount, obtained in that way, and which could have been obtained in no other way, that sustained Jackson's army, and enabled it to reach New Orleans; and but for which, or an indispensable portion of it, it could not have moved at all. The world is entitled to a life of this patriot.

The General Post-Office Department at Washington, was for a long time in a state of great dilapidation—I refer to the period which preceded Mr. M'Lean's administration of its affairs. At the time to which I refer, Mr. M'Lean was Commissioner of the General Land Office. Coming down Pennsylvania avenue one day, I met Mr. M'Lean, with whom I had been for a long time on terms of close intimacy, and thinking I saw something in his countenance that indicated depression of spirits, I asked him what was the matter. He replied, "I am going to leave Washington, and return to Ohio to practice law. My situation as Commissioner of the Land Office, being subordinate to the Treasury Department, is by no means agreeable; besides, the salary is not adequate to the support of my family, &c."

I immediately said—Why go to Ohio for these reasons? A Post-Master General is about being appointed, and surely, if it is your pleasure to accept that office, there can be no difficulty in having it conferred on you. "You are mistaken," he replied; "the Ohio delegation have been with the President this morning, and have ascertained that he has fixed upon Mr. Anderson, of Kentucky, (then recently returned from a foreign mission.) There is no chance, therefore, of my being chosen for that place.

We parted—he to go to his residence, and I (without his knowing it) to the President's. I found Mr. Monroe at leisure. As usual, he was glad to see me, and began talking about foreign and other matters of like import, when I told him, by his leave, we would talk of these on some other occasion; and if it were his pleasure, I would refer to a subject interesting alike to himself as President of the United States, and the country. "You know, Colonel McKenney," replied this good man, "that any subject that concerns our country cannot be otherwise than interesting to me." Then, sir, I continued, have you so far made up your mind as to the citizen you are about to nominate for Post-Master General, as to preclude any reference to the subject? "I have," he answered, "thought of nominating Richard Anderson, of Kentucky, for that place." Is your determination final? "No—it is not—if I can hear any good reason for changing it."

I proceeded to state, that I hoped he would not consider anything I might say as being unfriendly to Mr. Anderson—for I was sure he possessed every qualification for the place except one, and that was an exception over which he had no control, nor had any body else. What is that? inquired the President, with much earnestness. His health is too feeble for the toils which any man must endure who assumes to bring order out of that department, and so re-organize it, and administer it, as to make it what it ought to be—an instrument of good to the people at large, for whose convenience it had been created. Mr. Anderson, I proceeded to say, cannot live a year; he is now in such feeble health as to justify that opinion; to call him to the discharge of such heavy duties as must devolve upon him, in the General Post-Office, would, should he attempt their execution, hasten his transit to the grave; if he should not, for lack of health, be able to attend to the duties of the station, then it had just as well remain as it is.

A pause for a moment ensued—when the President looked at me, saying—"Colonel McKenney, I am very glad you have called"—when, at the moment, the servant announced dinner. He asked me to accompany him, after which we would resume our conversation. I declined, having company to dine with me that day—when he called the servant, directing him to tell Mrs. Monroe not to wait for him. The conversation was continued for an hour longer, when I left him.

The next day, when crossing Rock Creek bridge, which separates Washington from Georgetown, on my way home, I met George Hay, Esq., son-in-law of Mr. Monroe, on his roan horse. He spoke, saying, he was glad to meet me—that he had been riding about all the morning, looking after Mr. M'Lean, and had not found him. "I will thank you, if you see him, to say the object of my search is, at Mr. Monroe's instance, to tell him that his name has been this morning sent into the Senate as Post-Master General; and that it is Mr. Monroe's wish, that he would appoint you his First Assistant Post-Master General." I told him we were to dine that evening at Foxall's, when I would deliver to him the message.

On arriving at Foxall's, I found Mr. M'Lean was there, when, taking him into the office, I announced to him what Mr. Hay had charged me to make known to him. The President's reference to myself was responded to with great cordiality.

The nomination was confirmed, of course, and Mr. M'Lean entered upon the discharge of the duties of his new station. Some weeks went round, when he referred to the relations that the President desired I should stand to the office and to himself—saying he could not feel free to dismiss the incumbent without cause; that Mr. Bradley was competent and efficient, although he had found the department in great disorder, &c.; that he would, on the first occasion, should any delinquency happen, make the change.

I told him I respected his feelings and his principles, and had not a doubt he would find Mr. Bradley all he could desire; and that, from that moment, to think no more of me in relation to the appointment. He was put at ease, and we parted friends.

The same organization that had given such efficiency to the War Department, introduced into it, for the first time, by Mr. Calhoun, was adopted by Mr. M'Lean for the government of the Post-Office Department. It proved no less operative. The entire plan consisted in dividing the business into appropriate parts, and assigning a bureau to each branch, with an officer at the head of each, who was held responsible for the right and prompt management of the duties assigned to him; all the bureaux connecting into one common centre, whose supervisory and controlling power was in the head. If ever there was perfection carried into any branch of the public service, it was that which Mr. Calhoun carried into the War Department; and it was the same admirable organization which made the War Department the most effective and most popular branch of the government. And it was the same system that imparted such efficiency to the General Post-Office. And yet neither would have produced the popular results that distinguished both, if each had not been governed by heads that comprehended, and knew how to give direction to both. The War Department was a literal chaos when Mr. Calhoun took it in hand; and so was the General Post-Office, when Mr. M'Lean succeeded to its management. Both rose out of this chaos into order, and harmony, and usefulness.

I have recorded this anecdote, if it may be called one, for the purpose of showing how personal predilections were made to give way, in Mr. Monroe, to the higher claims of public utility. Mr. Anderson was his choice, but Mr. M'Lean was the better qualified man to advance the public interests as Post-Master General, when, of course, all that was personal gave way, and the "general welfare" alone was consulted.

A time came, at last, when Mr. M'Lean was considered

a stumbling block in the way of party. The "*reward*" and "*punishment*" system was to take the place of qualification, patriotism, and experience. Personal rewards, and not the public good, had now become the practice of the government. The friends of General Jackson were now to be "rewarded," and those who were not "of his party," were to be "punished." But how, it may be asked, could this system affect Mr. M'Lean? Was he not favorable to the elevation of General Jackson? The general impression was, that he favored the result. Then why was he moved upon? Because, I answer, he declined to make the General Post-Office an instrument of party; and to become an executioner, and chop off heads as he might be commanded. To the question asked of a member of the Hickory club in Washington—What are you going to do with Mr. M'Lean? the answer was, "D—n him, we'll bench him." The alternative left for Mr. M'Lean, was to quit with an appointment as judge; or quit without any thing. Nor would the office of judge have been tendered to him, if his popularity had not forbade his expulsion. So, at least, it was understood at Washington. The judgeship was not, at that time, what best suited Mr. M'Lean. He had been long out of the practice of law, as member of Congress and commissioner of the General Land Office. But the same industry, sustained by moral rectitude, and strong natural talents, enabled him, in a few years, to occupy a respectable position on the bench of the Supreme Court, and now to rank with its most able and honored members.

Mr. Barry succeeded Judge M'Lean. There was one act, at least, of this functionary, that gave great notoriety to his official character as Post-Master General. It was the issuing of an order through the heads of the departments, which was distributed among the several bureaux, by order of the secretaries, directing that no letters, from and after its date, should be sealed with wax, but with wafers only; wax, it being alleged, adding so much to the weight of the mails!

When I saw this order, I took it with me to Mr. Secretary Eaton, and asked if it was intended to apply to the correspondence of the Indian department. "Why not?" he inquired. Because, I answered, much of that correspondence has to traverse the wilderness, and portions of it to be swam with over rivers, tied to the heads of Indians; and in various other ways to be exposed to the weather, and to the rough usage of a border circulation. "I suppose," he answered, "the Post-Master General knows his own business best; conform to the order."

I was curious to know how much weight the mails were relieved of by this change, and ascertained it to amount to something less than five pounds, daily! there being an average of about a pound and a quarter of wax used in each of the four departments—State, Treasury, War, Navy, and in the office of the Attorney General. There was much speculation at the time, as to the real object of this order. Nobody believed then, and nobody will believe now, that it was what it was avowed to be.

CHAPTER III.

THE BUREAU OF INDIAN AFFAIRS. COMMISSIONS TO TREAT WITH THE INDIANS. VOYAGE ON THE LAKES. GREEN BAY. BUTTE DE MORTS.

Organization of the Bureau of Indian affairs—Dilatory legislation—Living on half pay—Effects of severe labors upon health—Appointed commissioner to negotiate a treaty with the Indians at Fond du Lac—Other commissioners to the Choctaws, Chickasaws and Creeks—Arrival at Detroit, and departure for Green Bay—First steamboat ascent of the Neebish Rapids—Sault de St. Marie—White fish, and the fishery—Canadian voyagers—Gale on the Lake—Sea-sickness—Boat aground—Detention at Green Bay—Le Petit Butte de Morts—Return to Mackinac—A patient—Doctor Monroe and lady—A contrast—A romantic wife—Return to Green Bay—Hazardous voyage—A night on shore—Another patient—The medicine man superseded—A cure—Arrival at Green Bay—Alarm in the fort—Allayed by the arrival of General Cass—Apprehensions of an attack—The big gun brought up—Portage at the Grand Kockalas—"Short guns"—An experiment—Lighting an Indian's pipe with the sun—Firing at a target in the lake—Indians coming in—Toils of the women—An exception—An Indian's gratitude—Passage of the Rapids of the Grand Kockalas—Talk with the Winnebagoes—Anecdote of General Leavenworth.

In the month of February, 1824, Mr. Calhoun being Secretary of War, that gentleman made known to me his wish, which was also the President's, to organize a Bureau of Indian Affairs, in connexion with the Department of War, and offered me the appointment of chief. He said the duties were peculiar, and required experience in their performance, and that I had that. I was engaged in the incipient stages of a departure for a trip to Mexico, and thanking him for his confidence, told him I did not think I could accept of the proposal. I made the offer known to some of my friends, who thought it better for me to forego my contemplated trip to Mexico, and resume under this new form, my relations to the government and the Indians. At another interview with Mr. Calhoun, I learned that all the means at his disposal, which he could make applicable to my salary, were sixteen hundred dollars. This I declined to accept, upon the ground that it was inadequate to my support, and would not be a just equivalent for the services which I knew the office would require at my hands. He admitted the justness of both—but added, the President and himself had talked the matter over, and that, if I would undertake the trust, the President would recommend in his next message to Congress, the organization of an Indian Department, with a salary equal to that paid to auditors, expressing a hope that this would be satisfactory. I finally consented, and on the 11th of March, 1824, had assigned to me the duties of the Bureau of Indian Affairs.*

---

* DEPARTMENT OF WAR,
March 11th, 1824.

SIR—To you are assigned the duties of the Bureau of Indian Affairs in this department, for the faithful performance of which you will be responsible. Mr. Hamilton and Mr. Miller are assigned to you, the former as chief, the latter as assistant clerk. You will take charge of the appropriations for annuities and of the current expenses, and all warrants on the same will be issued on your requisitions on the Secretary of War, taking special care that no requisition be issued, but in cases where the money previously remitted has been satisfactorily accounted for, and on estimates in detail, approved by you, for the sum required. You will receive and examine the accounts and vouchers for the expenditure thereof, and will pass them over to the proper auditor's office for settlement, *after* examination and approval by you; submitting such items for the sanction of this department as may require its approval. The administration of the fund for the civilization of the Indians is also committed to your charge, under the regulations established by the department. You are also charged with the examination of the claims arising out of the laws regulating the intercourse with Indian tribes, and will, after examining and briefing the same, report them to this department, endorsing a recommendation for their allowance or disallowance. The ordinary correspondence with the superintendents, the agents, and sub-agents, will pass through your bureau.

I have the honor to be your obedient servant,

[Signed] JOHN C. CALHOUN.

THOMAS L. MCKENNEY, Esq.

I found the business of our Indian relations greatly in arrears. It required the most laborious efforts, for nearly the whole of the first year, to bring it up. The President was faithful to his promise, and recommended the passage of an act for the organization of a department. At the request of the Chairman of the Committee of Indian Affairs, I prepared a bill, submitted it to the Secretary of War, who wrote on it, in pencil, "*All right—alter not a word.*" I left in it a blank for the committee to fill with the sum they might agree upon for the salary. It was filled with the sum of three thousand dollars. The bill was reported to the House, and passed to a second reading, and there it stopped, not from objection to it, or its provisions, but because it was taken precedence of, by other matters, deemed by Congress to be of more importance. This was its fate for several successive sessions; I being left, meantime, to get along as well as I might on the *half pay*, which was at the disposal of, the department. Afterwards, Governor Cass and General Clark, by direction of the executive, drew regulations for the government, in detail, of the Indian department, which, however, contained little else than an embodiment of the system upon which the bureau had been previously governed. Still the salary was not reached, nor was it appropriated till my successor was in place, and ready to receive it. To him, and to his successors, it has been paid to this day.

I addressed a letter to Mr. Calhoun, after he had left the department, calling his attention to my unrequited labors, and received from him the following answer:— "No one better knows than myself, how inadequate your salary is, as a compensation for the varied and important duties of your office. There is no branch of business in the War Department, which requires more minute and laborious attention, or to which greater responsibility is attached. I would rejoice to see your compensation placed on a more respectable footing." Nothing, however, has ever been done to reimburse me, and I remain to this day without having received a copper towards the difference between what I did receive, and that which, by every rule of equity and justice, I was, and yet am entitled to receive.

Such were my labors, so constant and oppressive, and so weighty the responsibilities which devolved on me, as to have very nearly cost me my life. My health gave way under the pressure, and but for the confidence of President Adams and Mr. Barbour—the latter, at the period to which I am referring, being Secretary of War—in referring to me the duties of joint commissioner with Governor Cass to negotiate a treaty with the Indians at *La Fond du Lac, Superior*, and again with other tribes at Green Bay, the year following, I should, in all probability, have died at my post. Twelve senators and representatives in Congress united in a request to President Adams to join me in those commissions. The late President Harrison, being at that time senator, was one of them. (See Appendix, D.)

It was not, perhaps, the state of my health that operated to produce this request, so much as a belief which they expressed, in the benefit that would result to the public service, from the information which I might obtain in a personal intercourse with the Indians, and which would give me greater power over the varied and complex duties of my office, when I should return to resume them.

The first year's travels to Lake Superior restored me my health; though it was not until some time after the expedition had entered that lake, that the officers in command of the military escort gave over their more than half-made preparations to give me a magnificent burial on its shore. Of this kindness, however, I knew nothing at the time, but was often reminded of it after my health was restored. I threw together in a volume of some five hundred pages, under the title of "*Tour to the Lakes*," the incidents of that expedition, which I dedicated to my friend and patron, the Hon. JAMES BARBOUR, Secretary of War. Besides the duties enjoined on me, jointly with Governor Cass, in that year, it was made my duty, by special commissions, after concluding our labors at Green Bay, to proceed in my individual capacity, to the performance of others, as disclosed in the following commissions:—

DEPARTMENT OF WAR,
March 28, 1827.

To COLONEL THOMAS L. MCKENNEY:—

SIR—With the view of obtaining local and other information of the country between the lakes and the Mississippi, the condition and disposition of the Indian tribes which are scattered over it, and especially to ascertain the disposition of the tribes within the States, the Chickasaws and Choctaws, and, if practicable, the Cherokees, on the subject of emigration to lands west of the Mississippi, the President directs that after the council is closed at Green Bay, and the business entrusted to you and Governor Cass settled, that you will cross the country from Green Bay in such direction as you may esteem it to be the most eligible, either by way of Fox and Ouisconsin rivers, or by descending Lake Michigan to Chicago, down the Illinois to the Mississippi, and thence to the States, noting whatever incidents you may esteem valuable, and that in any manner may be connected with our Indian relations, and that may tend to enlighten the department in matters pertaining to their judicious disposition and application.

To your discretion is referred the best mode of approaching the Choctaws and Chickasaws, and, if you can reach them, the Cherokees, on the subject of emigration; but any convention you may make with them, will be understood to be only conditional, and subject to the approval of the President, to be afterwards confirmed by the more formal stipulations of treaties. The extent to which you are to go in these visits and councils, will reach no farther than an ascertainment of the disposition and will of the Indians, and the nature and extent of the terms on which they will consent to emigrate; which may be made binding on them, on being approved by the President, and thrown afterwards into treaty form.

You will also visit agencies, and such Indian schools as may be within your reach, and inform yourself of their condition and prospects; and generally collect such information as may be necessary to a prompt and efficient discharge of the duties arising out of our Indian relations.

Your compensation will be fixed on your return, and made equivalent to the extent and value of your services. Your expenses, (together with any reasonable amount, not exceeding one thousand dollars, which you may find it necessary to expend among the Indians for the promotion of the objects in view,) will be borne, and a requisition will issue on your estimate of what they mav probably be, for which you will, as is usual, account on your return.

I have the honor, &c.,

JAMES BARBOUR.

Department of War,
April 10th, 1827.

To Colonel Thomas L. McKenney:—

Sir—Referring to my instructions to you of 28th March, I now add the particular desire of the President, that if it be practicable for you to return by the way of the Creek country, that you do so, and that you employ all proper means in your discretion, to procure of the Creeks a cession of the remaining strip of land in Georgia; and for this object the President hereby empowers you to act, either separately or jointly, as you may esteem it best, with the agent, Colonel Crowell, who will be, meanwhile, authorized if possible to accomplish this object.

I have the honor to be, very respectfully, your obedient servant,

James Barbour.

I left Washington in due season for Detroit, there to join Governor Cass, having in my *suite* a secretary, physician, my son, and a servant; where, on my arrival, I found all the preparations made, and a day appointed for our departure for Green Bay. Our conveyance was a steamboat, in which, besides a goodly number of passengers of both sexes, were Major General Scott and suite. General Scott was to make his first visit to the post at the *Sault de St. Marie*. It was proposed, on our way to Mackinac, and agreed to, to allow the captain some additional pay to try the ascent of the *St. Marie*, and test the power of his boat in a contest with the Neebish rapids. The bargain was concluded, and the experiment was decided to be made; when, leaving Mackinac, we were soon in the *Detour*, and very soon after amidst the whirl and agony of the rapids. The power of the descending water, and its whirlpool-like surges, would often bring the boat to a stand, then force her first to one side and then to the other, the rocks, meantime, as seen through the transparent water, being often near aboard, when she would again shoot ahead, and again become stationary, like a thing taking repose, or gathering strength for another onset, and a new triumph. At last we reached the more level and tranquil surface, when coming suddenly in view of the village and its population, of the fort and garrison, and the Indians, an expression of universal astonishment marked every face, at this unlooked-for appearance of the first steamboat that had ever reached that place. The inhabitants looked spell-bound, whilst the Indians eyed the boat in silence, and listened, half horror-struck, to the whizz and deafening roar of the steam, as it escaped from the vent. In every face was depicted a mute, but bewildered surprise, such as one might be supposed to feel if brought suddenly in contact with his Satanic Majesty, invested with all the trappings, and set off with all the appendages with which our youthful fancies were wont to invest that personage.

Having been at the *Sault* the year before, when on my way to *La Fond du Lac*, *Superior*, I had made acquaintances. Among these was the proprietor of the only public house in the village of which these remote regions could then boast, where I well remember the white fish was cooked in perfection. My first move was to this long, low, log house, where I forthwith requested a dinner to be prepared for our company—white fish, that were then swimming in the rapids, to form part of it, and the principal dish, *of course*. In a moment the order was passed, and in another moment the Indians, some of them boys, were out among the rapids, balancing their little bark canoes, with a foot upon each gunwale, and in their hands a scoop net, with its handle some ten feet long, reaching down into the whirling and foaming rapids, taking in the white fish as fast as they could be thrown into the canoe. Our repast was a sumptuous one.

Taking a bark canoe and some voyagers, I gratified part of our company with a view of Lake Superior. These dexterous Canadians knowing the party, with an exception or two, to be unaccustomed to the canoe, and to its movements among the rapids, on our return, ran the frail vessel along the very edge of the curve, over which the water tumbles in its first plunge, but with a skill which only the voyagers can exert, enlivening the scene, meantime, with their boat songs, and a jabbering of their Canadian French.

Returned to Mackinac, and thence on to Green Bay. When off Lake Michigan, a terrible gale arose. Its severity and duration were unusual, even in this region of storms. Such was its violence, that both anchors proved insufficient to keep the boat to her moorings, and being driven ashore; when the steam was let on, and the wheels kept in motion, which alone, it was thought, saved us from being stranded. So billowy were the waters, as when the boat would wear round, and expose a quarter to the surge, it would strike her with such force as to roll her well nigh over, the bell, meantime, keeping up a continual toll, as if noting the time that was hastening to engulf us all.

A fine opportunity occurred during the storm, for testing my skill in the management of that most prostrating of all afflictions, sea-sickness. We had three physicians on board, but they were all as dead men. Nearly all the passengers, and several of the hands and attendants, were paying the customary tribute to the gale; myself and son, and faithful servant Ben, being excused from the contribution. Even the cabin girl, when making her way to the companion door, gave signs that her time also had come, for she had scarcely delivered to me a message from my cousin, Mrs. Doctor T–b–r–k, of New York, which she did by gasping out, "You're wanted down here"—when she fell backwards flat on the cabin floor. Going down, I found some seven or more of the lady passengers also on the floor, having been tumbled from their berths, whilst others who had been able to keep their places, were not the less victims to the overwhelming nausea. Among the latter was my cousin, whose husband was among the helpless ones in the gentlemen's cabin. Those who were upon the floor, had arrived at that condition of helplessness, as to have no power over their movements—not a muscle seconded their will to take hold and steady themselves. When the boat would lurch, they would roll across the cabin, and fetch up in one confused mass on the opposite side, to remain there till another lurch from the other side would send them all across the floor in an opposite direction.

I made signal to Ben, who with great effort reached me. I directed him to cut open a bale of blankets—separate, and pass them to me as quick as possible. It was done; when, holding a blanket in one hand, and with the other supporting myself, as the mass began to separate to find its lodgment on the opposite side of the cabin floor, I would, as the openings between the bodies were made, thrust in a blanket. I continued the process till I had the sufferers all wedged in, so as at last they became stationary. Fresh air was indispensable, to obtain which, I hoisted one of the stern windows. A few moments after, a sea broke in, bringing with it enough of terror to arouse a few of the prostrate party to some extra efforts—and these were accompanied by cries of "*Oh, we're lost!*"

I next caused to be procured from my medicine chest, a bottle of laudanum, with another of brandy. I poured portions of each into a tea-pot—all guess-work, for such was the rolling and pitching of the boat, as to make it difficult to hold on, much more so to count drops, or measure proportions—and so, from various positions which I sought and obtained, to hold on to something with one hand, I employed the other in divers attempts, (in not over one in a dozen did I succeed,) to get the spout of the tea-pot into the mouths of the sufferers, always involving the hazard to pour in more than might be useful. In less than thirty minutes after I had gone the rounds, all my patients, except one, who was in a berth, were as tranquil and composed, and free from sickness, as the circumstances would permit. I had my fears for the safety of that one—an interesting young lady, a Miss S–b–n–s, from the South, who, in company with her aunt, was on her way to visit her sister, wife of Captain B., of the army, stationed at Green Bay. Spasms had blackened her, and changed into this dismal hue, the hitherto rose and lily tinge of her cheeks—telling in language not to be mistaken of suspended circulation, and threatening to stop it forever. I had no one to assist me, and my only alternative was to tear (cut I could not, without danger, from the motion of the boat, of the knife's taking a direction other than the one intended) her corsets loose, which, being done, I applied bread saturated with laudanum and brandy to the pit of her stomach. A warm bath, my next resource had this failed, could not of course be commanded. In a few minutes after the application of the laudanum and brandy had been made, and about a spoonful taken, the face resumed much of its natural color, and the sufferer gave signs of doing well.

The storm having in part subsided, the anchors were weighed, and we were heading it on to Green Bay. When within some five miles of the village, and about two from the fort, the boat grounded; and such was the rapid recession of the waters which the gale had blown into the bay and river, that before the appropriate means could be put in operation for heading her off, her paddles were out of water. We were conveyed to the village at Green Bay in boats.

I thought I saw in this revulsion of the waters, the cause of the apparent tides that rise and fall, with an almost periodical precision, in those lakes. The winds keep the waters in constant agitation, and force them in the direction in which they blow. These falling or blowing from an opposite or any other direction, the waters fall back, seeking their level; and to this constant action, thus caused, I attribute the ocean-like ebbing and flowing of the waters of these lakes.

Every body, except the captain, was delighted at the stationary, and for some time at least, permanent situation of the boat. Our company had been so very agreeable as to make it quite hard to separate. This grounding of the boat gave us the opportunity to remain together some days at Green Bay; and but for it, all, except Governor Cass and myself, and suite, and a few who lived at the bay, would have the next day returned in the boat to Detroit.

The ground which had been selected upon which to hold our treaty, was some thirty-seven miles above Fort Howard, on the Fox river, and just below the opening into the Lake Winnebago. There could have been no more beautiful position found in all that region. The rise to it from the river is gradual, and reaches to some thirty feet. The level, when reached, widens out into the form of an irregular circle of some three hundred yards in circumference, and in nearly the centre is a mound called by the French, *La Petit Butte de Morts;* the mound being conical in form, about a hundred feet in circumference, and some twelve feet high. To this spot, all our supplies in provisions for the treaty, and presents for the Indians, &c., were forwarded; and leaving our party to put up the necessary log houses in which to store the property, and to give time for the Indians to come in, Governor Cass and myself agreed to separate—he to go to the Mississippi, and I to Lake Superior; the chief object being to send runners among the Indians to secure a full attendance from as many bands as could be reached. The governor took to his bark canoe, and I, as far as Mackinac, to the steamboat.

Arriving at Mackinac, where I parted from friends in whose society I had enjoyed so much pleasure, I took with my company a barge conveyance to Drummond's Island and the *Sault.* The waters of Huron becoming a little billowy, another scene of sea-sickness was witnessed, which made a longer pause at Drummond's Island, at that time a British post, than was contemplated necessary. I was, as before, the ministering physician. Arriving at the quarters of Captain Anderson, it was thought my fair patient could not survive. Indeed, so thought Doctor

Munroe, of the British army, who, with his accomplished lady, had just arrived, to exchange the polish of courts of Europe for a bark lodge on Drummond's Island, to which barren and desolate station he had been appointed surgeon. About the doctor's neck, suspended by a riband, hung a medal, the badge of distinction which he had won at the battle of Waterloo.

The previous remedies, with the addition of a warm bath, and the kind offices of Mrs. Anderson and Mrs. Munroe, succeeded in restoring the patient to health, and enough of strength to enable her the next morning to breakfast with Mrs. Munroe in her bark-thatched cottage. Rough as was this little lodge in its exterior—for its sides, as well as its roof, were of bark—there was an enviable comfort within. I could not refrain from questioning the accomplished Mrs. Munroe upon the state of her feelings, when, for the first time, and only a few days before, her eyes were met by the rocky, barren, exposed, and inhospitable exterior of that island—for so little of space was there upon the rock-wedged surface for the formation of earthy matter, and so little of vegetation of any sort out of which to form it, that, to have a garden at all, Captain Anderson had been compelled to employ his command in scratching about in crevices for earth, and conveying it in hand-barrows to a space which he had marked out for a garden. To my questions, this charming lady gave the most winning answers. "Oh," said she, "I am just where my fancy has often been before me. I love everything that is wild in nature. London has no charms for me, compared with this island; and its palaces, smothered in smoke, fade away, to give place to these Indian wigwams, and this fresh air, and this delicious water, and this sweet and cozy little cabin." Happy man, I could not help ejaculating, to be blessed with such a wife! I saw, in all her revelling amidst these new scenes, that there was a charm even more endearing than all beside, and that was derived from the possession and presence of the man she loved; and how the presence and sight of such happy contentment must have balanced the loss of that world of fashion, of taste, and luxury, which the accomplished Doctor Munroe had left.

Arriving at the *Sault*, runners were put in motion, as they had been elsewhere, to invite the Indians to attend the treaty. This being done, I took a bark canoe, which, in honor of my fair cousin, I called "THE MARY OF THE LAKES," and with eight Canadian voyagers, wended my way back to Mackinac and Green Bay—the entire distance being some two hundred and fifty miles. At Mackinac I took in supplies, which, together with Ben and myself, and eight voyagers, left out of water, of this frail vessel, not over four inches, except at the bow and stern, of her beautiful form. All being ready, and just as I was going to embark, a storm arose. The good folks at Mackinac urged me not to attempt to put out. But my time had nearly expired, and there was barely enough left for me punctually to meet Governor Cass on his return to the bay; and so I gave orders to embark. The kind friends with whom we had parted at the landing, or many of them, ran down to the point of the island, to see, as some of them afterwards told me they were sure they should, the canoe and all in it go to the bottom. I had no such fears, for I had the year before been billow and storm-tossed on Lake Superior, and had reached the conclusion that if there is anything specially secure in a gale of wind, when one happens not to be too far from shore, and not exposed to a rock-bound coast, it is in a bark canoe, thirty-six feet long, and five feet wide across the middle—and these were the dimensions of mine—managed by eight experienced Canadian voyagers.

Night coming on, I ordered a landing made on the sheltered side of an island. The canoe was soon in about two feet of water, her side to the shore, and a voyager out, steadying her stern and bow, whilst myself and Ben were borne to the beach on the backs of two others. The provisions and baggage being conveyed on shore, the canoe was lifted out of the water, and conveyed there also—where it was placed bottom upwards, furnishing beneath a shelter for these hardy men, who were soon under it, munching their raw pork and hard biscuit. My tent having been meanwhile put up, all was made right for the night. Presently I heard the barking of a dog. Stepping from my tent, and looking in the direction from which it came, I saw in the distance, amidst the thick foliage, a light. Advancing a little, I heard an Indian's drum. I knew from the beat upon it, what it betokened. Somebody was ill, and the medicine-man was engaged with his incantations, and drum, and mummeries, to drive out the bad spirit. Taking along with me Ben and an interpreter, I wended my way through the dark and tangled undergrowth, till presently a full glare from a flambeau burst upon me, and the beat of the drum fell more distinctly on my ear, confirming my first impressions. The dogs had now all come out in full cry, and a tall Indian revealed himself by the torch-light at the door of the wigwam, accoutred in the habiliments of his tribe, with a rifle in his hand. He hailed us, and received from the interpreter, in his own language, the answer that we were friends, and on our way to the great treaty which was soon to be held at the foot of Winnebago Lake. The dogs were called in, when we met and shook hands. The pipe was lighted, handed round, and smoked.

Upon a mat much worn, with nothing but the ground beneath it, lay a fine-looking Indian woman. On one side, near her head, sat, in pensive mood, a middle-aged man, and beside him a young man. On the other side sat two girls, and at the head stood the medicine-man, thumping his drum, and performing those mystic rites that belong to his craft. My sympathies grew strong for the sufferer, till finding it impossible to remain longer a spectator of such a scene, and not employ what skill I had, and my means, to save life, I determined to interfere. I knew there was hazard in the attempt—for I should have to encounter, first, the ire of the medicine-man, it being a no greater calamity to deprive such a one of his "occupation," than it was in the days of Shakspeare for Othello to lose his; next, should the patient die on my hands, there might be an account to settle with the husband, who would have no difficulty in arriving at the conclusion that she had been killed by me. But my mind was made up; so I said to my interpreter—Tell this man, (the woman's husband,) if he will stop that drum, and allow me to medicine his squaw, I think I can make her well. These words were scarcely out of the interpreter's mouth, when the medicine-man threw upon me from his black eyes, which were shining amidst the torch-light of the wigwam, and exceeding it in brightness, a look of fierceness, which nothing but my previous intercourse with the Indians could have enabled me, without great apprehension, to endure.

The husband hesitated—then looking at me, then at the medicine-man, and then at his suffering wife, said, "*I will be glad;*" when, making the signal, the drum was hushed, and the insulted operator, with a scowl at me, rushed from the wigwam, in all the fiery temperament that such a stroke at his art was so well calculated to enkindle.

A brief examination of the case satisfied me that there was no time to be lost, and that the remedies must be of the most powerful class. My first impression was that the patient was laboring under *puerperal* fever; but a further testing of the symptoms satisfied me that it was *pleurisy.* The inflammation was great, and the suffering extreme. Blood-letting gave partial relief. Warm applications, in the form of fomentations, not being at hand, I directed a hole to be dug at the door of the wigwam, and filled with water; meantime a large fire was kindled, and stones were thrown into it, which, on becoming hot, were put into the water, till, by this means, it was sufficiently heated, when the patient was drawn down upon her mat, till her feet and legs were immersed knee deep. Blankets from my stores were then wrapped round and over her. In five minutes the perspiration literally rolled down her cheeks. Meantime, I directed Ben to make a good bed out of blankets, with a pillow of the same, when she was drawn back again, and placed upon it, her ragged mat of a bed being left at the door of the wigwam, and then thrown away. Her symptoms were greatly improved, which, added to her more comfortable bed, caused this poor destitute daughter of the forest to look volumes of gratitude, though without uttering a word. Twelve grains of calomel that night, and a dose of magnesia in the morning, concluded the treatment, which I took care to sustain by light diet, in the form of tea, with crackers broken in it. All being so well, I left in the afternoon of the next day, placing by her a nourishing diet, with a superadded bottle of sweetened water, dashed with claret wine. Tea and crackers, bottled, which she was to warm before taking, was to be her food till what I left was gone, when a certain portion of the wine and water was, afterwards, to be taken. Dog-soup and fish were prohibited, until she felt very hungry, and then these were to be eaten in moderation. This being all arranged, I embarked. Having lost time, I proposed to the voyagers to go on all night, which they agreed to, on condition of being paid additional rations, including, of course, tobacco.

These hardy adventurous fellows never rose from their paddles, nor stopped, except to "*pipe*," from four o'clock, P. M., of one day, till eleven o'clock, A. M., of the next, a period of nineteen hours, without rest or sleep, filling the air with their chanting, and giving new life to their efforts by their choruses. In coasting along the southern shore of the bay, I saw ample evidence, in the uprooting of enormous trees, that were lying in all directions, of the force and violence of the storm to which I have referred.

My attention, as I neared the fort, was arrested by the sudden opening of the gates, and the running down the pier of the officers and others. I was at a loss to divine the meaning. My destination was to the village, three miles beyond; but, on seeing this movement, I ordered my steersman to turn in, and bring up alongside the pier. It was done. When within speaking distance, I called to know if anything special was the matter. The answer was, "Seeing a canoe with a United States flag flying, and manned as this is, we thought it was Governor Cass, and are troubled to find that we are mistaken." What's the matter? "Two runners have been in, bringing intelligence that, as he was passing down the Ouisconsin, just beyond the portage, he was fired into by Indians, his cook killed, two of his men wounded, and himself and the remainder taken prisoners!" Then why, I asked, has not the force of this place been employed to rescue the governor and his party, and punish the outrage? No satisfactory answer being given, I proceeded on to the village, receiving, however, the assurance that the fort would be left in charge of as much force as might be deemed necessary for its defence, and with the remainder, an ascent of the Fox river would be made, and pursuit given after the murderers. I agreed to accompany the expedition.

On arriving at the village, I found the inhabitants in a state of the greatest alarm. Women were expressing their dread of an Indian incursion and massacre, and began to make ready to take refuge in the fort. I proposed a muster of the force of the place, an arming, and the throwing out of videttes, and stationing guards, &c. Preparations for embarkation at the fort, and a plan of defence at the village, were going bravely on, when a canoe was seen coming up the bay, and in the direction of Lake Michigan. All eyes were fixed upon it. A flag was seen flying at its stern. It drew nearer—when, by the aid of a glass, Governor Cass was recognized, his crew, the killed cook, and all! The panic was ended, and the joy universal. There had been no attack made upon the governor; but, on his arrival at Prairie du Chien, he found that murders had been committed there; and apprehending a frontier war, he pushed on down the Mississippi in his bark canoe to St. Louis, had an interview with General Atkinson, who, with his command, was soon in motion; then, continuing up the Illinois river, and through Lake Michigan to Green Bay, where our meeting took place, when our treaty operations were commenced.

Information had been conveyed to us by some of our people, that FOUR-LEGS, a distinguished Winnebago chief, and others, had shown symptoms of an unruly sort, and fears were entertained lest he might lead on an attack upon our party, and capture the property then on the treaty ground. On the receipt of this intelligence, I requested the commanding officer, Major Whistler, to have a six-pounder sent to the *Butte de Morts.* It was accordingly forwarded, and mounted just in front of the door of my tent, its muzzle pointing in the direction of Winnebago lake.

On the route to Butte de Morts, voyagers are impeded by the rapids at the Grand Kockalas—a shoot of water which stretches diagonally across the river, of an average descent of some four or five feet, producing a whirl and tumble of rapids below, which do not find rest for the distance of a quarter of a mile. A portage is made here by all who ascend this river. During this process, and while the men were busy in carrying the baggage, &c., around the rapids, I sat under the shade of a large tree, amusing myself with picking with a bristle the nipples of a pair of pistols, which were just large enough to be conveniently carried in my vest pockets. A young Indian of about twenty-five years old, stood leaning over me, watching the process. Presently he gave a shout and a laugh, saying, "Short gun—my father may shoot me—hurt nobody." I told the interpreter to tell him if he wanted to know what these short guns could do, just to go across Fox river and stand there, and if he desires to have a hole made through him, he can then be gratified. He shook his head and laughed, manifestly holding both myself, and my "short guns," in derision. I was compelled either to do something practically with my pistols, or forfeit the respect of at least one of those who were destined to be of the council at the treaty ground. There lay before me on the grass a bit of bark, some six inches long, and about four wide. I told Ben to put it in the ground, at about five paces from me. To the interpreter I said, now tell him I am going to let him see whether these "short guns" are to be laughed at. It was a desperate experiment, I knew; for should I miss the bark, I should have subjected myself to the scorn and contempt of this doubting Indian. I took aim, seated as I was, and fired.

The bark fell. The Indian sprang to it, took it up, and looked at it on the side that was exposed to my shot. The ball being only the size of a buck-shot, he could see no place of entrance, the filaments of the inner lining of the rougher outside having closed over the aperture. He laughed, and clapped his hand on his thigh, and pointed in derision at the pistol. I knew I had hit the bark, and felt satisfied that a piece had been split off on the opposite side, and so I told him to look at that side. He did so, and gave signs of astonishment. He then pushed his rifle-picker through the hole, and saw, sure enough, that it had been made by the shot from my "little gun," when he came up with a changed countenance, and asked permission to examine it. He was gratified, and seemed to think there was something more about it than met his eye.

An old Indian seated near me, took out of his pouch a bit of spunk, and flint and steel, and began to strike fire to light his pipe. I directed the interpreter to tell him he need not be at that trouble, that I would bring down fire from the sun, and light his pipe with that. He looked at me awhile, and shook his head, as much as to say, nonsense! I rose and went to him, drawing from my pocket a sun-glass, and, carefully concealing it from his view, drew through it the focal rays, and told him to smoke. He did so, when the tobacco being ignited, and the smoke from it filling his mouth, he first looked at me, then at the sun, then at his pipe, with eyes that danced in their sockets with amazement and awe. These two circumstances made of me almost a Manitou.

One other event tended very much to confirm this belief. We had arrived at the treaty ground, and were waiting to give time for as many Indians to come in as might be on their way to it. The delay caused, in those who had been there for several days, as is always the case, a tedium. To call them off from this state of idleness, I directed an empty barrel to be anchored in the direction of Winnebago lake, at a distance of about a quarter of a mile, and then summoned the Indians round to witness the power of the six-pounder. Very few of them had ever heard a report louder than the crack of their rifles. Everything being ready, I invited several of our party to take turns in firing. Each had a shot at the barrel. All missed it, but the water was ploughed up by the balls in columns and sheets, the foam and spray often for awhile obscuring the barrel from our view. I then said I would try. The gun being loaded, I drew what I thought was a true sight, fired, and shivered the barrel to atoms; when, turning short about, I walked leisurely to my tent, leaving the Indians to their own reflections—many of whom came to my tent and looked in upon me, not doubting what I knew to be quite an accidental affair, was something superhuman; and especially did those arrive at this conclusion who had heard of my hitting the bit of bark with a gun not larger than their little finger, and of my having lighted the old chief's pipe with the fire drawn from the sun, which latter circumstance I found had been much talked of.

The Indians were now pouring in—their canoes looking like fleets—some by the way of Winnebago lake, others by that of the Fox river below. I was seated in my tent-door observing these little fleets, and watching the movements of the Indians as they landed; the squaws laborious and busy, plying their paddles to reach the shore of their destination, and then foremost in the work of unloading, and conveying their poor stores and lodge-poles, and bark to cover them, their kettles, &c., to the beach—when they would take the canoe by one or more of the cross-bars, and walk with it out of the water to some secure place, where they would turn it bottom upwards, and then return for the materials for their lodges, convey them to some spot which their quick glancing eye would light upon, and then begin and end the process of putting up their place of repose during the continuance of the treaty; their lords, meantime, looking on with but seeming little concern; or, with blankets about their hips, standing or sitting, indulging in the luxury of the calumet.

It was in the midst of all this that I saw a canoe coming up the river, worked by two men, the woman and two girls doing nothing. This was so new a circumstance, as to call my attention from the general movements, to this single arrival. I thought there must be a sprinkling of civilization there; and that the men had been led by it to regard the women with a more appropriate tenderness. As soon as the canoe had approached the shore near enough for the party to step out, the men, I remarked, carried out this principle of tender regard for the sex, and were the first to step into the water, and the first to commence the process of unloading; in a word, the woman and the girls were but lookers on. All the articles, with the canoe, being disposed of, I saw the man stoop down and pick up a white fish of uncommon size; when he stepped forward, followed in Indian file by the rest, including some half dozen dogs. He wound round the little bluff upon which my tent was pitched, and when I saw him again rising to nearly a level with me, his eyes were in motion, looking in every direction, till presently they fell on me, when he made a short angle, followed still by his family, walked up to me, and stooping, laid the fish at my feet—then gracefully rising, he turned and walked away to the place where his canoe and his effects had been placed, and commenced putting up his lodge. This was the family from the island, and the woman was the same I had cured; the man was her husband, and the young man and girls were her children. This offering of the white fish, was an INDIAN'S GRATITUDE! Noble trait! Where this feeling has place, in no matter what bosom, whether it be red, or white, or black, all beside is apt to be right. Yes, and there is no doubt but if this poor Indian had possessed silver and gold, these richer offerings would have been as freely made, and in the same way. This was another proof, further confirming my previously conceived belief, that this noble race was never intended by their Maker to be trodden down and persecuted, after the manner in which this work of extermination has been carried on by our race.

I made a couple of trips to the village and fort before the council was opened. In one of them I prevailed on one of my voyagers—the rest declining—to go with me over the shoot, and down the rapids of the Grand Kockalas. There was one place which had been worn more smooth than the rest, of about ten feet wide, over which, at high water, barges descending the river could go. But it was low water now, yet enough remaining, over the shoot, to pass a bark canoe. My voyager was firm. I saw him to be so—when, taking my seat on the bottom of the canoe, and about midway, he pushed boldly out; then the current striking the canoe, a contest was begun between the skill of my brave, and this rush of waters. At last he had the head of the canoe on a line with the shoot, when down and over she went, with the velocity of an arrow, making a plunge of some four or five feet—the skill and self-possession of my voyager having governed him in making a single stroke with his pole, at the instant when it was required, just as the leap was about to be made, thus preventing the turning of the canoe's side to the current, and a consequent wreck. Never before had I seen anything upon the waters dance and bounce about as did this canoe, when fairly down amidst the rapids and breakers. The thing seemed like a joyous bird, after having escaped the toils of the fowler; or like some little blooming beauty of a child, after the restraints had been cut loose, and she was fairly in among her happy and delighted playmates.

We were prepared to open the council on Wednesday, the first of August, 1827, but concluded to defer it one day longer, and until tidings should reach us of the movements of General Atkinson. Meantime, however, we thought it proper to hold a talk with the Winnebagoes, of whom there were some five hundred present, and inform them that the murders that had been committed, were by individuals of their tribe, and urge upon them the surrender of the guilty persons, and thereby save themselves from the consequences of a war for their capture. At the moment when orders were about to be given to convene those present of the Winnebago tribe, we learned they were making ready for a feast—we therefore postponed assembling them until the next day. The following morning the talk was made, and they were urged to give up the murderers, it being no part of their Great Father's wish to punish the innocent; but that if their people would so far forget themselves as to kill our people, they must expect a road to be made through their country, not with axes, but with guns. The chief, *Four-Legs*, vindicated *his* band, asserting their innocence, and referring the murders to those living on the Mississippi. He did not think it just to bring guns among the innocent. This fine-looking chief occupied, with his village, the tongue of land which runs out between Winnebago lake, on the one side, and the Fox river on the other. When General Leavenworth, some years previous, was ascending the Fox river with troops, on his way to the Mississippi, on arriving at this pass, *Four-Legs* came out, dressed in all his gewgaws and feathers, and painted after the most approved fashion, and announced to the general that he could not go through; "*the lake*," said he, "*is locked*." "Tell him," said the general, rising in his batteaux, with a rifle in his hand, "that THIS IS THE KEY, and I shall unlock it, and go on." The chief had a good deal of the better part of valor in his composition, and so he replied, "Very well, tell him he can go."

Still anxious to hear from General Atkinson before we opened, formally, our councils, we deferred yet longer the opening of our negotiations, and sent a Winnebago runner with despatches, to meet that officer.

CHAPTER IV.

INCIDENTS OF THE COUNCIL AT LE PETIT BUTTE DE MORTS.

Sabbath amid Nature's solitudes—Christian Indians engaged in worship—Opening of the Council—A contrast—Treaty adjusted and signed—An alarm—Le Grand Butte de Morts—Indian tradition—Death of a medicine-man—Funeral ceremonies—Distribution of presents among the Indians—Breaking up of the encampment—Brutal attack upon a woman—Chargeable to whiskey—The man transformed to a woman—Moral effects of this punishment—Awful evils of the whiskey trade—Embarkation—Ascending the Fox river—Dangers of the way—Some of my party return—Number of our men—Incidents by the way—A chase.

The Sabbath of the 5th of August broke upon us in great beauty, and with an air tempered and calm. I have never been able, in my forest rambles, to disengage from my mind the impression that the Sabbath and these solitudes are in close affinity with one another. How rarely has it happened, in the course of my experience, that this holy day has been vexed with the strife of elements. On the contrary, all is still! The voice of their Maker would seem to have hushed river and forest into silence, and then to have bade the sun to wheel himself up from his depths in the east, and pour over all, unobscured by clouds, a tempered heat, and crown the world with special loveliness. The dawn of this morning was peculiarly beautiful. "Rosy fingers" did indeed seem, as Milton has it, to "unbar the gates of light." Violet and purple, with a wide and widening circle of "orient pearl," all met my eye with their charming and chastening influences—and then there was such silence! Not a leaf rustled, and the waves broke in softer murmur on the shore. The tree-tops now began to revel in the beams, and then the high-lands to drink in the falling glory, till the entire circuit of the heavens was full of the tempered splendors of this Sabbath morn!

Yet all this silence was broken in upon this morning—for just between the time when the eastern sky was made mellow with the sun's light, and when the light began to tip the tops of tree and mountain, and all was so quiet, my ears were greeted by sweet sounds of music! They came from a lodge of Christian Indians, which was hard by, in the woods. They had risen with the day, to "worship God!" They sang in three parts, base, tenor, and treble, and with a time so true, and with voices so sweet, as to add harmony even to nature itself. Notes of thrush and nightingale sound sweeter when poured forth amidst the grove; so sounded those of these forest warblers, in the midst of the green foliage, and in the stillness of the woods. I attended their worship, and was present again with them in the evening; and as I listened to their songs of praise, and their prayers, I felt humbled, and ashamed of my country, in view of the wrongs it had inflicted, *and yet continues to inflict*, upon these desolate and destitute children of the forest. There were flowers and gems there which needed only to be cultivated and polished, to insure from the one, the emission of as sweet odors as ever regaled the circles of the civilized; and from the other, a brilliance as dazzling as ever sparkled in the diadem of queenly beauty. And yet they were, and are, neglected, trodden down, and treated as outcasts!

At twelve o'clock on Monday, the signal gun for the assembling of the council, was fired—when were seen coming in from all directions, the great multitude of the sons of the forest, to hear what their fathers had to say to them. The bands represented were Chippewas, Menomonies, Winnebagoes, Wabanackies, &c., &c.—in all, about one thousand—all attired in their best apparel, ornamented and painted after the most approved Indian fashion.

The council square, towards which all who were entitled to a seat in it were wending their way, was covered with boughs of evergreen, resting on a frame-work of timber, supported by posts inserted in the ground. Seats of any sort would have been useless appendages; for Indians, who are not civilized, prefer the ground to sit on, and knowing nothing of the luxury of a sofa, or chair, or of the "three-legged stool," on which, as Cowper sings—

"————The immortal Alfred sat,
And swayed the sceptre of his infant realms,"

would have studiously avoided enjoying either, had the ground been covered with them.

A few slabs, resting on pungeons driven in the ground, served to accommodate those who were not so familiar with the earth's surface as are the Indians. These were placed around a rude table, at one end of the square, on which the necessary papers and writing apparatus were placed, and where the minutes of the proceedings were taken by the secretary, and at the head of which sat the commissioners.

Everywhere over the ground, in the woods, and on the open plain, were seen moving about in all directions squaws, and papooses, and dogs; of the two first, some were busy with their fires, over which kettles were slung, for boiling their pork and beans; others were nursing, whilst others again were running every way after the more than half-naked children of larger growth, to bring them in, preparatory to the breaking up of the council, to be in readiness for the meal that was to be eaten; whilst the dogs were not idle, some fighting, and others busy in the more agreeable occupation of smelling about for the fragments of the last meal—all of them gaunt as half-starved wolves, and not unlike them in form and action.

Everywhere, outside of the council square, there was life, and bustle, and confusion; all within was quiet and respectful. I could not help thinking how much many of our public assemblies, from the Capitol at Washington, through the States, all over the Union, might profit by observing the dignified silence and attention observed by these untutored savages, and following their example, at least in this particular.

The governor delivered the opening address, explaining the leading objects for which the council had been called. These embraced the adjustment and fixing of boundary lines between the different tribes, and to peace and harmony among them—the rupture of the last being almost always, and having been so from time immemorial, consequent upon the uncertainty of the first. A war of over a hundred years' duration had continued between the Sioux and Chippewas, which was terminated by the treaty of Fond du Lac, of the previous year, in which the boundaries were established between them.

The claim to lands set up by the New York Indians was also brought before the council, and finally adjusted; and another appeal was also made to the Winnebagoes, of a warning character, in which they were admonished to bring in the murderers, and save their people from the consequences of a war. The council closed, and the Indians retired to deliberate, &c.

Thump—thump—thump. A drum! It was the medicine-man's drum over a sick child, accompanied by the usual pow-wowing, which was begun at four o'clock, P. M., and continued till eleven at night. Rev. Mr. Flavell, a Roman Catholic priest, and the Rev. Mr. Jones, a Protestant Episcopal clergyman, the first settled at Green Bay, last destined to the St. Peter's, offered up prayers. The Christian Indians sang again this evening, their hymns being made more strikingly sweet by the yelling and whooping of the wild Indians by whom they were surrounded. What a contrast! The woods made vocal on the one hand by Christian music, and startled on the other by the wild yells of the uncivilized! And yet both proceeding from the same race.

From the 6th to the 11th we were busy with the details of the treaty, which, being adjusted and read, was agreed to, and signed. The Chippewa and Menomonie lines were designated, whilst the Winnebagoes and Menomonies agreed to have theirs in common.

Meantime, incidents were not wanting to give excitement, some of these being quite alarming. We were aroused at ten o'clock at night, on Wednesday, the 8th July, by Major R., who came to inform us that a Chippewa had given information of the intention of the Winnebagoes to rise upon and murder us. In confirmation of this purpose, another messenger came to say that a Winnebago squaw had been to a Wabanackie, to borrow some musket balls. The guard was doubled, and everything put in readiness for the attack, but all remained quiet. The 10th brought with it a violent storm of wind, rain, lightning and thunder. It seemed as if it would sweep us, with our log huts and tents, away. It continued until four, P. M. Our flag-staff, that was planted on the apex of Le Butte de Morts, was bent into a bow by it, but was neither broken nor uprooted.

Beside this Petit Butte de Morts, there is another on the western shore of Winnebago lake, and some ten miles above this, which the French call Le Grand Butte de Morts. The French having been the first to traverse these regions, have given names to almost everything that is distinguishable by a name. All mounds that I have seen, that are conical in form, as are these two hills of the dead, are full of the bones of men. I sought of aged Indians their tradition in relation to this little, as well as the great hill of the dead, and learned that a long time ago a battle was fought, first upon the spot upon which is Le Petit

Butte de Morts, and the grounds adjacent, and continued upon that, and the surrounding country, upon which is found Le Grand Butte de Morts, between the Iroquois and Fox Indians, in which the Iroquois were victorious, killing an immense number of the Foxes at Le Petit Butte de Morts; when, being beaten, the Foxes retreated, but rallied at Le Grand Butte de Morts, and fought until they were nearly all slain. Those who survived, fled to the Mississippi, and down that river to the country about the Des Moine Rapids, Rocky Island, Du Buques, &c., where they multiplied, and again became a formidable people. In those two mounds, it is said, repose the remains of those slain at those two battles.

Despatches were received from General Atkinson, bearing date July 31. At breakfast, Captain B. informed the general and myself that he had reasons for suspecting the Winnebagoes, and was under arms all night. In every direction were seen moving stealthily about, these irritated and war-loving people. It then occurred to me that I had heard some one busy in the night at our grindstone, which was near my tent, sharpening knives. Possibly the captain mistook the object of the movements of these people. We commended his vigilance.

After breakfast, Priest Flavell came to me, saying in broken English—"I have been, sair, to de governor, to say that one grand medicine-man be dead; and to ask him for someting to make shroud—and for some candle—and to say how much please I shall be, if he will give order for de band of music to play, while we march to de grave to bury him. He told me, sair, you would answer dese questions." I did, of course, answer them in the affirmative; when the good priest rubbed his hands, made his bow, saying, "Dis will be grand affair." He had not been gone an hour before he came back in haste, saying with great animation, "Tree more Indians be dead! It will make one grand procession. Will you give order, sair, if you please, for more muslin for shroud, and for more candles." Orders were given accordingly. Meantime, a tall tree had been cut down, and trimmed of its branches, when its larger end was inserted in a natural mound near by, to add to its elevation—upon its top was fastened a cross, and from beneath this, streamed various emblems, indicating to the Indians who might thereafter pass up and down the river, or through the country, that the dead lay buried there, and that the priestly offices had been there exercised. I went to see the dead. The medicine-man was as fat, almost, as Falstaff is represented to have been—with a neck very nearly resembling that which Knickerbocker describes as having belonged to *Wouter Van Twiller;* and, like this redoubtable governor's, too, the medicine-man's cheeks looked as if they "had taken toll of everything that had gone into his mouth." The others were young; two boys and a girl. Many others were on the sick-list, the result, doubtless, of the abundance of rations in beef and pork, &c., which were issued daily to these imprudent and gormandizing people; and whose appetites being whetted by previous fasting, had now become voracious—and then again, the usual exercise of the chase, or of fishing, being dispensed with, they become victimized by these new gastronomic relations. If the business of the treaty had been protracted a week longer, there is little doubt but the good Mr. Flavell would have gained a portion, at least, of that immortality, in his connexion with the dead, that SCOTT has conferred upon his "Old Mortality."

The morning following, the signal was given for the funeral procession to form. We all joined it, preceded by the priest and the music. The pensive notes of funeral dirges fell mournfully upon our ears; but, except the Christian Indians, the mass would have been, perhaps, more struck with a jig from a hurdy-gurdy.

The business of the treaty over, preparations were made for the distribution of presents. This ceremony is indispensable at all such assemblages, made so no less by usage, than by humanity and justice. It is humane to feed these impoverished people, and no more than justice, after calling them away from their homes, thus to supply their wants. One hundred and sixty-six new arrivals of Winnebagoes were announced on this occasion. They had doubtless been informed when the presents would be given out, by friends who had kept the run of the beginning and end of the business part of the ceremony. The distribution of presents having been gone through with, everything was in motion, preparing for the departure of all, to their respective destinations. The wigwams were seen first to present nothing but skeletons—the bark which had covered them being taken off and rolled up, to be used at the next encamping place. Here and there, the poles that had formed the frames of the wigwams, if very well turned and fitted, were also taken down, to form a flooring for the canoes, as well as to be put up as future occasions might demand them. Some canoes were undergoing the operation of being gummed, whilst the smoke of the fires ascended, filling the area with the incense odor, peculiar to them. This odor is the joint product of an occasional boiling over of the gum, and the burning of pine and cedar, and spruce boughs in their green state. At one place might be seen a group of squaws, and children, and dogs, all seeming to be engaged in huddling together, or hauling to the water's edge their provisions and effects; whilst others had their canoes in the water, and others again were in the act of gliding away upon the smooth surface of the river, enjoying the quiet satisfaction which the presence of rations and good fare are so well calculated to produce.

At this moment of general activity, a scream, wild and fearful, was uttered. It was by a female. A rush of a thousand Indians was made for the spot whence it proceeded. I looked, and saw in the midst of the crowd a man's arm raised, with a knife in the hand. It fell—and then was heard another scream! When I sprang towards the scene of what seemed to be a strife of blood, and just as I had reached it, Major F., having started from an opposite direction, was a few feet in advance of me; and at the instant when the third blow was about to fall upon the victim, he struck, and knocked down the man who was thus desperately employing the bloody weapon. There stood, trembling and bleeding, a fine-looking squaw. She was mother of the wife of the man who had made the attempt upon her life. The deltoide muscle of each arm, just below the shoulder, was cut with deep gashes. These were given, as each arm was raised, in succession, to shield her body from the impending knife. The first thrust had thus disabled one arm, the second the other; and if the third had been given, there being no shield in the arms for farther protection, (for they both hung powerless by her side) it would doubtless have gone, where the two first were aimed, to the heart!

I took charge of the trembling and agitated woman, giving order to the soldiers to take the offender, and lock him up in our provision house, until some suitable punishment should be agreed upon for a crime so flagrant and bloody. Our surgeons having left for the village, I cleansed and bound up the wounds, and by the employment of bandages, kept the arms stationary, giving her directions not to use them, and sent her in charge of her daughter and some friends to Green Bay, to our surgeon, to be attended to.

The cause of the outrage was as follows:—This woman and her daughter had carefully put away their supplies, &c., in their canoe, and were on the eve of embarking, when it was rumored among the Indians that a whiskey dealer had arrived in the woods, back of our treaty ground. The moment it reached the ears of this reckless Indian, he started with others, in quest of the whiskey. The mother-in-law, well knowing that their calicoes, and blankets, and strouding, and pork, and beef, and flour, &c., would soon be parted from, in exchange for this fire-water, followed him, entreating him not to go, but to go home and enjoy what had been given them there. She clung to him rather inconveniently, when he resolved on freeing himself by the use of his knife. For some time she kept off his blows with her paddle, but this being presently knocked from her hand, she had no shield left but her arms, and these were alternately disabled in the manner I have stated.

Governor Cass coming along, I narrated all this, and to the inquiry, what shall we do with this man? answered promptly, "*Make a woman of him.*" And so we did. The process was on this wise. The several interpreters were sent out to summon in the Indians, and to arrange them around the Butte de Morts—the women and children in front. This being done—from eight hundred to a thousand, perhaps, being thus assembled—the offender was brought from his confinement, and led by a couple of our voyagers to the top of the mound, and placed against the flag-staff; Governor Cass and myself, and the interpreters, being there also. Never before had I witnessed in Indians a feeling so intense. Every eye of chief, half-chief, brave, and squaw, aye, and of every child, and it seemed to me of every dog also, was beaming with concentrated lustre, and every eye was upon us. They had all heard of the assault upon the woman, but to a man justified it—alleging that a woman was nobody when the power and freedom of the man were attempted to be interfered with; and that the life of any woman would be no more than a just forfeit for such intermeddling.

The squaws entertained different notions, and were deeply interested, personally, in the scene before them, not one of them knowing anything farther than that some punishment was to be inflicted on the man for his conduct.

The offender stood unmoved. Not a particle of interest did he seem to take in what was to befall him. If he had been there alone, listening to the rustling leaves, and the moaning of the winds, and looking upon the woods, the sky, the river, and the lake, he could not have been more unmoved. He was dressed in his best. Moccasins ornamented, were on his feet; his leggins were of scarlet cloth, fringed and decorated, besides, with bits of fur, foxes' tails, and rattles. A good blanket was about his waist; his ears were ornamented with silver rings, his arms with bracelets, his face with paint, and his hair sprinkled with vermilion.

Attention being called through the various interpreters, the governor spoke, explaining the case—the innocence and kind designs of the woman—the propriety and usefulness of the interference, which was not rudely attempted—the noble object of keeping her daughter's husband from joining in drunken revelries, and being bereft of all their stores, and then going home poor, and naked, and hungry. That was her object; whilst the whiskey trader cared for none of these things, but sought only to rob them of their blankets and calicoes, &c., and give them nothing in exchange for them but fire-water. The Great Spirit looked down and smiled on this act of the woman, and was angry at the bad conduct of the man, and with the whiskey trader. It was for an attempt so kind, and so proper, on her part, that this man, the husband of her daughter, had seized her, and with his knife struck at her heart, to kill her, and but for her arms, with which she had shielded her breast, she would have been murdered. Her cries, and tears, and blood, were all unavailing—nothing could have saved her, but the timely arrival of help, and a blow that put it out of his power to consummate his bloody purpose. For this act, he shall be no longer a brave; he has forfeited his character as a man; *from henceforth, let him be a woman!*

At this annunciation, the chiefs and braves muttered

vengeance. We were told by the interpreters, they would resist us. But never before were hearts put more at rest, or did hope gleam in upon such a multitude of squaws; never did eyes dance in frames of such emotion, or smiles radiate faces with such animation. Never was the "*neaw!*" a term expressive of mingled surprise and gladness, uttered with such vehemence and joy. Even the papooses, turning from their sources of nourishment, looked round as if some new and blessed influence was felt by them, and the very dogs barked.

Meantime, a voyager had procured of an old squaw her petticoat, stiff with the accumulated grease and dirt of many years. As he ascended the mound with this relic, another mutter of vengeance was heard from the men, whose faces were black with rage; but it was literally drowned amidst the acclamations that broke, at this moment, from the squaws. Now they saw, for the first time, new light and new hope breaking in upon their destiny. Our burdens, they seemed to say, will be lighter, our rights more respected, our security more secure. There stood the voyager, holding the petticoat. The sight of both was far more obnoxious to the culprit, than would have been the executioner, armed with his axe. But still he was unmoved. Not a muscle stirred. Around his waist was a belt, with a knife in it, such as butchers use. Taking hold of the handle, I drew it from its scabbard, thrust the blade into a crack in the flag-staff, and broke it off at the handle; then putting the handle in the culprit's hand, I raised it well and high up, and said—No man who employs his knife as this man employs his, has a right to carry one. Henceforth, this shall be the only knife he shall ever use. Woman, wherever she is, should be protected by man, not murdered. She is man's best friend. The Great Spirit gave her to man to be one with him, and to bless him; and man, whether red or white, should love her, and make her happy. Then turning to the voyager, I told him to strip off his leggins and his ornaments. It was done, when the old petticoat was put on him. Being thus arrayed, two voyagers, each putting a hand upon his shoulders, ran him down the mound, amidst a storm of indignation from the men, mingled with every variety of gladsome utterance by the squaws; when, letting him go, he continued his trot, alone, to a lodge near by, rushed into it, and fell upon his face. An interpreter followed him, and reported his condition, and what he said. His first words, as he lay on his face, were—"I wish they had killed me. I went up the mound to be shot. I thought I was taken there to be shot. I'd rather be dead. I am no longer a brave; I'm a WOMAN!"

Now this mode of punishment was intended to produce moral results, and to elevate the condition of women, among the Indians. It was mild in its physical effects, but more terrible than death in its action and consequences upon the offender. Henceforth, and as long as I continued to hear of this "brave," he had not been admitted among his former associates, but was pushed aside as having lost the characteristics of his sex, and doomed to the performance of woman's labor, in all the drudgery to which she is subject, as well of the lodge, as of all other menial things. The whiskey trader had made off, or he would have been taught a lesson, which, with the proper using, might have been made useful to him for the remainder of his days. Upon these incendiaries among the Indians—these murderers of the Indian's health, and peace, and life—the law should have always, and ought now, to be armed with such frightful vengeance as to deter them from the exercise of their avarice under this form, *and under any form*, among the poor Indians, who know no better than to follow the cravings of their inordinate thirst, and to indulge, when they can command it, without stint, in that which makes brutes of them, involving them, at the same time, in every variety of wretchedness. And yet, with a full knowledge of these effects upon this hapless race, these whiskey traders follow these poor fellows from river to river, and from wilderness to wilderness, and from lake to lake, entailing, from year to year, this unmitigated curse upon them.

Who can account for the apathy that pervades the councils of this great nation upon this subject? And where shall be found a solution of the almost universal indifference with which a great portion of our race, *Christians*, as we profess to be, listen to the wails that reach them from the wilderness homes of these abused and cast-off people? The cry from the forests, from the beginning, and that which is heard to this hour, and which has never been hushed for over two hundred years, is, "PROTECT US—PROTECT US—PITY AND SAVE US!" But where are the practical responses that show that this cry has ever been properly regarded?

We were now to embark, and leave the theatre of our negotiations. The little fires to which I have referred, continued yet to send up their smoke—although the objects for which they had been kindled had been accomplished. The cross-sticks upon which the kettles were slung, yet remained. The ground was now at rest from the pressure of thousands of feet; the woods were no longer intruded upon by the confused sounds of Indian whooping and yelling, that had for so many days disturbed and awakened their echoes; and nothing was heard but the plash of the paddle, the beat of the drum, and the shrill notes of the fife, as our guard moved off to the tune of "Strike your tents and march away." True, there was also the chanting of our voyagers, just under way, and an occasional discharge of a gun. It was amidst scenes like these I left "Le Petit Butte de Morts." As I glided down the current, catching now and then a glimpse of the tree-tops, and of the priest's towering pole, crowned with the cross, I thought of the worship of the Christian Indians; and fancied I could hear the harmonies that had more than once soothed me, and which seemed so welcome even to nature herself—for I was wont to think the very groves listened, as I am sure the spirits did, that hovered invisibly over and amidst them—for

> "Millions of spiritual creatures walk the earth,
> Unseen, both when we sleep, and when we wake."

Other and subsequent despatches announced General Atkinson to be ascending the Ouisconsin. My commission having referred other duties to me, I determined to pass on; so Governor Cass referred to me the duty of addressing a letter to Major Whistler, urging him to embody a force and proceed to the portage of the Fox and Ouisconsin rivers, and there join General Atkinson. This was agreed to, upon condition that I would raise a hundred Indians to accompany the expedition as flankers. It was done. Force enough was reserved to protect the fort, and the remainder was organized, when the ascent of the Fox river was commenced.

The governor, and all of our party, except myself and servant Ben, were now off in a steamboat for Detroit, with whom I was strongly urged to return. The reasons assigned were, that I should certainly be killed on the way, there being some hundreds of miles of war country to go through; or, should I get through alive, there was no sort of chance of my effecting anything with the southern tribes, with whom it was made my duty to negotiate treaties. There was some force in this—since large appropriations had been made by Congress, and expended without effect, by the experienced Indian negotiators, Generals Clark, (Lewis's fellow traveller) Coffee, and Hinds, whilst I was going on a forlorn hope, single-handed, with no money to sustain and aid in the success of my operations. The whole undertaking was pronounced upon as rash. My answer to the governor was, I shall go. He then sought to obtain my consent to allow my son to return with him. This I referred to the pleasure of my son.

The governor succeeded in obtaining his consent to return to Washington by the way of Detroit, and he did so; and myself and Ben were all that remained of our party, except my trusty voyagers, with my bark canoe, and my clerk and interpreter, the estimable Mr. Kinzie.

The expedition being ready, I despatched an express to General Atkinson, on the supposition that he would be met by it at the portage, which is distant from Fort Howard, at Green Bay, some hundred and forty miles. The object of the express was, to inform the general that Major Whistler was in motion to meet him.

The embarkation of the troops took place on Tuesday, the 23d of July, 1827, at three o'clock, P. M. The force consisted of one hundred and one regulars; twenty-eight militia; one hundred and twelve Wabanackies and Menomonies; total, two hundred and ninety, besides Rolette, a trader, connected with the American Fur Company, on his way to Prairie du Chien, with an outfit, having fifty men with him, on whose co-operation we counted, with eight men in a canoe that I had provided for a guest from France, (who had brought letters of introduction from Cadwallader D. Colden, of New York,) Count de Lillier, and eleven of my own men, including Mr. Kinzie and Ben; making an aggregate of three hundred and fifty-nine. Rolette had passed on, and made the portage of the Kockalas, and was progressing, but was stopped by an order from Major Whistler, who apprehended that if he should attempt to go through to the Mississippi, he might be overpowered; and, having some thirty thousand dollars' worth of supplies with him, including a large number of guns and ammunition, his capture would enable the Indians to carry on the war with greater effect, and for a longer time.

The barges in which the troops were embarked being heavy, and their progress against the current of the Fox river consequently slow, whilst with my canoe I could overhaul them at pleasure, I concluded to spend that evening and the next day with friends at the fort and the village. I took leave of all on Saturday, the 25th July, and, as was the general belief, forever. The count, being full of the exploring fever, started with the military.

The climate of Green Bay is at all times pleasant, but at this season delightful. I was to have overtaken the count at the portage of the Grand Kockalas; but, on my arrival there, found he had gone on. Proceeding to the little Kockalas, about four miles higher up, I encamped. Fell in with two Indians in a canoe, fed them, and they kept us company. Heard guns in the direction of the fort, supposed it an arrival, as no attack was likely to be made upon it by a force that should not first pass us. Heavy dew that night; it dripped from my tent like rain. I had, without knowing it, pitched my camp within two miles of the military.

The morning broke in all its beauty. Never did the sun shine out with more brilliancy or loveliness, and never was there a sweeter day. It was the Sabbath—and here seemed another proof that our world, and those rolling orbs above us, and the ethereal, had combined to impart a more than natural beauty to this day of rest, by mingling with it those softer and quieter influences that would seem to belong to its sanctity. Such was the Sabbath—the 26th July, 1827. I had come in about nine hours a distance that it had taken the barges from three o'clock of the evening of Thursday, till nine o'clock of the following Sunday, to make; in all, *sixty-six hours*. This, however, is not the usual disparity of speed between a well-manned canoe and equally well-manned barges. The portage of the Kockalas had to be made, and the heavy material of war, with the provisions, &c., were also to be carried over it; and the current here is very rapid.

We passed Le Petit Butte de Morts. The buildings we had put up for the security and safe-keeping of our provisions and goods, &c., had been all fired by the Indians. A thick smoke hung over the ground—the top of the priest's pole and cross being above it, upon which the sun shone in his beauty, contrasting strongly with the murkiness of all beneath and around them. But there was Winnebago lake placid as a mirror, with not a breeze to ruffle its surface, or disturb its repose. A few Indians near the Butte, who had remained on the ground, on recognizing us, ran to the shore, and saluted us with their rifles. I found the count there, but in trouble. His canoe was not entirely the thing I had hoped it would prove to be, nor did those who were in it know how to manage it with skill, or work it with success. I found him a better, and provided him additional and more skilful help.

On reaching *the Grand Butte de Morts*, I discovered that Rolette had broken Major Whistler's orders, and gone on. To avoid all the consequences, as well those feared by Major W. as others that might arise between the parties, for this violation of military law, I resolved to give chase. So leaving a note with an Indian, for Major Whistler, informing him of my object, I proceeded to pursue and stop Rolette. I supposed from information given by an Indian, that he was about two miles ahead. This I found to be a mistake. The importance of stopping him increased as he advanced in the enemy's country; and my anxiety grew with it. I pushed on, hoping to reach him at an encampment. Night set in, but no tidings of Rolette. I kept on, and continued on all night, stopping neither to eat or sleep, except once to give the voyagers a half hour's nap, when I ordered the bowsman to stick a pole down in the river, tie the canoe fast to it, and then all hands to pull their blankets over them, lean forward, and go to sleep. I never knew an order more promptly obeyed. The dew was again heavy; it dripped like rain-drops from my umbrella. In about half an hour I awakened the sleepers, and we proceeded. The morning came, but Rolette was not in sight. Landed at sun-rise, and breakfasted. Heard guns on our right.

Supposed them to indicate Rolette's whereabouts. Kept on, when at about eleven o'clock, A. M., in one of the bends of this tortuous river, and in a broad part of it, saw his six barges with sails all set, looking like a fleet. My voyagers set up a chant, and within half an hour I was up with him. I made known the object of my pursuit, and the motives that had prompted me to engage in it, requesting him to go ashore. He complied cheerfully—when I addressed a letter to Major Whistler, stating our position, and also Rolette's entire readiness to acquiesce in his views; the reasons that had led him to disobey the order that had been addressed to him, &c., and despatched an Indian in his light canoe, knowing that this down-stream message would soon be in the hands of Major Whistler, and that his fears, if he had any, would be put to rest. I had come from Le Grand Butte de Morts, to where I overtook Rolette, eighty miles, against a strong current.

CHAPTER V.

EXPEDITION AGAINST THE WINNEBAGOES. SURRENDER, RECEPTION, AND APPEARANCE OF "RED-BIRD."

Encampment at Rush lake—Windings of the Fox river—Major Whistler and Rolette—A successful mediation—Remarkable celestial phenomenon—An omen—The snake and the bear—Ceremony of taking them—A fine position on the Fox river—Shooting a crane—Arrival at the portage—Encampment—Disarming and detention of a party of Winnebagoes—Object of the expedition—Indian diplomacy—Surrender of the murderers—Heroism of the act—Their arrival and reception—Noble appearance and dignified deportment of "RED-BIRD"—Solicitude of his people for him—His brief talk—Miserable appearance of WE-KAU, his accomplice—Mode of catching the rattle-snake—Preventive against his bite—Portage to the Ouisconsin.

OUR first business was to select a suitable position for an encampment. The grounds opposite the place of our meeting presenting, on neither side of the river, a favorable one, we continued five miles further on, and at noon encamped on the north-western shore of Rush lake. From this place, we were not over three miles, in a straight line, from the portage of the Fox and Ouisconsin rivers, and yet, such are the windings of Fox river, we were destined to go at least twenty miles before we could reach it.

At night we set a guard of twelve men, and ordered all hands to have their arms ready. We were not long in camp before four Winnebagoes came in, offering to sell squashes. I directed them to be detained. At nine o'clock the next morning the count arrived, well, and glad to see us. The military did not get up till August 31st—two days after the count, and three days after my arrival. Meantime, six squaws came in with potatoes and squashes. Bought them, and let the squaws pass on. The next day, five Indians arrived, with their faces painted black. They had been in battle, and had lost friends, and were in mourning, after this their fashion, for them. Took them in charge, and examined them. Finding they were not of the party who had committed the murder at Prairie du Chien, gave orders for them to pass.

The arrival of the military on the 31st, brought Major Whistler and Rolette together, and myself as mediator. My letter to the major, by the Indian, had been received, but his dander was up, as Major Jack Downing would say, and required something additional, of the soothing sort, to lay it. I had, on going ashore with Rolette, obtained of him guns and ammunition for our hitherto unarmed one hundred and twelve Indians, for which I gave a receipt, and the obligation either to return them as they were, or pay damages, or the price of the guns. I made use of this facility, and the cordial manner in which Rolette had assented to supply the arms, in connexion with the fact that he had not disregarded Major Whistler's injunction from any want of respect either for it, or for the commanding officer; and was happy to see harmony restored, and a mutual intercourse of friendly civilities forthwith take place.

A party of our Indians who were strolling about, had captured a rattle-snake, and found a fine bear in a trap. I had been in trouble with this part of our force, and feared we should lose it. Matters of fact with the civilized and enlightened, are made of no more stubborn materials, and have no more effect on the white man, and sometimes, indeed, not so much, as has superstition on the untutored Indian, in forming his purpose, and fixing his resolves. It was about this time that the heavens presented a remarkable phenomenon, in a belt of pure white, which crossed them from horizon to horizon. Its direction was across the line of our movements. This, the Indians, after consultation, had interpreted into a bad omen, and looked upon it as a barrier put across their path by the Great Spirit, in which they read his order, forbidding them to pass. It was in vain that I attempted to reason with them on the subject. There was the line of light, and they had seen it; its direction lay across the path of our movements, and that was clear, and what else could it mean, but a command to stop, and go no further? They augured evil results, also, upon those who should be so rash as to disregard this celestial omen. But when the party that had taken the rattle-snake and bear came in, all this reasoning, and all these conclusions, fell to pieces, like the diamond lustre of the ice-fringed forest, when the sun pours upon it his light and heat. They were looked upon as messengers that had been sent from the land of souls, revoking the order of the Great Spirit, as read in the belt of white; and, as by this time the white belt had become well-nigh blended with the ethereal, it was found to be no difficult matter to believe that the command was revoked, and permission granted them to proceed.

The ceremony of taking the snake and the bear, under these circumstances, was as follows: He who had first discovered the snake, made the usual signal that he had found one. This secured it as his property; when he addressed it thus: "You are welcome, friend, from the spirit-land. We were in trouble; our friends there knew it. The Great Spirit knew it. You are come to bring us rest. We know what your message is. Take this offering of tobacco;"—taking a pinch of fragments from his pouch, and rubbing them to powder between his finger and thumb, he sprinkled it on the snake's head—"it will make you feel strong after your long journey." Then reaching well down towards the tail, he ran his finger and thumb up the back of the snake, till they reached the neck, when, with a quick compression, he rose with the snake well secured, and giving it a jerk, broke every vertebra in the process. The head was instantly opened, the fangs carefully taken out, the skin taken off, and the body being quickly cut up into small pieces, was distributed to the Indians for their medicine-bags—thus furnishing a new antidote against evil agencies, should any happen, during the remainder of their march. The skin of the snake was seen in a few minutes after his capture, fastened by a root of the red cedar, called wattap, to a lock of the captor's hair, the tail reaching down his back, and nearly to the ground. This was a proud trophy.

While this snake capture, and what followed it, was going on, the bear was being disposed of. He who had made the discovery of the entrapped Bruin, set up his claim, in like manner, by announcing more formally his discovery of the prize. The bear was also addressed in terms of congratulation, in which he was told that his visit was one of great interest. He was questioned as to the condition of the departed whose spirits he had left upon this his errand of love, and then told that he would soon have the pleasure of going back to them with messages; that if the manner of sending him there should be harsh, he must blame the white man for it, since it was at his call they had left their squaws and papooses to come into that country, &c., &c.; so calling to him a couple of his friends, he gave the order to fire, at the same time pulling the trigger of his own rifle, when Bruin, receiving three balls, fell and died. He was soon released from the trap, skinned, quartered, cut up, and over the fires, in kettles, simmering away, preparatory to a feast, in which all joined. The obstacle to their march being now so clearly removed, and by the agency of friends from the spirit-land, and the Great Spirit himself, they announced their readiness to march on.

Broke up our encampment, and continued the ascent of this tortuous river. The count and myself, in our canoes, making the distance which I supposed the military would make, we encamped. The evening brought them up, when, for the first time since leaving Fort Howard, at Green Bay, we were all together for a night. Our position was a fine one. The bank of the river, of some ten feet elevation, was abrupt, and its base was washed by the waters. A fine level piece of ground stretched back of it, fringed in the rear with thick woods. Our tents were in a line, near these. In front, and between the line of tents and the river, and for a quarter of a mile, the level of the ground, and its freedom from undergrowth, were such as to give it the appearance of a parade-ground. Just before sun-down, a large crane was seen coming up at the slow rate which characterizes the flight of this bird. The line of its course being such, as to both height and distance, as to make quite a mark for a trial of skill of all hands, the thought seemed spontaneous, and in a moment every man with his gun was in line, on the edge of the river bank, at open order. The lazily moving crane, flapping slowly his enormous wings, arriving opposite the first man on the right, he aimed and fired; and so on, down the whole line, each man fired, but all missing the bird, which seemed as unconscious of the peril of its situation, as though not a gun had been within a mile of it. Indeed, so perfectly insensible was it, as to convey the idea that the thing was asleep. The count was on the left, the last man in the line, with a double-barrelled shot-gun; so, it coming to his turn, he fired, first one barrel, and then the other, both taking effect; when the sluggish bird's long neck became pendent, and his legs losing their horizontal position, fell into the perpendicular, the whole coming over, and over, to the river; which reaching, and even before it touched the water, I don't know how many Indians were off this ten feet bank, head foremost, after the prize. The one who had kept under water longest, coming up nearer the bird than the rest, seized his prey, and holding it up in one hand, out of the water, swam back to the shore, amidst the greetings and shouts of the whole company. His title to the crane was fixed, by Indian law. No matter who kills, the first to reach the game is owner of it.

Major Whistler embarked the next morning at day-break. My inclination led me to repose. I slept on, knowing I could overtake him, which I did at ten o'clock. The river now began to give signs that we were near the portage. Savannas of wild rice grew out of it in all directions, leaving a channel so narrow as to scarcely admit a barge, while its turns are so short as to make it difficult to follow their windings, except in a very short canoe. Ducks, pigeons, and blackbirds, numerous.

At four o'clock, P. M., of September 1st, 1827, arrived at the portage, and encamped on a high bluff which overlooks the country for a great distance, to the south and west. We had not finished the business of encamping, before seven Winnebago warriors came along, on their way from Green Isle to the four lakes, fully armed and equipped. It was a direction in which we did not desire any of that sort of force to go, the enemy being at the four lakes in great numbers. Major Whistler gave orders to disarm and detain them. They were told they should be fed well, and treated well, whilst they behaved themselves. They appeared to feel deeply, when their arms were taken from them; nor did they appear to like the strength and appearance of the military. An express arrived from General Atkinson, announcing his approach, and directing Major W. to halt and fortify himself at the portage, and wait his arrival, as the capture of the enemy could be made with his additional force, with more ease, and less sacrifice of life.

The object of the joint expedition of General Atkinson from Jefferson Barracks, below St. Louis, and of Major Whistler from Fort Howard, on Green Bay, was, as has been intimated, to capture those who had committed the murders at Prairie du Chien, and put a stop to any further aggressions of the sort. The Winnebagoes, it will be remembered, had been advised, prior to the opening of the council at Le Butte de Morts, that the security of their people lay in a surrender of the murderers. The first intimation that this primary object would be accomplished, was given the day after our arrival at the portage, in a very mysterious way. I was sitting at the door of my tent, when an Indian of common appearance, with nothing over him but a blanket, came up to the bluff, and walking to the tent, seated himself upon his haunches beside it. This was almost the middle of the day. I inquired through the interpreter, what was the object of his visit. After musing awhile, he said—"Do not strike—when the sun is there to morrow"—looking up, and pointing to about three o'clock, P. M.—"they will come in." Who will come in? I asked. "Red-Bird and We-kau," he answered. The moment he gave the answer, he rose, wrapped his blanket about him, and with hurried step returned by the way he had come. At about three o'clock of the same day, another Indian came and took his position in nearly the same place, and in the same way, when, to like questions, he gave like answers; and at sun-down a third came, confirming what the other two had said, with the addition that he had, to secure that object, given to the families of the murderers nearly all of his property. There appeared to me to be two objects in view by this Indian mode of managing the art diplomatique. One was, to prevent an attack, which our near neighborhood to the point where the Indian force was concentred, led them to apprehend; the other, to say all cause for an attack was, as they viewed it, removed by the treble assurance given, that the murderers will, and at a time specified, be brought in. There could be nothing more to the purpose.

There was, as I have said on a previous occasion, when referring to the subject of this voluntary surrender, something heroic in it. The giving away of property to the families of the guilty parties, had nothing to do with their determination to devote themselves for the good of their people, but only to reconcile those who were about to be bereaved to the dreadful expedient. The heroism of the purpose is seen in the fact, that the murders committed at Prairie du Chien were not wanton, but in retaliation for wrongs committed upon this people by the whites. The parties murdered at the Prairie, were doubtless innocent of the wrongs and outrages of which the Indians complained, but the law of Indian retaliation does not require that he alone, who commits a wrong, shall suffer for it. One scalp is held to be due for another, no matter from whose head it is taken, provided it be torn from the crown of the family, or people, who have made a resort to this law necessary. If these Indians had multiplied their victims to ten times the number slain by them at the Prairie, it is highly probable the balance of suffering and of blood would have been greatly on the side of the Indians—and yet we find, under such circumstances, a readiness on the part of the murderers, rather than have "a road cut through their country with guns," which would subject the innocent to both affliction and death, to make a voluntary surrender of themselves!

At about noon of the day following, there were seen descending a mound on the portage, a body of Indians—some were mounted, and some were on foot. By the aid of a glass, we could discern the direction to be towards our position, and that three flags were borne by them—two, (one in front and one in rear,) were American, and one in the centre was white. They bore no arms. We were at no loss to understand that the promise made by the three Indians, the day before, was about to be fulfilled. In the course of half an hour, they had approached within a short distance of the crossing of the Fox river, when, on a sudden, we heard singing. Those who were familiar with the air, said—"it is a *death song!*" When still nearer, some present who knew him, said, "it is the *Red-Bird singing his death song.*" The moment a halt was made on the margin of the river, preparatory to crossing over, two *scalp yells* were heard.

The Menomonies, and other Indians who had accompanied us, were lying carelessly about upon the ground, regardless of what was going on, but the moment the "scalp yells" were uttered, they sprang as one man to their feet, seized their rifles, and were ready for battle. They were at no loss to know that the yells were "scalp yells;" but had not heard with sufficient accuracy to decide whether they indicated scalps to be *taken* or *given;* but, doubtless, they inferred the first.

Barges were sent across to receive, and an escort of the military to accompany them within our lines. The white flag which had been seen in the distance, was born by the Red-Bird. During the crossing, a rattle-snake passed me, and was struck by Captain D., with his sword, and partly disabled, when I ran mine through his neck, and holding up the slain reptile, a Menomonie Indian cut off his head with his knife. The head was burned, to keep the fangs from doing injury by being trodden upon, and his body cut up, after the fashion of the one previously spoken of, and disposed of in the same way. This was looked upon as another good omen by the Indians.

And now, the advance of the Indians had reached half up the ascent of the bluff, on which was our encampment. In the lead was CARIMINIE, a distinguished chief. Arriving on the level, upon which was our encampment, and order being called, Cariminie spoke, saying—"They are here—like braves they have come in—treat them as braves—do not put them in irons." This address was made to me. I told him I was not the big captain. His talk must be made to Major Whistler, who would, I had no doubt, do what was right. Mr. Marsh, the sub-agent, being there, an advance was made to him, and a hope expressed that the prisoners might be turned over to him. There was an evident aversion to their being given up to the military.

I told him Mr. Marsh should be with the prisoners, which composed them. For the remainder of the incidents, I must resort to a letter which I addressed to the Hon. James Barbour, Secretary of War, giving an account of this most imposing, and by me never-to-be-forgotten ceremony.

"The military had been previously drawn out in line. The Menomonie and Wabanackie Indians were in groups upon their haunches, on our left flank. On the right, was the band of music, a little in advance of the line. In front of the centre, at about ten paces distant, were the murderers. On their right and left, were those who had accompanied them, forming a semi-circle, the magnificent Red-Bird, and the miserable looking We-kau, a little in advance of the centre. All eyes were fixed upon the Red-Bird; and well they might be—for of all the Indians I ever saw, he is, without exception, the most perfect in form, in face, and gesture. In height, he is about six feet; straight, but without restraint. His proportions are those of the most exact symmetry, and these embrace the entire man, from his head to his feet. His very fingers are models of beauty. I have never beheld a face that was so full of all the ennobling, and at the same time the most winning expression. It were impossible to combine with such a face the thought that he who wore it, could be a murderer! It appears to be a compound of grace and dignity; of firmness and decision, all tempered with mildness and mercy. During my attempted analysis of this face, I could not but ask myself, can this man be a murderer? Is he the same who shot, scalped, and cut the throat of *Gagnier?* His head, too—sure no head was ever so well formed. There was no ornamenting of the hair, after the Indian fashion; no clubbing it up in blocks and rollers of lead, or bands of silver; no loose or straggling parts—but it was cut after the best fashion of the most civilized.

His face was painted, one side red, the other intermixed

with green and white. Around his neck he wore a collar of blue wampum, beautifully mixed with white, which was sewn on to a piece of cloth, the width of the wampum being about two inches—whilst the claws of the panther, or wild-cat, distant from each other about a quarter of an inch, with their points inward, formed the rim of the collar. Around his neck were hanging strands of wampum of various lengths, the circles enlarging as they descended. He was clothed in a *yankton dress*—new and beautiful. The material is of dressed elk, or deer-skin, almost a pure white. It consists of a jacket, the sleeves being cut to fit his finely formed arm, and so as to leave outside of the seam that ran from the shoulder, back of the arm, and along over the elbow, about six inches of the material, one-half of which was cut into fringe; the same kind of fringe ornamenting the collar of the jacket, its sides, bosom, and termination, which was not circular, but cut in points; and which also ran down the seams of his leggins, these being made of the same material. Blue beads were employed to vary and enrich the fringe of the leggins. On his feet he wore moccasins.

"A piece of scarlet cloth of about a quarter of a yard deep, and double that width, a slit being cut in its middle, so as to admit the passing through of his head, rested, one-half on his breast, (and beneath the necklace of wampum and claws,) and the other on his back. On one shoulder, and near his breast, was a beautifully ornamented feather, nearly white; and about opposite, on the other shoulder, was another feather, nearly black, near which were two pieces of thinly shaven wood in the form of compasses, a little open, each about six inches long, richly wrapped round with porcupine's quills, dyed yellow, red, and blue. On the tip of one shoulder was a tuft of horsehair, dyed red, and a little curled, mixed up with ornaments. Across his breast, in a diagonal position, and bound tight to it, was his war-pipe, at least three feet long, brightly ornamented with dyed horse-hair, the feathers and bills of birds. In one of his hands he held the white flag, and in the other the calumet, or pipe of peace.

"There he stood. Not a muscle moved, nor was the expression of his face changed a particle. He appeared to be conscious that, according to Indian law, and measuring the deed he had committed by the injustice, and wrongs, and cruelties of the white man, he had done no wrong. The light which had shone in upon his bosom from the law which demanded an eye for an eye, and a tooth for a tooth, so harmonized with his conscience, as to secure its repose. As to death, he had been taught to despise it, confiding in that heaven, that spirit-land, where the game is always plenty—the forests always green—the waters always transparent, tranquil, and pure—and where no evil thing is permitted to enter. He was there, prepared to receive the blow that should consign his body to the ground, and send his spirit to that blissful region, to mingle with his fathers who had gone before him.

"He and We-kau were told to sit down. His motions, as he seated himself, were no less graceful and captivating, than when he stood or walked. At this moment the band struck up Pleyel's Hymn. Everything was still. It was indeed a moment of intense interest to all. The Red-Bird turned his eyes towards the band; the tones operated upon his feelings in such a way as to produce in his countenance a corresponding pensiveness. The music having ceased, he took up his pouch, (which I forgot to say was a handsomely ornamented otter-skin, that hung on his left side,) and taking from it some *kinnakinic* and tobacco, cut the latter in the palm of his hand, after the Indian fashion, then rubbing the two together, filled the bowl of his calumet, struck fire into a bit of spunk with his flint and steel, and lighted it, and smoked. All the motions employed in this ceremony were no less harmonious and appropriate, than had characterized his other movements. He sat after the Turkish fashion, with his legs crossed.

"If you think there was anything of affectation in all this, you are mistaken. There was just the manner, and appearance, and look, you would expect to see in a nobly built man of the highest order of intelligence, and who had been taught all the graces of motion, and then escorted by his armies to a throne, where the diadem was to be placed upon his head.

"There is but one opinion of the man, and that I have attempted to convey to you. I could not refrain from speculating on his dress. His white jacket, having upon it but a single piece of red, appeared to indicate the purity of his past life, which had been stained by only a single crime; for all agree that the Red-Bird had never before soiled his fingers with the blood of the white man, or committed a bad action. His war-pipe, bound close to his heart, seemed to indicate his love of war, in common with his race, which was no longer to be gratified. The red cloth, however, may have been indicative of his name.

"All sat, except the speakers. The substance of what they said was—We were required to bring in the murderers. They had no power over any, except two—the third had gone away—and these had voluntarily agreed to come in, and give themselves up. As their friends, they had come with them. They hoped their white brothers would agree to accept the horses—of which there were, perhaps, twenty—the meaning of which was, to take them in commutation for the lives of their two friends. They asked kind treatment for their friends, and earnestly besought that they might not be put in irons—and concluded by asking for a little tobacco, and something to eat.

"They were answered, and told, in substance, that they had done well thus to come in. By having done so, they had turned away our guns, and saved their people. They were admonished against placing themselves in a like situation in the future, and advised, when they were aggrieved, not to resort to violence, but to go to their agent, who would inform their Great Father of their complaints, and he would redress their grievances; that their friends should be treated kindly, and tried by the same laws by which their Great Father's white children were tried; that for the present, Red-Bird and We-kau should not be put in irons; that they should all have something to eat, and tobacco to smoke. We advised them to warn their people against killing ours; and endeavored, also, to impress them with a proper notion of their own weakness, and the extent of our power, &c.

"Having heard this, the Red-Bird stood up—the commanding officer, Major Whistler, a few paces in front of the centre of the line, facing him. After a moment's pause, and a quick survey of the troops, and with a composed observation of his people, he spoke, looking at Major Whistler, saying, '*I am ready.*' Then advancing a step or two, he paused, saying, 'I do not wish to be put in irons. Let me be free. I have given away my life—it is gone—(stooping and taking some dust between his finger and thumb, and blowing it away)—like that'—eyeing the dust as it fell, and vanished from his sight, then adding —'I would not take it back. It is gone.' Having thus spoken, he threw his hands behind him, to indicate that he was leaving all things behind him, and marched briskly up to Major Whistler, breast to breast. A platoon was wheeled backwards from the centre of the line, when Major Whistler stepping aside, the Red-Bird and We-kau marched through the line, in charge of a file of men, to a tent that had been provided for them in the rear, where a guard was set over them. The comrades of the two captives then left the ground by the way they had come, taking with them our advice, and a supply of meat and flour, and tobacco.

"We-kau, the miserable-looking being, the accomplice

of the Red-Bird, was in all things the opposite of that unfortunate brave. Never, before, were there two human beings so exactly, in all things, so unlike one another. The one seemed a prince, and as if born to command, and worthy to be obeyed; the other, as if he had been born to be hanged. Meagre—cold—dirty in his person and dress, crooked in form—like the starved wolf, gaunt, hungry, and blood-thirsty—his entire appearance indicating the presence of a spirit wary, cruel and treacherous. The heart, at sight of this, was almost steeled against sympathy, and barred against the admission of pity. This is the man who could scalp a child, not eleven months old, and in taking off its fine locks as a trophy, and to exhibit as a scalp, cut the back of its neck to the bone, and leave it to languish and die on the floor, near the body of its murdered father! But his hands, and crooked and miserable-looking fingers, had been accustomed to such bloody work.

"The Red-Bird did not appear to be over thirty years old, and yet he is said to be past forty. We-kau looks to be forty-five, and is no doubt as old as that. I shall see, on my arrival at Prairie du Chien, the scene of these butcheries; and, as I may write you upon all matters connected with my tour, I will introduce you to that. The child, I forgot to say, by the latest accounts, yet lives, and promises to survive. The widow of *Gagnier* is also there, and I shall get the whole story from her mouth, and shall then, doubtless, get it truly. You shall have it all, and a thousand things beside, that, when I left home, I never expected to realize; but having once entered upon the scenes I have passed, no matter with how much of personal risk they were to be encountered, there was no going back. I see no danger, I confess, especially now—but, any how, my way is onward, and I shall go."

I never, however, made good my promise to narrate the incidents of my travels, further than as these were embraced in my official returns. The above account of the surrender of the Red-Bird will not lose any of its freshness here, I hope, from its having been published in pretty much the same dress in the newspapers, a short time after its reception by the Secretary of War, and again, in the work on the Aborigines of North America, by myself and James Hall. As it formed part of the varied occurrences of my tour in 1827, which I am now for the first time embodying, I can not, in justice to the connexion which I wish to preserve of the whole, omit it.

On the morning of the 3d, having little else to do, I busied myself to find out, if I could, how the Indians could, without danger, capture the rattle-snake. This whole country is full of them; and so constant is the noise of their rattles, when anything happens to molest them, that the ear is kept half the time deceived by what seems to be the ticking of watches, in a watch-maker's window. I was honored by a visit from one in my tent that morning, and was prompted by that call, perhaps, to find out in what way my civilities might best protect me from their too close attention. I was told the smell of tobacco made the snake sick; and this explained why, in two instances in which I had witnessed the taking of this reptile by Indians, tobacco was employed—as in the case of the one that had come from the land of souls, at the time when the march of the Indians was impeded by the white mark in the heavens. They also employ a root, but of what herb or shrub I could not find out, which they pound and put on a stick; then they excite the snake to bite it, when the poison of the root being taken into the snake's mouth, kills it. I was told they take from the neck of the turkey-buzzard a piece of the flesh, and dry and pound it, and rub their bodies with this powder. Thus guarded, the snake will not bite, or come near them. How true all, or any part of all this is, I cannot vouch, never having made trial of either.

At nine in the morning, after the surrender, I took leave of the military, and in company with the count, Judge

Lecuer, and Rev. Mr. Jones, started for a descent of the Ouisconsin river. Having crossed the Fox river to the opposite landing, on the portage, an ox-cart was provided for our transportation across to the Ouisconsin—the width of the portage being about twenty-five hundred paces. The entire way was miry, and full of rattle-snakes. The veteran interpreter, *Pauquet*,* was employed to drive us over. The wheels of the cart, though broad, sank deep in the mud, and the sturdy beasts bent to their duty; but without the constant employment of Pauquet's powerful arms, and the exertion of his great strength in applying to their sides repeated strokes from what seemed like a hoop or a hop-pole, exciting them, meantime, with his stentorian voice, and giving vent to anathemas, in Winnebago, with almost every breath, we must have been forced into some other conveyance, or taken to our feet in mud a foot deep, to have, in any reasonable time, reached the Ouisconsin. But by the aid of the hop-pole and the Winnebago anathemas, both well understood, doubtless, by the oxen, we were carted over in safety. When about mid-way, and during one of the numerous pauses which the oxen were wont to make, the man bearing the flag-staff of my canoe struck, with the lower end of it, a rattle-snake that lay near by where Pauquet was standing—for he walked the entire distance. The snake, enraged at the blow, gave signs of resistance, and apprehending it might dart its fangs into Pauquet's legs, I stooped from the cart, and ran it through with my sword, when one of the men cut off its head with an axe. Whether Pauquet trusted to his leather leggins and moccasins, or their being well imbued with tobacco smoke, or to the powdered root, or the buzzard's neck, I did not learn; but he was as composed in regard to these reptiles, as if he had been mailed in brass or iron.

Having crossed the portage, our canoes, and supplies, and baggage being all over, we embarked at eleven o'clock,

* Since murdered.

A. M., on the Ouisconsin. The current which we had been opposing, the entire length of the Fox river, was now in our favor; the waters of the Ouisconsin running from its source to the Mississippi, as do those of the Fox river, on the other side of the portage, into Green Bay. The first find their way through the lakes to the ocean by the St. Lawrence, the last by the way of the Mississippi and the Gulf of Mexico. Whether, after having started for those diverse directions, from sources so near one another, they ever meet, and mingle more in the deep blue sea, is a problem which I do not pretend to solve. I could not help thinking how closely they resembled early friends, who in boyhood were hand in hand with each other, and rarely, for a series of years, out of one another's sight; when, at last, "some current's thwarting course" separated them, to meet no more forever!

CHAPTER VI.

PASSAGE DOWN THE OUISCONSIN AND MISSISSIPPI RIVERS.

Passage down the Ouisconsin—An accident—Scenery of the Ouisconsin—A parley with the Indians—Visit to their village—Distribution of presents—Meeting with General Atkinson at Le Petit Roche—Difficulties of navigation—Changes in the river—Junction with the Mississippi—Prairie du Chien—Origin of the name—Description of the Prairie—Scene and story of "the murders"—Apprehensions of another attack—Mystery of "Red-Bird's" outrage explained—Passage down the Mississippi—Grave of Julian Du Buque—Galena—The lead-mines—Trespass upon Indian lands—Causes of the Black Hawk and Seminole wars—Rents at Galena enormously high—Rock Island—Exceeding beauty of the place—Boundary between civilized and savage life—Familiar sounds—Wrecks in the river—Fort Edwards—Encampment on an Island—Visit to the farm-house of a settler—A peep at the newspaper—Pelican Island—Shooting—Panic of the inhabitants—The milk-sickness.

Our voyagers felt now, upon this onward current, as the mariner feels, when both the wind and tide, after having been long contrary, turn in his favor—and when he is assured there will be no change, till he reaches the port of his destination.

I had engaged a fine-looking Indian to join the count as a voyager, hoping thereby to add to the speed of his canoe, and that we might, in our descent to the Mississippi, keep close company. I had heard much of the scenery of the Ouisconsin, and felt that my admiration of it would be stimulated, if the count, with his lustrous eyes, could be along to see the beauty and grandeur of the scenes, and in such close neighborhood to me, as to interchange sentiments and feelings in their contemplation. An accident deprived the count of the services of the Indian

The Rev. Mr. J., being unpracticed in the handling of fire-arms, was sitting on a log with the count's double-barrelled gun across his lap—the muzzle pointed in a line with another log, at some twenty paces distant, upon which sat the Indian—when, as luck would have it, one of the barrels was discharged, the shot rattling against the log, and scattering the sand about, besides a few penetrating the Indian's leggins. Up sprang the astonished brave and voyager, and eyeing Mr. J. for a second or two, said—"That man don't know what he's about"—then, looking over his shoulder at Mr. J., walked off.

We had not been long under way, before I saw the count's force was inadequate. I made a pause till he came up, and transferred to his canoe one of my men; the force proving yet too feeble, I assisted him with another—when onward we went, to the music of the voyagers' songs—happy in the reflection that our expedition had, so far, terminated otherwise than in blood. We were charmed, too, at having escaped the monotony, as well as the tedium of the ascent of the Fox river. There are, it is true, upon its shores, many beautiful upland views, where the trees grow apart, and without undergrowth, conveying to the eye the almost certain presence of civilization and cultivation. But, in the main, its shores are level, and its waters are dark, and filled with the *folle avoin*, or wild rice, and various aquatic plants besides; some of them, the lily, especially, very beautiful. Nature would seem, even here, to have made provision for the gratification of man; and, if the way was monotonous, she kindly scattered flowers to diversify the scene, and regale the voyager. Here, on the Ouisconsin, are sandy shores, and sand-bars, and islands, and rolling and verdure-capped shores, and hills and mountains—with valleys of the richest green, in which there would seem never to have been a war, even of the elements; and these again were relieved by miniature representations of the pictured rocks of Lake Superior.

The water of the Ouisconsin is of the color of brandy, with less sediment than is found in that of the Fox river. Neither, however, should be drunk, in my opinion, without having first undergone the process of boiling. Every mile of our descent increased the variety, and grandeur, and beauty of the shores. Hills shooting up into more towering heights, without a tree, but clothed in the brightest green; others again, with summits resembling dilapidated fortifications, and so like them, as to cheat the observer into the belief that they were, sure enough, once, what they now seem to have been. In one of these, we noticed a tall, leafless, and dead pine, so exactly resembling a flag-staff, not in exterior, only, but in its position, as to convince at least one of the party that a fortification had once crowned that hill, and in its destruction, the flag-staff had escaped the conflagration, by being only charred. Many of these elevations rise from the river, in the terrace form; the lower, all soft and green, and beautiful; the upper, crowned with dark evergreens, arranged so as to wear the appearance of having been planted upon a regular plan, the whole conception and execution of some mind richly stored with all the elements of a practical science. And was it not

> "NATURE, enchanting nature, in whose form
> And lineaments divine, I trace a hand
> That errs not?"

We had not been many hours on the Ouisconsin, before, on looking to my right, I saw some hundred or more Indians appear suddenly on the summit of a hill of some sixty feet elevation, overlooking the river, and form in line, with their rifles. What their object was, I could not divine, but every movement seemed to indicate a purpose to greet us with a shower of leaden deaths. There was not a second to spare; so I ordered my steersman to turn in, instantly. The head of the canoe was in a moment changed from its line down the river, and brought in one to the shore. This movement brought all their rifles across the arms of the Indians, who, being suddenly struck by this prompt movement, were at a loss to comprehend its meaning, and seemed resolved to await its issue. Our guns were concealed. On reaching the beach, I ordered the men to be ready for any emergency; and so, buckling on my sword, and putting a pair of pistols in my pockets, I directed Ben to fill his pockets with tobacco and Indian jewelry, and follow me and the interpreter up the steep ascent.

Ben's color changed from its fine and glossy ebony to a sort of livid paleness, and a trembling seized him. He had often predicted, as well the year before, as now, that we should never see home again; and this he verily believed was to be the hour when his prophesy was to be fulfilled. This change in his complexion was nothing new to me, having had occasion to observe it frequently; and, in my "Tour to the Lakes," to record it.

On arriving at the summit of the hill, I stood a moment. The Indians had all changed their position, and were now facing me. Not a word was spoken, nor did a man of them stir. After a short pause I inquired, through the interpreter, if their chief was present. He was. "Tell him to come and shake hands with me. I am from where the sun rises, and near his Great Father's lodge, in the great village of Washington, where I have often seen and shaken hands with many of the great men of the Indian race. I have come a long way to see them in their own country, that when I go back to their Great Father, I may be able to tell him how his red children are—what are their wants—and before I go, if I can, to make peace among them." The moment this was interpreted, the whole party gave a *grunt* of approbation, long, loud, and emphatic; when a tall, aged, and good-looking Indian, from his position on the extreme right, walked up and shook hands with me most cordially. I asked his name—and then calling him by it, said, "*You hold in your hand, the hand of a friend and brother*"—when the whole party advanced and shook hands with me.

Seeing their village at about a quarter of a mile back, on the plain, I asked to be allowed to go there, that I might shake hands with the squaws and papooses, and make them some presents. We marched to the village. A buffalo robe was spread out for me to sit upon, the calumet lighted, and we smoked—I, according to my custom, (for I never smoke,) blowing the smoke out of the bowl of the pipe, like a steam-engine. I was never suspected of not relishing this great luxury, the prized, and cherished, and enjoyed, alike by savage and civilized man. This ceremony over, I directed Ben to cut up the twists of tobacco into smaller portions, and divide it among the men. Ben was so much relieved of his terrors, as to be specially prompt, on this occasion, and he so employed his eye in counting, and his judgment in cutting up the tobacco, as to make it hold out exactly; for this I gave him great commendation. The distribution of the tobacco having been made, and to the high gratification of this tobacco-loving people, I proceeded to distribute the jewelry, consisting of finger-rings, made of cheap metals, set with variously colored glass, and ear-bobs, &c. These I threw, by the handful, on the ground, which produced an excitement, and a display of muscular dexterity, which told well for the activity of these, at other times, indolent-looking squaws. The scene was a literal scramble; and it was carried on with the energies of the prize-fighter, and amidst expressions of mingled joy and surprise, that made the affair quite a circumstance in the lives of these poor destitute people. I was made happy myself, in seeing them so.

After an hour spent in these ceremonies, I told the chief I was short of hands, and wanted two of his *braves* to accompany me to Prairie du Chien. He shook his head, and said, "Sac and Fox Indians kill them." Never, I assured him, while they were with me; and that I would promise they should come home in safety, laden with presents. He assented, when there was a general rush of young men as volunteers. I put a hand on the two who were nearest to me, and said,—I take these, because they came first, and not because of any preference; for I know they are all brave men and true. I now felt secure for the remainder of the distance to the Prairie, and immediately embarked, and continued my voyage.

At *Le Petit Roche*, forty-five miles from the portage, at eight o'clock in the evening, fell in with General Atkinson, and his command. His barges were ranged alongside the bank of the river, and moored there. These long keel-boats, some as much as thirty tons burden, with the sails of several of them hanging quietly in the calm of the evening against the masts; the numerous fires that lined the shores, around which a large portion of the general's command of seven hundred men were gathered, gave to the place the appearance of a seaport. The general hum of voices, the stroke of the axe, with the confused noises, made of it, in so out-of-the-way a place, where never before had such circumstances combined, a sort of spirit-scene; especially as the moon's light invested the whole, being made pale by the many lights, and yet paler with an occasional half-obscuration caused by the rolling up of denser portions of the smoke from these numerous fires. Everything in nature by which we were surrounded was still, save only the sounds that proceeded from this spot, and the plash of the paddles of our canoes. Presently a sentinel challenged, and demanded the countersign. I told him who I was, and that I was bearer of tidings from Major Whistler's command, (which I had left that morning at the portage,) to General Atkinson. The sergeant of the guard was called, who making this message known to General Atkinson, we were invited to come alongside his barge, and (he being confined to his berth by a slight attack of fever) down into the cabin to see him.

We were received with the courtesy that always distinguished this gallant officer, when I went rapidly over the events that had transpired, and informed him of the surrender of the murderers; commended the Red-Bird to all the kind usage which his unfortunate condition would permit, and especially urged that he might not be put in irons. I did this, because I very well knew that he would suffer a thousand deaths rather than attempt to regain his liberty. There was no mistake in this matter. The man had literally already parted from life, and had his eyes fixed more upon the spirit-land, than upon coming in contact again with the bitter realities of the world around him. All this passed, and pledging each other in a glass of wine, and our best wishes for the general's health, we continued our voyage till ten at night, when we landed on a sand-bar for repose. Myriads of mosquitoes assailed us. Finding it impossible to endure their assaults, we determined to fly; so at two in the morning we struck our tents, and were again afloat, and going finely to the tune of the boat songs.

At seven the next morning we were thirty miles below our encampment, and forty-five miles from *Le Petit Roche.* The varied and bold shores of the river continued still to increase in interest. The color of the water is the same, and so is the loose and moveable material of the bottom of the river; the sand of which it is composed being so fine, as when touched by anything, is seen to stream off in the direction of whatever current may be the strongest. To this cause may be attributed the formation of the numerous sand-bars and islands that abound in this river. General Atkinson doubtless knew the nature of the passage he would have to make, and how difficult is the navigation of the Ouisconsin, owing to the ever-varying course of its channel, and its shallowness; and hence he secured boats that did not draw over twelve or eighteen inches of water.

Everything indicates a recession of the waters of this river. The water-marks, sometimes high up on its shores, and bluffs, and hill-sides, as well as the form and fertility of the bottom lands and prairies, all tell, in very plain language, that this river was once—but when, who knows?—capable of swimming navies. Many a tall ship might have rested on the bosom of this once wide and deep, but now narrow and shallow river; and anchors might have been let go, the noise of whose chain cables would have resounded amidst those hills like rumbling thunder. Hills, vast, towering, irregular, many of them circular-crowned, increased as we approached the Mississippi; and between them, stretching far off in the interior, are beautiful savannas, widening as they recede from the river, and then terminate in fertile and richly-clad table lands.

At about sun-down, arrived at the junction of the Ouisconsin with the Mississippi. Being in advance of the count, we landed, taking from our canoe as much baggage as would make room for him and the remainder of the company, Ben, on the arrival of the count, being transferred to his canoe, and left in charge of the baggage; when we rounded to, upon the Mississippi, and against the current of the river, arriving at Prairie du Chien at eight o'clock, in the softest, and brightest, and purest moonlight I had ever beheld. I thought of every scene of the sort I had ever seen, and of which I had ever read; of that hour when Shakspeare watched and loved the beams of this beautiful orb, until he said—

> "How sweet those moonbeams sleep on yonder bank;"

of those nights when I used to sit on the shore of Lake Superior, where I thought light so pure, so all-encircling, never came from the moon before, and where the rainbow also took precedence, in the gorgeousness of its dies, in the breadth and nearness of its bases, so near, sometimes, as to produce an irresistible motion to wash my hands in the falling glory. I have often since sought to give precedence to that lovely bow that spanned the Potomac, the frigate Brandywine immediately beneath the centre of its arch, on board of which we had, but a few hours before, placed the good La Fayette, on his final return from this country to his *La Belle France*. But it was vain. The rainbow of Lake Superior has had, can have, no equal; but the moonlight of the Mississippi, on that night when I first beheld this father of rivers, will take precedence of all I had ever seen before. How I wish I could paint it! The moon above, and the river beneath me; the glory of the heavens, and the silver-tipped ripples of the Mississippi, and the pearl-tinged forests, made brighter by the contrast of the dark recesses into which the moonlight had not entered, with the associations of the scenes around me—Pike's Hill, so named in honor of the gallant officer of that name, being just opposite—all combined, as the canoe was wheeled out upon the river, to fill me with emotions strange, bewildering, yet soothing; and then there was the grateful sense which my heart cherished for the security which the unseen, though ever-present God, had blessed us with. I had no language to express all these then, and I have none now; but the memory of it all will never die!

We were now on the theatre of the recent Indian murders, tidings of which had gone forth; and reaching St. Louis and Jefferson Barracks, upon the one hand, and Green Bay and Fort Howard upon the other, had put in motion about a thousand men, to interpose the appropriate shield to arrest and extinguish the spirit that had led to these butcheries. Well would it have been, if, when the bayonets of the nation had been despatched to punish the unenlightened, the untutored Indian, for the execution of the provisions of the *Lex Talionis*, the only law known to him, a corresponding energy, and the adequate power, had been employed to compel the civilized of our own race to treat these unfortunate people as human beings; and if there could be found no place for *kindness* in these relations, to enforce the obligation to treat them with at least common justice.

Prairie du Chien is said to have been once the seat of a Fox chief, named "THE DOG." The level land, upon part of which the village stands, was once, doubtless, part of the bed of the Mississippi. When forsaken by the waters, the channel of the river running close to the opposite or southern shore, the deserted lands became a prairie. Being now shorn of its native grass and flowers, the entire area has become a waste. When a *prairie*, "the Dog" was its principal occupant, with his band perhaps, and its owner—when the French gave it the appellation it yet bears, of *Le Prairie du Chien*, or the Prairie of the Dog.

This area is composed of several thousand acres of land. From W. S. W. to N. N. E., (the Mississippi running at this place due N. N. W., and being not over four hundred yards wide) it may be one mile and a half in breadth, and in length from four to five miles. The hills opposite rise abruptly out of the river. They are irregular, but covered with trees. On the east, are hills corresponding in height, but wearing no foliage. The rocks rise to some three hundred feet above their base, with a show of the blue and the white of the lime of which they are composed, and with many a water-mark to tell how high up their towering ascent the waters of the Mississippi once reached. And then, the most hasty glance will satisfy any one that the two sides were once united; but in what age of the world, nobody can tell. Ages may have been required for the waters of the Mississippi to have worn away the opposing masses, making for their transit to the ocean so wide a passage as is now opened at that spot; and yet, only about four hundred yards of it are now occupied by the descending waters.

The buildings of the Prairie are of wood, are old, and generally in a state of decay. The only two good houses here, are Rolette's, and a trader's, by the name of Lockwood, I believe. There appeared to be about one hundred of these decaying tenements, the old picket fort standing on the plain, a little north of the village, quite a ruin.

My first duty on arriving at the Prairie, was to fulfil my promise, made to the Indian chief, by returning to him safely his two young braves, laden with presents. I took them to the public store, and literally loaded them with good and useful Indian supplies, and of every variety. This done, I procured an escort, to attend and protect them on their journey across the country to their village. They arrived, as I afterwards learned, in safety. I have often heard since, of the inquiries which these people make after "the big captain," as their Indian term applied to myself, being interpreted, imports; the prefix "big," not relating so much to my size, as to their conception of my capacity to confer benefits upon them, and from my relations to the government.

This duty performed, I rode to the scene of the recent murders, attended by my companions, including Ben, who manifested great anxiety to see the place where the Indian had actually carried out, upon others, those plans of destruction, which he had so often anticipated would be made personal to himself. The scene of these butcheries is distant from the village, in an easterly direction, about three miles. I received the whole story from the widow of one of the murdered men, *Gagnier* by name, who was, at the time, proprietor of the log house in which he was killed. Gagnier was a half-breed, his mother having been Indian, and his father French. The door of this one-story log tenement fronts east, and a window opposite, of course, west. A large tree grows near its southwestern corner. *Gagnier* was sitting on a chest, on the left of the door. At the window, his wife was washing clothes. On her left was the bed, in which a child, eleven months old, was sleeping. On her right, and a little back of her, sat a discharged soldier, named *Liepcap;* and this was the situation of the family, when Wan-nig-sootsh-kau—the Red-Bird—We-kau, or the Sun, and a third Indian, entered. Visits of Indians being common, no particular attention was paid to them. They were, however, received with the usual civility, and asked if they would have something to eat. They said yes, and would like some fish and milk.

Gagnier had, meantime, seen something peculiar in the looks and movements of these Indians, as is supposed, which led him to reach up, and take from brackets just over his head, his rifle, which, as Mrs. G. turned to get the fish and milk, she saw laying across Gagnier's lap. At the moment she heard the *click* caused by the cocking of the Red-Bird's rifle, which was instantly followed by its discharge. She looked, and saw her husband was shot. At the same moment, the third Indian shot old Liepcap, when Mrs. G. seeing We-kau, who had lingered about the door, about to rush in, she met him, made fight, and wrested from him his rifle. He ran out, she pursuing him, employing all her energies to cock the rifle and shoot him, but, by some mysterious cause, was rendered powerless—"feeling," as she expressed it, "like one in a dream, trying to call, or to run, but without the ability to do either." To save himself, We-kau kept running round the big tree at the corner of the house, well knowing if he should put off in a line, she would have better aim, and be more likely to kill him. After a few turns round the tree, and finding she had no power over the rifle, she turned short about, and made for the village, bearing the rifle with her, to give the alarm; which, being given, she returned, followed by a posse of armed men, and found her infant, which she had left, covered up in the bed on the floor, scalped, and its neck cut just below the occiput, to the bone. This was the work of We-kau, who, being intent on having a scalp—the other two having secured theirs—there being no other subject, took one from the head of the child. The knife, from the examination made of the head, was applied in front of the crown, and brought round by the right ear, and far down behind, and up again on the other side, the object seeming to be, to get as much hair as he could. In the turn of the knife, at the back of the head, the deep cut was given, which found its way to the bone.

The child, when I saw it, was comfortable, and I believe it recovered—but the sight of a rifle, even at that tender age, when one might suppose it could not distinguish between a rifle and anything else, would terrify it almost into fits. Young as it was, it must, from its place in the bed, have seen a rifle, in connexion with what it was made itself, so immediately after, to suffer. I made the mother presents for herself and child.

Governor Cass, after our first parting at Green Bay, arrived at the Prairie just after these murders had been committed. The inhabitants being, as was natural, in a state of great alarm, he devised the best means of defence in his power, and, as has been stated, descended the Mississippi with tidings of the outbreak, to General Atkinson. From the day the governor left Green Bay, till his return to it, which was four weeks, he had voyaged in a bark canoe *sixteen hundred miles*—this was going at an average rate of about sixty miles the day, including a tarry of one day at the Prairie, and three at St. Louis.

Notwithstanding we bore to the Prairie the tidings of the surrender, there still remained, in the minds of the inhabitants, some lingering apprehensions that more of the same kind of bloody work might await them. They thought the war-cloud had not yet spent itself. But nothing surprised them so much as that the hitherto peace-loving "Red-Bird" should have been guilty of such conduct. He was not only well known, but was, also, the pride of the Prairie. Such was the confidence reposed in him, that he was always sought after as a protector, and his presence was looked upon as a pledge of security against any outbreak that might be attempted. Indeed, when husbands, and brothers, and sons, had occasion to leave their homes, the families considered themselves quite secure, if the Red-Bird could be procured to see to their safety. What had happened to induce him to act the part he had acted, was a mystery to all. As to We-kau, he was known, and abhorred, as one of the most bloody-minded of his race. Of the third, whose name I could not learn, they knew but little.

All this mystery, however, was, at last, solved. There had been great indignities offered to the band near the St. Peters, to which Red-Bird had become allied, and personal violence committed upon some of their leading men, and by those whose station ought to have taught them better; and whose authority and power should have been differently exercised. The leading chiefs counselled upon those acts of violence, and resolved on enforcing the Indian's law—*retaliation.* Red-Bird was called upon to go out, and "take meat," as they phrase it. Not wishing to appear a coward, he undertook the enterprise, secretly rejoicing that the business had been referred to him; for he resolved to make a circuit, and return, saying he could find no meat. He did so, and was upbraided, and taunted, and called "*coward,*" and told he knew very well, if he had the spirit to avenge the wrongs of his people, he could, by going to the Prairie, get as much meat as he could bring home. This fired him, and he resolved to redeem his character as a *brave!* when, beckoning to We-kau, and another Indian, he told them to follow him. They proceeded to the Prairie. Gagnier's was not the first house they entered, with the view of carrying out their purpose. If I mistake not, their first visit was to the house of Mr.

Lockwood, who was then absent. His interesting wife was at home, and her life was undoubtedly saved by the presence of an old Frenchman on a visit to her, who not only understood the Winnebago language, but knew the parties; and he, also, was known to them. They had respect for him—he had been their friend. So, after lingering about the house for a season, they quit the premises, and crossed the Prairie, to Gagnier's, and there executed their bloody purpose, as I have narrated.

Addressing a few lines to General Atkinson, still urging a lenient treatment for the Red-Bird, I prepared for the descent of the Mississippi; and accordingly, after having partaken of the hospitality of Rolette, I embarked with my party in my bark canoe, and at three, P. M., of the 8th September, was again upon the bosom of the Mississippi, and going, with its descending current, onward, to St. Louis. Continued on till six o'clock, P. M., and encamped twenty miles below. What had been selected as a place of repose for the night, proved to be a mosquito hive—for they literally swarmed there. At six in the morning, after a night of suffering, caused by the stings of those pestilent lancers, and of inconvenience occasioned by the rain, we pursued our voyage. The bed of the river had now widened to about two miles—the shores on the eastern side broken, scolloped, and barren of trees, with nothing of verdure but grass; whilst on the western, they were crowned with trees, and altogether very beautiful.

Arriving at Du Buque's, sixty miles below the Prairie, we stopped, and visited his grave. This grave is on a high bluff, or point of land, formed by the junction of the Black river with the Mississippi, on the west side of the latter. A village of Fox Indians occupied the low lands, south of the bluff—of these Indians we procured the guide who piloted us to Du Buque's last resting place. The ascent was rather fatiguing. Over the grave was a stone, covered with a roof of wood. Upon the stone was a cross, on which was carved, in rude letters—"*Julian Du Buque—died 24th March*, 1810—*aged* 45 *years*." Near by, was the burial-spot of an Indian chief. We returned to our canoes, embarked, and proceeded sixteen miles further, to Fever river, and up that river to Galena, arriving after nightfall. The river sent forth a most disagreeable odor. It appeared to be the very hot-bed of bilious fever. At Galena, I visited the mines and smelting establishments, at that time in their infancy. In the previous July, eight hundred thousand pounds of lead had been smelted; and perhaps a million of pounds in August.

The Winnebagoes were in a state of great excitement, caused by the intrusions of the whites on their lands. They had, after having remonstrated for a long time in vain, made up their minds to endure it no longer, and had so informed Mr. Conner, the sub-agent. A warning was circulated among the miners, who replied, "We have the right to go just where we please." Everything appeared threatening. Two thousand persons were said to be over the lines, as intruders, upon lands belonging to the Indians. The Indians had fallen back, and sent word to the sub-agent that "he would see them no more"—meaning, as friends.

The white population were supposed to be at that time from three to five thousand, the larger portion at Galena. At least fifteen hundred, alarmed for their safety, caused by the apprehended disturbances, had quit the country. There appeared to be no time to lose; and as justice was all these harrassed people desired, I adopted measures, at once, to secure it to them, by restoring to them their rightful possessions. A general return to a peaceful order of things immediately ensued.

This *overt act, this trespass on their grounds, was the egg out of which the Black Hawk war was hatched.* There was no necessity for that war, when, some few years after, it did break out. It was only needed that *the same justice* should be continued to the Indians; the same regard shown to their rights, and that war would never have occurred. At the time it broke out, the places that had hitherto been filled by those whose experience had fitted them for the rightful and harmonious adjustment of such difficulties, were filled with strangers. Hence the Black Hawk war; and hence, also, the Seminole war. *Injustice* and *bad faith*, combined with the absence of the needed intelligence, and that indispensable pre-requisite, experience—were the causes of both these wars, and of the waste of the blood and treasure that attended upon them; but the loss of this blood, and of this treasure, could be endured, if, in the origin, and progress, and termination of these wars, the national honor had not been tarnished, and our name, as a people and nation, held up to the civilized world as *unjust—cruel*—and *treacherous*. It is painful to recur, even thus slightly, to the history of those wars—and, for the present, I pass on, first recording my judgment against them, against their necessity, and against *the policy* that originated them; as well as against *the measures* that were adopted for carrying them on.

I found rents at Galena enormously high—the certain index of prosperous times. One log house, one story high, sixteen feet by twenty, I was told, rented for thirty-five dollars a month. Another, in which the tavern was kept, also of logs, fifty feet by twenty, rented for *one thousand dollars per annum!* The village consisted of about two hundred houses, all small, and all ranged almost against the western bank of the river—the river being narrowed, at this point, to a mere stream. The reader will bear in mind that I am describing Galena as it was in 1827.

Left Galena at three, P. M.; proceeded twenty miles, and encamped. Evening cool; morning also very cool; wind fair and free. Embarked at six, A. M.; run up a little sail, and took in paddles. Ran twenty-three miles in three hours. Breakfasted at nine, and at five, P. M., reached Fort Armstrong, having run, since six in the morning, sixty-five miles. Numerous villages of Fox Indians on our route. Found a large number of this tribe at Rock Island. This spot is one of most enchanting beauty. The fort occupies a rocky elevation on the west side of the island, and at some thirty feet above the level of the river. The officers' quarters front west, and from these a view opens, caused by a bend in the river, that cheats one into the belief that what is seen of water is a beautiful lake, of about three miles one way, by half that distance the other. The hills on the opposite shore are high, and of great beauty; sloping down to the river with a grace so easy, as to captivate the eye of every beholder. They are thick set, down to their bases, with the richest grasses, unobstructed by undergrowth, and unbroken by ravines, seeming to my eye to have been cut only a short time before, by some skilful hand, and left, as well-shaven grass will, wearing the appearance of velvet. I was never weary in looking at this rich scene. We were entertained by the garrison with great hospitality.

Embarked the 12th of September, at six, A. M. Weather cool and cloudy; wind ahead, and blowing fresh. Encamped at sun-down. Thursday, 13th, at half-past six, A. M., put out against a strong head-wind. The river wide, and quite ocean-like, rolling its huge waves into billows, whose tops were whitened with foam. The current and wind being opposed, caused this roughness; and yet, against this wind, and amidst these billows, we made fifty miles, encamping that evening three miles above *Rapide Des Moine*. The world seemed everywhere filled with mosquitoes! There was no escaping from them; and in fierceness and venom, they surpassed their more northern kindred of Lake Superior. Up with the dawn, the next morning, and out upon the broad waters, where the rapids commence. There was something life-like in these rapids, as contrasted with the usually smooth current of the river.

It was not the animation of the rapids, only, that proved inspiring to us, but the superadded feeling caused by our having reached the line where the civilized and savage limits meet. The fruits of the labor of the hardy pioneer now began to greet us, in the sight of here and there a log cabin, with its flaxen-headed urchins, and the hardy, and sun-burnt, and coarse-clad parents. And here, too, we began to hear the lowing of cattle, and to see the half-tamed horses and hogs, and to be charmed with the singing of birds. How natural were these sounds, and how sweet! How composing was all this; and how rapidly arose the associations of civilization, of refinement, and of home! How all this hushed the feelings! We passed the steamboat Mexico, of Cincinnati, at stationary moorings—she having, in ascending the river, about three weeks before, struck a rock, and sunk. Four miles lower down was another, the Pilot. She had parted her cables, and gone ashore.

Fort Edwards was now in view. It occupies a bluff on the Mississippi, of some eighty or one hundred feet above the level of the river. Here we landed, and breakfasted, having come about twenty-three miles. The opening into the rapids, ten miles above Fort Edwards, is beautiful. The river is wide, and the cultivation on the Illinois shore is grateful to the eye—for there the dottings of civilized life, which had begun to cheer us above, had thickened into a more general combination of the cultivated scenery; and man, and beast, and nature, all seemed to have undergone a cleansing, and been subjected to the hand of the artist, in all the variety of the civilized exterior. The birds were the same, but more numerous, and apparently more gay and happy. How man can make war upon these sweet songsters, and stop, in wanton sport, so much, and such variety of music as they pour forth; and who do not contribute with their notes, only, to regale him, but assist him, also, in his crops, in both field and garden, by devouring the worms and insects that tend to make both barren, I could never conceive. Such a war upon this interesting portion of God's creation, always indicated, to me, the absence of the better feelings of human nature, and its approximation to cruelty, in all other things.

> "I would not enter on my list of friends,
> (Though grac'd with polish'd manners, and fine sense,
> Yet wanting sensibility,) the man
> Who needlessly sets foot upon a worm."

Leaving Fort Edwards, we took the right of the river, and into a channel varying from one-half to a mile in width. The water was calm; the hills on the western side high and rolling. A fringe of low ground stretched along our left, whilst in the middle of the river, an island of great beauty stood full in our view. When I first saw this island, it resembled a castle, with three distinctly formed terraces, and as many turrets, each terrace about twenty-five feet above the other. Beyond, and upon its right and left, the eye passed far onward over the waters, till it rested on distant mountains, that seemed like blue mist curtaining the further distance from view; the nearer waters reflecting the scenery from their mirror face, made green by the foliage medium through which the light passed. Everything was tranquil here, and a sober grandeur rested on castle, woods, and water, till, presently, the castle-like form began to lose its distinctness, turret after turret disappearing, with the magic-like removal of the terraces, when the island stood forth divested of its formidable aspect, simple, and true to nature; and with this change were lost, also, the associations to which its first appearance gave rise, as light clouds melt into the air, and disappear.

> "'Twas distance lent enchantment to the view."

Encamped on an island five miles below, and, as is my

custom, took to the water, and bathed. It was somewhere about here, when, seeing a light on the Illinois shore, away off in the woods, that I concluded to pass over to it, climb up the ascent, and purchase some milk, and other necessaries. The night was dark. Ben, having reached the cultivated region, and being now within sight of houses, and fields, and of domestic animals, was nothing loth to accompany me. We reached the place, and commenced the ascent. When at the top, the light seemed to have receded, but was still visible in the distance, through a thick foliage. The undergrowth was heavy and tangled, and our way was impeded by the darkness, and by the brush-wood which lay scattered over the ground, in all directions; but, keeping my eye upon the light, I continued on, for about a quarter of a mile, when I found we were in a clearing. The bodies of huge trees lay in all directions, between which the earth had been disturbed, and the crop was growing. I knew this to be a new settlement. Presently the dogs began to bark, when a tall, gaunt man came to the door, demanding to know "who comes there?" A friend, I answered. "Advance!" The dogs were called off, whilst he stood in the door-way to receive me. "Two of you, I see." Yes, sir; this is my servant. "Ah, from the States, I suppose?" Yes, sir.

I had observed, in my advances to the house, through the only window in it, a woman of large size, who appeared to be seated, and around about her the tops of the heads of some half dozen children, their hair standing, as if in fright. Now and then, I could see their hands rise and fall, with quick motions; whilst the head, and neck, and shoulders of the woman, being all visible, I could see and comprehend better the meaning of her movements, which were like those indicated by the children. I could see her strike her face, and then her neck, first with one hand, and then the other, the hands of the children, as I have said, being in constant motion, performing, as I supposed, corresponding ceremonies. It was a perfect pantomime, which did not, however, explain itself. But on entering, I saw they were all busy in warring with the mosquitoes, against whose bites I was guarded by a green veil over my face, a cloth coat and pantaloons, boots, and thick leather gloves.

My great object was to get some milk. Those only who have been brought up where this article of diet abounds, and are then separated from it, for a length of time, know how strong the desire becomes to taste it again. "Sit up, sit up, stranger, and join us," said the hardy settler. I had noticed, on coming into the room, a large wooden bowl in the middle of the table, with the handle of a wooden ladle lying on the rim—the lower part being buried in something, I knew not what; and yet, when one and another of the children were to be helped, and I saw the thick, dark surface disturbed, there was milk brought up from beneath it. Just as I was about joining the repast, my eye being on the constant slapping of the mother and the children of their own faces, and hands, and necks, I saw, at every stroke, the crippled and wing-broken mosquitoes falling into the big bowl, and that the beverage they were all eating with so much *gout*, was, sure enough, milk, heavily sprinkled with crippled and dead mosquitoes—when I excused myself on the ground of haste, asking if I could be obliged with a few dozen of eggs; my milk mania having been effectually cured.

During the absence of the man to get the eggs, I re marked to the woman—You appear, madam, to have a good many mosquitoes here. "What!" she said, with a look of surprise, still slapping her face, and neck, and shoulders, the children being no less busy in the same way—"what! mosquitoes? You don't call what we have here, in this clearing, *many*, do you? If you had stopped in that bend just above here, about forty miles, I guess you wouldn't call what few we have here, *many*."

The eggs having been procured, paid for, and handed over to Ben, we made our way back to the canoe and our camp. "Did you ever see such a fight, before?" inquired Ben, as we entered the woods. "And then the milk, how it was covered with the dead ones. Well, give me Washington," he continued, "or any other place in the old settlements, in preference to these new countries. But there don't seem to be any *Indians* along here." I told him we should have the pleasure of seeing a goodly number, before we should see Washington. "Not *wild* ones, I hope, sir."

Saturday, 15th, embarked at day-light. Made a call at Louisiana, a little town, thirty miles below our encampment, and after taking breakfast on the beach, walked to the town, hoping to find some newspapers—another article after which one who has been accustomed to their daily presence, is no less hungry, when deprived of them for several months, than for milk. I found there about half a bushel of Duff Green's Telegraph, directed to numerous persons, who had not, for some reason, as the man told me, called for them. As many of these as I wanted, were placed at my disposal. Taking a few, and being favored with some of another quality, making up quite an assortment, I proceeded on to Clarksville, which is about one hundred miles above St. Louis. I literally devoured the newspapers; and every name I saw that was known to me about Washington, and elsewhere, seemed to be invested with new charms. I read every article, in every paper, and even the advertisements, and many of them over and over again. No wonder Selkirk sighed as he did after

"Society, friendship, and love."

Zimmerman, I know, has invested solitude with charms; but to one who, like myself, had been in its midst, and who also knew what was included in "*society*," and "*friendship*," and, I suppose, I might as well say "*love*," there could be no time required to weigh the attractions of the two conditions, unless, indeed, as some one has said, a beloved one was present, when in solitude, to whom I might say,

"How charming is solitude!"

At Clarksville I essayed to procure something fresh to eat—but could find nothing but eggs. Thirty miles lower down, we saw, on a small island, at least three hundred pelicans. They were so numerous as literally to cover the island, giving to it (the island was a sand island, with nothing of vegetation growing out of it,) the appearance of being covered with snow. The rage for shooting whatever came in their way, had seized the count, and the rest of my companions, including Ben, when nothing would do but to have a shot at them. The bird, I knew, was as useless as it was harmless. But no remonstrance could divert them from their purpose, when they were landed amidst the undergrowth of a contiguous island, from the point of which they fired—killing three, and winging two. The winged ones were brought on board the canoe, and being not much injured, I concluded to take them to St. Louis; and, if I could, to Washington.

Encamped at eight at night, forty miles above St. Louis; and succeeded there in procuring some fresh supplies, including milk. This being in bottles, to keep it cool, I tied cords around the bottles' necks, and fastening these to the canoe, towed them after us. Here, too, we were so lucky as to get some peaches. What delicious fare! The apprehension of a border war, proceeding from the Prairie du Chien murders, had just reached these settlers, who fled at the approach of our canoe, as would children from an apparition. The wildest panic had seized the entire population! One entire family, on seeing us approaching the shore, were with difficulty kept from running away, leaving their all behind them—not doubting but we were Indians.

At five next morning, embarked, and ran twenty-two miles, when we landed for breakfast. A settler came to our encampment. I asked if he could supply me with some milk. He answered—"We don't use it." I asked why? "The people," he replied, "about these parts, were afraid of the *milk-sick;* and never used milk after early spring. They do not even permit the calves to suck it; if they do, the calves die, as well as the people." I sought information touching the nature of this "milk-sick," and to find out what it was that, after "early spring," imparted such deleterious qualities to the milk of cows—but found my settler not one of the sort out of whom answers to such abstract questions could be extracted. All he knew was, that, after a certain season, those who partook of cow's milk, whether human beings or calves, were made sick, and many died from the use of it. I interpreted the poisonous quality of the milk to be produced by some weed that was indigenous to these parts, which the cows ate; and I suppose that to be the fact. It was fortunate that the man had come to our camp; for Ben, seeing some cows in the distance, was just about to put off, to take, *sans ceremonie*, as much milk as his bucket would hold.

CHAPTER VII.

SOJOURN AT ST. LOUIS. PASSAGE DOWN THE MISSISSIPPI. HARD JOURNEY FROM MEMPHIS TO CHICKASAW BLUFFS.

Mouth of the Missouri—A toast—The French count—Meeting of the waters—St. Louis—General Clark—Hospitalities—Sudden illness of the count—Kindness of Mrs. Clark—Departure and destination—Compagnons de voyage—Screw-mills—The channel ever shifting—Abrasion of the banks of the Mississippi—A town falling into the river—The cause explained—Sawyers—Planters—Duty of government to remove them—Profits of two acres of onions—Memphis—Journey to the Chickasaw bluffs—Missionary stations—Drunken Indians—Power of General Jackson's name—Halt in the middle of a stream—Ti-esh-ka—Tockshish—Monroe—Barren tract of country—Arrival at Colbert's—An Indian's gratitude and regard—Designs of the government at that time—Different principles afterwards adopted—Jeremiah Evarts, and his papers, signed "William Penn"—A "blow-gun"—Counting time—"Red-sticks"—Anecdote of Tecumthé—Preparations for the grand council.

At half-past twelve, we were opposite, indeed in, the mouth of the Missouri river. This being the first time I had seen this river, I directed the voyagers to fetch a compass, and go into it. When upon its waters, unmixed with those of the Mississippi, the paddles were taken in, and all were at rest. While thus stationary, there remaining, as reported by Ben, one bottle of claret wine, of the stores that I had taken with me from New York, I directed the cork to be drawn—"the sun being," in nautical parlance, "past the foreyard," and told all hands to prepare for a sentiment—voyagers, Ben, and all. On filling our cups—a few of us had tumblers—I gave, "*The memory of Napoleon Le Grand*"—a compliment I thought due to my guest, the count, who had served under that great captain. I had scarcely given utterance to the sentiment, when the count cried out—" Stop, stop, Monsieur Le Colonel, one moment, if you please. Benjamin, hand me the brandy. The wine is good, but not strong enough for that sentiment." When pouring his wine into Ben's cup, he said, " Now colonel, with all my heart ;" when, standing in our bark canoe, in the mouth of the Missouri river, we drank to the memory of " Napoleon Le Grand ;" and by the count it was done with a *gout* that told, in language not to be mistaken, how undying was the devotion of the French to the memory of their great idol.

I beg to make, here, a short digression. Being in my office in the War Department, one day, the door was thrown open by my messenger, when a remarkably fine-looking young gentleman entered. He advanced to me, saying, " Colonel McKenney, I believe ?" Yes, sir. He drew from his pocket a letter directed to me, saying, " From Doctor Black, of Nova Scotia." The object of the letter was to introduce to me this young Englishman, named STAR.* From his brilliant and animated countenance, and fine, manly form, he appeared to be appropriately named. Having read the letter from my venerable friend, who was a bishop, I believe, in Nova Scotia, I said to Mr. Star, You will do me the honor of dining with me to-day, at five o'clock ? He declined, urging that " he had come all the way from his home to gratify a single feeling ; that the ship in which he had arrived was at New York, and nearly ready to sail ; and that all the time he had at his command he must devote to the sole object which had brought him here—and that was to visit what was once the home of the greatest and best man that had ever lived, and the tomb that contains his remains. I need not say, sir, that I refer to your WASHINGTON ; nor that my call on you is to obtain counsel as to the best and speediest route to Mount Vernon." The Supreme Court was then in session ; so I wrote a line to Judge Washington, asking for this young Englishman a permit, &c., &c. My messenger was des-

* Hon. J. Leander Star, subsequently member of the council of her majesty in Nova Scotia.

patched to the Capitol, who soon returned with a note from the judge to his major-domo, the substance of which was, to refuse the bearer no request he might make.

The moment young Star had run his eye over tne note, he sprang from his chair, rubbed his hands, his eyes sparkling with delight, and, with many acknowledgments, started for Mount Vernon, by the way which had been, meantime, agreed upon.

The next day he returned, called on me, repeating his acknowledgments, and charmed with his visit. Availing himself of the judge's note, he had made two "requests"—one was, to be admitted into the room in which General Washington died, and the other to visit the tomb where reposed his remains. A pause in the major-domo, for a moment, produced a fear that these requests could not be complied with; but the note being looked at, they were. On entering the tomb, and the coffin being pointed out to Mr. Star, that contained the remains of Washington, he put his hand on its breast, and on a sprig of *arbor vitæ*, which he took from its resting-place, saying, "Can I take this?" If you request it, was the answer. It was placed there, (pointing to the spot where it had lain,) by General Lafayette, on his visit to this tomb; and, till now, the door has never since been opened.

Meantime, taking the sprig of evergreen from his pocket-book, he said, "This is it, sir—this is it. What a relic! From the breast of the coffin of Washington, and put there by Lafayette!" The treasure was carefully returned to its place of safe-keeping; when this fine youth, declining all further offers of civility, left me, looking as if the circle of his happiness was now completed, and as though no other incident of his life were needed to make it more perfect.

The French count had lavished his heart's best feelings, as was meet he should, over the memory of the great captain under whom he had been led to victory; whilst the young Englishman revelled in the fame, and gloried in the patriotism and purity of our Washington.

The waters of the Missouri contrast strongly with those of the Mississippi, being clay color; whilst those of the Mississippi are lighter and brighter. There were floating about, and being driven with the current of the Mississippi, numerous fragments of trees, which made it necessary, whilst in their midst, to guard well our canoe of bark, from being crushed by them. The waters of the Missouri, when there is anything of a descent, drive those of the Mississippi far across to the Illinois shore, and would seem to be the master-river of the two—where, by a well defined line, each is separated from the other, and continue so for many miles, when the clay color of the Missouri at last becomes blended with the less turbid Mississippi. Still, a perfect commingling is not consummated, until they pass St. Louis, some forty miles below, when the color of the Missouri water is lost, and the Mississippi carries what would seem to be its own tribute to the Gulf of Mexico, and onward to the "deep blue sea."

The mouth of the Missouri, at its junction with the Mississippi, is about a mile wide—my eye being judge—the lands on both sides are flat, and quite unbecoming the noble river which passes out between them. There are heights some eight miles back of the mouth of the river. Upon part of these, *Bell Fountaine* is situated, and this is the only object of a bold nature that greets the eye around this place.

Landed at St. Louis, at three, P. M. We were met and greeted by many; and among them, by that good man, and faithful public officer, General William Clark, whose name has acquired celebrity as the companion and fellow-traveller of Lewis, in the expedition planned by Mr. Jefferson, to the Rocky Mountains, and the Columbia river. Quarters having been arranged for me at General Clark's, my companions and myself parted company, they occupying rooms at the hotel. Dined at Camp Jefferson, with Colonel Leavenworth and others. The civilities of those hospitable people, I can never forget—those of Colonel John O'Fallon, and his brother, Major Benjamin O'Fallon, were made especially acceptable. With the latter I made excursions round the country back of St. Louis, and saw enough to satisfy me then, that St. Louis was destined to become a great and populous city. It is yet destined to outstrip the most sanguine anticipations of those who look farthest. Nothing can be more beautiful than is the country back of the city, and nothing more fruitful.

A party was made at General Clark's, to which we were invited. Going over to the count's room in the afternoon, I found him seated on the side of his bed, caparisoned and ready for the evening's entertainment, except his coat, which lay beside him, ornamented with the insignia of his rank. He was dressed in white cassimere shorts, white silk stockings, and shoes mounted with buckles set in diamonds, a rich vest, and ruffled shirt. His fine black hair, and whiskers, never looked so well before. All these, with a person over six feet, of finely proportioned form, seemed to qualify him, together with his rank and character, to figure with *eclat*, in the lovely Mrs. Clark's drawing-room. But all this exterior was lost to my eye, in an instant, when, on looking at his countenance and complexion, I saw he was in a perilous state! I put my finger on his pulse, looked at his tongue, and was satisfied nothing could save him but *instant bleeding*.

I had no lancet at hand; but calling in Ben, I directed him to assist the count in getting to bed, whilst I went out in search of a physician. I asked everybody for a doctor, and desired all I met to send one, forthwith, to the hotel, and to the count's room—making my way as fast as I could to Doctor Farrow's. He was not in; so I returned, still looking for aid, when I met the doctor, (somebody having despatched him to the hotel,) coming down stairs. I asked eagerly after the count, and got for answer, "His case is a bad one." Did you bleed him? "In a moment after I saw him." Will he recover? "I hope so." This implied doubt. I had learned to love the count. He was, besides, a stranger, and far from home, and family, and friends. He was in a strange land. He had been my companion in peril, in storm, and in calm; and he was, besides, a glorious fellow. I could not endure the thought of his dying. I sat by him—watched him—ministered to him. Ben, too, was all attention. The next day the disease was broken, and the symptoms all favorable. I was to leave on the 22d, but delayed till the 24th. The count being young and vigorous, once upon a level with his disease, I felt sure he would master it.

On the evening of the 23d, Mrs. Clark, one of the most estimable of women, lovely, and beloved by everybody—(alas! she is dead, and knows nothing of what I am recording to her memory, nor will she ever know)—said to me, "Your friend, the count, Doctor Farrow tells me, is sitting up. You are to leave to-morrow. One promise I must exact of you; and that is, to leave your friend in my care. The room you will vacate is large and airy, and better suited to an invalid than the one he is in. Now this is my plan. Tell him, with my respects, that, the day being favorable to-morrow, I will call for him at eleven o'clock, and take him riding in my carriage, and give him an airing. You must accompany us. While we are gone, Ben must pack up his trunks, and transfer them to your room. On our return, I will stop at my door. We must unite our invitations, and prevail on the count to make a call, when you will introduce him into your room. There he must remain, till he gets well. You see I employ *the positive*—MUST. You can then leave with more quiet of mind, and he will have a home, and friends who will delight in attending upon him." Never did woman's loveliness break forth in charms so captivating. She looked like an angel. I could scarcely speak. And this, I could not help ejaculating, is

"Being mindful to entertain strangers."

All this was done according to the programme of this excellent lady, and the count put in possession of his new abode.

In the meantime, I had taken leave of the estimable Mr. Kinzie, my tried friend, clerk, and interpreter; and of my trusty voyagers, and of my favorite canoe, having seen them off, on their way up the Illinois river, thence on, by the way of Lakes Michigan, Huron, and Erie, to Detroit, where they all arrived safely. My destination was, by the way of the Mississippi, to the Chickasaw bluffs; thence through the country of the Chickasaws, Choctaws, Cherokees, and Creeks. With the first three it had been made my duty to enter into conventional arrangements, for an exchange of their country, east, for a country west of the Mississippi; and with the latter, to negotiate a treaty of cession of a strip of land which remained in Georgia, and by this means put to rest the excitements that had been so long kept up between that State and the federal government. Honest and earnest efforts had been made, by the federal Executive, to satisfy and pacify Georgia, by obtaining the consent of the Creek Indians to relinquish *all* their claims to territory within that State, and those efforts had proved successful, until arrested by a refusal of the Indians to relinquish their last foothold; when I was sent on this forlorn hope, without resources in goods, or money, or resort of any sort, even for the expenses attending the experiment, except to the limited provisions of the contingent fund, so far as, in my discretion, it should be proper to draw upon it.

Taking leave of my hospitable friends of St. Louis, and of the count, I embarked at four o'clock, P. M., on Monday, the 24th September, 1827, on board the steamboat

Crusader. At a quarter past four, we were under way. On passing General Clark's house, the windows were occupied by its inmates, and among them I caught a glimpse of the count's face, fine black head, and large dark eyes, all expressive of the courtesy which had always characterized this polite and finished gentleman. A moment passed in the waving of handkerchiefs, in token of the parting, and the boat, impelled by her wheels, and borne onward by the current, shut from my view all these kind manifestations, and I was once more on the bosom of this father of rivers; but now in a state of enlargement from the limits of my canoe, and amidst new, and some of it strange company. We ran eighteen miles, and came to for wood, and for the night, such being the difficulty of navigation about here, as to render any attempt, except by day-light, unsafe.

The boat was a fine one, in all respects, but I had never before travelled with such company. One of the lower decks was appropriated, from stern to bow, for the transportation of live stock. Noah's ark, it appeared to me, could not have contained a greater variety. Horses, cows, bullocks, sheep, calves, hogs, mules, chickens, geese, turkeys—in a word, everything that had life, seemed to be there; and all were so huddled together, as to create in each a feeling of self-protection that would, every now and then, break out into acts of open hostility, accompanied by the cries of the frightened or hurt, so as to make of the whole a perfect Babel. And then there was the *ammonia!* And yet the boat, in all other respects, was first-rate, and the accommodations very superior.

I noticed along the shore of the river many mills that were kept going by a screw in the water, operating as a propeller, performing a similar duty, that of turning, and acting upon the same principle with that known as *Erickson's propeller;* the difference being in the motive power, or in a modification of it; the mills being turned by the current of the Mississippi operating upon the screw that was passed into it, and the boats by a similar screw, put in motion by steam. My attention was arrested by the constant change in the direction of the boat. The object, I learned, was to find the channel, it being rarely the case that a boat goes down to New Orleans from the upper Mississippi, and back again in the same channel. The current makes the channel, and the current is made constantly to change, by the undermining action of the water upon the banks of the river, and the falling into it of many acres of land at a time, and by the lodgment of trees and floating matter upon sand-bars, &c. It is not unusual for a log house of the settler, after having stood a mile from the Mississippi for a few years, to find itself, by the gradual advances of the river, first upon its bank, and next a wreck amidst its waters. The very house I had gone to, and at which I witnessed the fight with the mosquitoes, furnished, almost, an example of this sort; and long before now, I have no doubt, it has been floated down the Mississippi. While the good man was out getting the eggs, I chanced to say something of these invasions of the river upon the land, when the wife answered, "Oh, yes; Lord bless your soul, old Mississippi does just what he pleases with the land. When John first made this clearing, we were two miles from the landing, away off in the country, and that wasn't over two years ago; and now we're a little over a quarter of a mile from the river. I told him it would be so, but he wouldn't mind me, and now he sees I am right."

Another example. New Madrid once occupied ground which, at the time I passed it, was the main channel of the river. When at the place, Hon. Mr. S., whom I had known as a member of Congress, said to me, "We are now over the spot once occupied by New Madrid. That," pointing to a house near the shore, "is the only house now left of those that once (in 1805) formed the town of New Madrid; and yonder barn, that was then three-quarters of a mile from the landing, is, as you see, not now over four hundred yards distant." A line being at hand, I threw it over, but found no bottom.

This New Madrid, the reader will recollect, had been the seat of an earthquake, I believe in 1812. The cause of the incursion of the water upon the land was before me, at this place. It was an island that had been formed by materials brought down the river, and lodged in shallow water opposite New Madrid, forming a nucleus for sand, and sediment, and trees, &c., &c., till, in the lapse of time, it became an island. The current striking against it, was changed in its course, and thrown diagonally across the river, and against the bank on which the town was built, and there it ran, till the ground was undermined, caved in, and carried away, to form some new deposit, or some new island; or, if it should not be thus disposed of, to enlarge the Delta at the mouth of the Mississippi. The river, where New Madrid once stood, was about a mile wide; it may, from the causes stated, be now wider or narrower.

We passed innumerable sawyers, engaged in that perpetual swing, from side to side, caused by the action of the current upon them; from which motion they derive their name. They are formed by trees, that fall, frequently by acres at a time, with the soil in which they grew, into the water, as I have stated, and these are brought down the Missouri and Mississippi, with others from numerous other rivers which empty into them, and floated in every direction, till the roots become impeded, when sediment and drift-wood form around, and fix them deeply and firmly at bottom, their upper ends being above the water. A descending vessel will pass over these sawyers without injury. The tree yields under the pressure of the boat; and, when relieved from that pressure by being gone over, rises with a rebound, throwing a large portion of its length out of the water; when, presently, it resumes its swinging or sawing motion, as before.

Planters are trees, also; and, like sawyers, are also firm set at bottom, but are either too short to be seen above water, or have been, by some cause, broken off, at or near, and sometimes some feet below the surface. The first, in ascending the river, by being visible, can be avoided; but the last is that hidden enemy to both property and life, which are so frequently destroyed by their agency on these waters. Their position is generally favorable to the nature of the work they perform; it being inclined, and pointed, as if by a skilful engineer, so as to receive the boat's bow, or bottom, just where there is the least possibility for escape; when it ploughs through and through, making a breach, and opening numerous seams for the admission of water, and holds on, till the work of destruction is complete. There would be scarcely less danger were as many cannon mounted in the same positions, and pointed, at like angles, and so contrived that, when a boat should strike the muzzle, a trigger should be drawn, and the load discharged.

The vast and increasing commerce of the Mississippi, and the wide-spread interest of the mercantile community in property that floats upon its waters, as well as of that of almost all other classes, would seem to make the business of ridding this great highway of these invisible enemies a national duty, not to be begun, and ended, as has been the case, but to be continued, and under a system that should last as long as the evil it was intended to extirpate should endure.

Whenever a national spirit shall actuate Congress, this great business will be properly regarded, and attended to. Nothing tends so effectually to paralyze the "general welfare," as the presence, and exercise, in Congress, of sectional or local jealousies. It seems, in great part, to be overlooked, that we are one people; that a benefit conferred upon one section of this wide-spread domain is, to a greater or less extent, a blessing diffused among the rest; and yet it has often happened that an admitted good has been withheld from the people of one quarter of this common country, by votes in Congress, because some corresponding amount of money, proposed to be expended for its accomplishment, was not appropriated to be expended among the citizens of another part of the same country. No one who looks upon his country as a patriot, and upon the American people as one great family, though of different members, can contemplate this sectional jealousy with any feelings other than those of deep regret.

We had taken in tow, at St. Louis, a keel-boat laden with one thousand five hundred bushels of onions, bound to New Orleans. These onions were part of the product of ten acres of ground--the entire quantity raised upon it, being two thousand bushels. The labor was performed by two men. The charge for towing the boat to New Orleans was one hundred and fifty dollars, where they expected to receive for their onions one dollar and fifty cents per bushel. Estimating the entire cost of raising the onions, in labor and transportation, &c., at four hundred and fifty dollars, including the cost of the return of these two men to St. Louis, and the nett product of these ten acres of land, for that year, would be eighteen hundred dollars.

At sundown, the 28th, arrived at Memphis. Memphis stands on the fourth Chickasaw bluff. The position appeared to me to be a fine one, except, only, the ascent to the town from the river was too great for either profit or convenience. The distance from St. Louis to this place, is four hundred miles. The next day, wrote home; and by the kind offices of Mr. A., I succeeded in procuring a one-horse wagon, a couple of horses, a guide, and an interpreter. I had procured the customary outfit, at St. Louis. This consisted of crackers and tea, a cooked ham, a tongue, a tea-kettle, &c. My tent, of course, I brought with me from Green Bay. The day was sultry, and Ben thought there were "strong symptoms of disease there, (a couple of funerals being under way) which, if taken, would carry one off in a jiffy." "The elements," he thought, "looked sickly." He knew his destination was now once more among the Indians. He dreaded this, but he was more alarmed at the climate at the bluffs, and was glad to be under way. All things being ready, I mounted him on the baggage, in the little wagon, took to my horse, and at twelve at noon, in company with my guide and interpreter, made for the country of the Chickasaws. There had never before left these bluffs a shabbier-looking set of travellers. Clothing, wilderness and river-worn; faces sunburnt, hair long, horses common, and wagon, and gear, saddle and bridle, even worse than common.

Made twenty miles, and encamped for the night. Rose early the next morning, (the Sabbath,) and proceeded thirty miles under a burning sky, before we come to a drop of water—when at last a stream, called *Cold-water*, greeted us, by the side of which we boiled our tea, and broke our fast; when, after proceeding ten miles further, and at half an hour after sunset, we arrived at *Martyn*, a missionary station. Met by the Reverend Mr. Blair, with the cordial welcome of a Christian, with the words—"You are indeed welcome, colonel, to Martyn." Every manifestation of kindness was shown to me. Discharged my guide and interpreter. How green this little spot looked! How full of comforts—and there were the fledglings of the forest, being tamed, and blessed, and made to feel the blessed influence of Christian teaching, and of Christian hope. The wagon had become rickety, and Ben was fearful it might break down, as "he was sure it would, if we had many more of such roads to go over." Ben's fears were, for once, well based; for it required all of Monday to vamp up the wagon—so, instead of pursuing my journey, I was obliged to defer it till Tuesday, when Mr. and Mrs. Blair agreed to accompany me to Monroe, another missionary station among the Chickasaws, about eighty miles distant.

The morning of Tuesday was fair and fine. Various little impediments delayed our movement till twelve at noon, when I bade adieu to Martyn. Proceeded ten miles; when, coming to a stream of water, we stopped, and dined on its margin. At sundown arrived at an Indian farm. I chose for my tent a beautiful green spot near to a water-course, Mr. and Mrs. B. keeping on to some house in its neighborhood. A fire, as usual, was struck, and applied to an old tree that lay near by my tent, and Ben had gone with his tin-bucket to fetch water, in which to boil our tea—when, coming suddenly back, and with looks of wild amazement, he rushed into the tent where I was reposing on my pallet, saying—"Indians, sir, Indians, as sure as you're alive—I heard their yells!" At that moment the yells were repeated. "There," said Ben, "there they are again; and, as I believe, they are drunk, and here we are with nobody but ourselves. Your pistols, colonel, are under the head of your pallet, and your sword, also." Why not take part, yourself, Ben? Why put them all away up here out of your reach? "I was thinking, sir," he replied, "when I put the tent up again, that is, if I ever live to do it—I would take a couple of the pistols, and keep them near me." Another yell, and close at hand. "I am certain, sir," said Ben, "we shall never see Washington. Don't you think we had better take down the tent, and go on?" No, Ben, I answered, we might travel all night, and not come across such a nice bit of ground to encamp on, as this. "Yes—but what's the use of a bit of nice ground, if one is to be killed upon it?" Put on the kettle, Ben.

He had scarcely reached the fire, which, by this time, was a large one, before half a dozen drunken Indians came staggering up to it; one of them passing on, came to the door of my tent, and pulling aside the curtain, began to reel in, with gestures of a sort that intimated his intention to take possession. The light from the fire made everything bright, almost, as day. I knew one side or the other must be master; so I ran my fingers through the guards of two of the pistols, and springing to my feet, took him by the neck, and gave him a shove. He lost his balance, and tumbled heels over head; when the remaining five, seizing, some their knives, and some their rifles, made for me. Seeing my pistols cocked, and pointed in the direction of the two foremost, a pause was made, accompanied by silence; when one, who had been too drunk to come up with the rest, rose upon his feet, and stretching out his arm, and pointing at me with his finger, said, in a loud voice, "JACKSON!" That moment knives were put up, and rifles lowered, and I became the object of a general gaze. Shortly after, they all, in tolerable quiet, left the ground.

My hair being grey, and having grown unusually long, and it having been always my practice to wear it thrown up from my forehead, this Indian, having doubtless seen General Jackson, and his hair being also grey, and worn after the same fashion, concluded that the general was sure enough before him. He had not only seen General Jackson, but was, there is little doubt, acquainted with his manner of handling Indians, and thought it best, therefore, with his comrades, not to place himself in a situation where the same sort of treatment might be enacted over again.

The kettle boiled, we took our tea and crackers, when I repaired to my pallet; and Ben, coiling himself up in his buffalo robe, laid himself down at my feet. I was soon asleep, but was not long enjoying my nap, when Ben, shaking one of my feet, aroused me, saying, "There they are again!" And sure enough, so they were, in increased numbers, and all of them on horseback. For more than an hour, these fellows were yelling and shouting, and trying to ride their horses over my tent. I felt quite sure they could not accomplish this manœuvre; so it did not give me much concern. At last, they all galloped away, leaving me to enjoy the remainder of the night in very comfortable and refreshing sleep.

Breakfasted at half-past six; mended the wagon, and moved on. Stopped at twelve, and ate something. A rattle-snake crossed our path, his rattles admonishing us that we were trespassing. Alighting from my horse, I ran him through with my sword. I cut off his rattles as a trophy, and carried them with me to Washington. He was three feet long, and twelve years old, his rattles being ten in number.

Mr. and Mrs. Blair had preceded us—for, truly agreeable as was their company, I could not exact it, at so great a sacrifice of time and comfort to them. We came to a swamp, in an Indian settlement, and when about midway of the stream that passes through it, our horse refused to pull the wagon an inch further. I had employed a new guide, by the way. I told him to follow, and overtake Mr. and Mrs. Blair, and tell them we were unexpectedly delayed; and if he could, to bring some assistance. So, leaving the horse and wagon in the stream, Ben waded out; when my tent, being carried over on my horse, was pitched on the other side; then, going into a cane-brake, we cut cane for our horses; then, wading into the stream, we ungeared the obstinate animal, and led him out, leaving the wagon in its position, in the middle of the stream. It was now night. The moon was full, and the sky clear; the hooting of owls our only requiem. Kindled a fire, boiled our tea, partook of the refreshing beverage, and went to sleep.

Early the next morning, I joined Ben, and wading into the stream, took manfully hold of the wagon, and by our joint efforts, drew it upon dry land. We packed up, and putting my saddle-horse in the wagon, I mounted the other, and rode to Ti-esh-ka's, whither Mr. and Mrs. Blair had preceded us.

Ti-esh-ka, an Indian, by his extraordinary natural endowments, had surrounded himself with a farm, well fenced in, and well stocked. Besides his success as a farmer, he was an artist, and worked in iron and silver. His character for talents, and exemplary conduct, had combined to give him great influence. He was, in all respects, a noble specimen of man; one of whom many in civilized life might have learned, and might yet learn, virtues which are rarely excelled among the civilized. Breakfasted with this noble Indian; and, in token of my high respect for his character, left him and his family a few evidences of my regards. Proceeded to Tockshish, (which word means "*Root of a tree*,") a missionary station, in charge of Rev. Mr. Holmes. Leaving Tockshish, where Mr. and Mrs. Blair tarried for the night, I proceeded on to Monroe, another missionary establishment. Wagon broke down.

Nearly the whole of the country of the Chickasaws, through which I had, so far, passed, was poor. Wild turkeys plenty. Tarried at Monroe, and mended the wagon. This delay furnished the opportunity to send out runners to invite the chiefs of this district to meet me at Levi Colbert's, on the Tombigbee, the place I had selected at which to hold the council with the Chickasaws.

Monroe, I found to be beautifully situated, high and healthful, it being on a ridge of land. All the arrangements for the mission were excellent. A horse-mill, worked by two horses, had been put up by the family, which proved of great value, as well to the Indians as themselves.

Left Monroe on the 6th, for Levi Colbert's, with whom I had been long acquainted. He had been to Washington, and I had brought up one of his sons, Dougherty, in my family. Was accompanied, part of the way, by Mr. L., Mr. B., and Mr. A., who made the journey, so far as they went, highly agreeable. On parting with them, I continued on across what is called the old Natchee trace, and by the way of Major James Colbert's. This whole tract would be well named, if called *the barrens;* for wood, and almost everything, was taken off, leaving a naked and poor soil, out of which nothing but extraordinary culture, and enriching contributions, could make anything grow; and yet, these lands had been settled by the Indians no longer ago than the year 1795.

Stopped at seven o'clock, P. M., to feed horses, at McCleeches'. Halted there an hour, then continued on till twelve o'clock, when I laid down at the root of a tree, and slept. I awoke in a rain, at two; got up, and pitched my tent, turned in, and slept till day. Rose with the dawn, and reached Colbert's, my place of destination, at ten o'clock, to breakfast. I had been preceded by Major James Colbert, and Mr. McGee, who were there by sunrise, having received the call to meet me.

The chief, Levi Colbert, could not find language to express the joy of his heart, on my arrival. "It makes my heart glad, brother," said he, "to see you. I feel as if some good thing was to happen to us." Then grasping my hand, he continued, "Yes; and never since, about three years ago, when I left my son with you, have I gone to sleep, without having you before my eyes. You are our friend, and we all look upon your visit as a great blessing, for we are in trouble."

With a view of making known the principles which governed me in this embassy, and they were the same which, at that day, governed the administration of the general government, I record, (in Appendix, E.,) my official correspondence with the Hon. James Barbour, Secretary of War, and which President Adams transmitted to Congress in his message, at the commencement of the first session of the twentieth Congress, containing all that took place at the council held with the Chickasaws, at Colbert's, with its results. The leading objects in the proposal to this people to exchange their lands, east, for lands west of the Mississippi, were, first, to relieve them from the then existing and increasing causes that had operated to render them miserable where they were, and which, owing to the relations between the federal and state governments, could not be obviated by the federal government, by the introduction of an adequate protection, without coming into collision with state sovereignty, and state rights; and, second, to secure them in their possessions west of the Mississippi, against the recurrence of such anomalous relations in the future; with the full design of superadding, in those new relations, all the elements needed to improve and elevate their condition, and ennoble and bless them, as a people. And yet, it formed no part of the views of the President, nor did it of any other member of the Executive Department, to employ force to effect the removal of these suffering people, much less to mingle in the cup of their sorrows another drop of humiliation, or of bitterness, *with the intent, by such indirect and cruel means, to rid the states of their Indian population.* If it had been made my duty to open a negotiation with these people, upon any other basis than that which included their freedom to remain, or to remove, as they might deem best, I should firmly, but respectfully, have declined to undertake it. The documents in the appendix will vindicate the administration under which I had the honor to act, from any feelings or purposes, towards this hapless race, other than those of the most *just*, the most *humane*, and the most *parental* nature.

How happy should I be were it in my power to record the continuance, towards the Indians, of a like spirit! Alas! alas! the hour was even then rapidly approaching, when, on the question of their removal, they were to have no will of their own. The mandate went forth, and submission, or death, was all that was left to them! Their absence was demanded, and they must go; their lands were wanted, and they must surrender them. Mock treaties, as that of *New Euchota*, and that at *Payne's Landing*, were transformed into honorable compacts ; and the voices of petitioning thousands praying to be heard, in the solemn appeals made, that the Cherokees, as a people, had no agency in making the first, and the Seminoles no agency in making the last, were drowned by the rumbling of the war-drum, and hushed into silence by the array of armies to enforce unqualified submission ! Deep were the wrongs inflicted on these sorrowing people ; and dark and dismal were the days when ligament after ligament which bound them to the homes and graves of their fathers, was made to crack and give way, as they were thus *forced*, by a power which they were too feeble successfully to resist, to take a last sad look at scenes hallowed by every association that enters into the composition of life's happiness !

I would rather be one of these persecuted sons of the forest, and have been, as many of them were, transported in chains, than to have had any agency in thus forcing them, under such forms, from their country ; even though its exercise would have secured to me a sceptre and a crown.

It is true, I was anxious for their removal ; and I sought diligently so to enlighten them, that they should see, as I saw it, the cloud that did, at last, burst over them, and secure to themselves a shelter from its violence ; and for their posterity a position that would, forever thereafter, preserve them from the desolating ravages of kindred elements. I know they were counselled differently, and by men who sought their well-being with a zeal no less ardent than my own, and with a friendship for them as sincere as that cherished by me, but I never could see their counsels in any other light than I should the counsels of parents, who, because the house in which their children were, was justly and legally their own, should advise them not to come out of it, though it were in flames over their heads.

One among the best men I ever knew—a man of education, of intelligence, and humanity, and a zealous friend of the Indian race, Jeremiah Evarts, who was connected with the American Board of Commissions for Foreign Missions, wrote and published some very able articles in opposition to an exchange of country, by the Indians, signed "William Penn." I knew he was honest, but I knew he was mistaken. It fell to my lot to reply to these papers. (See Appendix, F.) Like views were entertained by certain other good men, missionaries among the Cherokees; who, making themselves obnoxious to the laws of Georgia, were consigned, by the authority of that state, to the penitentiary. The elements that had been kindled against the Indians could not be restrained in their fierceness until, in this way, they were made to seize upon their friends. It was the visible presence of these elements that led me to counsel the Indians to escape from their fury, and at the same time stipulate for terms that should secure them from their consuming effects in the future. A union of counsel of the friends of the Indians, of this sort, would have gone far towards reconciling them to an exchange of homes, *but no acquiescing spirit could be looked for, on their part, whilst the federal government continued towards them the irritating and grinding policy, which was at last consummated, by an appeal to force*, and a literal *driving* them from their country.*

The poor lands which I have noticed, continued, with but very little change for the better, all the way to Colbert's—the water, too, was bad, but the air fine. There are prairies in that district, large and level. Pretty groves occasionally rise out of them, wearing the appear-

* What our duty is towards this people, in their new homes, will form the subject of part of the second division of this work.

ance of islands, whilst a fringe of woodland belts them round, so far, at least, as the eye can reach—for you look out upon some of these prairies, as you do upon the ocean; the boundary being, in both, the horizon. But there is no water there. The soil, which is light and loamy, is about ten feet thick, and rests upon a stratum of soft limestone; and such is the general character of the soil of these prairies, as well as of their substratum.

I had never before seen what those Indians call a blow-gun. Here, among the little boys, it was in common use. It is a reed, of from eight to ten feet long. The arrow is about a foot in length, the smaller end being wrapped round with thistle down. When put in the hollow of the reed, this down fills it. The arrow, being pushed into the reed about the length of the finger, leaves that depth of the hollow for the impelling power—which is the breath. The reed being light, these little fellows find no difficulty in holding it up at arm's length. With the end in which the arrow is lodged in their mouth, a sight is drawn upon the object to be shot at; when, with a sudden blow into the reed, the arrow is darted out at the other end, and with a force sufficient to kill, at twenty or thirty feet, birds, rabbits, squirrels, and often wild turkeys—and so practiced are these Indian boys in the use of the blow-gun, as to shoot them with the precision, almost, of a rifle. Indeed, I have known them to snuff a candle at twenty paces, upon an average of three times out of five. I soon became owner of one, and when an hour of leisure occurred, was as much amused with it, in shooting at a mark, as any little boy in the Chickasaw nation.

I was sorry to find my protegé, Dougherty Colbert, who had returned to his home a year or so before, was absent on a visit to some of his friends. To improve time, I sent, on the 8th October, an express to the Choctaw agent, directing him to assemble the chiefs at his agency, at a specified time. Both nations, the Chickasaws and

Choctaws, were all agog for a ball-play that was to come off on the 17th, and fears were expressed, lest this exciting occasion might prevent them from responding, as generally as they otherwise would, to my call. I saw a chief take from his pouch a bundle of reeds, about an inch long, very carefully and compactly tied together, draw one out, and throw it away. I asked what that meant, and received for answer, "He is counting the time." Each of the reeds tied up in that bundle counted a day; every morning, one was thrown away, and so continued, until the day arrived for which the reckoning had been made, and on which the duty or ceremony was to be observed, to which the reckoning referred. I asked to look at the bundles; and, on counting the remaining reeds, found the last would bring the 17th of the month, the day of the great ball-play, and to mark which, these reeds had been originally prepared. The same plan is observed to mark any future event; not the day only, but any portion of the day, is noted with the same precision, and even any given hour. It was by this mode the celebrated Tecumthē had fixed on a day for a general rising of the Indians from the lakes to Florida; and it was to secure their co-operation in this design, that he left Detroit, and travelled all the way to Florida. The sticks he distributed on that occasion, being painted red, secured for those who agreed to co-operate with him, the title of "Red-sticks."

A remarkable instance of the boldness and promptness of this chief occurred when he was engaged on this mission of combining the power of those Indians, at Tuckhabatchee, then in the Creek nation. He had been south as far as Florida, and was on his return to Detroit, when he sought to enlist in his plan the Creek Indians. The chief of the Tuckhabatchees was the "Big Warrior;" so, of course, his visit was made direct to him. Like all Indian movements, Tecumthē conducted this great one with a corresponding caution—he asked the Big Warrior to go with him into the upper room, or loft, of his log house. When seated, Tecumthé eyed him with great keenness, for a while, in silence; then, taking from under his dress a tomahawk, and a bundle of red sticks, asked if he was a *brave*. The Big Warrior, of course, said he was; when Tecumthé revealed his plan, telling him he had been sent on this errand by the Great Spirit—and cautioning him, meanwhile, not to let any white man know anything about it—but to tell such as might inquire what he was doing there, that he counselled them to attend to their crops, to be industrious, and sober, and live in peace. He then presented him with the tomahawk, and the bundle of sticks, telling him, in substance, with a look of lightning, that he was a coward, and did not mean to do what he had promised; that he (Tecumthé) should leave Tuckhabatchee, forthwith, for Detroit; and that he might know the Great Spirit had sent him, he would, on his arrival, stamp upon the ground, and shake down every house in Tuckhabatchee. This remarkable announcement was soon noised abroad among the Indians of the village, who began making up the time, with great care, at which Tecumthé would arrive at Detroit. A certain day was fixed upon, when, sure enough, on its arrival, a rumbling was heard, and the shaking of the ground was felt, and the log tenements of the Indians began to totter and fall, and all hands were satisfied, not that Tecumthé had reached Detroit, only, but that he had been sent on the mission he had announced, by the Great Spirit. The shaking of the ground, and the demolition of the log cabins of the Indians, at Tuckhabatchee, were, not, however, produced by the stamping of Tecumthé's foot, but by the earthquake, which, singularly enough, happened on that very day at New Madrid.

In the interval between the sending out of runners to invite the chiefs to the council, I rode to Cotton-Gin Port, a little log town on the east of the Tombigbee, and about a mile, in a direct line, from Colbert's, whose house occupies an eminence on the opposite side of that river, and in full view of Cotton-Gin Port—a wide bottom interposing, which was once, doubtless, the bed of the river, now narrowed to less than one-third of what once was its width. Here I purchased presents, in articles of necessity, for Colbert, whose premises were soon to be a theatre for the consumption of a good many of them, and drew a bill for their cost upon the agent. On my return, met Mr. L., Mr. H., and Mr. B., on their way to Cotton-Gin Port, having come on, at my request, to be present at the council, which was to be opened the next day. Tremendous storm at about seven, P. M., and soon after my return, accompanied by vivid lightning and heavy thunder. Kept to my tent, which I had pitched in Colbert's yard, preferring it to a room in the house.

CHAPTER VIII.

INCIDENTS OF TRAVEL FROM THE CHICKASAW BLUFFS, THROUGH THE CHOCTAW COUNTRY TO TUSCALOOSA. THENCE, THROUGH THE CREEK COUNTRY, HOME.

Opening of the council at Colbert's house—Its results—On the way to the Choctaws—Beauty of the prairie—A Choctaw "rain-maker"—Espy outdone—The secret of the art—A thunderbolt wrapped up in a blanket—The sorcerer—On the wrong track—Ben in a prairie—An Indian camp surprised—A bargain—In difficulty—A false guide—A night among the cane-brake—A copperhead-snake for a pillow—A new guide—Safe arrival at Folsom's—Opposition of Indians to selling their lands—Colonel James Johnson—His brother, Richard M. —Proof that Tecumthé was killed by R. M. Johnson—Result of the Choctaw council—A burnt child—Great Indian ball-playing—Columbus—A beautiful sufferer—Governor Adair—Passing by the Cherokees—Horrible roads—Woods on fire—Guide to Tuscaloosa—A Sabbath of rest—Journey to the Creek agency on the Chattahoochee—Results of conference with the Creeks—Two Indian boys adopted—Home sickness—Effect of a change of dress—Scene at a public house—Subsequent history of the Indian boys.

The next morning broke away, revealing a bright and beautiful day. My anxiety became great, as the time approached for holding the council. I knew that much, every way, depended upon my success with the Chickasaws. It was my conviction, that never, whilst these hapless people continued to retain their then relations to the whites, would they be otherwise than harrassed, and afflicted, and miserable; for I had seen too many proofs of the determination of the States, to rid themselves, at all hazards, of the presence of their Indian population. Nothing was needed to carry out this determination, but a change in the policy that had, always, up to that hour, governed the Executive branch of the general government. With a deep sense of my responsibility, both to the government and the Indians, I opened the council on the morning of Tuesday, October 9, at ten o'clock, A. M., in an upper room of Colbert's house. I proposed that the council should be held there, to avoid the counteracting influence of intermeddlers, there having arrived some such characters; and besides, I knew there were certain grievances of which it was the intention of the Indians to complain, that would involve the character of at least one individual who was connected with the government; and therefore I determined the council should be held where none could intrude. The appendix (E.) already referred to, will tell what was done, and how it was done; and it will show, also, what sort of principles, on the question of Indian emigration, influenced me.

Having by twelve o'clock at night finished, to my entire satisfaction, as also to the satisfaction of the chiefs, my business with the Chickasaws, I was up, and ready for a start for the Choctaw nation, by the break of day, the next morning; but was delayed by the horses having, during the night, broken out of the stable, and being off, somewhere, grazing in the fields. Meantime, I addressed a hasty note to the Secretary of War, stating the result of the council—(see Appendix, as above.) By eleven o'clock I was off, accompanied by the Rev. Mr. Bell, for Mayhew, another missionary station, in the Choctaw country.

Rode across part of an immense prairie, supposed to be over a hundred miles long, (so, at least, my guide told me,) and from one mile to ten miles wide. No one that has not seen a prairie in the season of flowers, can form the slightest conception of its grandeur and beauty. It is, literally, *an ocean of flowery billows!* Such this was, as the south wind blew over it, producing undulations like those which characterize the ocean. Encamped on the other side of it. The dew was heavy, and the night cold. Rose at day-break, and continued on, arriving at Mayhew, at about ten o'clock; where I was most cordially received by Rev.

Mr. Kingsbury, the principal of the mission. Wrote to the Secretary of War, as the reader will see, in the Appendix, (E.) a more full account of the proceedings at the Chickasaw council, and its results, &c.

It was somewhere in this district that I had a most interesting interview with a Choctaw "*rain-maker*." This country is remarkable for its long droughts; and this circumstance, it is supposed, set the wits of some cunning rogue of a fellow to work, to find out how to profit by it. And so, from earliest times, there have been "rain-makers" among, at least, the Choctaws. I had seen an Indian far off, west from my position, who seemed to be pow-wowing; his peculiar costume, combining with his motions, satisfied me that he was at work with some of the mysteries of the juggling art. On inquiring who he was, and what he was about, I received for answer, "He is a rain-maker, and is engaged with the Great Spirit, to procure his consent to give the people rain." The season was an exceeding dry one; and if such agency, I thought, was ever required for the benefit of both man and beast, it was required then. I requested a messenger to go and tell the rain-maker that I wanted to see him, and received in return a shake of the head, and an assurance that nothing could move him from that spot, until he made it rain. I added —Go, and tell him I have some presents for him. I very well knew that a message of this sort was potent in relaxing previously formed conclusions among most people, but especially so among Indians. The messenger left me. I kept my eye upon the meeting. There appeared to be much talk. At last, they both started down the hill together. "This," said the interpreter, as the singularly clad personage approached me, "is the rain-maker;" and to the rain-maker he said, "This is Colonel McKenney, from Washington, who sits near your Great Father, the President, and manages all the Indian affairs."

I shook hands with him, and told him I was glad

to see him; that I had heard of his greatness—that he was not only a great man among his people, but that I was told he had great influence with the Great Spirit. This seemed to please him. I asked him if he had any objection to instruct me in his art of rain-making; saying, we had in my country many seasons of dry weather, and as I was going so far away, I should not interfere with him in his business of making rain for the Choctaws. He shook his head, saying, (all this through the interpreter,) "the Great Spirit would not like him to tell how he made it rain." I asked if he had any objection to go with me to the edge of a prairie that commenced about a mile off. He said no—when we all started. On arriving at the prairie, I alighted from my horse, and sat down on a log, inviting the rain-maker to sit by me, and also the interpreter; the rest I directed to move on, and I would overtake them.

As soon as they were well out of sight, I began by saying I was so anxious to know the secret of rain-making, that I would give him an order on the agent for a pair of scarlet leggins, a pound of tobacco, a string of wampum, a pound of powder, two pounds of lead, and a blanket, if he would tell me all about it. He stood up, and looked around him; and then, holding his head first on one side, and then on the other, listened; when, looking well round him, again, he sat down, saying to the interpreter, "Ask him if he will give me these things." Most certainly, I replied, upon the condition that he will tell me all about his art as a rain-maker. He stood up again, and looked, and listened, and then seating himself, began:—

"Long time ago I was lying in the shade of a tree, on the side of a valley. There had been no rain for a long time—the tongues of the horses, and cattle, and dogs, all being out of their mouths, and they panted for some water. I was thirsty, everybody was dry. The leaves were all parched up, and the sun was hot. I was sorry; when, looking up, the Great Spirit snapped his eyes, and fire flew out of them, in streams, all over the heavens. He spoke, and the earth shook. Just as the fire streamed from the eyes of the Great Spirit, I saw a pine-tree, that stood on the other side of the valley, torn all to pieces by the fire. The bark and limbs flew all round, when all was still. Then the Great Spirit spoke to me, and said, go to that pine-tree, and dig down to the root where the earth is stirred up, and you will find what split the tree. Take it, wrap it carefully up, and wear it next your body, and when the earth shall become dry again, and the horses and cattle suffer for water, go out on some hill-top, and ask me, and I will make it rain. I have obeyed the Great Spirit; and ever since, when I ask him, he makes it rain."

I asked to see this thunderbolt that had shivered the pine-tree. He rose upon his feet again, and looking well around him, sat down, and drawing from his bosom a roll which was fastened round his neck by a bit of deer-skin, began to unwrap the folds. These were of every sort of thing—a piece of old blanket; then one of calico; another of cotton—laying each piece, as he removed it, carefully on his knee. At last, and after taking off as many folds as were once employed to encase an Egyptian mummy, he came to one that was made of deer-skin, which, being unwound, he took out the thunderbolt, and holding it with great care between his finger and thumb, said, "*This is it!*" I took it, and examined it with an expression of great interest, telling him it certainly was a wonderful revelation, and a great sight; then handing it back to him, he carefully wrapped it up again, with the same wrappers, and put it back in his bosom.

The reader is no doubt curious to know what this talismanic charm—this thunderbolt—was. Well, it was nothing more, nor less, than that part of a glass stopper that fills the mouth of a decanter—the upper, or flat part, having been broken off!

I wrote, and gave him an order for the presents, when he shook hands, and left me, doubtless much edified, as well as benefited, by the interview, to carry on his operations as a rain-maker, till it should rain.

This class of persons make quite a living out of their occupation. They do nothing else. If the rain shall fall quickly, they give out the Great Spirit was in a good humor; and they get the credit, besides the pay, of making it rain. If, however, the drought is a long one, they say the Great Spirit is hard to move; meantime, they are fed, and made comfortable; and when it does rain, they satisfy the people by telling them of the difficulty that attended their toils, but that, at last, the Great Spirit yielded, and there was the rain.

But among the most extraordinary of the race, was the sorcerer of whom Brainerd gives an account.

Brainerd had the opportunity of visiting many different tribes of Indians, each having some peculiarities, in which they differed from the rest; but he says that, of all the sights he ever saw among them, or anywhere else, nothing ever excited such terror in his mind, or came so near what he imagined of the infernal powers, as the appearance of one of these sorcerers, who had the reputation of a reformer among them, being anxious to restore the ancient purity of their religion. His pontifical vesture was a coat of bear-skin, with the hair outside, falling down to his feet; his stockings were of the same material; and his face was covered with a hideous mask, painted with different colors, and attached to a hood of bear-skin, which was drawn over his head. He held in his hand an instrument made of a dry tortoise-shell, with corn in it, and fitted to a long handle. As he came up to Brainerd, he beat time with this rattle, and danced with all his might, suffering no part of his form, not even his fingers, to appear. Brainerd tells us, that when this figure came up to him, he could not but shrink from it in dismay, though he knew that the sorcerer had no hostile feelings or intentions. If it were so with him, it must be easy to imagine how the credulous Indians must be affected.

At his invitation, Brainerd went into his house with him, and conversed on the subject of religion. Some parts of his doctrine the sorcerer seemed to approve, but from others he strongly dissented. He said that the Great Spirit had taught him his religion, which he did not mean to abandon, but, on the contrary, wished to find some, who would join him in sincerely professing it; for the Indians were growing so corrupt and degenerate, that he could no longer endure them. He believed that there must be good men somewhere, and he intended to go forth and travel, in order to find them. Formerly he had acquiesced in the prevailing corruption; but, several years before, his spirit had so revolted from it, that he had left the presence of men, and dwelt alone in the woods. While he was in solitude, the Great Spirit had taught him, that, instead of deserting men, he ought to remain with them, and endeavor to do them good. He then immediately returned to his associates, and, since that time, he had no other feeling than that of friendship for all mankind. The Indians confirmed the account which he gave of himself, saying that, when strong drink came among them, he warned and implored them not to use it; and, when his counsels were disregarded, he would leave them in sorrow, and go crying into the woods.

At eleven, A. M., Thursday, October 11th, left Mayhew, after early dinner, for the residence of my old friend, David Folsom, a chief of great worth and distinction of the Choctaws, distant about fifteen miles from Mayhew. The way was represented as being so plain, as to make it unnecessary for me to employ a guide. A diverse trail, however, misled, and took me out of the line of my journey. Having rode five hours, I on my horse, and Ben in the wagon, I began to suspect the way to Folsom's had been left; and, sure enough, it was. Night came on; but being on an Indian trail, which I concluded would fetch me up somewhere, I concluded to keep on. Eight o'clock came, which I ascertained, not by seeing, but feeling the hands of my watch, for it was total darkness. No light from moon or stars, and none from Indian camp-fires or wigwams. I told Ben to halt, his movements over grounds where wheels had, perhaps, never been, being necessarily slow, and I would gallop ahead, on the trail, it being a pretty good one, and keep on till I should find somebody. I had not gone over half a mile, when I heard Ben hallooing at the top of his voice. It sounded as if he were in distress. I paused a moment, and heard him again, more and more loud; when, putting spurs to my horse, I was soon back to where I had left him. What's the matter, Ben? "Just as sure as I'm alive, I heard Indians off here on the right, treading softly among the leaves, and muttering something; and I know I'm not mistaken." Well, what if you did? Do you expect to meet with anybody else but Indians, while you are in their own country? and are not these the very people I am trying to find? "If I am ever spared to reach home," was the response, "this time, I'll never venture among such dangers again!" I told him to follow me, and keep his eye upon the tail of my horse, which was remarkably white, and very long. We continued slowly on.

By and by, on rising a small ascent, and at about a mile's distance, flared up an Indian camp-fire. I immediately made for it. On nearing the camp, I saw, by the light of the fire, some ten or a dozen Indians. A dog barked; when one of them who had been seated, sprang to his feet, fetching his rifle up in his hand; then throwing around his neck his powder-horn and shot-pouch, stood looking for a moment in the direction in which the dog was yet barking, and that of my approach. He stepped quickly forward, some of them still seated, but resting on one hand, and looking in the direction in which their comrade had gone, the rest of them standing, and all looking the same way. The entire group was fully revealed to me by the light of the fire, but I was yet concealed from their view, by the surrounding darkness. Presently the Indian who had advanced towards me, spoke, but I did not understand what he said. I replied, however, by answering, "*Friend.*" We soon met, both within the range of the light from the fire, when I said—Folsom—chief—me—(pointing to my own person)—go—(pointing in another direction)—see Folsom—chief. He put his finger to his breast, saying, "*Me;*" then pointing to his left, added, "*Folsom.*" Again pointing to his person, he said, "Me—money." I struck my hand on my pocket, and said—Yes, money.

This half pantomime over, he stretched forth his arm, pointing to his left, and, giving me a sign to follow him, strode off through a thick, dark wood. I did so, Ben making the best of his way after me, with his charge. We had not proceeded over a quarter of a mile before the front axle-tree of the wagon, striking a stump, broke one of the shafts. I dismounted, and putting the split parts together, Ben bound them round with raw hide, some of which I had brought with me from Colbert's, in place of rope, to provide against such contingencies. I told Ben he must walk and lead the horse, and thus relieve the wagon from so much of its weight, thereby rendering us less liable to similar casualties. Having gone about a mile further, I heard the Indian upon a trot in a direction to our left, and calling a halt, found that we were on a trail, but that he had left it. I paused awhile to ascertain, if I could, what that manœuvre meant; then moved on, when, having gone half a mile further, and turning a point round a hill, I saw another fire, and coming in the direction of my march were two Indians, at a trot, both having rifles. They presently came up to us, when I halted, the light from the fire giving a tolerable light, by which I recognized one of them to be my guide; the other, of course, a stranger. They came up to the wagon, and began to pull about its contents, when I sprang from my horse, throwing a rein over my arm, and with the other hand drew out from a basket a couple of pistols. I held one in each hand, and told Ben to move on. The moment I alighted from my horse, they stepped back a few paces from the wagon, and stood side by side.

I knew I was upon the lines where the vices of the white men are constantly practised before the eyes of these poor, persecuted Indians, and that there, as all along the border, they had been corrupted, and made savage by them; and this thought impressed me with a sense of danger. My firm belief was, that as I moved off, these Indians would discharge their rifles at me; and the only ground of safety left me was in the possibility that they might miss me. I was satisfied the second Indian had been gone after to make more sure the plunder, which I was convinced was the object of both. I had been often on the shores of Lake Superior, surrounded by hundreds of what are esteemed to be men more fierce, and more savage, but never had the least occasion of entertaining fears for my personal safety. Those remote Indians had not been degraded, and made reckless and barbarous, by the deleterious influences of a proximate border population. The remark made to me by President Monroe, on his return from his tour along the borders, I had, on more occasions than one, seen verified. To the questions which I put to him, How did the red people appear to you? Were they savages, as so many people think they are; or have they put off this character, in whole, or in part, so far as your observation extended? "The *worst* Indians I have seen in my travels," he answered, "are the *white people* that live on their borders."

I looked back upon the two Indians with no little anxiety, until I had got so far in the thick darkness as to lose sight of them, and at the same time I got rid of the greater portion of my apprehensions. At a distance of a mile or so from where I left them, I discovered, by the descending surface, that I was getting into a morass, or valley of some sort, which, upon a little examination, I found to be a cane-brake. It occurred to me, that this being a favorable place for a rencounter, the attack had been put off, until I had got fairly into it; when I halted and listened. Hearing nothing, I told Ben to turn short off to the right, and keep on the level ground as well as he could. I continued in this direction for a quarter of a mile, and halted; struck fire into an old tree, piled a large quantity of wood upon it, and travelled three or four hundred yards further on, when coming to a large tree with overshadowing branches, I concluded to stop there for the night. Ben ungeared his horse, and tied him to part of the wagon; I unsaddled mine, made a pillow of the saddle, threw down my pallet, and a couple of blankets, tied my horse to a limb of the tree, and descended with Ben into the cane-brake, and cut cane for our horses, out of which we extracted quite an agreeable repast for ourselves, for our provisions were exhausted. Having fed the horses, and made our repast, I stretched myself out upon my pallet—telling Ben to take care of himself—pulled the blankets over me, and went to sleep.

My object in building the fire where I did, and leaving it, was intended to mislead the Indians, should they follow us. The place I had retired to was beyond the range of the light of the fire, which made it quite certain that, unless by the veriest accident, I should not be discovered. Another of my contrivances was, to hoist my umbrella over me, to keep off the dew; which I made stationary, by connecting the top of it to the branches of the tree that impended over me.

Ben chose, as a place of greater security, a retreat beneath the wagon. When I awoke, day was just breaking.

I called Ben, who had scarcely cleared the wagon, before he gave a look of horror at the place he had just left; then, making a spring of six feet, he seized a bit of wood, and to my question—What's the matter? answered, "A copperhead-snake!" The fury of Ben's onset was such, as, in very quick time, to kill his companion for the night. "This is hard," said Ben; "we scarcely make ourselves secure from the Indians, before we are met by such poisonous rascals as this." I told him I thought the snake, having behaved so well as to lie by him all night, and do him no harm, was entitled to his thanks, and not his maledictions. But, as you have shown great courage, Ben, I continued, in the attack upon the snake, go now into the cane-brake, and cut cane for your horse, and I will go back to the trail, cross the brake, and try if I cannot find a guide.

I had just crossed the brake, and was rising the hill on the opposite side, when my eye caught the head of an Indian. I was soon up with him. He had a bridle in his hand. I asked him where he was going. Fortunately, I was answered in English, "I'm horse-hunting." I then told him who I was, and where I wanted to go, and asked him to guide me. He held out his hand, shook hands with me, and said, "Follow me." He took the track I had travelled over to where Ben was. I opened a box containing some articles for presents, and took out a pair of silver arm-bands, and a silver gorget, and presented them to him. We were soon under way, *and over the same track by the two camp-fires we had passed the night before.* This confirmed my impression that fair play had not been intended by my guide; and that, but for the state of preparation for defence in which the two Indians found me, I might have been, at least, plundered.

Arrived at Folsom's at eleven o'clock, A. M. Such was the apprehension of these people at being suspected of selling land to white men, made more so after the summary punishment inflicted by the Creeks on McIntosh, a principal chief of the Creek nation, that, on arriving at Folsom's, my guide, taking him aside, asked if I was not a land trader? and why, if I did not want land, I had, for so small a service, made him such costly presents? He was poor, he said, and the Indians would know, if he should wear these arm-bands, and that gorget, he had never bought them; and fearing the worst, he begged Folsom to keep them for him, and explain to the council, when it should meet, how he had come by them; all of which was done.

After dinner, rode down the federal road to the Choctaw agency. Met there a brother of Colonel R. M. Johnson, and several others. The Indians were coming in, in great numbers. Spent the Sabbath at the agency, and on Monday went back to Folsom's, and dined there.

The presence of Colonel Johnson's brother revived many reminiscences of the late war; and among these, the battle of the Thames, where the two Johnsons, James and Richard M., both behaved with such gallantry. Perhaps there was nothing more desperate in the history of that war, full as it is of deeds of valor, (with perhaps the single exception of the readiness with which General Miller consented to sacrifice his life, when, to the question of the gallant Brown, "Can you take that battery?" he answered, "I'll try!") than the charge of cavalry on the British line, led by Colonels James and R. M. Johnson, at the battle of the Thames.

It was in that battle, as is known, that the brave Tecumthē fell; and it is also known that much has been said about "*who killed him.*" Generally, the death of this chief has been attributed to Colonel R. M. Johnson, but no evidence of that fact, I believe, has been ever yet published. Those who claimed this honor for Colonel Johnson, have, in the main, been led to do so, to make political capital out of it; thinking, doubtless, that a feather of this *tall sort*, being stuck in the colonel's cap, would captivate such eyes as were fitted to be charmed by it, and lead to an increase of his popularity. It would be well for the country, its prosperity, and its hopes, if other and more substantial claims to popular favor were urged, than such as are derived from the mere circumstance of killing an Indian—which a chance shot, discharged by the veriest coward, might do as effectually, as if aimed and delivered by the bravest of the brave, or indeed an idiot. I have never been able to contemplate this downward tendency of things—this making political capital out of mere clap-trap circumstances—without a feeling of regret. Other, and loftier qualities, were required by our patriotic fathers. When the army of the Revolution was to be furnished with a chief, WASHINGTON was instinctively turned to; and when, after our independence was achieved through his instrumentality, a President was required, the bright, and sterling, and well-tested virtues of Washington, were the attractions that led the people, with an almost unanimous voice, to confer upon him this highest of civil trusts.

There were qualities of both head and heart in Colonel R. M. Johnson, and these had been made manifest by his patriotism in the war, and by his zealous labors, and the highly respectable position he occupied in the councils of the nation, out of which legitimate claims could be set up, for the popular favor. He has served the republic faithfully, in both the Congress and the field, pouring his blood out like water, in defence of his country's rights. Here, surely, was ground enough upon which to rest his claims upon popular gratitude, and popular favor, without descending to make capital out of the death of Tecumthē; and especially when not a single one of his adherents knew whether Colonel R. M. Johnson, or any other colonel, had killed him; (indeed, Colonel Johnson never claimed the honor;) and many of them without knowing who Tecumthē was, or whether, in fact, he had been killed at all.

I have known Colonel Johnson, and, for a large portion

of the time, intimately, since 1812. We saw the necessity for the war through the same medium, and, indeed, belonged to the same school of politics, until about the close of Mr. Monroe's administration. We have never been in political fellowship since; and the probability is, never shall be. But that is no reason why I should not appreciate the many good qualities which I know him to possess, and put a just estimate upon his patriotic efforts, wherever and whenever these have been displayed, whether in the Senate or the field. And now, without looking upon the man who killed Tecumthē as being entitled, for that reason, to my vote for the Presidency, or any other place of honor and profit, I state that *Colonel R. M. Johnson* did kill Tecumthē, and that none other than his own hand consigned that brave and wonderfully-endowed Indian to the dust; and these are the circumstances out of which I derive the proof:—

A Pottawattamie Indian being at St. Louis, was asked by General Clark, "Were you at the battle of the Thames?" "I was." "Did you see Tecumthē in that battle?" "I did." "Did you see him shot?" "I did." "Where were you when he fell?" "Close by him." "Who killed him?" "Don't know." "Did you see the man who killed him?" "Yes." "What sort of a looking man was he?" "Short, thick man." "Was this short, thick man, on horseback?" "Yes." "What was the color of the horse he rode?" "White." "How do you know the short, thick man, on a white horse, killed Tecumthē?" "I saw him shoot him." "When did you first see the man on the white horse?" "When he was galloping up in front of where Tecumthē stood, his horse got tangled in the top of a tree that was blown down; and while he was there, Tecumthē raised his rifle, and fired. Saw the man go so—(reel on his horse, imitating the motion)—horse got out of the bushes —the man spurred him—came galloping up—came close —Tecumthē raise his tomahawk, just going to fling it—

white man raise pistol—fire—Tecumthê fell—we all run away."

On hearing this statement, which I did from General Clark himself, I wrote a letter to Colonel Johnson, in which I inquired (without his knowing my object) what was the color of the horse he rode at the battle of the Thames? To which he answered, a white mare. Where were you, when you received the rifle-ball in the fore-knuckle of your bridle hand? To this he replied, in substance, (I have not his letter at hand) my mare was at the time entangled in the branches of a tree that lay across the line of my advance to the British line; and while there, I saw an Indian aim at me, and fire. I received the ball near the upper joint of the fore-finger of my bridle hand. Getting out of the difficulty, I spurred the mare, drawing a pistol from my holster with my right hand, having thrown the reins of the bridle over my left arm, and, as I neared the line, the same Indian raised his tomahawk; when, with what little strength I had left, I raised my pistol, and fired—and from that moment lost all sense of what was going on." Colonel Johnson knew nothing of the effect of his fire. His mare, he was told, wheeled with him, at the moment of the discharge of his pistol, galloped to the American lines, and fell, being pierced through with many balls. The Indian further told General Clark, that Tecumthê was hit in the forehead, or near the corner of one of his eyes, with a ball. I learned afterwards, that, besides the bullet wound, near the eye-brow, there were three oblique cuts on the person of Tecumthê, as if made by a knife—one down his thigh, and two others in other front parts of his body. To the question put by me to Colonel Johnson, how was your pistol loaded? he answered, "with one ball, and three buck-shot." The ball, therefore, took effect in the head of the chief, and the buck-shot, scattering, cut his flesh, in a descending line, as they must needs have done, as stated, Colonel Johnson's position being above Tecumthé's.

The foregoing are the *circumstances* which furnish the proof—to my mind amounting to demonstration—that Colonel Richard M. Johnson killed Tecumthé.

On the evening of Tuesday, 16th, opened the council with the Choctaws. For the ceremonies of that council, and its results, see Appendix, (G.) If my power had been *plenary*—in other words, if I had been authorized to treat with them for an exchange of country, and in all other matters to have adjusted our relations with them, I should have succeeded. Their words were—"*If* YOU *had the power to do everything, and it had not to go into other hands, it (their decision) might be different. We have confidence in you,*" *&c.* See Appendix, (G.)

A runner came to announce that a child had been badly burned at a house just below the agency. I hastened to see it. I found the poor little thing in the greatest agonies—but there were no remedies at hand for its relief. How such a case of human suffering lifts to the mind the enriching excellencies of civilized and contiguous society! I asked for lime—the meaning of the word was hardly comprehended. I called for eggs, and for sweet oil—the first were handed me, the last I obtained at the agency. I made a mixture of the yolk of the egg and of the oil; and, by means of bandages made of my pocket-hankerchiefs, dressed the wounds of the little sufferer, as well as my means would allow.

Thursday, the 18th October, left the agency for Columbus, twenty-five miles distant. Called, by the way, at Folsom's, and Major Pitchlyn's. Overtook numerous Indians of both sexes, going to the ball-play. The whole nation seemed to be in motion, pushing for the theatre where the great fête was to be performed—women, often, in their anxiety to get there, on a trot; men on horse-back, at half speed. On these occasions, a large portion of the property of the two nations, the Chickasaws and Choctaws, changes hands. They bet their all. The strife is intense; the excitement, excessive. Such are the exertions, as sometimes to dislocate joints, break bones, and life, in various ways, is often put in jeopardy.

Fell in with flocks of wild turkeys, frightened from their retreats, doubtless, by the rush of the ball-play-goers, through all parts of the country. Crossed the Tombigbee—paid one dollar and a quarter toll for two horses, and a small wagon, over the stream.

Arrived at Columbus, where I found Mrs. M., of the Mayhew mission, a beautiful sufferer—beautiful in her person, and beautiful in her resignation. She looked like one of those white fleecy clouds, that are sometimes seen in a summer's day, when just on the eve of vanishing, and mingling with the ethereal. Prescribed for her, but with little expectation that she would be long retained from her heavenly rest, for which her pious life and gentle spirit had fitted her.

I found, there, a brother and sister of Colonel Abert, the distinguished topographical engineer, at this time, I believe, in charge of the Topographical Bureau at Washington. They were charmingly situated, and I was charged, on my arrival at Washington, to say so to the colonel. Met, also, Governor Adair. This venerable man, and patriot, I found in a very inferior state of health. It had fallen to his lot to command the Kentucky troops, in the last war, at New Orleans. I had seen an authenticated statement of his services on that memorable occasion, shown to me by his son-in-law, "Florida White," as it was the custom to call him. History will, I have no doubt, do this pure patriot and gallant officer justice. A great wrong will be done to his memory and fame, if it shall not.

I was piloted out of Columbus by the venerable Judge Cocke—and took the wagon-road for Tuscaloosa. The name of this gentleman reminds me that I might as well state here the reason why I omitted to go with any message to the Cherokees. Congress had made an appropriation of a sum of money for the purpose of holding a treaty with the Cherokees, to obtain their consent to open a way, by means of a canal connecting the waters of the Canasaga and Highwassee. Commissioners were then in the Cherokee country to carry out this object. I did not feel at liberty to call off the attention of the Indians from this negotiation; and so I passed on to the Creeks. General John Cocke was a commissioner to treat with the Cherokees. I was satisfied the attempt would prove a failure, and was the less willing, therefore, to go among them, lest it might be inferred that I had been the cause of it.

The way to Tuscaloosa was horrible. Twenty-five miles of it were over rugged mountains, and almost impassable roads. I was two hours after night, literally *feeling*, not *seeing*, my way; and the darkness was so great, that I could not see my horse's mane, though it was white. The wagon, with the intrepid Ben, were constantly in difficulty. It was one mud-hole after another, and our united strength was often put in requisition to disengage the wheels from their deep-set connection with unknown depths of mud and water. Our progress was about a mile an hour. Encamped somewhere, but know not where, and never expect to know. Saturday, 20th, rose at day-break, did the best we could, over thirty miles of similar roads. On nearing the Black Warrior, saw a fire. It looked like a city in a blaze. The woods were in flames. The country was lighted by them for many miles; and, on nearing this grand spectacle, the ear came in for part of the effect, in the cracking, and snapping, and the terrible crash made, ever and anon, by the falling of trees; when the corruscations from each crash would illumine, as it seemed, the whole universe. By the light of this fire, I reached the Black Warrior, when it almost instantly faded, and darkness fell suddenly upon everything. The ferryman refused to ferry me over—alleging it was too dark, and the current, he said, was too rapid. I told him I must go over, and if he found it inconvenient to ferry me across, I would go without him. He then lighted some pine-knots, and ferried us over. When about midway, the fire in the woods blazed up again, and continued till I ascended the hill on the Tuscaloosa side of the Black Warrior, amidst an almost dazzling light; which, however, soon went out, leaving me again in thick darkness. Passing a small house, I rode up, and inquired the way, and whether there were any ditches, or bad roads, of any sort, and received for answer many things that made everything uncertain; so I asked for a guide, and procured one in the person of a little, old, Virginia, Orange county negro. Without him, or somebody just like him, I felt, as I progressed, that I should never have found my way, till the day should break, and reveal it to me. By the aid of this little old blackey—the very image of "*little Billy*," who is known to everybody in Portland, besides to half the people of the globe, according to his account, I reached Tuscaloosa at nine o'clock, P. M., horses jaded, and almost broken down, Ben in a condition not much better, and myself ready for rest. How composing was the thought that to-morrow will be the Sabbath! Oh, how welcome is this day of rest to the weary! How demonstrable the wisdom and love of that Good Being who ordained it!

After a charming night of the most refreshing sleep, arose, breakfasted, and wended my way to the Methodist church. I could not recall to mind a Sabbath of greater rest. I luxuriated in it.

Tuscaloosa reminded me of Detroit—the ground level, the apparent dimensions of both alike, the houses being in about the same proportion, built of brick and of wood; streets wide. If the Black Warrior ran north of the town, it would answer for the river Detroit.

Proceeded on Monday, rode thirty miles, and encamped. Tuesday, to Cahawba Falls, by nine, A. M., to breakfast. Day fine. Thence on to Sawyer's Mills, where I encamped. Reached Foreman's, on the pine flats, on the 24th, and tarried there for the night. Crossed the Alabama on the 25th, and arrived at Montgomery, where I remained all night. Met there with the number of the North American Review containing a review of my "*Tour to the Lakes.*" Read it with eagerness, and with satisfaction. The commendations were far above what I had hoped for.

Rose early, and pushed on for my place of destination, the Creek agency, at Fort Mitchell, in Alabama, on the Chattahoochee. Fell in with the agent, Colonel Crowell, some ten miles from the agency, who accompanied me to his home, where, as soon as I arrived, I commenced operations for convening the Creeks, in council, at Tuckhabatchee. Despatched a messenger with a talk, to Opothleyoholo, he being the organ of communication, as speaker of the Creek councils, to the nation, inviting him to come and see me. His answer foreboded difficulties. He could not come, assigning as the reason that he was not well enough. I succeeded, however, in getting him to meet me. The result was a call of the council, and a final arrangement by treaty, and settlement of all the difficulties that had for so long a time existed between the Creek nation, the State of Georgia, and the federal government. Every foot of land remaining to the Creeks, of what was once their immense domain in Georgia, was now ceded; and henceforth they were to be confined to their possessions in Alabama.

Having disposed of my horses, and travelling and camp equipage, to Colonel Crowell, I took the stage at the door of the agency, having adopted, at the request of their parents and friends, two Indian youths, *William Barnard* and *Lee Compere;* the first a Creek, the other a Uchee; and these, with the Honorable William R. Ring, then a senator in Congress, now minister to France, were my companions.

My little Indian boys were about ten and thirteen years old, Lee being the youngest. His Indian name was *Arbor.* After leaving the agency some thirty miles, this little fellow gave signs of great restlessness, and kept muttering something in Uchee, which William interpreted. "He wanted to go home." This was the burden of his muttering. So I thought I would test the self-relying feeling which I had often heard attributed to Indians, even of his tender age, as also their trust in their instinct. I knew he could have no knowledge of the way he had come, for he, and William, and Ben, had occupied the front seat of the stage, and had travelled backwards. I called to the driver, requesting him to stop. He did so. Now, William, tell Lee he can go home, if he wishes to go. This was scarcely said, before the little fellow, who had learned some English at the missionary school, seized his bundle, and was, in a twinkling, out at the side of the stage, and going down over one of the fore-wheels; when, seeing him determined to go, I told Ben to reach out and take him in. He was inconsolable, and remained so till we reached Augusta, in Georgia.

On arriving there, I sent Ben out with them, with directions to clothe them in the best manner, and to buy for each a plaid cloak, and a handsome cap. Ben was fortunate in securing quite a handsome and perfectly well-fitting suit, including the cloaks and the caps. I then had their hair cut. Ben took them into a chamber of the hotel, and gave them a thorough cleansing; when they were brought to me, dressed, not in a very handsome suit of clothes, only, but in smiles. A couple of prettier boys could be found nowhere.

I had rode all night, after leaving Augusta; and stopping at a public stand to breakfast, I directed Ben to go with the boys to the breakfast-table, and attend to them there, while I shaved. On going in myself, I saw the two boys with Ben, standing at the back door of the passage. What, Ben, I inquired, through with breakfast already? "Oh, lord, sir," said Ben, "I was sent out in a jiffey." Why, what's the matter? "The *lady*, sir," answered Ben, "says she don't allow Indians to eat at *her* table." I took the boys, each by a hand, and went in, and as I was about seating them, each on one side of me, the good lady, at the head of the table, sprang to her feet, gave her chair a push backwards, threw her head well up, and, with her arm extended, and her fist clenched, accompanied by a wild and vengeful expression, her lips compressed, she looked at me, saying, "*Sir, I will not allow Indians to come to my table.*" I am sorry, madam, I replied, to be obliged, on this occasion, to trespass on your rules, but these little boys must have their breakfast, and just as they are now seated, with me. I am their protector, and have taken care of their persons, so as to render them quite prepared for your table, or any other table in Georgia.*

She flew out of the room, saying—"*I'll send my hus-*

* On my arrival at home, these little boys were made part of my family; and were adopted by the government. Their education, and the supervision of their entire circumstances, devolved on me. I sent them to a school, at that time kept in Georgetown, and upon the principle of the West Point Academy. The uniform required to be worn, I knew, would furnish a tie to this school, of the most agreeable sort. Both these children made the usual progress in learning, and were tractable, and well disposed. The little one, Lee, had in him a portion of obstinacy which never showed itself in William. He was, however, younger, and had not been favored with so many advantages in instruction, at school and otherwise, as had been enjoyed by William. Strong attachments were formed in them, both for me and my family, as the sequel will show.

When I was dismissed from office, I included in my arrangements for leaving Washington, a plan for the furtherance of the welfare of these children. They had been confided to me by their parents and friends, and I felt bound, besides the interest I took in their welfare, to carry out what I knew was the will of their parents, as well as to make good all their expectations, so far as it might be in my power to do so. In a word, I felt the trust to be a sacred one. Accordingly, I applied to President Jackson, for his permission to take them with me to Philadelphia. It was refused. On making this known to the boys, they grew sad, and *band after you.*" By the time Ben had poured out the coffee, the good man of the house entered, saying, "*Sir, this is against my rules.*" I can't help it, sir. Your's is a public house. We are travellers. Those little boys are very near to me, and I shall see, wherever I go, that they occupy the same level which I do; and my advice to you, as a friend, is to keep cool, and leave the room. I shall pay you for our fare. "Well, sir," said he, "I suppose it must be so," and went out!

---

gave signs of great distress. At last, of their own accord, they wrote, and took to the President the following note:—

"*Great Father*—

"We are in trouble—our friend Colonel McKenney is going away—we want to go with him. We don't want to stay here without him. He is our friend. We love him, he is good to us—do not, Father, let us be taken away from him. We ask you to let us go with Colonel McKenney. He is like a father to us. We came from our nation with him. When we leave here, we want to go back; but we do not want to go back, if we can go with him. We come to see our Father with this talk—we hope he will not deny what we come for.

William Barnard,
Lee Compere."

There is no date to this. It is in the hand-writing of William. The original is now before me; and I have copied it, in all respects. They kept together, and avoided seeing anybody—and would not come to their meals till after the family had separated. I said to them, perhaps your Great Father, if you were to see him, and tell him you wish to go with me, would gratify you—he may not know it is your wish. William replied—"We have been to see him, and (pulling from his pocket the foregoing letter,) handed him that." After I had read it, I asked what his answer was. "He said you can't go with him—you must go home to your people." I retained the paper.

In making my arrangements to leave Washington, I concluded such as embraced the comfort of these poor boys, until the President should dispose of them, by taking board for them, and continuing them at school. The day I left Washington, they were inconsolable, and wept bitterly. I soothed them by telling them I should come again, before long, and see them—when the carriage drove off. Just as we were ascending the capitol-hill, a gentleman called. The coach was stopped. "Colonel," said he, "your little Indian boys are trotting after the carriage, and seem much fatigued." I stepped out, and told them, if they loved me, they must go back. I reasoned with them, and they became more composed, when I called a hack, put them in it, and we parted. I have never seen them since. They were sent home to their country soon after. Of William, I heard that he never recovered from his depression—became desperate—and, getting into an Indian quarrel, a fight ensued, in which some of the parties were killed, he left the Creek country, and joined the Seminoles in Florida. Of Lee, I have never heard anything.

CHAPTER IX.

RETURN TO WASHINGTON. CHANGE OF ADMINISTRATION. POLITICAL EXCITEMENT. CORRUPTION AND FAVORITISM IN HIGH PLACES.

Arrival at Washington—Mr. Barbour's estimate of my services—Adjustment of my accounts—Political agitation—Personal abuse—Duff Green's account—His "mark"—The work of proscription going on—Pledges honestly given—How fulfilled—Duff Green's first appearance at Washington—How he went ahead—Strife for office—Interview with President Jackson—Charges—Satisfactorily answered—Result—A call at my office—An office not wanted—The office of Indian affairs—General Eaton and Duff Green—General Houston—"Proposal"—A second and third interview—Proposals for contracts to supply the Indians—Ben Hawkins, alias General Houston—A rat behind the curtain—"Bids"—Actual cost of rations, and removal of the Indians—Extracts from documents—Bold favoritism—General Houston in a rage—A scene with my clerks—Almost displaced.

On my arrival at Milledgeville, I announced the adjustment of the difficulties. See Appendix, (H.) The annunciation that a treaty had been made, preceded me by a day. I had scarcely time to reach Washington in season for the President's message; but, by constant travelling, night and day, I arrived there just three days before the message was sent in—leaving me time only to make up my official report. The appendix, as referred to, contains my report to the Secretary of War, embracing, in an official form, all that had been accomplished under my commissions, during those travels, since parting from General Cass.

On reaching the War Department, I was met in the passage-way, by the Hon. James Barbour, then Secretary of War, who, reaching out both hands, grasping one of mine, said—"Is it indeed so, that you have concluded a treaty with the Creeks?" It is, sir. "Then, sir," he added, "there is not money enough in the treasury, to pay you for what you have accomplished"—when he left me, and went over to the President's. The treaty was ratified by the Senate, and the exciting circumstances that had so long continued to vex Georgia, and trouble the Executive of the Union, so far, at least, as the Creek Indians were concerned, were put to rest, and forever.

My special commission (that of March 28, 1827,) referring to me the duties which I left Green Bay to execute, stipulated that my "*compensation should be fixed on my return, and made equivalent to the extent and value of my services.*" After having been some time at home, I suggested to the secretary, that when he should be at leisure, I was prepared with my accounts, and ready for their adjustment. "Sir," said he, "I have been thinking of this. I know the terms upon which you undertook this almost hopeless mission; and I know, also, that your services have been immensely valuable; and whilst I set an almost priceless value on them, I am compelled, that no cry of favoritism may be raised, to limit your compensation to the pay of a commissioner." I am perfectly satisfied, sir, I replied, and will make up my accounts upon that basis.

I sent my messenger to the office of the Second Auditor, with a request to Mr. John Peters, the ablest and most efficient clerk in the office, to come to my room. So taking down a United States map, I requested him to mark and measure my route—from Washington to Green Bay, and from Green Bay by the way of the route I had returned home. It made, (I write from memory,) *seven thousand miles*. He knew the day I had left home for Green Bay; and now having the distance, I referred to him the making up of my account for my per diem allowance, and for the mileage. I was gone about seven months. He stated my account, certifying that he had measured the distance, and that it was made up, and correctly, upon the basis of the pay to a commissioner. I handed it to the Secretary of War, who said, "I have no doubt it is all right—but that I may be able to say I examined the route myself, bring in your map, and let me go over your track." It was done. He went over the whole, making also the calculations, and found all was right; when he took his pen, and wrote upon it, "*Approved—J. Barbour.*"

Political agitation, and of a sort more bitter and more fierce than any that had ever preceded it, had now become universal. Mr. Adams and his administration, the ability and economy, and purity of which, no honest and intelligent man doubted, was to come down, "*though it was as pure as the angels at the right hand of God!*" The Washington Telegraph, edited by Duff Green, took the lead in this war, and was the caldron in which the elements were concocted, that were to be employed by the party in opposition to Mr. Adams, to overthrow his administration. Every day sent forth fulminating matter, until the country rang with the fierce cry of "intrigue—bargain—and corruption;" and this was the battering-ram chosen by the party in opposition to the administration of Mr. Adams for its overthrow. I shall be excused, I hope, for giving it as my firm belief, that not one of the original contrivers of this master-stroke of the political engine, believed it to be true.* Names, intended to be opprobrious, were invented and applied to functionaries of the government, with the clap-trap purpose of taking the *fancy* of those whose capacity was too shallow to be stirred by things of more solid or truthful import.

Humble as was my position in the government, I was not permitted to escape. Day after day, the Telegraph teemed with abuse of me. In vain did two of General

* This charge has been anaylzed by Mr. Colton in his life of Henry Clay. It is now put beyond all doubt, that my opinion of it was correct.

Jackson's friends interfere to stay these onsets, by representing to Green their injustice, etc. The answer given by him to one of them was—"He (meaning me) was the author of a letter signed P. B. K., wherein my name and my course were assailed; and, whilst I can hold a pen, he shall feel its power." This might have been the spark that fired the magazine of this gentleman's wrath, but it was, by some, shrewdly suspected that my inability to make a *certain account, amounting to some sixty thousand dollars,** square with the provisions of either the intercourse law of 1802, or with my conscience; and the reference which I recommended of that account to the Committee of Indian affairs of the Senate—the chairmen of which, Colonel Benton and General Green, being not on terms of the most harmonious sort—as Green told me—and which reference had been "*approved*" by the Secretary of War, and acted upon, was at least *one* of the reasons of all those assaults upon me. Two accounts had been handed to me by General Green, at the same time—that to which I have referred, and which claimed, in the names of numerous settlers, remuneration for spoliations *alleged* to have been committed upon them by certain Indians; and another, amounting to some five or six hundred dollars, (I write from memory,) for cattle that General Green had furnished to the garrison at Prairie du Chien, as contractor, and which had been driven off by the Indians after they had been turned over to the proper officer. This last account, as the certificate of my agent at Prairie du Chien, Nicholas Boilvan, at the Prairie, I recommended for payment. It was paid. It was to inquire after these accounts, and shortly after their reference to the Senate Committee, that General Green came to my office. On learning the disposition that had been made of the large account, he flew into a passion, and after giving vent to much wrath against myself, and making known the sort of relations that exist-

* I write from memory. The sum was enormous.

ed between him and Colonel Benton, "a man," he said, "whom I cannot approach," and receiving from me an appropriate response, he left the room, shaking his finger at me, saying, "*I'll mark you, sir!*"

Now it might have been this circumstance, or Mr. Key's letter, or both, that had kindled General Green's wrath, and made it burn so fiercely, and with such constancy, in his Telegraph, against me. When the ordinary means of assault failed, the resort was had to the *extraordinary*—and I was known by the title of "KICKAPOO AMBASSADOR!"

General Jackson having succeeded to the Presidency, and General Duff Green, with his Telegraph, becoming the organ of "the government," I saw, from the known influence that Green exercised over the President, that among the officers who were destined to be struck down, I was one. General Jackson had not been long in power, before one after another of the officers of the government were dismissed. The promise, that "*General Jackson will reward his friends, and punish his enemies*," was now in a course of rapid fulfilment; and ever and anon, as one and another of the faithful, experienced, and long-tried officers, were struck down, the cry went forth from "*the Telegraph*," "THE WORK GOES BRAVELY ON!" No matter how long, or how faithful had been the service rendered by the victim; nor how indispensable was his "experience" towards the right action of the government, or the protection of the public interests; nor how dependent his position, for the means of support for himself and family, nor how unblemished his character, if those who held "*the list*" resolved to put "*the mark*" to his name, *he was sure to go*. Had some of these been appointed by Washington? No matter—even if it be the venerable and pious Register of the Treasury, Joseph Nourse, the honored of Washington, the cherished of Madison, of Monroe, and of Adams—down with him! The promise must be fulfilled—the "reward" must be bestowed—"to the victors belong the spoils."

It was foreseen that such havoc made among the tried,

and competent, and faithful incumbents, might lead the public to suspect that the loss of all this "experience" might prove hurtful to their interests. To quiet all such apprehension, it was announced, by high authority, and under the most imposing form, that "experience was not a necessary qualification for office," etc. And then, again, it had been announced, that persons were to be selected, whose "*diligence and talents*" were to "*insure*," in their respective stations, "*able and faithful*" co-operation, whilst *more* reliance was to be placed on the "*integrity* and *zeal* of the public officers, than on their *numbers*."

Now, all this, I cannot bring myself to doubt, was honestly meant by the distinguished functionary who gave utterance to these doctrines and purposes; nor can I question his honesty of intention to fulfil *all* the promises that he made—even to that which announced that mighty "*reform* in those abuses that had (as it was alleged) brought the *patronage of the federal government into conflict with the freedom of elections*." Nor were the causes which, it was also alleged, had "*disturbed* the rightful course of appointment," and "which had *placed*, or *continued* power, in unfaithful or incompetent hands," to be permitted to remain, but were to be "*corrected*." This, too, was, no doubt, honestly spoken by the distinguished personage who thus pledged himself before the American people. He was fresh in his place. But there were those who had been hackneyed in artifice, who, knowing the avenues of approach to his confidence, took care to prepare the way, not only for the foregoing flowery openings, for the quieting and repose of public opinion, but for the ultimate results of Executive favor to themselves, with all their enriching results.

Among the first to profit by this state of things, was General Duff Green, whose "reward" was conferred in the job-printing of the government in his paper, and in his appointment as printer to Congress. I was present when this gentleman first came to Washington, with a view of settling there, *if he could*. I was dining with a distinguished citizen, who was called from the dinner-table to see "a gentleman," who had declined the invitation to "come in." Soon after, I joined the stranger and the gentleman with whom I had dined, and was introduced, for the first time, to "GENERAL DUFF GREEN." The general had brought a letter of introduction, I believe, from Governor Edwards; and this was deemed a sufficient passport. The object of General Green being to transfer himself from St. Louis to Washington, as a publisher of a newspaper, the gentleman with whom I had dined turned the general over to me, as his adviser; and by invitation, the general dined with me the next day, *en famille*, when his entire object was disclosed. The substance was, that he wished to leave St. Louis, and come to Washington; but having no means, he desired, if he could, to find some one with a press in Washington or Georgetown, who would be willing to exchange with him. I went to work, with sincerity, to promote the general's views, and after various attempts, he succeeded in making a bargain of some sort—I never knew what it was—with JONATHAN ELLIOT, who had printed a paper in Washington, the *quality* of which had secured for it the title of "*the mud press*." Upon this General Green engrafted his *Telegraph*.

I can never forget the general's costume and appearance when I first saw him. They were both indicative of great embarrassment. His eye, which was black and animated, seemed the only live thing about him; and that indicated, by its flashy and lustrous motions, a good deal of mind, which General Green certainly possesses. From the state of great embarrassment in which I found him, General Green became, under the system of "*rewards*," a man of wealth; or, at least, a large property-holder.

How far this "reward" system was calculated to alienate from professional duties, and from the various departments of labor, so many thousands of citizens, and start them as competitors, upon the political race-course, for Executive patronage, I pretend not to know. One thing, however, is certain. Before this lure was held up, and the proof given that it meant what it promised, viz: that political gladiators should be rewarded, there was no such rush after office, as well by the unqualified, as the qualified, as has continued to distract the country from that day to this. To it, also, may be fairly attributed those reckless assaults upon private character, and the employment of the most degrading and demoralizing means, to break down an opposing candidate, and, indeed, whatever else might happen to be in the way of this burning thirst after the spoils of office, and the ephemeral glory of occupying a place in the government. Nor has this spirit proved less vindictive in the candidate for the office of tide-waiter, or keeper of a light-house, than in others whose eyes were fixed upon foreign missions, and cabinet offices. The glory of contending for principles, and the toils of the patriot, to secure for his country measures of a useful and enriching sort, have become, to the eye of the beholder, so blended with the selfish ends of the mere demagogue, as to place all alike, in their common view, upon the same level, and subject all to the degrading suspicion of following after political candidates, led by pretty much the same instincts that took so many of old into the wilderness, viz: that they might be fed.

It is only when the strife is past, that the patriot can be known from the demagogue—the whole-souled lover of his country, from the man whose only motive, in all of his burning zeal for his favorite candidate, is confined to the expectation of being rewarded with a part of a loaf, and *a few little fishes!* If there were no other consequences than the foregoing, to rebuke, and render odious, this system of "rewards," these ought to be sufficient. But there are others—in the alienation of friend from friend, and of family from family; and in the annihilation of that whole system of equal rights in which *every American* is entitled to participate, by virtue of the constitution, as well as his birth, and from which he can never be deprived, by anything short of their unjust invasion and down-treading, by the foot of despotism. Where can the right be found, either in the system of privileges inherent in every American, or in justice, or the constitution, in any man, who, on proclaiming himself a candidate for office, or being so proclaimed by others, whether of the Presidency or any other, shall announce that "*rewards*" shall be conferred on all those who may contribute to his success; and that "*punishment*" shall be inflicted on all who shall fail to join the army of his friends? And yet, an *exile* is known to await every man, so far as he can be reached, who may not happen to have fallen in with the views of the dominant party; and this has become an affair of such common occurrence, hideous as it is, as to have lost, to the general observation, all of its viciousness! This strife becomes the dignity, as it is also the duty, of the citizen, and crowns him with honor, as it has done, and will continue to do, when it is the result of a contest for *principle*, and for *measures* that are essential to the "*general welfare.*" It only becomes degrading when it is engaged in for mere *party* ends, and *personal* advantages.

I well remember the time, when a head of a department, having been deprived, by death, of a valuable chief clerk, inquired of me where he could obtain a *qualified* successor—so wholly unknown was the practice then, (and this was during the latter part of Mr. Madison's administration, or the first of Mr. Monroe's,) for a thousand applicants to make a rush at the same time for the place; or, for a vigilant looker-on, having caught from the doctor's looks an expression of doubt whether his patient would recover, to hie away to Washington, as has been done, present the claims of "*party*," receive a commission, and be back to

Philadelphia in time to be present at the dead man's funeral! It was my fortune to know a gentleman who was qualified for the place to which I have referred. I named him; he was appointed, and was all that the head of the department required of him; and that gentleman is the same who now fills with such distinguished ability, the office of Secretary of the Senate of the United States. The place he was called to fill at the time to which I have reference, was Chief Clerk of the office of Commissary General of Prisoners, whose head was GENERAL JOHN MASON.

But General Green, whose success had been so triumphant, was doomed himself to drink of the same bitter cup that he had so often mingled, and caused to be drank, by others. A cloud fell over his prospects, even before General Jackson's Presidency was closed. This change was caused by the suspicion that General Green favored another personage for the successor of General Jackson, other than General Jackson's own choice. The success of Mr. Van Buren was the signal of General Green's downfall; for in walking "in the footsteps of his illustrious predecessor," Mr. Van Buren took especial care not to cross the track which his "predecessor" had, doubtless, marked out for the guidance of his steps in relation to General Green—who went, so far as public patronage was concerned, literally, on Mr. Van Buren's accession to the Presidency, into exile, where he remained till recalled by his ancient friend and ally in the cause of Jacksonism, Mr. Tyler.

That General Jackson permitted himself to be surrounded and influenced by others, regardless of the means they employed to carry their ends, the following statement of facts will show:—

Some time after General Jackson had been inaugurated, the Secretary of War, Major Eaton, inquired of me, *if I had been to see the President?* I said I had not. Had you not better go over? Why, sir? I asked—I have had no official business to call me there, nor have I any now; why should I go? You know, in these times, replied the secretary, it is well to cultivate those personal relations, which will go far towards securing the good-will of one in power—and he wound up by more than intimating that the President had heard some things in disparagement of me, when I determined, forthwith, to go and see him, and ascertain what they were. On arriving at the door of the President's house, I was answered by the door-keeper, that the President was in, and having gone to report me, returned, saying the President would see me. On arriving at the door, it having been thrown open by the door-keeper, I saw the President very busily engaged writing, and with great earnestness; so much so, indeed, that I stood for some time, before he took his eyes off the paper, fearing to interrupt him, and not wishing to seem intrusive. Presently, he raised his eyes from the paper, and at the same time his spectacles from his nose, and looking at me, said—"Come in, sir, come in." You are engaged, sir? "No more so than I always am, and always expect to be"—drawing a long breath, and giving signs of great uneasiness.

I had just said, I am here, sir, at the instance of the Secretary of War, when the door was thrown open, and three members of Congress entered. They were received with great courtesy. I rose, saying, you are engaged, sir, I will call when you are more at leisure; and bowed myself out. On returning to my office, I addressed a note to the President, of the following import:—"Colonel McKenney's respects to the President of the United States, and requests to be informed when it will suit his convenience to see him?" To which Major Donaldson replied, "The President will see Colonel McKenney to-day, at twelve o'clock." I was punctual, and found the President alone. I commenced, by repeating what I had said at my first visit, that I was there at the instance of the Secretary of

War, who had more than intimated to me, that impressions of an unfavorable sort had been made upon him, in regard to me; and that I was desirous of knowing what the circumstances were, that had produced them. "It is true, sir," said the President, "I have been told things that are highly discreditable to you, and which have come to me from such sources, as to satisfy me of their truth." Very well, sir, will you do me the justice to let me know what these things are, that you have heard from such respectable sources? "You know, Colonel McKenney, I am a candid man—" I beg pardon, sir, I remarked, interrupting him, but I am not here to question that, but to hear charges which it appears have been made to you, affecting my character, either as an officer of the government, or a man. "Well, sir," he resumed, "I will frankly tell you what these charges are, and, sir, they are of a character which I can never respect." No doubt of that, sir, but what are they? "Why, sir, I am told, and on the best authority, that you were one of the principal promoters of that vile paper, "We the People;" as a contributor towards establishing it, and as a writer, afterwards, in which my wife Rachel was so shamefully abused. I am told, further, on authority no less respectable, that you took an active part in distributing, under the frank of your office, the "*coffin hand-bills;*" and that in your recent travels, you largely and widely circulated the militia pamphlet." Here he paused, crossed his legs, shook his foot, and clasped his hands around the upper knee, and looked at me as though he had actually convicted, and prostrated me; when, after a moment's pause, I asked—Well, sir, what else? "Why, sir," he answered, "I think such conduct highly unbecoming in one who fills a place in the government such as you fill, and very derogatory to you, as it would be in any one who should be guilty of such practices." All this, I replied, may be well enough, but I request to know if this is all you have heard, and whether there are any more charges? "Why, yes, sir, there is one more; I am told your office is not in the condition in which it should be." Well, sir, what more? "Nothing, sir; but these are all serious charges, sir." Then, sir, these comprise all? "They do, sir." Well, General, I answered, I am not going to reply to all this, or to any part of it, with any view of retaining my office, nor do I mean to reply at all, *except under the solemnity of an oath*—when I threw up my hand towards heaven, saying, *the answers I am about to give to these allegations, I solemnly swear, shall be the truth, the whole truth, and nothing but the truth.* My oath, sir, is taken, and is no doubt recorded—— He interrupted me, by saying, "You are making quite a serious affair of it." It is, sir, what I mean to do, I answered.

Now, sir, in regard to the paper called "*We the People*," I never did, directly or indirectly, either by my money, or by my pen, contribute towards its establishment, or its continuance. I never circulated one copy of it, more or less, nor did I subscribe for a copy of it, more or less; nor have I ever, to the best of my knowledge and belief, handled a copy of it, nor have I ever seen but two copies, and these were on the table of a friend, amongst other newspapers. So much for that charge. In regard to the "*coffin hand-bills*," I never circulated any, either under the frank of my office, or otherwise, and never saw but two; and am not certain that I ever saw but one, and that, some fool sent me, under cover, from Richmond, in Virginia, and which I found on my desk among other papers, on going to my office; and which, on seeing what it was, I tore up, and threw aside among the waste paper, to be swept out by my messenger. The other, which I took to be one of these bills, but which might have been an account of the hanging of some convict, I saw some time ago, pendent from a man's finger and thumb, he having a roll under his arm, as he crossed Broadway, in New York. So much for the coffin hand-bills. As to the "militia pamphlet," I have seen reference made to it in the newspapers, it is true, but I have never handled it—have never read it, or circulated a copy or copies of it, directly or indirectly. And now, sir, as to my office. That is my monument; its records are its inscriptions. Let it be examined, and I invite a commission for that purpose; nor will I return to it to put a paper in its place, should it be out of place, or in any other way prepare it for the ordeal; and, if there is a single flaw in it, or any just grounds for complaint, either on the part of the white or the red man, implicating my capacity—my diligence, or want of due regard to the interests of all having business with it, including the government, then, sir, you shall have my free consent to put any mark upon me you may think proper, or subject me to as much opprobrium as shall gratify those who have thus abused your confidence by their secret attempts to injure me.

"Colonel McKenney," said the general, who had kept his eyes upon me during the whole of my reply, "I believe every word you have said, and am satisfied that those who communicated to me those allegations, were mistaken." I thank you, sir, I replied, for your confidence, but I am not satisfied. I request to have my accusers brought up, and that I may be allowed to confront them in your presence. "No—no, sir," he answered, "I am satisfied; why then push the matter farther?" when, rising from his chair, he took my arm, and said, "Come, sir, come down, and allow me to introduce you to my family." I accompanied him, and was introduced to Mrs. Donaldson, Major Donaldson, and some others who were present, partook of the offering of a glass of wine, and retired.

The next morning, I believe it was—or if not the next, some morning not far off—a Mr. R–b–s–n, a very worthy, gentlemanly fellow, and well known to me, came into my office. "You are busy, Colonel?" he said, as he entered. No, sir, not very, I replied; come in—I have learned to write and talk too, at the same time. Come in; sit down; I am glad to see you. Looking round the office, the entire walls of which I had covered with portraits of Indians, he asked, pointing to the one that hung over my desk, "Who is that?" *Red-Jacket*, I answered. "And that?" *Shin-guab-O'Wassin*, I replied; and so he continued, till, pausing a moment, he asked, "And which is the *Kickapoo Ambassador?*" Oh, sir, I answered, rising, he has the honor of standing before you, in *propriæ persona.* "Come, come, Mac," said he, a little put out, "and have you really no Indian here, called the Kickapoo Ambassador?" None, I assure you, except myself; and that is the title by which I have been honored, and which, believe me, I cherish with becoming pride, and a corresponding pleasure. "Excuse me, Colonel; I really was honest in supposing that a chief was among your collection of paintings, so called." He then asked, "Who wrote the treaties with the Indians, and gave instructions to commissions, and, in general, carried on the correspondence of the office?" These are within the circle of my duties, the whole being under a general supervision of the Secretary of War, I answered. "Well, then," after a pause, he said, "the office will not suit me." What office? I asked. "This," he replied; "General Jackson told me, this morning, it was at my service; but before seeing the Secretary of War, I thought I would come and have a little chat with you, first."

I rose from my chair, saying—Take it, my dear sir, take it. The sword of Damocles has been hanging over my head long enough. "No," said he, "it is not the sort of place for me. I prefer an auditor's office, where forms are established." This worthy citizen had, in the fulness of his heart, doubtless, and out of pure affection for General Jackson, made that distinguished personage a present of the pair of pistols which General Washington had carried during the war of the Revolution. The general could not fail, of course, to feel grateful for so distinguished a gift; and, as times had become now, it was not unreasonable to expect that a suitable "reward," or token of the general's high estimate of the present, would be given. It so happened, however, that Mr. R., and a personal friend of General Jackson, had a fight somewhere down the Pennsylvania Avenue, the latter being, as it was reported, much worsted. I never learned that the offer of any other office, than the one I held, was afterwards made, by President Jackson, to Mr. R.

The office of Indian Affairs had, in like manner, been proffered to others; and the only reason why I had not been, at a very early period after General Jackson's succession to the Presidency, summarily disposed of, was, that the Secretary of War, Major Eaton, opposed it. He very frankly told the President that the duties of the Indian Department were heavy and complex, and that great experience was necessary to their proper discharge; and that I was familiar with those duties, and that the business of the department was well attended to, &c. On other occasions, when new applicants were favored with the President's approbation, Major Eaton would speak of the increased labors that my removal would impose upon him; and sometimes, of the danger that was justly to be apprehended, should the office fall into incompetent or inexperienced hands, of dissatisfactions being caused among the Indians, and a consequent border war. General Green having ascertained, I suppose, that Major Eaton had been the barrier, hitherto, to his exertions for my ejection from office, came in person to him; and, in terms rather more bold than was consistent with the relations of the two parties, insisted on my removal; and was very significantly referred, by Major Eaton, to "*his own business.*"

But it had been my lot to incur the displeasure of another of General Jackson's personal friends. I refer to the then General Houston, since President of Texas. Proposals had been issued by the department, of the 18th February, 1830, for rations for the support of emigrating Indians; the seals to be opened by the War Department on a specified day. Some few days previous to the date of the proposals, General Houston came into my office, and commenced a conversation by referring to the intention of the Executive to supply rations to the emigrant Indians by contract; when, drawing his chair near my desk, he said, "It is my intention to make an attempt to engage in this business. I wish you to aid me. You can do much in accomplishing my intentions. Everybody knows your acquaintance with this business, and you can have the matter attended to, pretty much as you please. If I succeed, as I am pretty sure I can, by your aid, you shall lose nothing by it."

I replied—General Houston, I regret your mode of approaching this subject, and the terms you have employed in presenting it. Waiving further remark in regard to these, I have to say that I have no power whatever over the subject. My place is subordinate; I can do no more than execute such orders as the Secretary of War may direct.

He said, in general terms, that he had no particular object in the remarks to which I had taken exception; that he nevertheless held the opinion, if I chose, I could be essentially useful to him; when he asked me to come and see him at his lodgings. He came again the next day, and asked if I had seen the Secretary of War. I answered—I had. "Has he said anything to you about issuing proposals for supplying rations to the emigrating Indians?" I replied—He has not. He appeared much surprised, adding, "It is d—d queer."

The next day he called again, when, in reply to similar questions, about my seeing the Secretary of War, and whether anything had passed between us touching the publication of proposals, &c., and receiving similar answers to those given the day before, he said he was satisfied the

Secretary of War had forgotten it, for that he had promised to see me, and give orders, &c., &c.—promising him that they should appear that morning in the Telegraph. I repeated that the secretary had said nothing to me on the subject. He asked if I would not see the secretary on the subject. I replied by referring to my subordinate position, and that I could not, with propriety, move upon the Secretary of War, but must wait his movements upon me. He said this was exceedingly embarrassing to him, as he wished to get off, and this was delaying him beyond his convenience; that "it was the more vexatious, as he had prepared proposals, given them to the Secretary of War, and received his assurance that he would hand them over to you. There was no reason, that he could see, for this delay." He continued to call, sometimes as often as two or three times a day; and at last insisted, with vehemence, that I must see the Secretary of War. I declined; when, looking at me, evidently much excited, he said, "McKenney, you have sustained Major Duval (the then Indian agent for the Cherokees in Arkansas, than whom the government never had a more capable, zealous, or faithful officer,) too long. You have issued to the delegation (meaning the Cherokee delegation) that was here before the last, without proper or justifiable reason, fifteen hundred dollars;" and, shaking his finger at me, added, "*I know certain things, of which I have said nothing.*"

I answered—My support of Major Duval is matter of record. That he (Houston) ought to know that I had the same power, without the knowledge and "*approval*" of the Secretary of War, to issue fifteen hundred dollars, or any other sum, to the Cherokees, or to any other person, that my door-keeper had, and no more. That, as to his insinuations of knowing certain things, of which, however, he had said nothing, he was at liberty, and I urged him to move upon me in any manner, and under any forms, that he might see fit to adopt—when he left the office.

On reflection, I considered it due to myself, to address to him a temperate, but firm letter, which I did. In this, I relieved him from any sense of delicacy, which he appeared to entertain towards me, and urged upon him to move upon me, touching any matters which he might suppose to involve my title to the respect and confidence of the Executive, or the world.

One of the points that Houston had urged upon me, as being important to himself, was that of limiting the time for the offer of the bids, for the contracts for rations, to thirty days, and which I very pointedly met, by saying that, as these supplies, in my opinion, would come from Arkansas and Missouri, there would be no time for the people of that quarter to respond to the call. To this, he urged his inability, owing to his poverty, to remain longer in Washington, and he wished, at the earliest possible period, to return home. To all which, I replied—It is an affair over which I have no control.

I received no *written* answer from General Houston, to my letter to him, but being in my office, some two or three days after, he said in pleasant words—"You know, McKenney, that what I said on the occasion to which your letter refers, is not worth entering into, as a subject of dispute between us; therefore, let it drop, and come down and see me. I shall be happy to see you at my room. I am having my likeness taken in Indian costume, and I want you to tell me how you like it." *Of course*, I never went. I understood, or thought I did, both moves; the first, I interpreted to be an appeal to my hopes, in the *implied* promise of being benefited in return for my co-operation, in obtaining the contract for Houston; the last, to my fears that these, as the first had failed, might urge me into a compliance. Neither prevailing, the good humor of the general was resumed; and a closer intimacy sought by the invitation to visit him at his room, and see his likeness, &c.

At about three o'clock on the day of the date of the

proposals, being in the secretary's room, and about returning from it, the secretary asked me, if I had seen Houston? I told him I had, and added—My interviews with him have not been of the most agreeable sort. He made no reply, but taking from his pocket a paper, he said—"I have forgotten, for some days, to hand you this paper. It is a paper containing proposals for rations for Indians, written by Houston, and handed to me by him; take it, and examine it, and if correct, have it copied, and sign it, and let it appear in the Telegraph to-morrow morning." I opened the paper, and saw at a glance that it was not a proper notice. Seeing me open the paper, the secretary said, "It is late now, take it home, and examine it." I said it was incorrect and imperfect, and a few words would explain in what. I then pointed to the imperfections; when the secretary said, "Well, take the paper home with you, and prepare a form, and bring it in in the morning." I did so.

I left a blank for the time within which bids would be received; stating that, as thirty days had been named, I wished to call his attention to it, it being too short a time for bids to reach the department from Arkansas, whence the supplies could be had at less price, than if obtained on this side the Mississippi. The secretary thought differently, and directed the blank to be filled with "*thirty days*," saying, "Houston is waiting," and "he believed few men were so well qualified for the discharge of such a trust." Besides the "thirty days" limitation, which, as it appeared to me, excluded a fair competition, there not being time enough for the citizens of Arkansas and Missouri to respond to the call, the secretary added an almost insuperable barrier to any reliance on the *permanency* of the contracts, in these words: "The right to be reserved to the Secretary of War to enlarge, or alter the quantity of rations to be issued, and the right of continuing the contract to any period of time he may think proper, and to deter-mine it at pleasure, when any of the conditions shall be broken. The points of delivery, not to exceed three in the country of either of the tribes, to be designated by the Secretary of War."

Besides the power reserved for the Secretary of War, to enlarge the quantity, or alter it, and to fix periods for concluding the contract; and the right, also, without any appeal, to decide when the conditions were complied with, or broken, there was no data in the advertisement, upon which the price of the ration could, with any certainty, be fixed upon, seeing "the points of delivery" were not named. All that was made known publicly was, that the rations were for "such Indians as might emigrate to their lands west of Arkansas and Missouri." There could, therefore, be no certain estimate made of the cost of the "transportation," because there were no depots named at which the rations were to be delivered. They might be a hundred miles in one direction, or a hundred miles in another. And yet there were some dozen bids sent in, I believe; the whole of which, however, were by persons then in Washington, except one from Louisville, Kentucky. Not one of these, however, so far as they were made public, was in the name of Houston, or in the name of any one for him.

The "thirty days" having expired, which set limits to the time of receiving bids for contracts, I was called upon by several persons, at my office, who inquired what decision had been come to on the bids? To all which, I gave the answer—I do not know; when a good deal of surprise was expressed; the applicants supposing that, as the proposals had emanated from my office, and bore my signature, I must, of course, be in possession of the decision of the department, and knew to whom it had been decided to give the contract. I referred the parties to the Secretary of War.

I was soon after in the secretary's office, and mentioned to him that such inquiries had been made of me, when he replied, "I have received no offers, except Houston's, in the name of Ben Hawkins.* I expressed surprise, and said—This is throwing responsibilities too heavily upon me. I was here interrupted by the secretary, who said—"If men will not be prompt, and hand in their proposals in time, they have no one to blame but themselves;" when I continued my remarks, by saying, I had received several packages in my office, having written on them, "Proposals for rations," which I had, *with my own hand*, on the afternoon of the day previous to the time fixed for opening them, placed in the hands of his chief clerk, Dr. Randolph, saying—These are proposals or bids, for supplying rations to Indians, the time expiring to-morrow; you will, therefore, be careful to place them before the Secretary of War, in time for his action upon them. If these proposals, I added, have not been placed before you, it is not owing to any fault of mine.

I had no knowledge, from any source, of what was going on, touching this ration business, from the time the proposals were issued, to the interview, as above referred to, with the Secretary of War. There had been great derangement in every branch of our Indian relations, caused by the intermeddling of the Second Comptroller, and which greatly embarrassed the right action of that important branch of the public service. When the Indian Bureau was organized, it was made the repository of all transactions relating to this branch of the public service; and all transactions, and of every sort, whether between the government and the Indians, or the Indians and our citizens, passed through it. It so continued, until a short time before Mr. Barbour's administration of the War Department had ceased; when, without his knowledge, or my own, the Second Comptroller issued a circular, directing the superintendents and agents to make their returns direct to either the Second Comptroller, or Second Auditor.

* Ben Hawkins was a half-breed Indian.

The effect of this order was, to divert from the Indian Bureau, and from the knowledge of the officer having charge of it, that very business, which, by his commission, he was required to act upon; taking from the Indian Bureau, at once, both its action, and its responsibility. The records of the office will show the efforts that were made by me to restore to the Bureau its proper action, and re-establish the responsibility of the officer having charge of it. The evil, however, was never cured, but grew worse and worse, until I left it.

Over this ration business, however, I had no control. It belonged, legitimately, to the Secretary of War to judge of the bids, and to decide upon them. But this action, on his part, over the entire duties of carrying out his decisions, devolved, not of right, perhaps, but in some sense of necessity, upon the Indian Bureau—it being impossible for the Secretary of War to attend to the details of the business. My action upon this ration business had ceased, when I put in the hands of his chief clerk such proposals as had been committed, by those who made them, to my charge; but it should have revived immediately after "thirty days" for receiving bids, and a deciding upon them, had expired. I very soon discovered, however, that difficulties of some sort had arisen to embarrass this business. The first light thrown upon this darkness, was by Luther Blake, of Alabama, who, coming into my office a few days after the expiration of the "thirty days," in a state of excitement, said he had just parted from Houston, who had told him that he (Houston) had seen all the bids, and that his (Blake's) was the lowest; that if Blake would withdraw his bid, he (Houston) could secure the contract, and that Blake should make more out of this step, than he could realize if he should get the contract. Blake's anger had been kindled, as he told me, at the permission which had been given to Houston "to see behind the curtain," and at his attempt, by a collusion of the sort, "to defraud, (as he phrased it,) the government."

The expenditure contemplated under these contracts for rations for emigrating Indians, was enormous. In view of it, I had given the subject my closest attention, and the result was, that a ration (under a system of contracts which I had recommended, as preferable to the previous system of referring the procuring of the supplies to the agents,) need not have cost over six cents and two-thirds. I derived this estimate from a thorough examination and average of previous expenditures, chiefly from accounts of agents on expenditures actually made, and returned to the office of the Second Auditor. On the 6th April, 1830, I made a report to the Secretary of War, from which what follows is an extract. I give it, to show that there was no lack of information in the proper Bureau, touching the cost of rations, if it had been thought proper to call for it. This information was elicited by a resolution of Congress, if my memory serves me, calling on the Secretary of War for the information contained in the extract—such calls being uniformly sent to the Indian Bureau, to be responded to.

EXTRACT.

"Department of War,
"*Office Indian Affairs*, April 6, 1830.

"To Major Eaton, *Secretary of War:*

"The average expense, per head, of removing the Creek Indians, who have emigrated, has been thirty-three dollars; but it is believed, under the system of contracts which I had the honor to recommend in my annual report of the 7th of November last, the cost may be considerably reduced. The cost of supporting the Indians for a year after their arrival, has been, in application to the Creeks, at the rate of six cents per day, each.

"The incidental expense which has attended the removal of the Creeks, is embraced in the foregoing; from which it appears the entire cost of removing each Creek, and supporting him, has been fifteen cents per day, or fifty-four dollars per year. But subsequent experience in taking over the last party, has shown that, under the present system, it need not amount to more than about half the cost of the first movement; and it may, as I have stated, be still reduced, by a system of contracts. The value of improvements abandoned by the Indians, is not included; nor is it supposed it was intended to be, since what is paid for these will be reimbursed, it is fair to presume, in the additional value which these improvements will give to the land.

"If fifty-five dollars be assumed as the cost attending the removal of each Indian, and supporting him for a year after his removal; and if there are, as is presumed to be, eighty thousand Indians east of the Mississippi, the entire cost will be, for removing them, and supporting them for a year, four millions four hundred thousand dollars. If from this be deducted the difference between the actual cost of the first and the last party, it would cost two millions eight hundred and eighty thousand dollars; and if one-third be deducted from this, under a system of contracts, which I think would be a fair reduction, it would be two millions two hundred and ninety-four thousand dollars.

"It is proper to remark, that this estimate is based on the removal of eighty thousand Indians. This number has been assumed, because the inquiry contained in the resolution of the House of Representatives embraces "*all* the Indians on the east of the Mississippi." If, however, it were confined to the Indians which it is presumed may have been *intended* to be embraced, viz: the four southern tribes—Chickasaws, Choctaws, Creeks, and Cherokees—the Seminoles in Florida, and the fragments of bands in Ohio, Indiana, &c., those numbering about fifty thousand, it would be proper to deduct one-fourth, which would leave one million seven hundred and twenty thousand dollars.

This sum would be a charge upon the treasury for so much expended in *removing* the Indians to, and *supporting* them for a year in the country heretofore described; but, if the inquiries embraced the question of reimbursing it, there would be no difficulty in showing that the lands abandoned by those Indians would, when sold, reimburse not only this sum, but furnish a fund, besides, for their improvement in the west, for many years. As, however, this information is not called for, I forbear to enter upon a calculation of the number of acres of land that are now claimed by those eighty thousand Indians, and to show the probable value of the same."

It was the duty of the Indian Bureau to operate upon all such elements, and be prepared, at the shortest possible notice, to furnish this, and all other information which came within the sphere of its legitimate operations; and yet, pending this contract business, embracing so vast an amount of expenditure, and when, to know the price of the ration, was indispensable to an enlightened, as well as just action upon the subject, I was never inquired of, directly, and, I may say, or indirectly, for information which, in view of the call for proposals, I had prepared myself to furnish.

The bids, for this large business, varied from eight cents per ration, to twenty. I gather this from the public and published documents; for I knew nothing of who bid, or of the prices bid, until a committee of the House of Representatives published them. Luther Blake's bid was the lowest, viz: eight cents. There were others at nine cents, nine and a half, ten, twelve, thirteen, &c., up to twenty. Houston's, it appears, was *eighteen cents per ration.*

I extract the following, from Document No. 502, House of Representatives, Twenty-Second Congress, First Session. It is Duff Green's testimony, on oath, before the committee of Congress, appointed to investigate this business. To the question, "Do you know anything in relation to a contract, said to have been attempted to have been made between Samuel Houston, and the late Secretary of War, to supply the emigrating Indians with rations? If you do, state that knowledge."

"*Answer.* About the time that the advertisement was published in the Telegraph for proposals, which advertisement has been referred to, in the testimony of Mr. McKenney, I was at the President's, and saw Major Eaton, then the Secretary of War, and General Houston, sitting together in earnest conversation; one of whom (I believe the secretary) beckoned me to them, and asked at what time an advertisement intended for publication on the next day should be sent to the office. I replied, at any time before ten o'clock. He said, I will send you one to-morrow. General Houston said, 'No, I will call and take it.' The advertisement was inserted; and some time thereafter, I believe on the 18th of March, I was in conversation with Major Eaton: he told me that he was about to close an important contract for supplying the emigrant Indians with rations; that he had ascertained that the ration had heretofore cost about twenty-two cents; that General Houston had gone on to New York, and, having obtained a wealthy partner, (or security,) would take the contract at eighteen cents. He estimated that the rations, at that rate, would amount to twelve thousand dollars per day, and seemed desirous to impress on my mind a belief that the difference between twenty-two cents and eighteen cents per ration, would be so much saved to the government on the issue to that extent. He spoke of the number of Indians whom he expected to emigrate, which, as well as I recollect, he estimated from sixty to eighty thousand.

"I told him that I was satisfied that, instead of a saving, there would be a great loss to the government. I told him that I knew that beef could be purchased in Missouri and Illinois, on foot, at from one dollar to one dollar and fifty cents per hundred pounds, and that, without further inquiry, I should suppose that the ration ought not to cost more than six cents. He manifested considerable impatience, and seemed unwilling to listen to me. I believe that I then urged him to advertise again, and thus give to the western people an opportunity to bid, assuring him that the result would be a great saving on the contract. I left him under a firm conviction that he had determined to give the contract to Houston, and that his object in speaking to me was to induce me to make a favorable mention of the contract in the United States Telegraph. Upon reaching home, I consulted with a friend from Missouri, then at my house, and expressed my wish that some one could be induced to put in a lower bid. He suggested that Mr. John Shackford, then a respectable merchant at St. Louis, and now the door-keeper of the Senate, then in the city, would be a proper person to do so; and I immediately sent for Mr. Shackford. I explained to him my suspicions; told him what had transpired between Major Eaton and myself, and urged him to put in a lower bid, saying to him that my object in sending for him was, first, to induce some one to bid the contract down as near as possible to a fair price, so as to save the money of the government; and, next, to prevent the effect which I plainly foresaw such a contract as that contemplated with Houston would have on the character and popularity of the administration; and that, knowing that he was not a partisan of the administration, I relied upon his honor not to use the facts then disclosed, to the prejudice of the administration, if we could prevent the contemplated contract. He told me that he had invested a large amount of his property in the Louisville and Portland canal, and, that the stock being unproductive and below par, he was not in funds, and that his disappointment made him fearful to enter into any enterprise attended with uncertainty. We examined the proposals, and he commented upon the power which the secretary would have over the contract, and the danger of embarking in it against *his* wishes, and seemed unwilling to put in a bid at what I considered a fair price. He agreed, however, to think of it until the next day, and did call on the next morning. Finding that he would not consent to put in a bid at such a price as I believed the government ought to accept, I resolved to see the President, and, if possible, to prevail on him to extend the time of receiving proposals.

"When I entered the President's room, I found him in conversation with Governor Branch. (It is my impression, although the governor, the other day, told me that he thinks he entered the room after I did.) I apologized for calling, by referring immediately to the contract; said that I was confident that it could be furnished for much less than I understood the department was about to give. The President said that they had ascertained that the ration had cost twenty-two cents; General Houston had gone on to New York, and had brought with him (or obtained) a wealthy partner, (or security,) and that the contract would be given to him at eighteen cents. I then referred to the price of beef, corn, &c., in the west, and said that I was confident the rations could be furnished at six cents. He replied, quickly, 'Will *you* take it at *ten?*' I said, no, sir. He then said, 'Will *you* take it at twelve cents; if you will, you shall have it at that?' I told him that I was not a bidder for the contract; that, although I was satisfied that I could realize an immense sum upon such a contract, I was influenced to call upon him by a desire to serve him and the administration, and not by a wish to speculate; and left him. Upon reaching home, I wrote to Major Eaton a letter, which I gave to my youngest brother, then living with me, to copy in my confidential letter-book, with instructions to carry it to Major Eaton; which he told me that he did. The letter was as follows:—

"WASHINGTON, *March* 19, 1830.

"TO MAJOR EATON:—

"After leaving you last evening, I examined, for the first time, your proposals for rations. From my knowledge of the prices of beef and corn in the Western States, I am confident that the proposed rations ought not to cost ten cents; yet I understand you to say that you expect to give from eighteen to twenty cents, and that the issue, at these prices, will amount to twelve thousand dollars per day.

"That a contract of such amount should be made without giving notice to the Western States, where provisions must be purchased, will be a cause of attack; but when I read the advertisement, and see that it is so worded as not to convey any idea of the speculation it affords, and connect it with the facts, which are within my own knowledge, that it was prepared under the special advisement of General Houston, who has gone on to New York, and has brought from there a wealthy partner to join him in the contract, I should be unfaithful to the administration, to General Jackson, and to myself, if I did not bring the subject before you in such a shape as to guard against the consequences which I foresee will follow any such contract as the one he contemplates.

"Such a contract may enrich a few who are concerned in it, but will destroy the confidence of the public, I fear, in the administration, and impair the fair fame of the President, which it is your duty and mine to guard. Will it not be well to extend the time, so as to enable the people of Missouri and Arkansas to bid?

"Yours, &c., D. GREEN."

Duff Green swore further, that "he had no doubt, at the time of examining the proposals, that they were so framed as to prevent competition, by presenting difficulties, as well in the fulfilment of the contract, as in the control which was reserved to the department. The tendency was to prevent bidders from making accurate calculations of the cost, inasmuch as he believed that the contract could have been made at six cents, allowing a fair profit to the contractor, in case he had full confidence in the department. He had no doubt, that, even under the proposals, a contract could have been made, if due notice had been given in the Western States, to furnish the rations at ten cents." And further—

"When I found that Mr. Shackford would not put in a bid at what I considered a fair price, I then appealed to the President (General Jackson) for the same purpose, (which was to defeat the contract with Houston.) During my interview with him, I became satisfied that he would interpose no obstacle to the contract with Houston."

The bidders at eight and nine cents—being the lowest—became restless. One of them, William Prentiss, opened quite a sharp correspondence with the Secretary of War.

Colonel Sevier, United States Senator, of Arkansas, testified that "he was a good deal provoked, and took every step in his power to defeat the contract. He thought the citizens of Arkansas, who had the supplies of beef and corn among themselves, were shut out from making bids; the advertisement allowing but thirty days for the reception of bids, when it would take nearly thirty days to reach Arkansas. He saw the Secretary of War, and remonstrated; wrote to him, &c.; and learned from him something about turning it (the providing of rations) to the management of General Gibson, of the Commissary Department."

I had not only incurred General Houston's displeasure, in the preliminary steps of this business, as recorded in this narrative, but on learning from my chief clerk, Mr. Hambleton, that he was in the habit of going into his room, pending this ration business season, and asking for papers, and taking them out with him; and in reply to my question whether he brought with him the order of the

Secretary of War, and receiving for answer that he had not, I directed that such unauthorized liberties should be granted to no one.

The next day General Houston entered my office through the door leading to the clerk's room, in a highly excited state, and demanded to know if I had forbidden to him the use of such papers as he might want. I replied—I have given such orders. He gave vent to much threatening, and retired, grating his teeth, saying, "*You shall suffer for it.*" I reported to the Secretary of War the nature of this interview; told him that I had directed my chief clerk to allow no one, without his orders, to take from the office any paper belonging to it, as I felt myself responsible for the safe-keeping of the records, &c. I received no answer; but pointing to a sofa which was in the room, the secretary said, "There are some papers;" (and I think a letter-book,) "you had better take them." I did so, and restored them to their proper places. Mr. Hambleton told me these were the papers that had been taken from the office by General Houston.

The conclusion of all this ration business, was, to recognize no one who had made proposals; but, overlooking the bids that had been made, the duty of providing the rations for the emigrating Indians was referred to the Subsistence Department.

Whether before, or after this transaction, I forget, my chief clerk, Mr. Hambleton, came into my room one morning, soon after I had taken my seat at my table, and putting his hands upon it, leaned over. I looked up, and saw his eyes were full of tears! To my question—Is anything the matter, Mr. Hambleton? "Yes, sir—I am pained to inform you, that you are to be displaced to-day! We all feel it. Our connexion has been one of unbroken harmony; and we are grieved at the thought of a separation. The President has appointed General Thompson, a member of Congress, of Georgia—he boards at my mother's, and I have it from himself. He says I shall remain, but the rest of the clerks he shall dismiss, to make room for some of the President's friends."

Well, Mr. H., I replied, it is what I have been constantly looking for. Your annunciation does not at all surprise me; indeed, it puts an end to my suspense; and, apart from the pain of leaving you all, and the thought that others are to be cut adrift, as well as myself, I feel relieved. He walked a few times across my room, and then retired to his, which joined mine. Two hours after, I heard walking, and earnest talking in the passage. They continued for half an hour. When they ceased, Mr. Hambleton came into my room, his face all dressed in smiles, saying, "*It is not to be!*" What is not to be? "You are not to go out. When General Thompson came to the secretary this morning, with the President's reference to him, to assign him to your place, he was told, before he could act, he (the secretary) must see the President. The result of the secretary's interview with the President was, you were to be retained, and General Thompson is referred back to the President, for explanation, &c. Thompson is in a rage about it—and among other things said, "*It's a pretty business, indeed, that Eaton thinks he can command a frigate, and I can't manage a cock-boat!*"

CHAPTER X.

PLANS FOR IMPROVING THE CONDITION OF THE INDIANS. HINDRANCES IN THE WAY OF THEIR EXECUTION.

Organization of "the Indian Board" at New York—Address before the Indian Board—Claims of the Indians presented—Massasoit—Pocahontas—Benevolent designs of the Pilgrims—Obstacles to be overcome—The Indian vindicated—The Indian a victim to the vices of civilization—Some of the obstacles to his improvement removed—His anticipated progress—Destiny of our country—Duty to the Indians—Views of President John Quincy Adams—Different views of emigration—Diminution of the tribes—Some wholly exterminated—An erroneous impression corrected—Terms of the proposed removal—Imaginary talk with the Indians—Conclusion—Letter of "the Indian Board" to the Executive—Reply by General Eaton—Comment upon this correspondence—Total failure of the objects of this organization—The causes of this failure—Protection promised the Indian—Promise fulfilled by force.

In July of the year 1829, the Secretary of War responded to a call made upon him by an association of distinguished and benevolent citizens (chiefly clergymen and laymen of the Dutch Reformed Church) of New York, for my presence in that city, and services, in aiding them in the formation of a Board whose object was, to advance the interest, and promote the well-being of the Indians, by authorizing me to meet them. These intelligent and philanthropic gentlemen saw the increasing dangers by which the Indians within our States and organized Territories were surrounded; and contemplated, with anxious solicitude, the perishing result, in the total extinction of the portions of this race who were thus situated, and sought to save them, by the only means which they believed were adapted to so noble an object; and these were, by a proper enlightening of the Indians, *to procure their assent* to change their relations to the whites, by emigrating to lands west of the Mississippi, and beyond the limits of our States, and to a condition, there—*social, political, moral, and religious*—that could, as they viewed it, never be realized where they were. *The entire scheme*, however, was based on the *voluntary consent of the Indians to remove, and upon the granting of the appropriate privileges and powers to them, in their new homes, by the government, for their security, preservation, exaltation, and happiness.* I repaired to New York, and met the gentlemen who had originated this benevolent scheme.

At a preliminary meeting, it was—"Resolved, That the Rev. Eli Baldwin, Colonel McKenney, and the Rev. Dr. Brodhead, be a committee to draft a constitution, which shall be to direct the proceedings of a proposed association for the salvation of the Indian race."

The following preamble and constitution were read in presence of a number of citizens of various denominations, from the Reformed Dutch, Episcopal, Presbyterian, and Moravian churches, at the consistory chamber, corner of Nassau and Ann streets, the Rev. Dr. McLeod being chairman, and Rev. Eli Baldwin, secretary:—

PREAMBLE.

The situation of the scattered remains of the Aborigines of this country, involving, on the one side, the wrongs, the calamities, and the probable extermination of an interesting race of men; and on the other side, the great perplexity of the government of the United States, arising from its unwillingness, as well as from its want of power, to interfere with the sovereignty of the States' governments, has for a long time employed the skill of the statesman, and the benevolence of the religious community.

Although what has been done, has neither accomplished the magnanimous and enlarged views of our government, nor realized the expectations of religious enterprise; yet, from the experience of the past, we have arrived at the conclusion that the harmony of these United States, the preservation of the American Indians from total extermination, and, consequently, the cause of humanity, require some prompt and decisive measures, calculated to carry into effect the only alternative left—namely, the final and speedy removal of the scattered remains of the Indian tribes from within the jurisdictional limits of sovereign States, to such place or places as will put them fully within the sovereign control of the federal government, so as to prevent the calamities of the past, and secure the perpetuity of their rights, in the future. Therefore, in order to promote an object so imperative and desirable, an Association is hereby formed, under the following

CONSTITUTION.

ARTICLE I.

This Association shall be known by the style of "THE INDIAN BOARD, FOR THE EMIGRATION, PRESERVATION, AND IMPROVEMENT OF THE ABORIGINES OF NORTH AMERICA."

ARTICLE II.

The acting members of this Association shall not exceed thirty in number; not less than one-half of whom shall be residents of the city of New York; all of whom shall have signed the Constitution; and seven shall constitute a quorum at a meeting regularly convened.

ARTICLE III.

The officers of this Association shall be, a President, five Vice-Presidents, a Corresponding Secretary, (who shall be authorized to employ a clerk,) and a Treasurer, chosen by ballot out of the acting members of the Association.

ARTICLE IV.

This Board engages to afford to the emigrant Indians, all the necessary instruction in the arts of life, and in the duties of religion.

ARTICLE V.

This Board is pledged to co-operate with the federal government of the United States, in its operations in Indian affairs; and at no time contravene its laws.

ARTICLE VI.

This Association invite the citizens of the United States, without respect to sect or party, religious or political, to co-operate with them in this benevolent enterprise.

ARTICLE VII.

This Board shall fill up vacancies, occurring from any cause, by ballot.

ARTICLE VIII.

This Board shall have power to elect honorary members by ballot; no choice, however, shall be made at the same meeting in which they are proposed. Persons so elected, shall have the privileges of members, with the exception of a right to vote.

ARTICLE IX.

No alterations or amendments of this Constitution shall be made, unless concurred in by three-fourths of the acting members; and no proposed amendment shall be acted upon, at the same meeting at which it may be submitted.

[Signed]

Alexander McLeod,
Philip Milledolar,
Jacob Brodhead,
Isaac Van Hook,
W. C. Brownlee,
R. McCartee,
N. J. Marcelus,
Thomas G. Talmadge,
Cornelius D. Westbrook,
Peter P. Rouse,
Hugh Auchincloss,
Joseph V. Varick,
Joseph M. Smith,
Stephen Hasbrouck,
Richard Duryee,
Samuel Van Wyck,
T. L. Ogden,
George W. Strong,
Jno. Clark,
Stephen Van Rensselaer,
Eli Baldwin,
S. H. Meeker,
Cornelius C. Cuyler,
Abraham Van Nest,
Cornelius Heyer,
Jacob R. Hardenberg,
Thomas DeWitt,
Abraham Bloodgood,
Wm. H. Van Vleck.

New York, July 22, 1829.

A ballot being cast, the following were chosen officers of the Association:—

Hon. STEPHEN VAN RENSSELAER, President.
Rev. Alexander McLeod, D. D.,
Philip Milledolar, D. D.,
Jacob Brodhead, D. D.,
Cornelius D. Westbrook, D. D.,
Abraham Van Nest, Esq., } Vice-Presidents.
Rev. Eli Baldwin, Corresponding Secretary.
Jno. Clark, M. D., Treasurer.

To a letter enclosing a copy of the constitution to General Van Rensselaer, the following reply was addressed to the Corresponding Secretary:—

"Albany, August 4, 1829.

"My Dear Sir:—On my return on Saturday, from an official tour to Lake Erie, I received Dr. Westbrook's letter, and the constitution of the Indian Board, &c. I congratulate you, and the friends of the poor Aborigines of our country, on the organization of the Board. I anticipate the happiest results. I only regret that my distance from New York will render me less efficient than I wish. To co-operate with the government in the laudable undertaking, will be my pride.

"My recent return from a fatiguing journey is my apology for not attending the meeting on Wednesday.

"Very respectfully your friend, &c.

S. Van Rensselaer."

It was resolved, at a meeting of the Board held at Dr. McLeod's church, Chambers-street, on the afternoon of the 28th, to invite me to deliver an address to the public meeting which was called to assemble at that church. In pursuance of which, the following letter was addressed to me, by the Corresponding Secretary:—

"NEW YORK, July 29, 1829.

"DEAR SIR:—At a meeting of 'the Indian Board, for the emigration, preservation, and improvement of the Aborigines of North America,' held yesterday afternoon, the following resolution was passed, viz:—

"*Resolved*, That the secretary invite Colonel McKenney to deliver an address at the public meeting, to be held at Dr. McLeod's church, in Chambers-street, on the 5th proximo, at half-past seven o'clock, P. M.

"Permit me, sir, earnestly to entreat your compliance with the above. From a long acquaintance with Indian affairs, (as the head of the department) you are doubtless conversant with many facts and circumstances, calculated to interest the feelings, and inform the minds of the public; these would be peculiarly grateful on that occasion, and facilitate the future operations of the Board.

"It is scarcely necessary to say, that a favorable answer to the above, will give personal pleasure to, sir,

"Your obedient servant,

ELI BALDWIN, Cor. Sec'y."

ANSWER.

"NEW YORK, July 30, 1829.

"To the Rev. ELI BALDWIN, Corresponding Secretary, &c., &c.

"DEAR SIR:—I am just favored with your letter of yesterday, informing me of a resolution of your Board, embracing an invitation to me to deliver an address at the public meeting, to be held in Dr. McLeod's church, in Chambers-street, on the 5th proximo; and conveying your own earnest entreaty that I would comply with the wishes of the Board.

"In reply, I have to state, that having been sent on here, by the Executive, in compliance with a request made by you, in behalf of the Association, then about to be formed, to aid you with such information as I might possess, in the furtherance of your benevolent intentions towards the Indians, I do not well see how I could, with propriety, decline to render any aid which you might consider important in its bearing on the great object you have in view; and, however convinced I may be, that more efficient service might be rendered in this part of the plan of your operations, by others better qualified for the task than I feel myself to be, still, I will be present at the meeting, and, as far as I may be able, act in compliance with the wishes of your Board.

"I am, Reverend sir, &c., &c.

THOMAS L. MCKENNEY."

ADDRESS.

There are, to use the words of a distinguished citizen of Virginia, two problems yet to be solved, both having, so far, puzzled the ingenuity of the politician, and baffled the wisdom of the sage. "One of these relates to the black population which we carry in our bosom; the other to the red population which we carry on our back." The inquiry is, how shall we, upon principles of sound policy, work out solutions that shall provide a remedy for the evils of the one, and a plan for the civilization and preservation of the other. These are questions, it must be admitted, of grave import. They are full of interest, and demand the untiring exertions of the wise and good, to answer them practically and satisfactorily.

Our business, on the present occasion, is with our red population—the remains of a once lofty and independent, but now degraded race; a people, who are, in all respects, entitled to our sympathies, and not to ours, only, but those, also, of the civilized world. Any appeal which can be made in behalf of the Aborigines of America, we consider as entitled to the privilege of passing, not the bounds of neighborhood, only, but of the republic. Every heart, no matter on what spot of earth it pulsates, must feel, if it have become humanized, the deepest interest in any proposition that looks to their rescue from the savage, and elevation into the civilized and Christian state.

Perhaps there are some in this assembly, who question the extent to which the sympathies of our race are claimed for our Indians. If so, we would refer such to Plymouth and to Jamestown; to Samoset and Massasoit, at the one place, and to Pocahontas at the other. It were not difficult to fancy these distinguished natives in the midst of this assembly, prepared to defend, by their own simple, but powerful eloquence, the claims assumed for their race. Massasoit would appear, doubtless, arrayed in the habiliments of his northern forests; with moccasins and leggins, made of the skins of beasts he had slain; and a robe over his shoulder of the same material. His porte, erect and manly. With one hand at his breast, he would grasp the partial and shaggy covering of his body, and with the other bared and extended, he would thus speak—

"When your pilgrim fathers approached the shore of my domain, I eyed them well. They were strangers. I knew not who they were, or whence they had come; but I saw they were men. The rock on which they landed, was my rock; and it was washed by the waters of my river. I stood up, and saw they were afraid. My heart felt pity for them. I bade my warrior-bands retire, and unstring their bows, and put up their arrows in their quivers. They did as I bade them. I, alone, advanced towards the strangers. Their faces were *white* with fear! They looked upon each other, and spoke not; and then looked upon me, and *trembled!* In this hand, I held an ear of corn; with it, I advanced towards their leader, and extended it to him. He understood me. It was the offer of peace, and the token of my friendship. I welcomed them to my lands, and gave them protection. Who doubts my power, by a single glance of my eye, to have sent a thousand deaths to quiver in the breasts of these your fathers, and to have strewed the beach with their dead bodies?"

"And what," we might fancy Pocahontas to say, "would have been the fate of Captain Smith, the leader of those who came across the deep waters to the lands of Powhatan, my father, had not a gush of pity forced itself on my heart, and impelled me to throw myself between that leader of your fathers, and the club that was uplifted to dash out his brains? And what the fate of those who attended him?"

"And where," we may fancy them both asking, "would now be their descendants, who, numerous as the leaves of our forests, fill our valleys, and sail upon our rivers, and hunt in our mountains?" And where, *we* ask, would have been the hundreds of thousands of the oppressed and distressed of the old world, who in later times, like the pilgrim fathers, have sought, and like them found, an asylum in the new? Who can doubt that those generous savages gave us this country; or that, with other dispositions than those which animated them, we might not have possessed it for centuries to come, if ever?

If this be so, and if this western world have, in its soil and climate; in its institutions, civil, and political, and religious, anything to endear it to the heart of man, then does the obligation exist, not in those only who possess this fair inheritance, but in those, also, who enjoy it in prospect, or draw lessons from our admirable institutions for the better regulation of their liberty, or the maintenance of their own peace and security, to feel for, and succor those who were once the proprietors of this domain—a domain on which is now acting the most engaging scenes in practical government ever presented to the observation of the world. The beautiful theory, long thought to be Utopian, of a government like ours, is no longer matter of speculation, but of practical operation. The predictions of its weakness and instability, have had their answers in the new and increasing glory which shines upon it; and which has been struck out by collisions, the prospect of which made many a patriotic and stout heart tremble.

The more exalted our state, and the more perfect our happiness, the deeper should we feel the obligation not to suffer those to whose country we have succeeded, to perish before our eyes. We have often, when surveying the wretched condition of our Indians, felt the apprehension, that perhaps enough of anxiety was not felt by our fathers for their condition; and that they were permitted to descend to us in a state unfavorable to improvement:—but the more we have examined into this subject, the more thorough has become our conviction that the reputation of the pilgrims for humanity and kind intentions, is unimpeachable. They meditated no exterminating designs;

they cherished no feelings of hostility, but the contrary, towards those untutored people. If we consult what remains of the records of those earlier, and we will add later, times, we shall find that so soon, and wheresoever it was practicable to begin the work of enlightening the natives, it was attempted. Let it not be assumed, that because those efforts failed, as they did, except partially, to accomplish the benevolent ends contemplated, that they were not cherished and acted upon. Never were labors more apostolic than were those which the Elliots, and Mayhews, and Brainards, and Kirklands, introduced into the wilderness of mind by which they were surrounded; nor purer, or more disinterested purposes formed, in reference to any object, than were those that contemplated to confer upon the Aborigines the blessings of civilization and Christianity. Roxbury, Nantucket, Elizabeth Isles, Martha's Vineyard, and numerous other places, attest the sincerity and zeal of those who labored to reform these people. Comparative success, only, attended those labors; when, from the failure to accomplish anything more than a partial change, arguments were drawn adverse in their conclusions to the Indian's capacity for improvement, and the question has often been asked—

Why, if the Indians are endowed with the faculties common to the whites, and are susceptible, like ourselves, to be improved by the lessons of civilization, have they remained uncivilized, as a people, to this day? Numerous, we answer, have been always the obstacles to such a change; but not one of these involves the dreary and disheartening conclusion that, by any law of his nature, the Indian is precluded from the benefits which civilization confers; or from a participation in all that is great and good amongst men. But what were those obstacles? We would enumerate, as constituting some of them—the almost boundless extent of the forests, and the easy means of subsistence furnished the Indian, in the game that abounded there; his passion for the chase, and for war; his conceptions of his own power and independence, and the consequent indisposition arising out of all these to submit to restraint; the preference he cherishes for the sports and pastimes, and the traditions of his fathers; the habits which become grafted on these; the indolence consequent upon such a state of being, and the aversion arising out of it to intellectual exertion. To these may be superadded various influences acting upon the Indian from without, and the infliction upon him, by avarice, of wrongs and outrages, which tended to destroy his confidence in the white man, and fill him with suspicion and jealousy.

Those are some of the obstacles which benevolence sought to overcome; but they are not all. Which of us has not listened with sensations of horror to the nursery stories that are told of the Indian and his cruelties? In our infant mind, he stood for the Moloch of our country. We have been made to hear his yell; and to our eyes have been presented his tall, gaunt form, with the skins of beasts dangling round his limbs, and his eyes like fire, eager to find some new victim on which to fasten himself, and glut his appetite for blood. We have been made to see the desperate onset; to hear the piercing war-cry, and the clash of arms, and the heavy, dead sound of the war-club, as it fell on the head of the victim—and then, from the midst of a partial stillness, we have been startled by the shrieks of the dying mother; and hushed, that we might hear the last sigh of the expiring infant—and then we have had disclosed to us the scene of carnage; and the Indian striding amidst the bodies of the slain; or beheld him seated over some favorite victim, with his fingers dripping with blood, and his face disclosing a ferocious smile, as he enjoyed the sight of the quivering limbs, and the agonies of the dying!

And thus were we, on our part, alienated from the Indian; and it was natural we should be—for amidst descriptions of savage barbarity like these, it was not to be expected that our feelings should be kind towards the authors of them. There was no time left us then to tear ourselves away from the resentments which were kindled in our bosoms, to inquire into the great moving cause of all this bloody strife; or whether these butcheries disclosed the *native* propensity of the Indian, or were the outbreakings of savage revenge, in retaliation for wrongs which it has not been given to human nature patiently to endure. Had it been given to us to know what we now know, whilst our infant feelings would have bled over the recital of those Indian cruelties, inflicted often on the unprotected, and unsuspecting, and unresisting, and deplored the sacrifice of innocent life, we must have indulged, also, a deep sympathy for the Indian.

We would take occasion here, in connexion with our reference to the Indian, and to his bloody acts, to vindicate him before this assembly, from any imputation that would go to establish *cruelty* as a *necessary* law of his nature; or any other feeling which we do not possess in common with him. We have had some opportunities of personally inspecting his character, and amidst his own plains and mountains, where are yet left to him some traces of the original domain, and where the face of his beautiful country has not yet been despoiled of its forests. Wherever we found him not yet imbued with the vices of civilization—for these are swift to reach him, and always reach him first—we found a being hospitable, kind, generous, with the natural affections, warm and constant. In his hospitality he vied with the most refined;—not, it is true, in the extent, or variety, or nicety of his accommodations—for these, alas! are always forbidding enough;—but in the promptings of the heart, and the freeness with which he would place before us all his little store of supplies, and in the gratification he would discover when he saw his offerings accepted. We have witnessed some rare examples of those virtues in the solitude of the desert, and never without feeling an anxious desire for the speedy arrival of the period that should bring with it a change in the condition of these people.

We have noticed some of the difficulties with which those had to contend, who undertook, in the earlier periods of our history, to reform the habits, and elevate the condition of the natives—many of these exist no longer. The forests, (we mean those within our States,) and their game, are gone. The Indian can no longer bury himself in the one, nor subsist on the other. He has become now a creature of necessity—he must labor, or starve. But not only are the forests and the game gone, but with these has disappeared also that feeling of independence which once made the native as uncontrollable, as he was invincible. Long and nobly did he struggle to maintain this. From the days of Pontiac, and long anterior to these, although often cut to pieces in their wars, and reduced in numbers, did this proud spirit display itself, until Tecumthé fell. Pontiac! What a noble specimen of man existed in the person, and displayed itself in the acts of this warrior-chief! He could not brook the idea of surrendering his relations to the French; and to which he and his bands had become reconciled, if not attached. So soon, therefore, as the French power fell, and that of the British succeeded, we find him mustering his legions, and with a spirit and enterprise that nothing could subdue, and a skill equal to that displayed by our most finished tacticians, aiming a death-blow at the newly established power. As long as history lasts, so long will the siege of Detroit be remembered, and Pontiac ranked amongst the most skilful and valiant in war. A like spirit, and under like circumstances, animated Tecumthé. His partialities were for the British, and his skill and power were arrayed against us. He sought, by a skilful combination of Indian bands, from the lakes to the Mississippi, not to fortify and defend himself, only, but by a sudden and simultaneous stroke upon our borders, to regain the territory of his people, and reign absolute,—not as monarch of his forests, only, but as lord, also, of his bands. His life paid the forfeit of the gallant enterprise; and with it vanished all hopes of all allied to him, of ever again becoming lords of their domain. Thus fell another of the obstacles in the way of Indian improvement.

It was to this state of things our fathers looked. We have found, they doubtless said, this singular being to be unmanageable;—but when this empire shall have become established, and the sceptre of freedom be swayed over its teeming population, then, surely, will that which is now literally a wilderness to the Indian, be made to blossom as the rose; and then will his solitary places become glad. No longer able to bury himself in his forests, or subsist on their game, or measure strength with the white man, he will yield to necessity, resort to the earth for his support, and practice gladly those lessons which are at present lost upon him. Then will be displayed before his eyes, the neat, well-cultivated farm, and the flocks covering the pastures. The earth will pour out her treasures in his very presence. He will imitate all he sees. The wigwam will be made to give place to the cottage, and thrift and comfort succeed to improvidence and want. Then will he and the white man be one in feeling,—one in principles,—one in friendship,—one in the enjoyment of the same happiness; and they will be seen together in the long vista of the future, brothers in the arts and conveniences of cultivated life. Then, too, will rise into her high distinction, and shine out in all her loveliness, heaven's best gift to man. No longer will woman be the drudge of her wilderness companion, and doomed to toil in abject and degrading servitude;—for the more man's faculties become improved, and the more he can analyze his relations to the things of earth, and the things of heaven, the more devotedly does he attach himself to woman, promote her comforts, and minister to her happiness.

This, doubtless, was the prospect so fondly cherished by our fathers. But, alas! what has experience brought along with it in regard to all these matters? How little of all that was hoped for, has been realized! True, as was anticipated, many of those obstacles which existed in earlier times, and which opposed, so successfully, the labors of our fathers, have disappeared; but these have been succeeded by circumstances arising out of the peculiar relations which it has been the fate of the Indian to have established between him and us, far more perishing in their effects upon him, than were those earlier difficulties with which our fathers had to contend. What these circumstances are, may be inferred from the sequel.

Shall we stop to indulge in useless lamentations over what has been done; or to arraign "the ways of Providence to man;" or question his merciful designs in peopling this land with a race such as ours?—The first would be useless, and the last impious. This country, in the plans of the Eternal, was to be the empire of freedom, and of mind. Here, in the purposes of infinite wisdom, it was determined, that science, and the arts, and religion, should flourish, and man attain, untrammelled by despotism or bigotry, the highest state of perfection and happiness, of which his nature is susceptible. All this was to be, and it has been. Nor were any of the consequences, which have attended the accomplishment of these purposes, unforeseen by Infinite Wisdom, even to those which have been so destructive in their effects upon the Indians. But it was not given to man to penetrate the mysterious purposes of the Infinite; we, therefore, resolve all this into those inscrutable dispensations, which, in the futurity, we may expect to see revealed in all their godlike forms.

> "Blind unbelief is sure to err,
> And scan his work in vain;
> God is his own interpreter,
> And he will make it plain."

But for any part we may have taken, as willing instruments in producing, or not taken, in preventing the miserable condition of the Indians, we must expect to be held accountable. Heaven, we doubt not, wills the happiness of man. Under this belief, it becomes our duty to look at the condition of the Indian, *as we see it;* and, it being one of great suffering, and degradation, seek for the best means for his relief.

Nothing, we think, can be more clear, than that there has been, and yet is, something radically, *fatally*, wrong, in the system of our relations with those people. We have seen that zealous efforts were made in times past, and with what effect, to reform them. And our own knowledge of those of later times, justifies the conclusion, that it has been a favorite design of our government, and a large portion of our citizens, to improve their destiny. That spirit animates the councils of this nation at this moment; and is more extensively felt among our citizens than at any other period. The Father of his Country was scarcely seated in the chair of state, before he fixed a kind and constant eye upon his red children. He counselled them zealously, and with a wisdom equalled only by his benevolence. These counsels, sustained by large appropriations of money to make them, if possible, effective, have been continued to this day, by every succeeding President, and by almost every Congress, varying only in some instances as to the course which, under all circumstances, it was considered best for the Indian to pursue. But the great object has been the same in all—to make better, and not worse, his condition. Those plans of improvement, however, could never have contemplated the carving out from the members of our confederacy, *against their will*, portions of their territory, on which to erect separate and independent Indian states. No such design could have been meditated; and apart from all abstract reasoning on the subject, the indications of late years may be referred to, as demonstrating that if it had been, it was not in accordance with either the genius of our institutions, or the prosperity of the Indians. And it may be assumed that whatever system shall not harmonize with the acknowledged principles of our Union, *must be defective*; and to suppose that any weaker power could withstand their opposing actions, would be adverse, not only to our conceptions of the high bearing of our system upon the hopes and the destiny of man, but to our notions of the relations of power; and, as applicable to the present question, altogether unreasonable. As well might it be assumed as a right inherent in the Senecas, and the other fragments of tribes of this state, to erect themselves into one or more sovereignties, and, under a constitution and laws of their own, exercise the corresponding attributes, and thus attempt the invasion of the sovereignty of this state, as for the same right to be argued in favor of any one, or all of the fragments of tribes, residing within the jurisdiction of the states in the south. The question is embarrassing; but the bearing of it, in any emergency in which the angry feelings may be excited, is wholly upon the Indians; hence, the constant anxiety which has manifested itself everywhere, but especially in our government, to devise some plan that should maintain the harmony of our beautiful system, and save those who, from the peculiarity of their relations, are every day liable to come into collision with it; and from the fatal consequences, to them, of such an event.

In a message of the President of the United States to Congress in 1825, may be seen the evidence of this anxiety. "Being deeply impressed," says the message, "with the opinion that the removal of the Indian tribes from the lands which they now occupy within the limits of the several States and Territories, to the country lying westward and northward thereof, within our acknowledged boundaries, is of very high importance to our Union, and may be accomplished on conditions, and in a manner to promote the interest and happiness of these tribes, the attention of the government has been *long drawn*, with *great solicitude*, to the subject." Again, "*experience* has clearly demonstrated, that in their present state, it is *impossible* to incorporate them in masses, *in any form whatever*, into our system. It has also demonstrated with equal certainty, that without a timely anticipation of, and provision against the dangers to which they are exposed, under causes which it will be difficult, if not *impossible*, to control, their *degradation* and *extermination* will be INEVITABLE !"

This is the language of humanity, dictated by wisdom and experience. It appeals to the understanding, and comes with the voice of warning to us all; but especially to those of us who profess to be friends of the Indian, and engaged to promote the welfare of his race. We are admonished to beware, and not permit a misguided philanthropy to give accelerated force to those causes which have been so long warring upon the happiness and lives of this people.

That men, and good men, should differ in their views of what ought to be done for the preservation and improvement of our Indians, is natural. We know there are men, and good men, who are opposed to the emigration of the Indians. We respect them, and their motives. They seek to save and civilize these people. We profess to aim at the accomplishment of the same end, and differ only as to the mode. We once entertained similar views of this question with them, and thought it practicable to preserve and elevate the character of our Indians, even in their present anomalous relations to the States; but it was "distance that lent this enchantment to the view;" we have since seen for ourselves, and that which before looked like a flying cloud, we found, on a near inspection, to be an impassable mountain. We believe if the Indians do not emigrate, and fly the causes, which are fixed in themselves, and which have proved so destructive in the past, they *must perish!* We might distrust our own conclusions, though derived from personal investigation, did not experience confirm them. But alas! it is the admonition of experience, more than anything else, that alarms, and urges us to employ all honorable means to persuade these hapless people to acquiesce in the policy which is proposed to them. Experience, did we say? Yes, experience.

Has it ever occurred to this assembly to reflect upon the period when this island was a wilderness? when it was the home of the Indians? when nothing was heard but the growling of the wolves and bears, the barking of foxes, and the yells of the savage, and the moaning of the winds of heaven amidst the forest, save now and then, in a moment of stillness, the twang of the Indian's bow, as he sped the arrow into some animal whose fur he needed to make him warm, or whose flesh he sought to appease his hunger? Nothing then disturbed the waters of your lordly Hudson but the winds of heaven, save when a canoe would cross its smooth bosom, and then the sounds were confined to the plash of the Indian's paddle, and the little murmur at the prow of his frail vessel. At night, who can fancy the stillness that prevailed? Then was there nothing of life here, that we call life; it was all the silence of the desert. The Indian was monarch here, and he saw no limits to his kingdom. Behold the change! And where now are the Indian and his canoe? They are gone! The one retired long ere your temples or your palaces were erected, or remained and perished under the influence of those vices which accompany the march of civilization;

the other waited not until your Hudson was put in a foam by your ships, but fell to pieces under the first undulations of your opening commerce. True, a few of the natives yet linger on your western limits, but they serve to attest the truth of what we are aiming to establish, viz: *the perishing consequences to the Indian, of a near connexion with a white population.* What are the remains of those once powerful tribes, but broken columns, mutilated fragments, of their once powerful confederacy? Look at them! Who sees any likeness in what is left to the Six Nations? Every vestige is gone! The race of the Skenandoahs is extinct! What *was* it, we ask, that destroyed the Indians of this island, and sent such a mildew, to exterminate those who yet hang upon your borders? The same causes, we answer, that have reduced the once countless bands that inhabited Maine, Massachusetts, Rhode Island, Connecticut, Pennsylvania, New Jersey, Maryland, Virginia, North and South Carolina, to a few over six thousand souls!

In Massachusetts, the great theatre of benevolence, where the missionary labors have been, both in early and later times, so unceasing; and where the spirit of kindness has never slumbered, and where the Indians, themselves, built churches and worshipped in them; and where the work of their complete reformation appeared so nearly accomplished; and where there was as much to cheer the heart of the philanthropist, as now exists in the most improved of the present day, there remain only about seven hundred and fifty souls! Penn was never suspected of cherishing unkind purposes towards the Indians, nor were his descendants; yet where are the natives of that district of country now comprehended in the state of Pennsylvania? And where are the bands of Jersey, and Delaware, and Maryland? All gone. And where the once powerful and numerous bands of Virginia? Where the descendants of Powhatan? Within the limits of that vast territory, there remain but *forty-seven* Indians! The plough, it is true, often turns up the stone axes, and arrow-points, once used by the natives, and in quantities to attest how numerous those were who once used them. These are all that remain now, to remind the traveller in Virginia, that the ground over which he rides, was once alive with an Indian population. But leave the Atlantic States, and go into the west—go to Ohio—linger among the tumuli of that great country, in which are the bones of so many thousands of the natives, and catch the echoes of the war-whoop, which resound through all the valleys; for it was but yesterday when it was sounded; and but yesterday, when the Indian exerted his power in triumph over all that country. Look for the savage bands. Go to the banks of that river that gives name to the State, and ask, where are the canoes that used to float down its tide, so filled with the painted natives. One, now and then, perhaps, may steal in silence along; and, here and there, upon the lands of their fathers, and clinging to the soil that covers their bones, you will find a few remaining;—but of all who once occupied that State, there remain, at present, but a few over two thousand. Here, then, is our experience; and, from it, we deduce the inference, that, whilst the Indians retain their present degraded relations to us, inhabiting a State, but excluded from all that is honorable in it, and even from the hope of any elevation of character and privileges in the future, he must deteriorate and go to decay; for there lives not a man, who is insensible to contempt and disgrace: and the more men become enlightened, to see the disparaging nature of the relations they bear to those around them, the more afflictive are those relations felt to be. It is important to provide different relations, if only for the one thousand three hundred Indian youths, who are at this moment enjoying the benefits of education; for to expect the Indians, circumstanced as they are, to advance and flourish as men and Christians, is to expect more of them than we should feel authorized to hope for, even of ourselves.

Under the operation of moral causes, does man rise or fall, in the scale of being? The whole mass of these, is against the Indian. Shut out from all participation in those ennobling connexions and pursuits, which give ardor to hope, and "fix the generous purpose in the glowing breast,"—why should we be surprised to find the Indian just such a being as he is? or doubt the fatal tendencies and termination of such a state of things? We confess, we tremble for the consequences, and feel, that if we are right, those who may have counselled the Indians to remain where they are, and in opposition to the kind designs of the government towards them, have assumed a tremendous responsibility!

We esteem it to be our duty on this occasion to correct an error which has obtained in regard to this business of emigration. It seems to be thought by some, that the Indians are opposed to removal; and that force is meditated to be employed to compel them to go. In regard to the disposition of *the great body* of the Indians within our States, we speak advisedly when we say, they are *anxious to remove.* The present excitement is occasioned, in great part, by the opposition of those persons, whose interest it is to keep the Indians where they are. Protection has actually been sought of the government by those who wish to better their destiny, against the threats of others, in which an *enrolment* for emigration has been forbidden on pain of death! This may be received as the real state of the case, obtained in good part by us, on personal opportunities, and from official information confirming our observation and experience. In regard to the employment of force to drive the Indians from the country they inhabit, so far from this being correct, they have been told by the Executive, in one of the documents read to you to-night, that if they choose to remain, they shall be protected in all their rights;* but they are advised to remove, for reasons relating wholly to themselves. Is there anything in this that looks like hostility to this people? There is nothing of cruelty cherished either by our government or people towards the Indians. The only point in controversy at present, is that which divides those who differ on the question of emigration. And surely this difference may be permitted without involving those of us who think the salvation of the Indians depends on a change of their relations to us, (and which cannot be realized, as we firmly believe, but on the basis of a removal,) in the charge of meditating evil, or cherishing a spirit of vindictiveness against this hapless race!

But it may be expected of us to state the terms on which we propose the removal.

It is proposed, in the first place, to give them a country, and to secure it to them by the most ample and solemn sanctions, suitable in all respects, in exchange for theirs; to pay them for all their improvements—and see them, free of cost, to their new homes—to aid them after their arrival there—and protect them;—to put over them, at once, the frame-work of a government, and to fill this up as their advancement in civilization may require it; to secure them the privilege of participating in it; to establish schools over their country, for the enlightening of the rising generation; and give them the Gospel. In fine, it is proposed to place them in a Territorial relation to us, and in all respects; and in the enjoyment of all the privileges consequent upon such a relation, civil, political and religious. Thus will they attain an elevation, to which, in their present relations, they can never aspire. And thus would new influences be created, ennobling in their tendencies, and animating in their effects. Under these, the

* Unfortunately for the honor and humanity of the nation, this "protection" was shortly after not only virtually withdrawn, but *force* was employed to compel the Indians to leave their country!

Indian would rise into the distinction to which he has always been a stranger; and live and act with reference to the corresponding honors and benefits of such a state.

We have in the United States, about three hundred thousand Indians, about seventy thousand of whom, it is proposed to advance at once, into this state of exalted privileges. The country on which it is proposed to settle these, is immediately beyond, and west of Missouri and Arkansas. It is believed to be unexceptionable in extent, and soil, and salubrity. Our information is derived from actual surveys which have been made of it.

Were the Indians present, we would address them thus:—

Brothers—We doubt not your sincere attachment to the country in which you live. Some of you believe you have a sovereign right over all within the limits designated for your occupancy. And suppose there was no dispute on this point, would you linger and die on it merely for that reason? Do you not see the degrading nature of the relation in which you stand to the whites? Do you not feel how perishing it is to you? Are you not aliens—and even worse, though living in the heart of the country? Has not this anomalous relation destroyed hundreds of thousands of your race; and unpeopled whole states of those of whom you are descended? Do you expect that you can escape a similar destruction—unless you fly from the causes which have heretofore proved so fatal? Do you not look in utter hopelessness on the destiny of your children?

Brothers—Whether is it wise in you thus to linger out a chafed, and impoverished, and disheartening existence, and die as your fathers have died, and leave the same destiny to your children; or to leave your country, and the bones of your fathers, (which cannot benefit you, stay where they are as long as you may,) and go to one where none of those perishing influences will be permitted to exist, and where upon you and your posterity shall be entailed all that is valuable in government, all that is exalted in privileges, and all that is refined in happiness?

Brothers—Be not deluded,—nor think us your enemy because we seek to advance your happiness. Listen to our voice. We have long felt for your sad condition, and mourned over it. Listen to us, and be advised. Yield up your prejudices. Try us this once. Do not distrust our object; it is your welfare, only, we seek.

But they are not present, and our voice is not heard; or if it were, the counsel it conveys, especially in the moment of excitement that prevails now, might be lost. But it is pleasant to know that we have done our duty. This consciousness, gentlemen, must, on an occasion like the present, be extremely grateful to you. We have witnessed your solicitude to save these hapless people; we have seen, and do highly appreciate your labors. We know your motive, and pronounce it pure. Like men zealous for the attainment of a great object, you have risen above the influences of political and sectarian feelings, and appreciating the importance of the work to be accomplished, and seeing it involves human happiness, and human life, you have given the invitation to all to unite with you in saving these people. You see, and truly, that the experiments of the past will not do to be further relied on, and you have adopted the only remaining alternative. You have thought well of this matter, and examined it with your accustomed energies of thought and action. Your conclusion is, that unless the Indians can be prevailed on to remove, and place themselves under the redeeming influences which you are ready, in their behalf, to see faithfully applied, *they must perish.* This conclusion has brought you together in the ardor of friendship, and with the hope of Christians; and you have associated, and now stand pledged to the world, and to heaven, to exert your best energies for the "emigration, preservation, and improvement of the Indians." We wish you, in a work so noble, and over which mercy will delight to preside, and on which you may with so much confidence implore the blessings of heaven, the most abundant success.

To Colonel McKenney.

NEW YORK, August, 1829.

DEAR SIR—Permit me, through you, to communicate to the distinguished individuals therein named, the following resolution of the Indian Board, &c., passed at their last meeting, viz:

"*Resolved*, That the thanks of this Board be transmitted to the President of the United States, and the Secretary of War, for their prompt compliance with the wishes of this Association, as conveyed in a letter addressed to the department, by the Rev. Eli Baldwin, soliciting the aid of Colonel McKenney, in the business which has engaged its attentions."

Allow me further to address to you personally, the following resolution, passed at the same time:

"*Resolved*, That the thanks of this Board be presented to Colonel McKenney, for his very eloquent address, delivered on the evening of the 12th instant; and that a copy of the same be requested for publication."

And to assure you of my hearty concurrence in the expression of gratitude, and in the request,

I am, dear Sir, very respectfully, yours,

ELI BALDWIN, Cor. Sec'y.

To the Rev. Eli Baldwin, Corresponding Secretary, &c.

NEW YORK, August 17, 1829.

DEAR SIR—I have received your letter of this date, embodying two resolutions of your Board. I will take great pleasure in conveying the first to the President and Secretary of War, who will, I am sure, duly appreciate the expression of the thanks of the Board in the matter referred to.

I am gratified that the Address delivered by me, in pursuance of a resolution of your Board, is acceptable to you; and highly appreciate the thanks of the Board, as conveyed in the second resolution of the same. The request for a copy for publication is complied with.

With my best wishes for the success of your Board in the noble object which engages its attentions, and for your individual prosperity and happiness,

I am, dear Sir, yours, most truly,

THOMAS L. MCKENNEY.

To the President of the United States.

NEW YORK, August 14, 1829.

SIR—The condition of the Indian tribes, and their present relations to the general and state governments, have occasioned, among the friends of these interesting people, feelings of deep anxiety; and awakened a disposition, among various citizens of the Union, to harmonize, if possible, the present discordant relations, and in a way that shall secure to the Indians peace and prosperity for the future. Participating in this common feeling, an Association of citizens of various denominations has been formed, with the view of contributing to ends so important.

The principles on which this Association proposes to act and be governed, are disclosed in the accompanying documents, which embrace the preliminary proceedings, the origin of the Association, and the Constitution of the Board.

By a resolution therein, you will perceive that it is made my duty to communicate for the information, and with a view to obtain the approbation and co-operation of the Executive, a copy of those proceedings to you.

The Board looks with confidence to the Executive of the United States for such patronage as it may have the power to bestow; and with deep anxiety to the Congress, to whom it doubts not the Executive will submit the subject for those ways and means upon which reliance is placed for the promotion of its benevolent intentions.

I am, most respectfully, your obedient servant,

ELI BALDWIN,

Corresponding Secretary of the Indian Board, &c.

To the Rev. Eli Baldwin.

RIP RAPS, VIRGINIA, August 25, 1829.

SIR—Last evening, by the steamboat Norfolk, from Baltimore, your letter to the President was received at this place, with a transcript of the Constitution, relating to the Indians, recently adopted at New York by your Convention. With the course pursued at your meeting, the President is much gratified, and desires me so to declare to you. He cannot but appreciate highly the views taken by you of a course of policy, which justice to principles recognized, and humanity towards our Indian brethren, constrained him, as a matter of conceived duty, to adopt. He regrets that so many inaccuracies, both as to object and motive, should have found a place in the public journals of the day, evidently misrepresenting, and calculated to produce incorrect impressions. The great consolation entertained by him, though, is, that time will prove that his only end, and object, and purpose, is to do full and impartial justice, to the extent that his official discharge of duty will sanction.

I BEG LEAVE TO ASSURE YOU, THAT NOTHING OF A COMPULSORY COURSE, TO EFFECT THE REMOVAL OF THE UNFORTUNATE RACE OF PEOPLE, EVER HAS BEEN THOUGHT OF BY THE PRESIDENT, ALTHOUGH IT HAS BEEN ASSERTED. The considerations which controlled, in the course pursued, were such, as he really and in fact believed were required, as well by a regard for the just rights which the State of Georgia was authorized to assert, as from a conscientious conviction, that by it, humanity towards the Indians would more effectually be subserved. Of this they have been assured, and in that assurance, no other disposition was had than to explain fully to them, and the country, the actual ground on which it was believed they were rightfully entitled to stand.

How can the United States government contest with Georgia the authority to regulate her own internal affairs? If the doctrine everywhere maintained be true, that a State is sovereign, so far as by the constitution adopted it has not been parted with to the general government, then must it follow as matter of certainty, that within the limits of a State there can be none other, than her own sovereign power, that can claim to exercise the functions of government. It is certainly contrary to every idea entertained of an independent government, for any other to assert adverse dominion and authority, within her jurisdictional limits: they are things that cannot exist together.

Between the State of Georgia and the Indian tribes within her limits, no compact or agreement was ever entered into;—who then is to yield, for it is certain, in the ordinary course of exercised authority, that one or the other must? The answer heretofore presented from the government, and which you, by your adoption, have sanctioned as correct, is the only one that can be offered. Georgia, by her acknowledged confederative authority, may legally and rightfully govern and control throughout her own limits, or else our knowledge of the science and principle of government, as they relate to our own forms, are wrong, and have been wholly misunderstood.

Sympathy indulged is a noble and generous trait of character; but should never assume a form calculated to outrage settled principles, or to produce in the end a greater evil than it would remedy. Admit it were in the disposition of the government at Washington to hold a course and language different from that they have heretofore employed; and to encourage the Indians to the belief that rightfully they may remain and exercise civil government in despite of Georgia? do those who are the advocates of such a course, and consider it reconcilable to propriety, dream of the consequences to which it would lead, or consider after what manner so strange an idea could be put in practice? Have they looked to the State of Georgia, conscious in the rectitude of her own construction of right, demanding of the United States their constitutional authority to interfere, and appealing to the States to sustain her against encroachments, which, if submitted to, might, in the end, prove destructive of the whole? If nothing else can be traced through such an appeal and in such an issue, I think the good and the humane may at least perceive that in it peril is to be discerned, and that the weak and undisciplined Indians, in such a contest, would be so utterly destroyed, that the places which now know them, would presently know them no more.

From the conversations had with the President, recently and formerly, on the subject of the Indians, I am satisfied that no man in the country entertains towards them better feelings, or has a stronger desire to see them placed in that condition which may conduce to their advancement and happiness. But to encourage them to the idea, that within the confines of a State, they may exercise all the forms and requisites of a government, fashioned to their own condition and necessities, he does not consider can be advantageous to them, or that the exercise of such a right can properly be conceded. What would the authorities of the State of New York say to an attempt, on the part of the *Six Nations*, to establish, within her limits, a separate and independent government; and yet their authority, to do so, would be as undeniable as that of the Creeks, or Cherokees, within the territory of Georgia, or Alabama? Would they agree, that the Indian law of retaliation on the next of kin, should be enforced for the accidental killing of one of their tribe? Or, that nothing of trade and commerce, by her citizens, should take place within their limits, except in conformity to the provisions of their muncipal code? Would they assent to have their citizens rendered liable to be arraigned at the bar of an Indian court of justice, and to have meted out to them the penalties of their criminal code? It is obvious, that no State of this Union would grant such authority. Concede, however, that these Indians are entitled to be considered sovereign within their own limits, and you concede everything else as matter of consequence. Admit the principle, and all is admitted—and what then? The sword, the alone arbiter in any community, where questions of adverse sovereignty and power are to be settled, would, in the end, have to be appealed to: and, when this shall be the case, the humblest prophet in our land cannot but discern what will be the *finale* of the contest. Is it not preferable, and does not their own peace, and quiet, and happiness, demand, that they should surrender, at once, such visionary opinions, and, by retiring beyond the Mississippi, place themselves where every conflict, as to State authority, will cease; and where the most enlarged and generous efforts, by the government, will be made to improve their minds, better their condition, and aid them in their efforts of self-government? For your efforts, and those associated with you in convention, furthering this liberal and only practical scheme, the time will come when all good and generous men will thank you.

In conclusion, the President desires me to thank you for the communication made to him, and to offer you an assurance, that every legitimate power of his, will be freely bestowed to further and assist the laudable and humane course which your convention has adopted.

I have the honor to be, with great respect,

Your obedient servant,

JOHN H. EATON.

This item of history may serve to indicate the spirit that was at that time alive, and active, for the enlightening and preservation of the Indians; also the basis upon which it proposed to operate. It looked to a rescue of this hapless people, by the agency of pacific and friendly influences, from the unhappy and perishing condition in which their residence within the jurisdiction of States had placed them. Those who had been moved to undertake, and carry out this work of mercy, held high rank as men of influence, and Christians—and the undertaking was wholly free from anything personal, sectarian, or selfish. It is only necessary for the reader to look over the names of members who compose this society, from that pure patriot and philanthropist, Hon. S. Van Rensselaer, the president, to its secretary and treasurer, to see proof positive, that the principles of the society were not only sound, but that there was intelligence and influence, and a power over the necessary means, sufficient to carry out their kind designs, provided the government would co-operate in the same spirit, and with a view to the same ends. And that pledge was given, and reiterated in Mr. Secretary Eaton's letter to the corresponding secretary, as above, in which the assurance was unequivocally given, that "nothing of a compulsory course, to effect the removal of this unfortunate race of people, has ever been thought of by the President."

There would seem, therefore, to have been perfect harmony between the Executive, and the objects of this Board, and this is declared by the Secretary, in the letter aforesaid, in express terms. "With the course pursued at your meeting," says the Secretary, "the President is much gratified." As for myself, I never contemplated any act touching the emigration of the Indians, that should not have for its object, first, their voluntary acquiescence; and, second, the immediate adoption of the appropriate measures for their improvement and happiness, and positive security in all the future, against a recurrence of the evils from which I sought to separate them.

The reader may feel anxious to know what were the fruits of the association, organized for these holy objects, and under such high auspices. I answer, *there were none!* So far as my knowledge extends, there went forth from that Board not a single influence towards the accomplishment of the great ends of its creation. It had being given to it, and life, but it was struck by paralysis! I never heard the cause for this assigned, either by the Board, or by any member thereof, but was at no loss myself to account for it. It was in the abandonment by the administration, not long after the organization of the Board, of the fundamental principle of its existence, viz: the operation, upon the Indians, by a policy that excluded everything like compulsion—both direct and indirect.

The fourth article of the constitution of the Board bound it "to co-operate with the federal government of the United States, in its operations on Indian affairs; and at no time to contravene its laws." The letter of the Secretary of War, Major Eaton, of the 18th April, 1829, to the delegation of Cherokees, then in Washington, was before the committee *when the constitution of the Board was adopted*, and was read to the assembly of the people, when it was ratified. In that letter he says, "An interference to the extent of affording you *protection*, and the *occupancy of your soil*, is what is demanded of *the justice* of this country, and *will not be withheld*." This was the guarantee, as well to the Cherokees as to the Board, that the quiet, at least, of this people would be preserved, during which, it was contemplated to operate by judicious and enlightened agencies, in convincing the Indians that it was better for their present and future happiness, to make terms, and accept a home where all things would be peaceful, and where the Indian Board was pledged, as well as the government, to follow them with all the means necessary for their advancement, and security, and happiness. Upon this branch of the question, the same letter that promised "protection," and "the occupancy of their soil," contained the following appeal to the Indians: "It must be obvious to you, and the President has instructed me to bring it to your candid and serious consideration, that to continue where you are, within the territorial limits of an independent State, can promise you nothing but INTERRUPTION and DISQUIETUDE. Beyond the Mississippi, your prospects will be different. There you will find *no* conflicting interests. The United States' power and sovereignty, uncontrolled by the high authority of State jurisdiction, and resting on its own energies, will be able to say to you, in the language of *your own nation,—the soil shall be yours while the trees grow, or the streams run.*"

These two quotations from the letter of the Secretary of War contained all of what the Cherokees, and other Indians similarly situated, had to hope for. Under the first, while in a state of "*protection*," though they should have nothing, under that panoply, but "INTERRUPTION and DISQUIETUDE" where they were, the Board saw it could operate; and employing this very state of "*disquietude and interruption*" as an argument, convince these harrassed people that it would be indeed better for them to escape from these evils, to where "the United States' power and sovereignty, uncontrolled by the high authority of State jurisdiction," could be exercised for their permanent welfare; and where, as was held out in another part of the same letter, "the government of the United States will be able to exercise over them a paternal and superintending care, to happier advantage; to stay encroachments, and preserve them in peace and amity with each other; while, with the aid of schools, a hope may be indulged, that ere long, industry and refinement will take the place of those wandering habits now so peculiar to the Indian character, the tendency of which is to impede them in their march to civilization."

The moment it became manifest that "*protection*" was *not* to be extended to them, but that a system of encroachments upon their lands, and upon their vested rights, would be tolerated, even to the driving from their own home the wife and children of the Cherokee chief, who were forced to build a shelter with branches of trees, in the woods; and on his return to it, (the Georgia guard, as it was called, yet holding possession,) the chief himself was refused corn from his own crib, to feed his own horse, and food from his own larder, to feed himself, unless he should pay for both;—I say, the moment it became manifest that elements of this oppressive sort were to be employed by those who sought to possess themselves of the Indians' domain, and that the general government was prepared to allow them, storm-like, to beat upon this harrassed people—the ground on which the Board had rested their hope, gave way, and with it, all their plans and purposes. It being an article in its constitution "to co-operate with the federal government of the United States in its operation on Indian affairs, &c.," if the Board should move at all, it must have been in concert with this oppression, this literal war upon the rights and peace of the Cherokees; and not having been organized for any *such* purpose, there was no alternative left, but to stand still, and not operate at all.

If the foregoing, or something like them, were not the reasons why the Indian Board of New York never advanced a step after its formation, towards carrying out the humane object of its creaton, then I know not what the reasons were. I had been cut off from all official relations with the government, by command of President Jackson, before those outbreaks had reached the height of their enormity upon the peace and happiness, and rights of the Cherokees; and with that severance, fell my official relations and intercourse with this Board.

CHAPTER XI.

ABOMINABLE ABUSE OF POWER IN OUR RELATIONS WITH THE INDIANS.

Protection guarantied by treaty to the Indians—Some extracts from these treaties—How interpreted by Mr. Calhoun—Trampled upon by General Jackson—A Circular Address to the Indians—A very essential modification—A thrust at the Cherokees—Newspaper comments—Dr. Randolph in the fidgets—Leave of absence—Dismissed from office—Charges of defalcation—Four years persecution—Mr. Berrien's influence in the treatment of the Cherokees—The treaty (?) of New Euchota—Repudiated by the Cherokees—Force to be employed—General Scott—Ridge's apology for the New Euchota treaty—Formation of a new government west of the Mississippi—The Ridges and Boudinot killed—Refusal to recognize the Cherokee delegation at Washington—My interview with Mr. Poinsett—A new treaty proposed—Mr. Van Buren's objections—A diplomatic way of getting round them—A plan proposed to bring the Seminole war to a close—More diplomacy, ending in treachery—Vindication of John Ross—Further developments of the injustice done to the Cherokees—The treaty of Payne's Landing—Jackson's "talk"—Outrages upon the Florida Indians—Indian talk—Micanopy—Jumper—Osceola—The mad policy which provoked the Florida war.

That all encroachments upon the lands not ceded by the Indians to the United States, and all trespasses, were forbidden by the treaty, and that the authority and power of the United States were solemnly pledged to protect the Cherokees from intrusions and trespasses, &c., the treaties with that tribe, as well as others, make manifest.

The fifth article of the treaty of Washington, of the 27th of February, 1819, between John C. Calhoun, on the part of the United States, and a delegation of chiefs and head men of the Cherokee nation, duly authorized and empowered by said nation, contains this provision:—"And all white people who *have* intruded, or *may hereafter* in-

PANIC PRODUCED BY THUNDER AND LIGHTNING.

See page 56, vol. 2.

trude on the lands reserved for the Cherokees, *shall be removed by the United States*, and proceeded against, according to the provisions of the act passed thirtieth of March, eighteen hundred and two, entitled an act to regulate trade and intercourse with the Indian tribes, and to preserve peace on the frontiers."

Well, what are the provisions of that act? There are several articles all binding upon the United States to protect the Indians, and under almost every variety of form in which these rights could be invaded.

The fifth article, however, contains enough of both obligation and power, for the full illustration of the Indian's rights and claims, and of the government's duty, in regard to them. It reads thus:—"*And be it further enacted*, That if any such citizen, or other person, shall make a settlement on *any* lands belonging, or secured, or granted, by treaty with the *United States*, to any Indian tribe, or shall *survey*, or *attempt* to survey such lands, *or designate any of the boundaries, by marking trees, or otherwise*, such offender shall forfeit a sum not exceeding one thousand dollars, and suffer imprisonment, not exceeding twelve months. And it shall, moreover, be lawful for the President of the United States to take such measures, *and to employ such military force*, as he may judge necessary, to remove from lands belonging or secured by treaty, as aforesaid, to any Indian tribe, any such citizen, or other person, who *has* made, or shall *hereafter* make, or *attempt* to make, a settlement thereon."

This act passed through all the forms of law, and was approved by Thomas Jefferson. So far as my experience went, or my knowledge, it was, from its passage till several months after General Jackson's accession to the presidency, regarded as *the law of the land*, and had been enforced, in good faith, by the government, as such.

One example, out of many, occurs to me. Trespassers had encroached on the Cherokee lands, put up cabins, and planted corn. Complaints were made by the Cherokees, to their agent. The agent proceeded, as was the custom, to drive them off. They resisted. He reported the case to me, and I to the then Secretary of War, Mr. Calhoun, who, forthwith, under the binding obligations of the treaty of 1819, and of the sanction of this law of 1802, ordered Captain Turk, then stationed somewhere in that quarter, to march with a competent force to the district that had been encroached upon, and order the intruders off; if they refused to go, to cut down their corn and demolish their cabins; if they resisted, to employ force. They did resist—a battle was fought, in which some one or more of the trespassers were killed. These intruders, being citizens of Georgia, the authorities of that State arrested Captain Turk for murder. The case was tried in a Georgia Court and by a Georgia jury, and he was acquitted. Thus were *the Indians* treated with good faith, and *the law vindicated.*

But this law was destined, at last, though unrepealed, to become a dead letter! The solemn compacts with the Indians, guaranteeing to them "protection," were treated as things obsolete, or regarded as mockeries. In the face, and in violation of the provisions of the one, and of the enactments of the other, surveyors were permitted to penetrate the Indian territory, roam over it, lay it off into counties, and to proceed, in all things, for its settlement, as though no Indians occupied it, and no laws existed, demanding the interference of the government to prevent it! In vain did the Indians implore the government to protect them; in vain did they call the attention of the Executive to the provisions of treaties, and to the pledges of the law. It was when these outrages first began to show themselves, and thinking President Jackson could not be aware of their existence, that I called on him, and referred to them, and also to the provisions of laws and treaties that guarantied to the Indians a freedom from such trespasses. His answer was, "*Sir, the sovereignty of the States must be preserved*," concluding with a termination so solemn, and the whole being spoken in a manner so emphatic, as to satisfy me that he had concluded to permit Georgia, and the other States in which the Indians were included, to take their own way in their plans, to harrass, persecute, and force out their Indian population.

Finally, General Jackson was to leave for the Hermitage, accompanied by the Secretary of War, Major Eaton,—the latter on his way to consummate, under the treaty form, the conventional arrangements I had established in 1827, with the Chickasaw and Choctaw Indians. They had not left the President's mansion more than an hour, when Dr. Randolph, chief clerk of the War Department, and who was brother-in-law of Major Eaton, and who had been left acting Secretary of War, came to my room, saying—"Colonel, the President and Secretary of War wanted me to see you, and request you to prepare a circular address to the Indians." What is the nature of the address, I asked; and to what Indians is it to be sent? "Why," he answered, "the General said you would know all about it." This is the first I have heard of this circular, Doctor, and how am I to prepare it? "Oh, that is nothing," he replied, "you have the business at your fingers' ends, and must know what he means." He retired. I wrote a circular of general import, but containing nothing very particular or very important, and taking it to the acting Secretary of War, asked if that was what the Secretary and President wanted? "*The very thing*," he answered.

I soon discovered that Doctor Randolph's position, as acting Secretary of War, was only nominal, and that there was a real, acting secretary at hand; for I had not been back to my chair ten minutes, when Frank, the colored messenger of the War Department, who deserves to have been born white, came to my room, saying, with his always bland and obliging manner, "Colonel, Judge Berrien is in the secretary's room, and desires to see you." (Judge

Berrien was then Attorney General.) I reported myself, when the judge, holding the circular in his hand, that I had awhile before taken to Doctor Randolph, said to me, "Colonel, do you not know that this—(holding the circular up to me)—is not what the President wants?" I know no more of the matter, I replied, than what Doctor Randolph has communicated to me. He brought me the order from the Secretary of War and President, and says, *it is exactly what they want.* He then put the circular upon the table before him, and added a paragraph, saying, "*This* is what is wanted." I saw at a glance, what was its object and aim; and that was, so far as that could go to accomplish it, to break up the Cherokee government, and resolve it into its former and scattered elements.

Many years before, and at the instance, if I mistake not, of Colonel Meigs, it was agreed by the then President, that the amount paid for rations to feed the Indians when they were called together to receive, each, his portion of the annuity, should, henceforth, be paid in money, to the authorities of the Cherokee nation; and that they would account to the nation for the same. The sum, I think, was about twelve hundred dollars; I write from memory. This amount had been remitted annually, for many years, with their annuities; and at last, when the Cherokees organized themselves into a regular government, with all the usual offices and their incumbents, this sum was put into their treasury, as part of the nation's rights.

An order forbidding this money to be any longer thus paid to the authorities of the nation, was an order which struck directly at their system of government, and looked to a return to the old system of the distribution of the amount among the Indians, reducing them, so far as this item went, to their original elements. *And this was the object of this circular.* As in the business of sapping and mining, to carry a fortress in war, a first entrenchment, unseen, if possible, by the enemy, must be made, so I saw in this, *a first step*, intended to be well covered, was taken, towards the overthrow of the Cherokee government, and a consequent breaking up of the power of this people.

I took the circular, with Judge Berrien's addition, to my copying clerk, Mr. Miller, and directed him to omit the customary heading of all writings emanating from my office—which was "*War Department, Office of Indian Affairs*"—and head it, WAR DEPARTMENT, only. The copy being made, I took it to Doctor Randolph, and told him, as this was an emanation direct from the War Department, it ought to be signed by him, as acting Secretary of War. "Certainly," said the doctor, when he signed it, and it was sent off.

By and by, the newspapers got hold of this move upon the Cherokee government, and spoke of it as unbecoming a government like ours, thus to vex and war upon a feeble people who were just emerging from barbarism into civilization, and from anarchy to a system of government, &c.; and some not very complimentary remarks were made upon the acting Secretary of War, for his manifesto. These assaults having reached the doctor, he came into my office, quite excited, and asked, "Why, sir, did you make me sign that paper?" What paper? "That circular to the Cherokees." I referred its signature to you, I answered, because it emanated from the department proper, and not from me. I did not deem it proper for me to sign it, nor do I now. If it has worked ill, I had no agency in it. The doctor continued some time to be annoyed by the newspapers, and did not seem, afterwards, to regard me with the usual civilities that had heretofore marked his intercourse with me.

I had at that time on hand the large work on the History, &c., of the North American Indians. It was in the hands of Samuel F. Bradford, of Philadelphia, as publisher. I needed rest from my labors, and withal I was not well. I requested and obtained leave of absence, to go and look after this work, and for relaxation, and to better my health—and extended my journey to New York. On my return to Philadelphia, and on my way from the wharf to the hotel, I stopped at the post-office, and took from it a letter from Doctor Randolph, informing me that, from and after the first day of October next ensuing, my services in the Indian Department would not be required. Returning to Washington, I inquired of him what the grounds of my dismissal were. "Why, sir," was his reply, "everybody knows your qualifications for the place, but General Jackson has been long satisfied that you are not in harmony with him, in his views in regard to the Indians." And thus closed my connexion with the government.

It was, immediately upon my dismissal, thrown out, through the party press, that my accounts were not settled; and the impression became general, that I was a defaulter. It is true, those very accounts to which I have referred, as having been adjusted, and "*approved*" by the Secretary of War, had not been carried to my credit, but remained in the hands of the auditor. I urged, entreated, prayed that they might be acted upon, but in vain! At last, and after I had been made to endure the persecution of the dominant press and party, and subjected to a withdrawal of confidence in the public mind, so far as that mind was affected by the implication of my being a defaulter, and *four years* had been allowed, that is, from 1829 to 1833, to pass on, leaving me thus exposed, *those very accounts* were passed upon, and allowed, without the variation of a cent, or any exception whatever taken to their correctness, not by the party, or by any officer, with which, or with whom, I was in political affinity, but by General Jackson's personal friend and auditor, William B. Lewis. The following is the copy of his letter to me, announcing the settlement:—

"Treasury Department,
Second Auditor's office, 16th November, 1833.

"Sir: Communication from the Comptroller of the Treasury, having been made to this office, on the 1st inst., that your accounts as late Superintendent of Indian Trade, had been closed on the books of that department, I hereby inform you that the balance of four hundred and fifty-five dollars, and thirty cents, arising out of an account presented by you, and sanctioned by J. Barbour, Secretary of War, for expenses incurred, presents made, and services rendered, under instructions from the War Department, of 28th March, and 10th April, 1827, on a tour among the Cherokee, Choctaw, and Creek Indians, in 1827, has been admitted. The above balance has been paid agreeable to your directions, viz: one hundred and thirty-eight dollars, and fifty-nine cents, to the American Fur Company, and three hundred and sixteen dollars, and seventy-one cents, to Major Trueman Cross. This transaction closes your accounts on the books of this office.

"I am, with respect, your obedient servant,

William B. Lewis."

I have referred only to the *indirect* assault upon the Cherokees, excepting the direct attack upon their system of government, through their treasury, in the paper written by Judge Berrien. If I am not mistaken, this distinguished gentleman published, on leaving General Jackson's cabinet, that his object in coming into that cabinet had reference, mainly, if not wholly, to that Indian subject. It is not therefore impossible, he being Attorney General, that his counsels in regard to the position the Executive ought to assume, as between the claims of sovereignty on the part of Georgia, and the treaties and laws which went to protect the Indians from its action upon them, were what influenced General Jackson to take the course he did. I am far from saying this *was* the case.

These distressing intrusions continued to afflict the Cherokees, who, in their midst, maintained their position in the best manner they could, down to the date of the instrument got up at New Euchota, and miscalled a treaty; when a stronger force was employed, and more direct movements were made, to expel them from their country. An instrument was found, in the person of *the Rev.* Mr.

Schermerhorn, for the making of a final move upon the Cherokees. This gentleman having secured the assent of Major Ridge, his son John, and Elias Boudinot, all men of influence among the Cherokees, called a council to meet at New Euchota, for the purpose of making a treaty for the final surrender of all their country remaining to them, on the east of the Mississippi. The instrument bearing the title of treaty, and purporting to be made with the Cherokee nation, was signed by the two Ridges and Boudinot, and a few obscure individuals, and sent on to Washington *as the act of the nation!* And in despite of the almost unanimous voice of the Cherokee population, declaring the act done at New Euchota, to *be a fraud*, and that it was the work of a few individuals only, and not of the nation, it was received, accepted, acted upon, and ratified!

The time limited in this mock treaty of New Euchota, for the removal of the Cherokees, approaching, and a steady determination having been expressed by them, that they would not regard the obligations alleged by the authorities of Washington to be imposed upon them by it, General Scott was ordered to move upon, and by force of arms, drive them from the country. At one time the Cherokees had well-nigh resolved to stand their ground, preferring, rather than have the provisions of an instrument, such as that framed at New Euchota, made binding on them, or to accept the provisions of any compact so base and so fraudulent as that, to bare their bosoms, and receive unresistingly the bayonet and the ball, and mingle their remains with the dust of their country, and the ashes of their ancestors. This purpose was, I know, seriously meditated by many.

The command to remove the Cherokees, fortunately for all parties, was referred to hands that moved in harmony with just dealings, and under the impulses of a humane heart. General Scott, appreciating his position, and the condition of the Cherokees, employed, and successfully, his influence to bring about a state of feeling, on their part, that should, at the same time, harmonize with the policy of the Executive in regard to their removal, and their own sense of their own rights; when such a compact was entered into, combining both, as led to the voluntary emigration, so far as the nature of the case would admit of the acquiescence of this long harrassed and suffering people. But their difficulties were destined to assume a new aspect; and those grew out of the relations which the party who signed the instrument at New Euchota, and the party who opposed it, might naturally be supposed to bear towards each other.

Major Ridge, and his son John, being on a visit to Philadelphia, spent some time with me, when the subject of their agency in consummating the New Euchota treaty, so called, was discussed. Major Ridge, in reply to my reference to the peril in which he had, in my opinion, placed himself, said, "*I expect to die for it.*" The treaty, he admitted, was not made by the nation, but in opposition to its known and expressed will. He admitted, also, that the only three names of influence attached to it, were his own, his son's, and Boudinot's, and that the remainder would have signed with the same freedom a paper of any other sort. Why, I asked, major, if you expected your life to pay the forfeit, did you take that step? "I thought my people," was his answer, "were very unhappy where they were. Georgia was pressing hard upon them; the government at Washington would do nothing to relieve them." He saw things getting worse and worse, and he thought if he could, any how, bring about *a removal* of his people, it would be for their present and future good; and that he was old, and his life would be of but little loss, compared with such gain to them. And yet, there is no reason for believing otherwise than that, when the nation agreed to remove under the arrangement made with General Scott, the enmity against the two Ridges, and Boudinot, had in a great degree ceased, if not altogether. 'Tis true, the wrong which had been done, was never esteemed to be the less deep or lasting; but if the purpose to avenge it in the mode common to these people, for such an offence, had ever been formed, it had been wholly abandoned.

The emigration being over, and the eastern portion of the Cherokees, (such as survived the Exodus, there having died in their passage, something like two thousand,) being now joined with their brethren who had preceded them under the treaties of 1817 and 1819, they called *a general council* of the whole nation, for the purpose of forming a government, and perfecting that which had been commenced on the east of the Mississippi. The council met, the Ridges and Boudinot forming part, when, to the surprise of the entire body of the late emigrants, except the party in the interest of the Ridges and Boudinot, the right of government was claimed to be *in the old emigrants*—who numbered about one-third of the whole—the Ridges and Boudinot taking the lead in this new opposition. This it was, that rekindled the fires of the previous enmity, which resulted in the killing of the two Ridges and Boudinot.

The federal Executive having taken sides with the Ridge or treaty party, when the Cherokee nation deputed its delegation to represent it at Washington, President Van Buren and his Secretary of War refused to receive John Ross and his accredited associates, in their capacity as representatives! Moreover, official communications, emanating from the officer in charge of the Indian Department, openly implicated Ross, the chief of the Cherokee nation, as accessory to the murder of the Ridges and Boudinot!!! Being in Washington during this state of things, Mr. Poinsett being Secretary of War, I called on this functionary. I had long known him personally, and knew him to be a gentleman, a man of talents, and, as I believed, sincerely devoted to the cause of justice. If he had not confided, under the honest impulses of his own heart, too much in others, for reports of facts and details, in this controversy, his decisions, I doubt not, would have been different, at least on several points, from what they were. I took the liberty of referring to the situation of the delegation of Cherokees then in Washington—to the notorious fact that they had been deputed by the Cherokee nation, to represent it at Washington—and yet, there they were, *under the ban*—having been refused to be recognized in their official capacity—literal wanderers! I referred to his having, as I had been informed, deputed Mr. Mason, the same who had been with him as Secretary of Legation, in Mexico, to the Cherokee country, to ascertain the relative numbers of the two parties, whose report, as I had been informed, was, in substance, that the Ridge party was merely a thing in name, and that the Ross party was literally *the nation*. Under such circumstances, I ventured to express the hope that the delegation then in Washington, headed by the chief, Ross, might be received; further stating, that, in my opinion, the certain way to harmonize all the distractions that had grown out of the New Euchota treaty, would be to annul it, and make a new one. There was precedent for it, I proceeded to state, in the treaty of Washington, of the 24th January, 1826, made with the Creeks. McIntosh had sold the country of the Creeks, at the Indian Springs, against the law and the will of the nation; for which he was summarily shot. Meantime, the treaty had been protested against, but was, by some haste in getting it through the Senate, ratified by that body, and approved by the President. The Creeks sent a deputation to Washington, who peremptorily refused, not only to acknowledge the validity or binding force of the treaty of the Indian Springs, made by McIntosh and his party, but to enter upon any negotiations for a new one, till, as they phrased it, "*the head of that treaty was cut off.*" In my interview with the delegation, I ascertained that, this condition being agreed to, they were not only prepared to make a new treaty, but such a one as I knew would be acceptable to the government—when the condition was agreed to, and, as a reference to the treaty of Washington will show, complied with, in the first article, in these words: "Article 1. *The treaty concluded at the Indian Springs, on the twelfth day of February, one thousand eight hundred and twenty-five, between commissioners on the part of the United States, and the said Creek nation of Indians, and ratified by the United States on the seventh day of March, one thousand eight hundred and twenty-five, is hereby declared to be null and void, to every intent and purpose whatsoever; and every right and claim arising from the same, is hereby cancelled and surrendered.*"

That, sir, I continued, is the precedent, and the cases are, in almost all respects, precisely similar. To which Mr. Poinsett replied, "*Colonel McKenney, Mr. Van Buren will never consent to undo anything that General Jackson has done.*"

Then, sir, that being the case, I propose another method. Make a treaty with this delegation, embracing, *without any reference to the New Euchota treaty*, such of its provisions as may be acceptable to both the parties to it, including all other matters which may be deemed important, and leave the offensive treaty to stand as a dead letter. "That," he answered, "might, possibly, be done." He then consented to receive the delegation, as such, and did so; I having, after a little further conversation, gone after them, and accompanied them to the War Department, giving the usual introduction. Mr. Poinsett accompanied them to the President's, who, after the usual ceremonies, (and which, as I learned from the delegation afterwards, were quite courteous,) said, "Whatever arrangements the Secretary of War might make with them, would be agreeable to him."

The further conversation which I had with Mr. Poinsett, had relation to the Seminole war, and the readiest way to bring it to a close. That way, I gave it as my belief, was, to interest the chief of the Cherokees, John Ross, in the matter, and procure his co-operation. I said, I was sure, if asked to do so, he would depute a delegation from his nation, of intelligent and prudent men, who, going as pacificators, would, in my opinion, secure a peace. "But to ask this of Ross," said Mr. Poinsett, "would be like acknowledging that the United States was not competent to subdue these Seminoles." Well, sir, I said, so far, they have not been, and the world knows it; and my opinion is, the conclusion of that war is yet a great way off—unless other means are resorted to, than mere force. To obviate your objection, then, suppose Ross shall *ask permission* to interfere in the way proposed—how then? "That would alter the case," replied the secretary.

I made known all this to Ross, who came very cheerfully into the measure, saying, it would afford him great pleasure to assist in restoring peace between the United States and the Seminoles. The result was, an understanding between the secretary and Ross, upon this subject; the appointment by Ross, of several of his most intelligent and prudent men; (the estimable and pious Jesse Bushyhead, afterwards judge of the Cherokee nation, being one,) their going among the Seminoles, and obtaining the consent of the chiefs to make a peace, (with the exception of Sam Jones, who said Micanopy was his chief, whatever he should do he would agree to,) the bringing these chiefs in to the American camp, for the purpose of making a treaty of peace; and in these chiefs being captured, and made prisoners of war of!

The effect upon the Cherokee mediators, of this proceeding, was, to expose them to the resentment of the Seminoles, and to their vengeance, *as traitors*. They all, however, reached their homes in safety, though not without enduring many hardships.

Meantime, Ross was, by the countenance which the Executive had given to the Ridge party—but more to the open charge that he had been accessory to the murder of the Ridges and Boudinot—exposed to the feelings which all civilized men entertain towards a murderer; and to the open or secret vengeance of those who were of the Ridge party; *and he stands thus exposed to this hour!* I have diligently examined the whole of this subject; and here make the record, that *John Ross, principal chief of the Cherokee nation, had no more agency, directly or indirectly, in procuring the death of the Ridges and Boudinot, than I had. Moreover, that if he had suspected the existence of any such purpose, on the part of any of his people, he would have put a stop to it.* No man deplored the tragedy more than he did. Great injustice has been done this intelligent, efficient, and excellent man.

There is, perhaps, no man living who is better acquainted with John Ross, than I am. My knowledge of him dates back as far as thirty years. I have known him in his official, personal, and private relations; in his official relations, from the time he succeeded the venerable Charles R. Hicks, as principal chief of the Cherokee nation; and personally, before that time, and ever since. It were a useless expenditure of time for me to dwell upon Mr. Ross's official character. This is stamped upon his entire career as chief of the Cherokees; and the ability, and firmness, and patience, with which he has vindicated and maintained the rights of the Cherokees in their relations to the general government, are matters of record in the archives of the government; whilst the influence which he has exerted over his people, for their good, are matters of public notoriety.

That divisions should exist among his people, is most

natural; that he should have enemies, implacable, bitter, relentless, is to share the lot of all who are patriotic and faithful, including our own Washington. But there is nothing more true, than if left to themselves, and to the enlightened, mild, and pacific counsels of Ross and his leading men; and intermeddling, and vicious, and avaricious white men had not originated the elements of strife, and thrown them in among the Cherokees, and promoted, for their own ends, the discords that have distracted that people, they would be, at this moment, harmonious, united and happy.

Mr. Ross is, and has always been, strictly temperate. In his private character he is without reproach. As a father, brother, husband, friend, he is beloved, and justly so. He is kind, and courteous, and unobtrusive—a man of few words, but of sound, deep thinking, a high sense of honor, and of indomitable firmness.

To his people, for whom he has endured much, and been exposed to all sorts of personal hazards, he is devotedly attached; and, except those who have been played upon and misled by intermeddling white men, is beloved and confided in by them. In proof of this, reference need only be made to their continued confidence, as shown in his election, for so long a period, as their principal chief, both east and west of the Mississippi. With less of confidence in him, on the part of the Cherokees, and less ability and foresight on his part, or less devotion in him towards them and their interests, the partizan strife which has been made to distract the Cherokees, must long before now have reduced them to insignificance, and resulted, finally, in their extinction. It is to Ross's great prudence, self-command, intelligence, and firmness, that this people owe their present freedom from far greater and more overwhelming calamities than have befallen them.

It is my firm belief that the United States owe to Mr. Ross a freedom from more than one outbreak on the part of the Cherokees, that would have produced great suffering along the frontiers, and immense expenditures of blood and treasure. His counsels have been always in favor of peace, and a patient endurance of the evils, with which the policy of the general government, for the last sixteen years, has overwhelmed them. Such was the stand taken by him, for the preservation of pacific relations between his people and the States, and so constant were his promises, that justice would finally be done his people, as to lead them, soon after General Harrison was elected, and when nothing was yet accomplished in their behalf, to the very brink of a rupture with the United States, attended by a full purpose to kill the chief, so soon as he should leave Washington, who had, as they now believed, so long deceived them. Fortunately, by the agency of General Scott, in his appeals to the War Department, in behalf of the justice of the Cherokee claims, Ross was enabled to carry home with him a large amount of money, though only a part of what was due to the Cherokees, thus restoring to himself the confidence, which, by the delays of the general government, he had lost; and with this confidence, came a state of, at least, comparative personal security to himself.

The reader has already, I am sure, traced all this painful business to its source. It proceeded from a fraudulent act, connived at by the Executive of the United States, *first*, in permitting the treaty (as it was styled) of New Euchota to be made at all; *second*, after it was made, in refusing to yield to the protestations of some sixteen thousand Cherokees, that the treaty was *not* made by the nation, but only by a few, who had no authority to make it; and *third*, in *the resolve*, at all hazards, to enforce its provisions, *vi et armis*. The *responsibility*, assumed by the Executive, in this view of the subject, was, indeed, most fearful!

But the whole affair assumes a yet more painful aspect,

when a treaty, *with the nation, was then*, and *had long been*, within reach of the Executive; and I am the witness. The Cherokee delegation, with Ross at its head, during a period of its greatest excitement, being in Philadelphia, I visited them at Mrs. Yohe's hotel, on Chesnut-street; and received the following from their own lips:—"It is true we do not wish to sell our country. The very thought is painful to us. But the injustice of the United States government, its total disregard of treaties, and our exposed and unprotected condition being such, we would not hesitate to negotiate for an exchange, that we might go where we would be free from the consuming policy which is permitted to be exercised towards us. And yet, what can we do? The President keeps sending among us, to negotiate for our lands, men for whom we have no respect, in whom we have no confidence; men, in a word, who are known to us to be our enemies. If it were referred to you, or to any one who was competent, and was our friend, and had our confidence, and who would co-operate with us in aiding us to obtain *justice*—we want nothing more—and would not seek to entrap, and deceive, and cheat us, we would consent to treat."

Being anxious to bring to a harmonious close the controversy that was being carried on for these people's lands, and securing for them a permanent and peaceful home west of the Mississippi, I wrote immediately to Governor Cass, at that time Secretary of War, and also to the Hon. William R. King, then United States Senator from Alabama, now Minister to France, communicating this conversation, and making known to the former my readiness to undertake, *if permitted, as a private citizen*, not as a commissioner, to lay the basis of a treaty which could be consummated by others. Governor Cass acknowledged the receipt of my letter. Mr. King afterwards told me he had replied to me also, but his letter never reached me; and there the matter ended. The resolve of the Executive *seemed* to be, to carry on all the business of the government by the agency of his political friends, only; and, as in the case of the Cherokees, when these, from no matter what cause, failed to accomplish the work assigned to them by the ordinary means, to assume the responsibility himself, and resort to those which were *extraordinary*. Whatever of suffering, therefore, or of blood, has succeeded that New Euchota treaty, including the murder of the Ridges and Boudinot, with all the subsequent afflictions and present distractions which agitate and distress the Cherokees, as also all the sufferings that may hereafter overtake them, and the shedding of blood, the result of this strife, it needs not the wisdom of Solomon to perceive, has come, and will come, as do poisoned waters from their source, *from the so-called treaty of New Euchota*. There lives not the man, with his intellects in order, and his moral balance adjusted, having a knowledge of all the facts, who will not put the seal of his condemnation upon that New Euchota instrument, and upon the power that was assumed for its ratification and enforcement. It was an open fraud, and is a foul blot upon the escutcheon of the nation, and will remain there forever. The same may be said of the treaty, and the means resorted to for its enforcement, of *Payne's Landing*, in Florida. The objection is not so much to the treaty itself, as to the usurpation of power to enforce at least one provision which it did not contain; or, in other words, to demand of the Seminoles to remove, under a *conditional* stipulation, as though they had made the article *unconditional*, and had offered no remonstrances against its fulfilment. "There is a condition prefixed to the agreement," says Colonel Gadsden, the commissioner who negotiated the treaty, in his letter to the Secretary of War, "without assenting to which, the Indians *most positively refused* to negotiate for their removal west of the Mississippi. Even with the condition annexed, there was reluctance, (which with some difficulty was overcome,) on the part of the Indians, to bind themselves to *any* stipulations, before a knowledge of facts and circumstances would enable them to judge of the advantages or disadvantages of the disposition the government of the United States wished to make of them."

Again, in the same letter, Colonel Gadsden says, "The final ratification of the treaty will depend upon the opinion of the seven chiefs selected to explore the country west of the Mississippi river. If that corresponds to the description given, or is equal to the expectations formed of it, there will be no difficulty on the part of the Seminoles. If the Creeks, however, raise any objections, this will be a sufficient pretext, on the part of some of the Seminole deputation, to oppose the execution of the whole arrangement." The Creeks did raise objections. The Seminoles wanted a separate country. The Creeks refused it, and wished them to live with them in common.

Again, the treaty, even if the Seminoles had not made known their objections to it—instead of having been passed through the forms of law at the proper time—was not ratified by the United States government, and its validity acknowledged, for *two years* after it was made. It was signed on the 9th May, 1832, and not ratified till 1834; and yet, one of its provisions stipulated, (that is, if it were finally accepted by the Seminoles, which, however, it never was,) that a removal of one-third of their population should take place in 1833. Not only did this delay of the ratification occur, but it was not for some time after, that means were appropriated to carry it into effect. It was, therefore, vitiated throughout—had lost every spark of its vitality—all of its binding force upon the other party—and was called by the Indians, in derision, "*A white man's treaty.*" And yet, in a talk sent to them by President Jackson, of the 16th February, 1835, he tells them, "I have ordered a large military force to be sent among you. I have directed the commanding officer, and likewise the agent, your friend, General Thompson, that every reasonable indulgence be held out to you. But I have also directed that one-third of your people, *as provided for in the treaty, be removed during the present season.*" Now the treaty provided for no such thing. It provided for such removal in 1833—the Indians ratifying it—but not in 1835. The talk proceeds—"If you listen to the voice of friendship and truth, you will go quietly and voluntarily. But should you listen to bad birds, that are always flying about you, and refuse to remove, I have then directed the commanding officer *to remove you by force. This will be done.*"

The Indians, however, could not comprehend the justice of this attempt to enforce upon them a compliance with obligations, on their part, that did not exist. Every species of outrage was committed on the Indians, the details of which are almost too shocking to be recorded. (Besides, by the then existing treaty of Fort Moultrie, they were guarantied in their right to continue where they were for twenty years from its date, of which time twelve years then remained to them.) Formal examinations were made into the causes of these outrages, and the results may be found, as also the details, in a work entitled "The War in Florida; being an Exposition of its Causes, and an Accurate History of the Campaigns of Generals Clinch, Gaines, and Scott"—"By a late Staff-Officer." In the straight-forward testimony of the Indians, is set forth, in one place, that "while six of them were encamped together, a party of whites arrived, *took their guns from three of them, examined their packs, and commenced whipping them,* and the Indians ran off," &c., &c. At another place, "six other Indians were at a camp. A party of white men came upon that camp, and began to whip the Indians, when two other Indians came up, and commenced firing on the whites. The arms of six Indians had been taken from them, and stacked against a tree. The six unarmed Indians were kept confined thirty-three days," &c., &c.

They were robbed of their money and their negroes. Chiefs, including Micanopy, their principal, were broke by the agent, for refusing to emigrate. Every possible indignity was offered them. Osceola was put in irons. Many were reduced to the greatest distress for want of provisions. They were forced, by their hunger, to go out in quest of subsistence. "On one of these occasions," says the author I have referred to, "three of the Long Swamp Indians were surprised, and two of them secured, by the owner of the land, who tied them by the hands and feet with a rope, and carried them to his barn, where they were confined without sustenance for three days, unable to extricate themselves, and obliged to remain in one position. Not returning to their homes, their friends became alarmed for their safety, and the chief of the town where they resided went forward and demanded them. Being refused, he returned to his town, and taking several of his people with him, he again demanded the release of the prisoners, and was again refused, with a threat by the white fellows, that if the chief dared to effect their release, complaint should be entered against him.

"Upon this, the whole party rushed to the barn, whence they heard the moaning of their friends; and there they beheld a most pitiable sight. The rope with which those poor fellows had been tied, had worn through their flesh; they had temporarily lost the use of their limbs, being unable to stand or walk; they had bled profusely, and had received no food during their confinement. The owner of the barn then fired upon the Indians, and slightly wounded one of the party; when their exasperation attained to such a height, that, in retaliation for this brutal outrage, they set fire to the barn, and would not permit the owner to take anything therefrom; nor did they leave the spot until the whole was consumed."

"These outrages," proceeds the narrator, "continued to increase with each succeeding week, and the Indians, discerning the hopelessness of their situation, at once concluded to oppose the efforts of the government, and call for a general assemblage of the nation."

There had been previous meetings between the agent and the chiefs; eight of the chiefs and sub-chiefs had signed a paper which the agent had prepared, in which the validity of the treaty of Payne's Landing, of the 9th May, 1832, as also that of Fort Gibson, of the 28th March, 1833, was acknowledged. It was then when Micanopy, through Jumper, refused to abide by the treaty, that his name was struck from the council of the nation, as also four others. It is not possible to read the petitions of these Indians to be saved from a connexion with those western Indians, to be mingled with the Creeks, and exposed to the treachery and thieving habits of the Pawnees, without feelings of the deepest sympathy. At one of the councils, convened by the agent to press upon them their removal, Micanopy said, "When we were at Camp Moultrie, we made a treaty; and we were to be paid our annuities for twenty years. That is all I have to say."

Jumper said, "At Camp Moultrie, they told us all difficulties should be buried for twenty years from the date of the treaty made there, (September 18th, 1823;) that after this, we held a treaty at Payne's Landing, before the twenty years were out, (by nine years,) and they told us we might go and see the country, but that we were not obliged to remove, &c., &c. When we went to see the land, we had not sold our land here, and we were told only to go and see it. The Indians there steal horses, and take packs on their horses; they steal horses from the different tribes. I do not want to go among such people. Your talk (addressing the agent,) seems always good, but we don't feel disposed to go west."

Charley Amathla spoke, and said, "The speakers of the nation are all dead, but I remember some of their words when they had the meeting at Camp Moultrie. I was not there, but heard that we should be at peace, and that we would have our annuity paid for twenty years. White people have told me that the treaty at Camp Moultrie, which was made by great men, and not to be broken, had secured them for twenty years; that seven years of that treaty are still unexpired. I am no half-breed, and do not lean on one side. If they tell me to go, after the seven years, I say nothing. As to the proposition made us by the agent, about removing, I do not say I will not go, but I think not; until the seven years are out, I give no answer. My family I love dearly and sacredly. I do not think it right to take them right off. Our father has often said to me that he loves his children, and they love him, &c. I do not complain of the agent's talk. My young men and family are all around me; should I go west, I should lose many on the path. As to the country west, I looked at it; a weak man cannot get there; the fatigue would be great; it requires a strong man. I hardly got there, &c. If I know my own heart, I think I am true. If I differ from the agent, he is a free man, and has his right to talk. I hope this talk will bring all things right; that hereafter we may all live well together." The council adjourned till the next day; when the agent said he was ready to receive their answers to the questions he submitted yesterday.

Holata Micco spoke—"I have only to repeat what I said yesterday, and to say that the twenty years from the treaty at Moultrie have not yet expired. I never gave my consent to go west. The whites may say so; but I never gave my consent."

Jumper—"We are not satisfied to go until the end of the twenty years, according to the treaty at Camp Moultrie," &c.

Micanopy—"I say what I said yesterday—I did not sign the treaty."

Agent—"Abraham, tell Micanopy that I say he *lies;* he did sign the treaty, for here is his name."

Charley Amathla—"The agent told us yesterday we did not talk to the point. I have nothing to say different from what I said yesterday. At Payne's Landing, the white people forced us into the treaty. I was there. I agreed to go west, and did go west. I went in a vessel, and it made me sick. I think that for so many people, it would be very bad," &c., &c.

At a previous private council of the chiefs and others, Osceola said, "My brothers! The white people got some of our chiefs to sign a paper to give our lands to them, but our chiefs did not do as we told them to do; they did wrong. We must do right. The agent tells us we must go away from the lands we live on—our homes, and the graves of our fathers—and go over the big river among bad Indians. When the agent tells me to go from my home, I hate him, because I love my home, and will not go from it.

"My brothers! When the Great Spirit tells me to go with the white man, I go; but he tells me not to go. The white man says I shall go, and he will send people to make me go. But I have a rifle, and I have some powder and lead. I say we must not leave our homes and lands. If any of our people want to go west, we won't let them; and I tell them they are enemies, and we will treat them so; for the Great Spirit will protect us."

There is much of the same sort of proof that the treaty of Payne's Landing was only conditional, as well as of the determined spirit of the Indians, as a body, to resist any attempt that might be made to compel a compliance with its alleged provisions. At the last council held with the chiefs, the agent, General Thompson, said, among other things, "I stand up for the last time, to tell you that you must go; and if not willingly, you will be compelled to go. I should have told you that no more annuity will be paid to you here. (Osceola replied that he did not care whether any more was ever paid.) I hope you will, on more mature reflection, act like honest men, and not compel me to report you to your father, the President, as faithless to your agreements."

Osceola said, "The decision of the chiefs was given; that they did not intend to give any other answer." Micanopy said, "I do not intend to remove."

It was at this "last council"—the last, in more ways than one, to General Thompson—that this fated agent committed an act, which, like the spark to the magazine, exploded it. I give the narrative as it has been, on several occasions, repeated to me, not from my personal knowledge of its entire correctness, or from any written account of it. But I have told it to gentlemen who, by the part they afterwards took in the Seminole war, and from their acquaintance with the circumstances that led to it, should be entitled to credit; and they all recognized the statement as one which was generally received as correct, about the parts where the provocative and the tragedy were enacted.

It was at this "last council"—the "last time" that General Thompson "stood up" in one—that during his address, Osceola, being a little distant from the speaker, stood with his arms folded, eyeing him with those mingled feelings of reproach and resentment, which the occasion was so well calculated to produce; when, being observed by General Thompson, he became indignant, and the emigration roll being open, and lying on the table, he commanded Osceola to come up and sign it. The indignant chief said he should do no such thing. "Tell him," said General Thompson, addressing the interpreter, "that I have a talk from General Jackson for him presently, which, when he hears it, will teach him better." To which Osceola replied, "Tell him I care no more for General Jackson, than I care for him; but," seizing his knife, and rushing up to the table, said, "if he must have my mark," driving his knife through the emigration roll, "*there it is!*" when, instantly, General Thompson ordered him seized and put in irons. The order was forthwith obeyed.

Sometime during the night, and after Osceola had been some hours manacled, and shut out from light and liberty, he called to the interpreter and said, "Go, tell my father, if he will take these off, (his irons,) and let me go, I will come in to-morrow, (pointing over his head to meridian,) when the sun gets up there, and will sign the paper, and will bring with me one hundred who will sign also." The message was delivered; when General Thompson congratulated himself with having subdued the refractory chief, and ordered him to be set at liberty.

True to his promise, Osceola came in, at twelve o'clock, bringing with him a hundred of his people, all of whom signed the roll, when all retired. This was a moment of triumph to the agent, who, it is due to his memory that I should state, acted in all this matter, not because he approved the work he had been sent to do, but to fulfil the orders of his superiors at Washington. There is proof of this in the official government documents.

The roll having been signed, Osceola, with the Indians he had brought in, retired to some distant and out-of-the-way place, where he thus addressed them: "Go, all of you, except these six, on the trail that leads to Fort King. Take with you all the Indians you can muster, and sleep not, and eat not, till you have collected a strong force, and reached about midway on the trail, and there wait my arrival—having your rifles and knives in good order, and your pouches filled with powder and ball."

They all retired, except those Osceola kept about his person. To these he said, "Never be out of sight of my finger; watch me, and keep near me."

They sauntered about until the second day after this, when the agent went to dine with the post-master. Osceola kept his eye on him. When the proper moment arrived, he gave the signal to his associates. They clustered about him. To one he said, "Do you take him," pointing to one of the party; to another, "and you him," and so on, till he had assigned a victim to each, when he added, "leave the agent to me." The positions being taken, the concerted signal was given, all fired, when General Thompson, and those who were with him, fell.

Immediately the alarm was given—the Indians have killed the agent; and so of the others. The war-cry went forth; Dade's command was put in motion for Fort King. Osceola had, meantime, joined his comrades. The attack on Dade was commenced, and every man of it, save one, was killed.

Now all this plan of attack, both at the agency, and on the trail to Fort King, Osceola contrived while he was in irons; and it was a double revenge that he meditated, the joint product of the heavy pressure upon him and his people of the government hand, which was forcing them from their country, and the degradation to which he had been subjected, by being put in irons and in prison. Upon whom, I ask, is blood thus shed, justly chargeable?

It is not possible to contemplate this picture, without experiencing a feeling of the deepest regret! A terrible retribution awaited the resolve of the administration to expel these people by force. It was little thought of, that the employment of it, to compel acquiescence to the terms of a treaty, which were never binding upon the Indians, would cost some thirty millions of dollars, and lead to as lavish a waste of as patriotic blood as ever the earth drank up, and that a train of disasters would follow, through nearly a seven years' war, reflecting anything and everything upon our arms and country, *but honor.* The war was alike unjust, inhuman, and inglorious. But the agony is over, and there remains no remedy but to study, in the future, to atone for the evils of the past. The Indians are now, nearly all of them, beyond the limits of our States and organized Territories. The means employed in placing them there, which have been resorted to *for the last sixteen years*, can never be approved by the good, the humane, or the just. And yet, the Indians, though through so much tribulation and suffering, and amidst such accumulated wrongs, are not only in a far better condition for their tranquillity and peace, than when surrounded by the whites, and in the midst of organized States, but where, under a suitable system, and one altogether adapted to their condition, they can rise in the scale of human advancement, to a level with those at whose hands they have experienced so many wrongs, and by whose agency they have been made to endure such deep sorrows.

It was in the hope of awakening the public mind to a proper sense of the duty which this nation owes to this persecuted race, that I conceived and executed the plan—in part, at least—of delivering addresses to such assemblies of the people as might be induced to hear me. The favor with which these addresses were received, from Maine to Maryland, and my inability, owing to certain causes, of travelling the entire rounds of the country with these messages—in connexion with a plan for the preservation of the remnants of the Indian race, and their advancement into the higher privileges of their nature—has led me, in connexion with the advice of friends, to publish them, and by this means send them round the entire country. They will form the second part of this volume.

END OF MEMOIRS, ETC., ETC.

APPENDIX.

(A.)

To the Editors of the National Intelligencer.

GENTLEMEN—I have a few remarks to offer to the public through the medium of your paper, on the speech delivered in the United States Senate by Mr. Benton, of Missouri, on the amendment offered by him to the bill to abolish the Indian factory system, as it appears printed in the National Intelligencer of the 10th inst. I offer no apology for this, as my object is to give *to the people*, by this public, and only direct route to their observation, the proper explanations of several positions which, it appears, were assumed in that speech, and which the people have a right to expect me to explain.

The object avowed by Mr. Benton, is to "look into the practical operation of the factory system." He proposes to examine, *first*, the conduct of the superintendent in purchasing goods; *second*, the conduct of the factors in selling them; *third*, the conduct of the superintendents in selling furs and peltries. The specifications are:—

First. In purchasing goods not adapted to the Indian trade.

Second. In purchasing goods of bad quality.

Third. In purchasing at improper places, and at extravagant prices.

In support of the first specification, Mr. Benton read, from a printed document, sundry articles of supplies which had been sent by the superintendent to the factories; among these, "eight gross of jews-harps;" all which, and other articles, he states are "adapted to a common country store, *but unknown* to the Indian trade."

The only reply I have to make to this is, that *every article* enumerated by Mr. Benton, even including jews-harps, was sent to the Indians in compliance *with their own request*, which request is forwarded, annually, by each factor stationed among them respectively, under the title of "a list of articles wanted for this trading-house for this year." This annual call is always complied with, so far as the superintendent may be able to command the articles enumerated. It is submitted to the public, which of the two, Mr. Benton or the Indians, is best acquainted with the wants and wishes of the latter. If the Indians do call for the articles which Mr. Benton has asserted are "*unknown* to the Indian trade," then it is fair to infer that Mr. Benton is not correctly informed on the subject; and that they do thus call, and for the very articles excepted against by Mr. Benton, I herewith furnish *the proof*, for your inspection, in *the original* annual requisitions made from the wilderness.

Specification 2. "In purchasing goods of bad quality." It is admitted that the factories do contain goods of bad quality, and that there are some articles to be found in the stock comprising them, not even suited to the trade. But this was explained by the Superintendent of Indian Trade, in the hearing of Mr. Benton, and afterwards written and printed for the information of the committee. For the information *of the public*, who have a right to know exactly what their public servants are about, I will, in as few words as possible, explain the charge included in this specification.

It is known to everybody, that, about the close of the war, merchandise of every description was *scarce* and *dear*. The articles required for our Indian supplies partook of this universal scarcity, and exorbitancy of price. It was, however, determined, and very properly, by the then incumbent, to procure *the best articles* the country could furnish, and upon the best terms. They were accordingly procured. It was thought better to send the Indians cloth, although some of it should be made of hair, than to let them perish for lack of something to cover them. It is also known that, soon after the war, an influx of merchandise overrun our country. It was the business and *duty* of the superintendent of the trade to go into this abundant market, get the supplies, regardless of what was on hand, and forward them forthwith. It was accordingly done. It follows, as a very natural consequence, that, whilst these better, cheaper, and more suitable goods were on hand, the Indians would prefer them to the old stock. Hence, the unsuitable articles, or a good many of them, remain undisposed of. Let this be taken in explanation of the numerous references made by the three gentlemen, (*among them Mr. Ramsay Crooks, agent of the American Fur Company,*) who were before the committee of the Senate, and who, as that committee know, *said nothing* implicating the honor or integrity of *any* one concerned, but afterwards *wrote* to Mr. Benton and the committee. It is from these written statements, that Mr. Benton has made such copious extracts in his speech. I will just stop here to remark upon the charge of remnants and cut goods being sent to the factories. It were strange if remnants were not *made* at the factories; and, therefore, doubtless remnants have been seen there. And it were equally strange, if a business of some twenty years had not resulted in the accumulation of at least the usual quantity of remnants. The existence of remnants at the factories is, therefore, admitted. So, also, is it admitted that "*cut goods*" are sometimes sent among the supplies. But could there be no reason assigned for this, but one worthy of being brought in to justify a specification involving an *abuse* of an honorable trust? It seems not! I will, therefore, furnish it. It often happens that an entire piece of an article is more than a supply for any one factory, and that it will serve three or four. When this is the case, the piece is cut into as many parts. Sometimes, too, *lots* of goods are bought at auction; among these, there will be, occasionally, "cut goods." But, under no other circumstances, are cut goods bought for the factory supplies.

Specification 3. "In purchasing at improper places, and at extravagant prices."

Here, the item of shot, amounting to $105, appears in the front, to support this specification; and which derives its chief odiousness from having been purchased in Georgetown, D. C., and from having cost, as Mr. Benton asserts, more than it could have been purchased for in St. Louis. *Seven cents*, he states to have been the price there in 1820; whereas, as the printed documents show, it cost here ten dollars *per hundred weight*, which is less than eight and a half cents per pound. *Now for the facts.*

First, then, owing to the nature of the transportation of dry goods, a wagon-load of which often cannot be made to weigh the amount which it is essential to bargain for, (to wit, 3,000 weight,) shot, and other heavy articles, are, therefore, added, which, whether added or not, never increases or diminishes the cost of the transportation as far as Pittsburgh. Thus, nothing, on account of transportation, is added to the cost of the price of shot and axes, corn hoes, knives, nails, frying-pans, and the rest, as enumerated by Mr. Benton, to Pittsburgh. There, the articles, in company with the body of the supplies, go on to their several destinations; but *shot*, BE IT REMEMBERED, always, (if purchased here,) *to the lakes*, and *never*, as has been charged upon this office, to St. Louis. But, suppose this article to have been purchased at St. Louis, and forwarded over the route pointed out by Mr. Benton; this office had no agencies on that route. It would require their appointment, before the shot could be got along with safety, or at all; and this implies *new commissions*. But would it be worth while, even admitting the price of shot to be a few cents cheaper at St. Louis than at Georgetown, to organize a new route, just to convey, annually, from the Herculaneum establishment, $105 worth of this article? But, then, I have before me a bill of shot, purchased at St. Louis, by James Kennerly, Esq., (brother-in-law to Governor Clark, both well known, no doubt, to Mr. Benton,) which bill is dated 14th August, *in this same year*, (to wit, 1820,) in which is charged two hundred pounds of shot, at *eleven cents* per pound. In Georgetown, it cost not quite eight and a half cents, and nothing for its transportation to Pittsburgh. The inference is, Mr. Kennerly being an honest man, of which I have not the least reason to doubt, Mr. Benton was not correctly informed as to the price of shot in St. Louis, in 1820.

Next comes the article of gunpowder. Many, and no doubt just eulogiums, are passed upon the manufacture of this article in the West. But, suppose it really was the best powder in the world, yet, if those for whom the purchase was to be made, (having tried it, as the Indians have the powder of the West,) direct their organ of communication to the Superintendent of the Indian Trade, to ask him to send the kind which used to be sent, the presumption is, there can arise out of this case no very serious charge against the Superintendent of Indian Trade for complying. The gunpowder of the West is, no doubt, very good; but that is no reason why the Indians should not prefer Dupont's. That they do, and that they have requested to have it sent to them, I refer for proof to documents in the office of Indian Trade, and to Mr. Sibley, of Fort Osage, who is now in Washington. But let us compare *the price*, with that which it has been found necessary to pay at St. Louis. For Dupont's best FF glazed rifle powder, I pay twenty-two cents per pound. I have a bill now before me, dated "St. Louis, October 1, 1820," in which is a charge of four hundred pounds best gunpowder, at forty-five cents per pound. In this same bill is charged five hundred and twenty-nine pounds of tobacco, at sixteen and two-thirds cents per pound. Mr. Benton excepts to the price paid by the Superintendent of Indian Trade, *for this same kind of tobacco*, at Pittsburgh, though it cost there only seven cents per pound; and says, "*in Kentucky*" it could be had for two and three cents. If so, it must be for the leaf tobacco, and that is not suited to the trade; or, if Mr. Benton means plug, or manufactured tobacco, then everybody knows it cannot be bought for those prices. Hence Mr. Benton is not correctly informed in relation to the price of tobacco.

I enclose you *the original bills* for those articles. It is best, in these times, when appeals are made to the law and the testimony, and when even these are not considered as being sufficient, to put such matters to rest by facts and documents.

Next comes the sale of deer-skins, and the letter from Mr. *George* Astor, of New York, complaining that, because of this private sale, he could not get a chance to bid. I will just remark, that deer-skins are a perishable article. They require to be sold immediately, else what the worms leave, the expenses are sure to devour. From the factories on the Sulphur Fork of Red River, and Fort Confederation, on the Tombigbee, a considerable quantity of this article was on its way to Mobile and New Orleans. I wrote to *New York*, to my agent there, to be informed of the state of that market for those articles. From Philadelphia, I received offers from *two houses*, and got the price of the Orleans market. I sold *to the gentlemen who offered most*, AS THE PRINTED DOCUMENTS BEFORE THE SENATE WILL TESTIFY. But, in addition to the extra price which I obtained, I inserted a condition in the contract, which provided, that, in the event of the skins having left New Orleans and Mobile before the purchasers' agent could receive them, the freight, &c., was to be paid *by the purchasers*. This saved the cost of freight on nearly $8,000 worth, which had actually left Mobile before the agent could arrest their departure. To have delayed selling a month longer, might have involved the loss of the whole amount; and it would have required more than that time to have notified the public of a public sale, when, by a combination of purchasers, the result might have been very different from that which has been realized. The commissions for selling, and storage, and all such charges, are understood to mean something when applying especially to the New Orleans market. The letters, and contract, and everything belonging to this sale, were furnished the committee, and may be seen and judged of, by referring to the printed documents of February 11, 1822, No. 60.

As to the remarks implicating the Georgetown market, as unsuited to the sale of furs and peltries, and the contrast drawn between it and the market at St. Louis, I am prepared to demonstrate, by actual sales which have been made in Georgetown for ten years, at least, that it has produced higher prices than were giving at any other point in the Union, at the periods when the sales were made. But I have an evidence more directly in point. Mr. Kennerly sold, of the parcel which was destined to this market, and which it was intended should constitute part of the annual sales of this last fall, and without instructions, (but doubtless with the best intentions,) rackoon, muskrat, and beaver, for $1,128 50, which would have brought here, at the rates at which the rest were sold, $2,078 81, *after deducting the price of transportation!* This is comment enough on the comparative prices, at least between this market and the market at St. Louis.*

Next comes the item of transportation. Mr. Benton was "*constrained*" to believe that the carriage of the goods from Georgetown to St. Louis cost more than I had reported, to wit: from four and a half to nine cents per pound—varying with the demand for the means of transportation. He states his reason for this belief to be derived from the exhibit furnished by me in 1820, and which is to be seen in Vol. II. of the State papers of that year, in which he finds that between the years 1811 and 1820, $110,543 had been paid for transporting $466,874 worth of supplies. Now, it might have occurred to Mr. Benton that there was a period of nearly three years, between 1811 and 1820, when the cost of carriage was enormously enhanced by the occurrences of those times; and which, falling into the average of ordinary times, would swell the amount above the customary limits. But everybody knows, including the wagoners themselves, that what once cost $300 to be conveyed tó Pittsburgh, can be got there now, and in ordinary times, for less than one-fourth of this sum.

Mr. Benton proceeds by conveying the imputation, that large profits have been charged on goods furnished on account of *treaties*, *annuities*, and *presents;* and asks, in this interrogatory of implication—"*and where are the profits?*" In 1818 he says, $165,611 96 worth of goods was sent to the Indians in presents. How much of this went through the factories, he professes he does not know, but says "*it must have been large.*" NOT A DOLLAR of the presents of that year went through the factories; and what went from this office *direct* to *the agents* (not the factors) of the *Indian Department* for distribution, amounted to $50,185 47, and on which the cost of transportation only was charged to *the original cost prices*, as the books of this office will show, and also the returns made to the office of the Second Auditor. The disbursements of the Indian Department for 1818, on Indian account, Mr. Benton puts down at $559,367 47. Of this I know nothing, further, at least, than the requisitions on me for that year go; and these amounted to $90,260 47; and this was all of that sum, except the pay to the superintendent, factors, and clerks, that went through the hands of the Superintendent of Indian Trade. No annuities are paid through the factories, save only the annuity to the Osages of the Missouri, and this is at their own request, and the amount of it is $1,500.

It is true, the law as referred to, Vol. IV., page 342, makes it the duty of the Superintendent of Indian Trade to purchase and transmit, on orders from the Department of War, all goods required for annuities, treaties, and presents. But he provides *no more* than the orders specify—and of late, since so much of this trans-

* Mr. Benton says, "Georgetown is, perhaps, the last place in the world that any person would think of for a fur market:" and, in proof of this, says, "the superintendent sold, during the year 1821, eleven hundred and eight pounds of beaver for $2,115 02, a fraction less than two dollars per pound. At St. Louis, beaver sells for three dollars per pound." It is true, the quantity mentioned by Mr. Benton was sold during that year, and produced the sum stated; but more than two-thirds of the quantity was southern beaver, a great proportion of which is little better than dog's hair. Of the quantity sold, however, *only four hundred and sixty-seven pounds* were *sold in Georgetown*, and produced $1,396 15, nearly three dollars per pound: that portion which was good northern beaver, averaged more than four dollars per pound. The rest was sold in New York, New Orleans, and Philadelphia—at New York, by J. L. Dias; at New Orleans, by Lieutenant Symington; at Philadelphia, by Price & Morgan.

mission has been made in specie, (a most impoverishing process to the Indians,) a very small part of the supplies go through the hands of the superintendent. But whatever is furnished by him, is furnished *at cost*, with the charge of transportation, *alone*, added. I refer to the office of the Second Auditor, where the original invoices may be seen.

So, then, Mr. Benton is no less in error as to the amount of goods which passes through this office, than as to the profits which have been added. If an Indian agent want, for the purposes of his agency, any articles *to give to the Indians*, or for any other purpose, and if fifty per cent. were charged upon them, which it is admitted has been the case, the profits go only out of one of the government pockets into the other. And the quarter returns from the factories account for such addition in the same satisfactory manner as they account for other sales.

As head of the Trade Department, and responsible for its support, I have no more option to give goods out of the factory, or to let them go at cost, to an *Indian agent*, than I have to any other person. The capital of the trade is to be preserved; and my business is with that.

Much error has originated by blending the Indian Department, and its operations, with the *Indian Trade Office*. And yet it should seem, every legislator, at least, should know the distinction, and at what points to apply the respective operations of these two *distinct* branches of the government.

Mr. Benton, in stating the amount of business which, he says, was done at several of the factories, must have confined himself solely to the abstracts, and omitted to read *the letter* which accompanied them. The abstracts set forth the amount "*received*," and no more; but the letter explains that what had been "*received*" was not all that had been *taken in* at the factories in that year. Mr. Benton's call embraced the terms—"*how much of each article has been* RECEIVED *by the Superintendent of Indian Trade in* 1821." Of course, only what had been "*received*" was put down in the abstract. But let the letter explain this.

It remains now for me to remark upon the manner of purchasing the supplies. It embraces calls for information of the markets of our principal cities; replies to some of which were sent in to the committee, and printed; reference to which is made, to show how far the imputation of "*purchases at improper places, and at extravagant prices*," is merited. I will just add an extract from a letter received by me from Governor Cass, to whom forty odd thousand dollars' worth of goods had been sent in one year, to show *his* opinion of this branch of the subject.

"*I have been much gratified to find the goods sent here for the Indians, are very well selected. Perfect justice has been done. I am informed by persons in the Indian Department, that such a selection was never sent to this country. In fact, I cannot conceive that they could be better suited to the objects for which they are sent.*"

In justice to the gentlemen engaged in the arduous duties of factors, it is due to them, that I should assure the public that I have no cause to doubt their honor, integrity, or ability; against whom no charge rests, except the vague rumors, from the disagreeableness of which no officer of the government, *if he be a disbursing officer*, need ever console himself with the hope of being free. For myself, I ask no favors in relation to the trust with which I have been honored, *but justice, only.*

I find, on looking over what I have thus very hastily written, that I have not noticed, in this place, the charge of selling goods to persons other than Indians.

This was fully explained in the printed reports and documents, and may be, in a condensed form, explained thus for the public.

First. It was thought good policy to open a way to get rid of unsuitable stores. This was attempted by granting the privilege to the factors to sell to white people any articles not needed for Indian trade, at an advance of 15 per cent. above the Indian prices.

Second. Outfits to Indians, *who requested them*, and to others who it was known *needed* them, was authorized, under *special directions*, on all the points necessary to guard the Indians from the fraudulent speculations of those to whom these supplies were entrusted. By this policy, the sphere of the public business was enlarged, and rendered thereby more useful. Reference is made to the documents furnished the committee of the Senate, by this office, and which are printed, and which explain, *fully*, this branch of *alleged* abuses.

I will close these remarks, by putting before the public an abstract of the account of property on hand at this office, and at the several factories, as made to the committee of the Senate, on a call made by it for this information, of the 27th of December, 1821. It will be seen that the capital being no more than $236,630 39, and the property, *at the original cost prices*, amounting to $295,632 36, (distributed thus, at the period when the statement was made out, to wit: 30th of September, 1821;) the gain is $59,001 97—the property was thus distributed in September last:

Amount merchandise in the stores of the Superintendent of Indian Trade, ...		$30,489 88
Furs and peltries in store, and on their way to the Superintendent's office, ...		12,500 00
Cash on hand, ...		5,483 00
Bills receivable, ...		8,744 94
Balances on the Superintendent's books, ...		6,455 10
		$63,672 92
Am't of merchandise in the hands of the transport agent at St. Louis,		10,100 00
Am't of property on hand at the several factories, as per their inventory, viz.:		
Prairie du Chien, ...	$52,041 77	
Fort Edwards, ...	15,205 76	
Fort Osage, ...	26,015 25	
Branch of do.	6,057 98	
Green Bay, ...	22,521 31	
Chicago, ...	13,164 33	
Arkansas, ...	14,074 09	
Choctaw, ...	40,613 10	
Red River, ...	15,736 41	
Merchandise on the way to factories, , .	16,429 34	
		221,859 44
		$295,632 36

I have presented this view of the trade fund to the public, merely as a set-off to these words at the close of Mr. Benton's speech—"that the capital be returned to the public Treasury, *so far as it can be found*," from which many persons in this "good-natured age" might infer Mr. Benton's meaning to be, *that it was not to be found at all.*

I have now performed what I conceive to be an act of justice to the people. They have had spread before them the speech on which I have endeavored to cast the proper light—and if there be errors in whatever may be given to the public, however innocent may be the intention of the speaker, or praiseworthy his motive, it is but justice that they should be *corrected.* It needs only, in a country like ours, where every citizen is born with the inheritance of freedom, and where the love of liberty and equal rights has not yet degenerated into the mere shadow of this mighty substance, to place any subject before *the people* in its true light, to insure a just decision upon its merits.

I do not intend that anything I have written should be interpreted an attempt to arrest any decision which the wisdom of Congress may lead that body to make, in relation to the continuance or discontinuance of the public Indian trade. I have no such object. My views have been given in official reports on that subject. I will just add, that my opinions have never been disguised—they have been frankly, and I think now, as I stated in an official report in 1818, that, unless *the proper support* be given to the public trade, it were as well to discontinue it. Nevertheless, no man doubts that trade, properly regulated, is *the best*, and, indeed, the only efficient power for the control and guidance of our Indian population, at least in their present state of improvement.

I trust the practice and policy of this office have been now freed from, at least, many of the imputations which have been, with so little ceremony, and with less justice, heaped upon them.

THOMAS L. MCKENNEY, S. I. T.

Office of Indian Trade,
Georgetown, April 26th, 1822.

(B.)

The charges preferred against me were, generally, as I was told, *anonymous.* My accusers were never produced. The charges embraced, in a general way, the implication against me, of "favoritism;" of a "corrupt abuse of my trust," in purchasing supplies of merchants in the District of Columbia, instead of from merchants in the larger cities, where better and more suitable, and cheaper goods, it was alleged, could be had; and that I had been led, as was asserted, to this favoritism, by collusions with those with whom I dealt, and the being paid certain douceurs, as the price of my alleged corrupt contracts.

The parties charged to be in collusion with me were named by these anonymous libellers, and were summoned, together with myself, before the Committee on Indian Affairs of the House of Representatives, when the following examination into all the charges took place. (See Gales & Seaton's collection of State Papers—Vol. II. of Indian Affairs, pages 418 to 427, inclusive.)

Examination of John Cox.

Question 1. Has Mr. McKenney participated, directly or indirectly, in any gains made by you on any merchandise applied for the Indian trade, annuities, or presents?

Answer. No, he has not.

Ques. 2. Have you at any time made presents to him, or to any member of his family; and if so, when, and to what extent?

Ans. Not to my recollection.

Ques. 3. Have you lent, or advanced to, or paid for him, any moneys, or for any of his family; and if so, when, and to what amount?

Ans. No.

Ques. 4. Do you know any other person who has furnished supplies for the Indian trade, &c., with whom Mr. McKenney has participated in any manner in any gain therefrom; or who has lent or paid for him, or any of his family, moneys; or who has made presents to him, or any of his family?

Ans. I do not.

Ques. 5. Do you know of any store, or mercantile establishment, in which Mr. McKenney was concerned, at the time of, or at any time subsequent to, his appointment as superintendent; if so, state what you know of the same.

Ans. I believe, but am not positive, that he was in partnership with a Mr. Hall, who had been living with him in Washington city before he received the appointment of superintendent; but not to my knowledge afterwards.

Testimony of John Cox, continued.

I have been an importing merchant during the time Colonel McKenney has been superintendent. My importations generally have been (since 1817) with a view to the Indian trade. I have supplied Colonel McKenney with goods to the amount of about $50,000 annually. I sold the goods in currency, without reference to sterling cost. Considered I sold them as low as they could be purchased at fair sale. I have not made Mr. McKenney any compensation, in any way, with a view to obtain the trade. I have endorsed some notes for Mr. McKenney, and Mr. McKenney has likewise endorsed for me. I am now on Mr. McKenney's paper as endorser, but am secured by his property.

Fifty per cent. on the sterling is equal to 150 per cent. Maryland currency; that is, suppose £100 sterling sells in this country for £150 sterling, that is equal to £250 Maryland currency. JOHN COX.

Second examination of Colonel Cox by Colonel McKenney.

Question 1. How long have you been a merchant in Georgetown?

Answer. Since June, 1798.

Ques. 2. When did you first turn your attention to the nature of the demand for Indian supplies, occasioned by the removal of the office from Philadelphia to Georgetown?

Ans. I think it was in the year 1809.

Ques. 3. Did you not sell, especially during the two or three years before I was appointed, large amounts to my predecessor?

Ans. I did.

Ques. 4. Did not your increasing ability to meet the demands of this office grow out of your increasing knowledge of the peculiar articles in which it dealt?

Ans. It did.

Ques. 5. Was there ever and even the least evidence of partiality shown you?

Ans. Not that I know of.

Ques. 6. On the contrary, did you not think the rigor of the inspection, and the closeness of the comparisons I made, were sometimes too pointed?

Ans. I did.

Ques. 7. Did there not, on at least one occasion, words pass between us, by reason of my strictness, in which you conceived I questioned too closely your statements?

Ans. There was one occasion, within my perfect recollection, in which Mr. McKenney and myself differed as to the relative value of some goods, in which I thought that Mr. McKenney was too tenacious of his own opinion and judgment.

Examination of J. W. Bronaugh.

J. W. Bronaugh, chief clerk in the store of the superintendent at Georgetown, says: That, when Colonel McKenney took the store as superintendent, an inventory was taken of all the goods on hand, agreeably to the original invoices. That the goods purchased since Colonel McKenney has been superintendent have been generally bought at Georgetown, of Colonel Cox, and of Mr. Wright, who were importers. Besides these, goods to the amount of from two to three thousand dollars per year have been bought at each of the stores of Messrs. J. & J. Cockran, W. Corcoran & Co., R. H. Fitzhugh, G. Gaither, and some others occasionally. That, besides those, goods were purchased for the trade at New York and in Philadelphia. That, when Mr. McKenney was appointed superintendent, he was in partnership with a Mr. Hall, on Pennsylvania Avenue; that, on his appointment, Mr. McKenney dissolved partnership with Mr. Hall. Does not know that Mr. McKenney has, since his appointment, had any interest with Mr. Hall in trade, or with any other person. That, since the dissolution, Mr. McKenney purchased from Mr. Hall an invoice of from ten to twelve thousand dollars' worth of goods, which were bought by Hall at Baltimore, on memorandum of Mr. McKenney. Knows of no other goods being bought of Hall by superintendent. The goods from Mr. Cox, importer, were bought without reference to sterling cost. Those from Wright were generally bought by the original invoice. Thinks the goods of Wright cheaper than those purchased from Cox, but not so good in quality. Thinks the goods purchased from the merchants in Georgetown, who were not importers, but who bought their goods in Philadelphia, Baltimore, and New York, as cheap as those bought of Cox and Wright. Understood that Mr. Cox was the endorser of Mr. McKenney on notes to be discounted at the banks. Has seen such notes, but does not know that this induced Mr. McKenney to purchase from him more than from others.

JER. W. BRONAUGH.

Second examination of J. W. Bronaugh, by Colonel McKenney.

Question 1. Were not due pains taken, by correspondence and intercourse with merchants, to ascertain yearly the state of the markets, before I decided to buy the annual supplies?

Answer. I think all necessary pains were taken.

Ques. 2. Was there ever, according to your judgment, an article bought of any man, when, after taking the pains to ascertain it, that article could have been bought, combining its suitableness and cheapness, for a less price of another?

Ans. I have no recollection that any article was purchased when it was known it could be had cheaper from another.

Ques. 3. Do you not believe that the Georgetown market was the best, for several years past, (say since 1815 and 1816,) for Indian goods, of any other market in the United States, especially for the *great and leading articles?*

Ans. I believe it was the best for blankets and strouds.

Ques. 4. Was it not the practice of the office to encourage competition, by giving samples to merchants, and every information touching the kind of goods in which we dealt?

Ans. It was.

Ques. 5. Was it not the business of the office to provide, as near as it was possible, and transport, the articles enumerated in the annual calls of the factors?

Ans. It was.

Ques. 6. Did you not, whilst packing in the spring of 1816, make out the list of articles enumerated in my letter to Mr. Edward Hall, of the 23d April, 1816, and report it to me as being then wanted? And were not the articles, including the blankets, which he offered, in all respects suitable and valuable goods, and wanted at the time?

Ans. I think I made out the list, and I know the articles were very suitable, and as cheap as others.

Ques. 7. When the articles arrived, did you not inspect them, and report on all of them that were bought that they were within the limits, were good goods, and suitable?

Ans. I did.

Ques. 8. Have not invoices been sent, year after year, from some of the older factories, containing the same quantity of the same articles, which, from their having been bought so long, and being unsuited to the trade, remained on hand?

Ans. I believe nearly so.

Ques. 9. Was not the advance of from sixty-six and two-thirds to one hundred per cent., the tested advance which had been adopted by my predecessor, essential, in the general operations of the establishment, to sustain the capital from diminution?

Ans. I think sixty-six and two-thirds per cent. was the maximum authorized by General Mason.

Ques. 10. Did not Colonel Cox show a good deal of feeling, and often declare, upon his honor, that he was not dealt as fairly by as he should be, by reason of the scrutiny which was exercised in buying goods of him?

Ans. He did.

Ques. 11. Was there not one occasion in which he told you he and I had had some words because of my exceptions to his goods, and perhaps questioning too closely his statements?

Ans. He did.

Ques. 12. Did you not, by my instructions, weigh, and examine, and adjust the parcel of goods referred to in my letter to Colonel Cox of the 10th April, 1821, and graduate the prices to a former purchase, to which this purchase referred?

Ans. I did.

Ques. 13. Was not the Georgetown market for furs and peltries considered by General Mason, and did you not believe it to be the best in the United States?

Ans. It has always been considered by me the best; and I have heard many dealers in the articles from New York, Philadelphia, and Baltimore, express the same opinion. I know General Mason believed it to be one of the best.

Ques. 14. Did we not uniformly realize more in Georgetown, for the sales made there, than was given at the same periods in any market in the United States ?

Ans. I believe so.

Ques. 15. Did not the purchasers attending, from Boston to Richmond, unite in this declaration ?

Ans. They did.

Ques. 16. Did not Mr. Kennerly, agent at St. Louis, in violation of my instructions, sell furs and other articles at St. Louis, in the year 1821, to wit: 625 rackoon skins, contained in packs Nos. 56, 57, 58, 64, and 65, from the Prairie du Chien factory; 2,500 muskrat skins, in packs Nos. 68, 69, 70, 72, and 73, also from Prairie du Chien; 80 wolf skins; 2,360 pounds feathers; 214 mats; 81 pounds beaver fur; 66 pounds deer skins; which, after deducting transportation from St. Louis to this place, would have sold for $3,597 11, according to the sale in Georgetown, to which they were destined ?

Ans. Mr. Kennerly did sell the furs at St. Louis, in violation of his instructions, and at lower prices than were obtained for them at Georgetown.

Ques. 17. And does not the said Kennerly now stand charged with said amount on the books of the Indian Office ?

Ans. He does.

Ques. 18. Did I ever, to the best of your knowledge and belief, apply a single cent, more or less, of the public money in my charge, to my own private affairs ?

Ans. Not to my knowledge.

Ques. 19. If I had so applied it, were not the checks and rules in the accounting system, which had been established, such as would have detected it ?

Ans. They would.

Ques. 20. Did I not make it one of these rules never to fill up or number a check; but, when payment was to be made, was it not made the duty, and did not you, or the book-keeper, or copying clerk, fill up the check, number it, and hand it to me for my signature, and then yourselves retire with it and apply it ?

Ans. We did.

Ques. 21. Was it not the rule of the office to write in the body of each check, and on the margin of the check-book, what each check was for, and to whom paid ?

Ans. It was.

Ques. 22. Were ever any payments made, except by checks thus prepared ?

Ans. Never, to my knowledge or belief.

Ques. 23. Were any moneys ever kept, except in bank, more than from ten to twenty dollars ? And did not the messenger receive this by a check ? and was he not held accountable for its disbursement in paying of dray and cart hire, and other incidental expenses ?

Ans. There never was.

A. B. Lindsley's statement.

A. B. Lindsley, agent to close the factory concern at Chicago, says: The samples exhibited were taken by him from the goods received from Mr. Varnum; and the prices affixed to them were those charged in the inventory. That the goods received from Governor Woodbridge, at Detroit, were equally high charged, and worse goods than received from Mr. Varnum, and worse damaged. Is of opinion that the goods received by him were generally charged from thirty to one hundred per cent. higher than they were worth in the Atlantic cities in 1822. This opinion is confirmed by comparison with goods bought by Indian traders in New York, in the spring of 1822, as well as by his previous knowledge of the market. A penknife, now shown to the committee, was charged at seven dollars per dozen, which was purchased in 1820, by the invoice, as recognized by Mr. Varnum, and which was not worth more than four dollars at private sale in Philadelphia in 1816.

A. B. Lindsley.

Second examination of Mr. Lindsley, by Colonel McKenney.

Question 1. Were you ever engaged in Indian trade?

Answer. Never, except in settling the United States' factory business.

Ques. 2. How much should a three point northwest blanket weigh, to be good? and how long and how wide should it be?

Ans. I do not know.

Ques. 3. Do you know how long the goods you have reported so unfavorably of were in the factory, the business of which you went to close; and by whom they were sent—whether by me or by my predecessor?

Ans. I do not.

Ques. 4. Did you not assign as a reason why the goods were sacrificed at Detroit, that of a *combination* among the purchasers?

Ans. It is probable; but I consider they generally brought their *present* value. But combinations existed, I believe, among the merchants, which I resisted all I could.

Ques. 5. Do you know whether the samples you have exhibited to the committee, of calicoes and baftas, were, or were not, from the *fag ends* of these goods?

Ans. I do not know that they were.

Ques. 6. Did you not sell some of the goods at cost? And how much more than cost? Of what articles?

Ans. I do not now recollect the articles, but some of the goods sold at Chicago brought more than cost, and others brought the cost. Some of them were not high; the flag handkerchiefs, for instance.

J. B. Varnum's statement.

Jacob B. Varnum produced several invoices received from Mr. McKenney. The first for merchandise forwarded from Philadelphia, in May, 1816, amounting to £315 1*s.* 9½*d.* sterling, on which an advance of 33⅓ per cent. was charged. Second, for merchandise forwarded from Pittsburgh, in 1816, being heavy articles, amounting to $495 33. Third, for merchandise forwarded by J. W. Bronaugh, by order of the superintendent, to Mr. Wooley, at Pittsburgh, to be forwarded to Chicago, amounting to $4,464 53; one per cent. advance charged as usual. Several other invoices were produced, none of which state from whence the goods were purchased.

Several samples of cloth, calico, &c., taken from the goods at Chicago by A. B. Lindsley, were shown Mr. Varnum. He could not recognize the samples, but is of opinion that the green cloth, from which the sample is said to be taken, was purchased in 1815, by General Mason; the calicoes in 1818, and the blue cloth in 1820, by Mr. McKenney. He was instructed, generally, to sell goods from 66⅔ to 100 per cent. advance, but much was left to his discretion. Finding he could not get that advance on the old stock of goods, he applied to Mr. McKenney for other instructions, who stated, in return, that his (Varnum's) situation would best enable him to judge of the propriety of reducing the prices, and gave discretionary power to sell at such prices as the nature of the case required, or to that effect. Mr. Varnum was not bred a merchant; was factor at Sandusky a short time before the war, and since the war had been at Chicago; has had no other practical knowledge of mercantile transactions than was acquired in those capacities; was in the habit of supplying Indian agents with goods from the factory; same profit as to Indian purchasers. Furnished Mr. Jouett, in one quarter, he thinks, about $1,800 worth, but usually not more than from $75 to $150 in a quarter; sold to officers and soldiers such articles as were not in immediate demand for the Indians. The powder received from the superintendent at $15 70 was accompanied by a letter from him, dated October 29, 1817, now produced, which shows it was purchased during the war.

JACOB B. VARNUM.

Second examination of Mr. Varnum, by Colonel McKenney.

Question 1. Were not the goods sent you by me, in general, good and valuable goods?

Answer. They were.

Ques. 2. After you selected the old and damaged goods for General Cass, were not those which remained on hand good and valuable goods, and suited to Indian trade?

Ans. They were.

Ques. 3. Were they not, generally, those sent by me?

Ans. They were, generally. JACOB B. VARNUM.

John Hersey's statement.

I, John Hersey, resident at Georgetown, late factor at the Choctaw trading-house, in the State of Alabama, testify and say: That in October, 1819, I was appointed factor at said trading-house, and continued to act in that capacity to October, 1822; that, on entering on the business at said house, as near as I now recollect, the amount of goods delivered over to me by my predecessor was about $14,000; many of which goods were so much damaged, or so unsaleable, as to render it impossible to sell more than $2,000 or $3,000, probably, of them during the time I was factor.

During the time I was factor, I received, as near as I now recollect, about $12,000 by the year, all which came to me through the medium of Mr. T. L. McKenney; about one-sixth of which came from New Orleans and Mobile; such as coffee, sugar, lead, and salt; the residue were from Columbia District and New York. When we received the goods at said house, we generally received accompanying invoices. I then thought most of the articles were of a fair price, and certainly of a good quality; except, in a few instances, some were damaged on their passage. From Colonel McKenney I received instructions to add from 66⅔ to 100 per cent. to the invoice prices; and the sales, on an average for the whole three years, were above 80 per cent. advance on the invoice prices. In payment of these things sold, I received deer-skins, furs, beeswax, tallow, and cash. The nett gains to government during the whole three years were between $8,000 and $9,000, after paying freight on such articles as were received from Mobile, and besides a remuneration of myself and all others employed there.

When I took charge of the house, I think, as near as I now can recollect, the amount of outstanding debts due the government was upwards of $13,000, not more than $1,000 of which were probably collected while I was there; and I now am of opinion that one-third of the remaining $12,000 may be collected.

I presume a majority of the debtors to government, when I went there, afterwards traded with me, many of whom might deliver me peltry and other things to an amount as great as the debts then due from them severally; each one, however, took other goods to an equal, and sometimes greater amount; so that, in most instances, the old debts remained on the books, uncancelled and unliquidated.

John Hersey, *Late Factor C. T. H.*

Mr. Hersey's second examination, by Colonel McKenney.

Question 1. Was there not in the Choctaw factory, when you took charge of it, a large quantity of old and unsuitable goods?

Answer. There was.

Ques. 2. Did I not, in my letters, direct that they should be disposed of at reduced prices, and on long credit, provided you could get unexceptionable security?

Ans. I was requested by you to dispose of the old and damaged goods, I think, at reduced prices, and on long credits, provided such security could be obtained.

Ques. 3. Were not the goods which you received of me in general suitable and fairly charged? and did you not do out of them your principal business?

Ans. To the best of my knowledge, they were charged at fair prices; they were of good quality; and out of them I did the principal business while there.

James Kennerly's statement.

I, James Kennerly, of St. Louis, do testify and say: That, about nine years ago, I was appointed transportation agent for the United States at St. Louis, and have transported all articles from said St. Louis to Fort Edwards, and to Prairie du Chien, on the Mississippi; Fort Osage, on the Missouri; and, within the last year or two, to Marie Decine. Among the articles transported were large quantities of powder and tobacco. In November, 1820, Colonel T. L. McKenney ordered into my hands forty packages of goods, supposed for the Indian trade, and the same are still in my possession unopened; and last spring I received the amount of $1,100, or thereabouts, in goods sent to me by Robert B. Belt, United States factor, from Fort Armstrong. Colonel McKenney never gave me any directions as to the disposal of these forty packages; but he told me they were purchased for the Indian annuities of the Chickasaw tribe; however, as they preferred specie, he agreed to take them again to the trade department. Four years ago, or thereabouts, I received several packages of goods sent to me by J. W. Johnson, United States factor at Prairie du Chien, which he considered as unsaleable in the Indian trade. I, by direction of Colonel McKenney, sold them at auction at St. Louis, and they went off at a great sacrifice, bringing, from the best of my recollection, not more than half invoice cost or price. Among the said articles sold, were coarse strouding, a large quantity of printed cotton shawls and of Madras handkerchiefs, a few pairs of morocco shoes, and a large number of gun screws.

All the furs and peltries which I sold at St. Louis were sold at a profit, without selection; but Colonel McKenney was dissatisfied at the sales made by me at St. Louis, and directed that the said furs and peltries might be sent by me to Georgetown. Accordingly, I sold only a small quantity at St. Louis, and forwarded the residue to Georgetown, which I could, without selection, have sold at a handsome profit at St. Louis. As to the goods at factories, Messrs. Johnston, Belt, and Sibley, told me they sold at sixteen per cent. advance on the cost and carriage. Three or four years, the fall supplies, intended for the Indian trade, did arrive so late in the season at St. Louis, that, in consequence of it, they could not be made to reach their place of destination till spring; by reason of which, the goods sustained damage, and the advantages of the trade with the Indians were not realized; though Colonel McKenney, on being informed of it, expressed his surprise, and said the goods were sent in season, and requested me to ascertain the reasons of the delay, in order that a prosecution might be commenced against the freighter.

JAMES KENNERLY.

Examination of Mr. Fitzhugh.

Question 1. How long have you been clerk and assistant packer in the Indian Office?

Answer. Between fourteen and fifteen years.

Ques. 2. Were not the heavy articles generally purchased at St. Louis and Pittsburgh? or, when here, were they not always put in with light loads, which weighed less than the weight for which payment must have been made, whether they had been sent or not?

Ans. Yes.

Ques. 3. Were not the supplies always sent off from the office, by the way of St. Louis, in season?

Ans. They were.

Ques. 4. Have you not copied many severe letters from me to Mr. Kennerly, complaining of his inattention to their transportation, with assurances that I could not, with all my good opinion of his integrity, permit the Indian supplies to be so delayed?

Ans. I have.

Ques. 5. Did not Mr. Kennerly reply, on one occasion, that he had not been as attentive as he ought to have been, and that he had trusted to others, but would in future be more vigilant?

Ans. I think he did.

Ques. 6. Did you help to pack the calicoes and cotton, samples of which Mr. Lindsley has produced?

Ans. I recollect having packed the knives and calicoes.

Ques. 7. Are they fair samples?

Ans. I do not know.

Ques. 8. Would you consent either to buy or sell by such samples?

Ans. I think the samples are rather too small to judge of the quality of the goods.

Ques. 9. Have you examined the invoices in regard to these goods?

Ans. I have. The calicoes sent to Chicago in 1818, at forty-five cents, were purchased in Philadelphia; and the knives in Georgetown, of Wharton & Grindage.

Mr. W. stated that the knives he sold to Mr. McKenney at seven dollars a dozen, he had retailed at eighty-seven and a half cents each.

M. Fitzhugh.

After the examination of the witnesses, Colonel McKenney addressed the chairman thus:

Mr. Chairman—I have, by your permission, looked over the several depositions of the gentlemen examined by the committee the other day, under the resolution of the House of Representatives of the 14th instant, " instructing the committee to inquire whether any, and if any, what abuses have been committed by the late superintendent of Indian trade, (Colonel Thomas L. McKenney,) in the purchase or sale of goods under the several laws formerly regulating the Indian trade, with power to send for persons and papers;" and I have submitted to the same gentlemen, to-day, such interrogatories as appeared to me to have a bearing upon the subject of the present inquiry.

I beg leave to trouble the committee with a few remarks, not because I have discovered anything in any of the statements going to sanction, in the smallest degree, the imputations which led to this inquiry, but because the occasion having been furnished by others, (I do not mean the committee,) in the expectation of detecting something in my official transactions which would tarnish my reputation, I cannot consent to let it pass without exhibiting such proofs as shall not only establish my claims to the confidence of the government under which, for six years, I was in the exercise of an important and responsible trust, (at least so far as the duties connected with that trust are concerned;) but, by disclosing *the principles* which governed me in the discharge of my duties as a public officer, place my integrity before the eyes of the committee, of the Congress, and the world, in the same light in which I have always had the happiness to contemplate it myself.

It is certainly very unpleasant even to appear to be one's own eulogist, but I trust to the nature of this inquiry to furnish the apology.

It may be proper for me to premise a few things.

1st. I was bred a merchant, and had all the advantages of information arising out of a large business, and frequent intercourse with our principal cities, as well since as during my initiatory progress in the counting-house of my father. From this, the committee may infer my competency to conduct a business entirely mercantile, as was the Indian trade; and not to *conduct* it only, but to judge of the suitableness or unsuitableness of the supplies required in its prosecution, and of their comparative cheapness.

2d. The calls for the articles constituting those supplies were furnished, annually, by the factors stationed at the several trading posts in the Indian country, and who, it is but reasonable to suppose, enumerated such articles only as were required in the prosecution of the trade. These calls, as far as it was practicable, were always complied with. From this, the committee may infer whether the articles forwarded were suitable or not.

3d. It was my good fortune to succeed to the superintendency of this trade a gentleman whose character for mercantile intelligence, and system, and integrity, needs no commendation of mine to give it weight. I found in the office the evidences of the most perfect system. I found in the several branches of it, among the agents, (so far as it was possible for me to judge of them,) intelligence and integrity, and, in the nature of their returns, the most perfect system of accountability. They were all, except the clerks in my office, strangers to me. I had never seen but one of them. I judged of them by their works. I supplanted none of them, neither those who were attached to the system, nor the purchasing agents in our cities, by others of my own selecting. When removals occurred, they were produced by death and resignations; when, with a view to the public interests, I recommended to the President such as I believed were "capable and honest." In doing this I consulted, as far as I was able, my own actual knowledge of the *ability* and *integrity* of the applicants. This was due to myself, for the *responsibility* was mine. From this the committee may infer whether my trust was made the instrument of "abuse" in conferring, so far as it relates to appointments to office, favors on my friends.

I have thought proper thus to premise; but I intend to show, before I have done, by something more than inference, what were the principles which governed me in the discharge of my duty as superintendent of Indian trade. My commission bears date the 2d day of April, 1816. I entered upon the duties of my office on the 12th of the same month. I had for some time, nearly two years before, disposed of my mercantile establishments, of which I was owner of two in Georgetown, and held an interest, till about the period of my appointment, in a store in Washington, under the firm of J. C. Hall & Co. *The obligations of my oath of office*, which forbade me to participate, directly or indirectly, in any trade or barter, except on the public account, made it necessary for me to give up my interest in that concern. I did so; and, in adjusting the preliminaries to that sale, I was kept from entering upon the duties of my office from the 2d to the 12th day of April, having solicited and obtained the superintendence of my predecessor, General Mason, till that concern was disposed of.

I had not been long in office before I heard the buzz of those insects whose business it is, according to Dr. Johnson, "to sting one, and fly away;" a kind of invisible agency of the prince of darkness, sent to annoy, and, if possible, to wound and destroy. They multiply in the atmosphere of public agencies, especially if they be *disbursing* agencies; and we have illustrated their activity and venom from their attacks upon the hero who first broke the charm of British invincibility, and who had established such claims upon the confidence and *gratitude* of his country, as one might suppose would have guarded him from such annoyances as these, even down to your door-keeper in a public office, who has entrusted to him no more of the public money than will suffice to purchase a straw broom or a mat. It was not for me, in the discharge of the trust with which I was honored, involving as it did disbursements of such various applications, to expect to live free from this kind of annoyance. I did not expect it. It was my duty, and I made it my business, therefore, to begin by providing such guards as should, at least, preserve me from any fatal consequences.

The first of these slanders was one which identified me, *after* my entrance upon the duties of my office, as a party in the concern of J. C. Hall & Co.; and again, if not a party, yet as deriving an indirect emolument in the purchases which it was circulated I was constantly making of that concern. And these slanders, after having remained in their elementary state for six years, have at last been embodied and made (and I thank the committee for bringing them within my reach) part of the subject matter of this inquiry.

So soon as I had ascertained that those insinuations were in circulation, I requested Mr. Edward Hall, through whom I had negotiated the sale, and who was interested, as he told me, in it, to embody the entire affair, down to the purchase of the only parcel of goods I ever made of him, (for, although there was a small invoice in addition to the first, yet it is *believed* to have been part of the principal purchase,) in a certificate, giving to it the solemnity and sanction of an oath. This was accordingly done, and signed in Georgetown, as the original, which I now submit, and which is the paper marked A, shows, on the 12th of November, 1817, and witnessed by John W. Rich, then book-keeper in my office. Mr. Hall being, as I learn, in Virginia, and Mr. Rich dead, I have procured the certificate of the brother of the latter, now in Washington, certifying to his brother's handwriting; and the oath of Mr. Richard Thompson, of Georgetown, identifying the signature of Mr. Hall. I have procured these, that no cavil may arise. I also beg leave to read the following letter (B) from my letter-book D, page 13, which will explain the *test* to which the goods he proposed to procure would be subjected, viz: an inspection and approval after they should arrive at the warehouses in Georgetown. They were subjected to this test, like all other goods which were ever bought in Georgetown, as Mr. Bronaugh has deposed; and, having passed it, were bought; and because I *had been* connected with the firm of J. C. Hall & Co., it has been insinuated that I participated in the profits of that transaction. I refer to paper A, just submitted, and ask if there be anything in it which would authorize such an insinuation? And I ask whether I must not have been constituted of more than degraded baseness, to have placed myself before Mr. Hall, who knew the binding obligations of my oath of office, as *a perjured man?* But I repel the insinuation; and, under the solemnities of the oath which kept the way to my passage to the office to which I was appointed, till I had "washed my hands" of all connexion with that concern, do I now swear, that I never participated one cent, either by profit or by present, more or less, in that purchase; nor, from the hour when the terms of sale were agreed upon, which separated me from that concern, in *any* transaction connected, either directly or indirectly, with the agency of either J. C. Hall or Edward Hall, or with any *other* individual who ever had transactions with the office of Indian trade during the period of my superintendency: and I challenge the worst enemy I have upon earth to convict me in this matter.

Let it be recollected that it was made my duty, by virtue of my commission, which constituted me sole judge of the purchases, to provide the *best* and the *cheapest* goods for the prosecution of this trade. For my attention to the state of the markets, I refer to my letter-books, and to the testimony of Mr. Bronaugh, in answer to questions touching this part of his examination. I never bought of *any one* without first satisfying myself that I was making the best purchases which the markets enabled me to make, taking the range of the New York, Philadelphia, Baltimore, and other markets, and bringing the prices and kinds of goods *into a just comparison* with the prices and kinds which were offered in our home market, and purchasing accordingly.

I beg leave to read to the committee a few letters, and the answers to them: say one to New York, to my agent in that city, J. L. Dias, (C,) with his answer, (D;) and another to Henry Simpson, agent at Philadelphia, (E,) with his answer, (F;) and to these I add a general reference to my letter-books, now in possession of the committee.

From the letters which I have read, and the replies to them, the committee may infer the state of those markets for Indian goods; I say *Indian goods*, because he who judges of the high or low cost of leading Indian articles, blankets and strouds, by a comparison, the blankets with any other kinds of blankets, no matter though the points be the same, or the strouding with any other kinds of cloth, and makes up his judgment from an *external* inspection, and not by *weighing* and *measuring them*, betrays at once his ignorance of the comparative value of these goods; and I appeal for the truth of this to the whole mercantile community.

Yet those goods, although, as these letters show, not to be had in either the New York or Philadelphia market, were to be had in Georgetown. My object in writing was to ascertain their value. The reason why the Georgetown market was the best, is plain: it was the place where the demand existed; and he must be a novice, indeed, in mercantile matters, who does not know the first principle of trade, "*that where a demand is, there will be also a corresponding ability to supply it.*" The progress towards this ability in the Georgetown market was gradual; and, by referring to the invoices, as did the committee of Congress, in 1817, of which the Hon. J. Pickens was chairman, it will be seen that, during the first years of the removal of the office to Georgetown, but few articles were purchased except in Philadelphia, where the office had been; but every succeeding year lessened the ability where the demand had ceased to exist, and increased it where it did exist.

I have one evidence in point, which I will submit to the committee, as to the ability of the Georgetown market to supply, (when the demand existed there, I mean,) the calls for Indian supplies. The arrearages of annuities occasioned by the war brought together, in 1816, the very first year of my agency, several of them; that is, for the years 1813, 1814, 1815, and 1816, all to be purchased and transported in one season, besides $20,000 worth of presents. Of these annuities and presents, *forty odd thousand dollars' worth* were purchased and transported to Governor Cass, at Detroit, for the purposes of his agency; but only about *eight hundred dollars'* worth were purchased outside of the District of Columbia. And what did Governor Cass say of those supplies? I will read an extract from the letter-book D, page 251, (G,) which I find incorporated in a report to the Hon. J. Pickens. Here, then, is *prima facie* evidence that it was not an "abuse" or corruption of office that led me to make purchases to so large an amount in Georgetown, *but the capacity in that market to supply the demand.* It may be well to remark, that a two-fold advantage was realized, which a purchase by agency, in other places, did not embrace: *first*, the selections were made under my own eye; and, *second*, the commissions were saved.

It may be asked, "Why, if I had such means of forwarding goods of such good quality, and upon such good terms, are there so many bad and high-charged goods at the factories?" The answer is plain. The factories contain goods which have been on hand from *seven* to *twenty* years. But for these goods, it is to be presumed, I am not accountable. I am, however, far from pretending that there never went, among the vast amount of purchases which I made in the six years of my superintendency, any high-charged and unsuitable goods. It would be preposterous: for where, let me ask, is the merchant, who, with all his care in supplying his single store, never gets, with his good and valuable goods, some which are not so?

But a short time before I received my appointment, the state of the markets throughout the United States was such as almost to forbid those who were of the mercantile community from purchasing at all. And as to the articles suited to Indian purposes, these were nearly out of the market. Powder, in those days, cost three times the price at which it has sold for since; and as to blankets, these were, of the proper kinds, entirely out of the question. Many of those which were sent among the Indian supplies, were manufactured with a texture like that of a hat, rolled out like a pelt; and cloth had to be bought, in some instances, made, in part, of hair! Yet this was the best that could be done; and no person will think of censuring my predecessor for sending those goods, because none better could be procured. We all remember to what a height, at about the period I refer to, all articles of merchandize had attained—from one to three hundred per cent. above what they have ever been since. But no one will think of laying the weight of such portions of these goods as are to this hour on hand at the factories, in the shape of censure, at my door.

It is asked, "Why I did not get rid of those old goods?" I appeal to my letter-book for the proofs that I made efforts to do so. But the difficulty in the way of accomplishing such an end is great—indeed, next to insurmountable. The merchants in our cities can, and do, disembogue their remnants and bad goods, through auctions, at any sacrifices. But there are no such facilities, let it be remembered, in the wilderness. Parts of the old stock at Prairie du Chien I did order to St. Louis, where they were sold at great sacrifices. (See my letter-book D, bottom of page 411.) The old goods at Chicago and Green Bay were sold to Governor Cass, for the Indian Department, at a sacrifice on the cost, (see letter-book G G, page 271;) and efforts were made at other points, as my letter-books will demonstrate.

But implications are made, and suspicion has been busy, because the great body of the leading articles for Indian supplies were bought at Georgetown; and because two persons, Colonel Cox and Thomas C. Wright, and not two hundred, had greater means, were better provided, and of course sold more to the Indian Office, than others. It is known to at least the citizens of this District, that these gentlemen have been at particular pains to provide themselves with the best supplies for Indian purposes; and Colonel Cox, in particular, for years, (as the testimony before the committee establishes,) before I had anything to do with these purchases, was a dealer with the office, and to very large amounts.

I have said, and I repeat it, and under the solemnities of the same oath under which I discharged my general duties as superintendent, that my purchases were made *wherever* and of *whomsoever* they could be *best* made. Nor did it become me to consider how little or how much was purchased of any man; but only whether what was bought of him was the best, the cheapest, and most suitable, which, at the time of buying, the markets could furnish. For the scrutiny that was exercised in my purchases of Colonel Cox, (and it was not peculiar to him,) I refer to the testimony of Mr. Bronaugh, and to a letter which I find in my letter-book G G, page 176, (H,) which I addressed to him on the subject of the supply of leading articles, which had been bought in the expectation, and with the understanding, that they were of the same quality and weight of the goods of the previous year. My terms in this letter were complied with. (See Mr. Bronaugh's testimony.)

I know no man, in my official relations, as a friend, *to be favored* at the public expense; and what my view of this subject is, and the principles which governed me, I have the evidence, and shall presently disclose it, to demonstrate. I will call the attention of the committee to another of the whispers which seldom fail to be made in relation to disbursing public officers: I mean those which embrace imputations of applying the public money to private uses. However this abuse may have sometimes occurred, yet, as the examination of Mr. Bronaugh has tested, it has no application to me. I never did, (and I add the awful sanction of my own appeal to the Deity in truth of it to that of Mr. Bronaugh,) apply, during the whole term of my superintendence of the Indian Trade Department, *one cent* of the public moneys, *more or less*—save those only which were allowed me for my salary—to my private uses. No; it was around this branch of my duty that I placed the most inflexible guards. And I defy the closest scrutiny into every transaction of the moneyed sort—and hundreds of thousands passed through my hands—to detect a single departure from the inflexible rule, *to keep the public moneys separate from what I might have of my own, and apply them* ONLY *to the purposes for which they had been entrusted to me.*

I will now, in conclusion, proceed to illustrate before the committee what the estimate was, which, as a public officer, I attached to my integrity; and how scrupulous I was in providing against the attacks of even the veriest veterans in the art of detraction and slander. I certainly feel how unpleasant it is to be compelled to speak of one's self; but, as I have said already, the occasion must furnish the apology.

I submit the oaths of two brothers; and I appeal for the testimony of their integrity and good name to General Reed, of the House of Representatives, who has known us all from our infancy, and who is himself known to be an honorable man; and also to the principal families of this District, among whom I will venture to take the liberty of naming General Mason, and Doctor Worthington, and General Walter Smith and his family, and the Rev. Mr. Addison, and the Rev. Henry Foxall; and I make these references, because the testimony I am going to submit is the testimony of my brothers. For these brothers I have the warmest and most affectionate attachment; nor did I ever decline, in a single instance, when it was in my power, and when my sense of duty authorized it, to do them any favor they asked. I submit their statements on oath, marked I, J, and ask that judgment be pronounced, whether, if I could be inflexible to an appeal like this—be driven from a compliance with the proposition, so reasonable in itself, by an instinctive dread of slander, and the imputations which I knew well enough would attach to, and perhaps tarnish my integrity—I could be influenced by corrupt motives to deal with others who, although acquaintances and friends, are, in the comparison of a brotherly relation, *strangers?* and whether, with these feelings on my part, I could consent, by participating, as has been insinuated, in the purchase made of Mr. Hall, to stand before him, he knowing the nature of my oath of office, *a perjured man?* No, sir; my good name was, and yet is, my all. Money is not the god of my idolatry, as those who know me will attest. It had been better for me to-day, perhaps, had I worshipped a little more devotionally at this shrine. My good name I have labored hard to preserve. I received it as a legacy from parents who died and left me little else with which to combat the roughnesses of this bleak and cheerless world; and the business of my life has been, and I trust will ever be to its close, to preserve that legacy, and to hand it over untarnished to an only son, to whom, although I may have little more to give, it may constitute a source of the most agreeable reflections; and, by a reference to the example which this very inquiry furnishes, he may be induced the more vigilantly to guard it, and hand it over in perfect purity to his posterity. I am concerned for its preservation. I will not, I could not, disguise it; but I shall expect it to be protected, on this occasion, only on the grounds of my having demonstrated that it has been unrighteously assailed.

A.

I do hereby certify, that, at or about the time Thomas L. McKenney was appointed superintendent of Indian trade, he was engaged in a mercantile business in Washington city with my brother, J. C. Hall; and that, of the term of said partnership, which was five years, about one only had elapsed when the appointment above named was made; that Mr. McKenney, aforesaid, stated to my brother his necessity, under his oath of office, to relinquish all mercantile affairs on his own account, and proposed to sell out to my brother. His terms were, for his interest in the concern for the four years then to come—the profits having been about $1,000 for the first year—five annual payments of $1,000, to include the proportion of profits that had arisen on the first year's sales; he (the said McKenney) to afford his endorsement on paper running in bank for Mr. Hall's accommodation, to the amount of $5,000. My brother declined giving as much as the sum required; but, through me, proposed to give a less amount, in similar payments, and on the same privilege of endorsement as referred to.

It was here I suggested to Mr. McKenney that my brother could be essentially served by any dealings he might have with him as a merchant for the public supplies, and that any promise of countenance to this effect would enable my brother to give more for the interest in the establishment about to be bought out; when Mr. McKenney replied, "I can make *no* stipulations on such a subject. I can hold out *no inducements* of the sort: if your brother have goods, such as my official duty requires me to procure, and his terms be as good as others, his chance will be equal. I cannot say *anything* to justify any *expectations of the sort.*"

Such was the manner and feeling of the said McKenney on the subject, that I feared he supposed me inclined to induce him, by an additional offer, to commit himself to deal with my brother upon terms which might include his own interests, apart from his official duty and obligations; whereupon I explained that my intention was not to insinuate that I thought he could be tempted to barter away his honor; far from it; but I only wished to get as much information as I could for my brother, as to the probable amount of purchases he might be able to make, as that would enable him to form a more correct estimate of the annual worth of the business he was in; to which Mr. McKenney replied, "*It is a point on which I cannot converse.*"

The bargain was at last concluded, by and through me, for my brother, and the sum agreed upon to be given was $2,000, in full of his proportion of the first year's profits, and for his interest in it for the four following years of the term of the partnership, in annual notes of $400 each: he (Mr. McKenney) agreeing to continue his endorsement on my brother's paper for $5,000.

Thus ended the purchase on the part of my brother, and the sale on the part of Mr. McKenney.

I do further certify and swear, that the notes above specified were all that were given, and that they were given solely as compensation for the said McKenney's proportion of profits that were then made, and for his interest in the business for four years then to come.

I do further swear, that Mr. McKenney urged me to come to some conclusion —I having undertaken to be the organ for my brother to Mr. McKenney—as he felt himself incapable to engage in the duties of his office until he had washed his hands of his own personal mercantile concerns; and further, that he—the said McKenney—always, during the negotiation, manifested the utmost repugnance to listen to the conversation which I had with him about selling to the Indian Department; nor did he ever justify the least expectations that any countenance, of any sort, would be shown to my brother or myself; and, finally, he "begged that no more might be said upon that subject."

Now, in justice to myself, it becomes me to say, that my whole motive in asking for information was to obtain, not any commitment from Mr. McKenney, but only to enable my brother to make his arrangements, by providing such goods as might be in demand, and to get some information of their kinds, and to place ourselves —my brother, Joseph C. Hall, and myself, I mean—before Mr. McKenney's view as sellers of goods, and to express a hope for a suitable patronage.

Finally, Mr. McKenney, some time after the sale, and when I called to offer him some goods, declined even to look at them himself; and then stated that "his having been in business with my brother would prevent him from ever making any purchases; that, whatever goods we might have to offer, we must present to Mr. Bronaugh," which we did.

I further swear, that I never in my life witnessed more circumspect caution, or apprehensions of suspicion, in any man, than I did in Mr. McKenney, nor did my brother ever sell but one parcel of goods to the Indian Department, and these were inspected and approved by Mr. Bronaugh.

EDWD. HALL.

Georgetown, November 12, 1817.

DISTRICT OF COLUMBIA, *County of Washington, to wit:*

On this 24th day of February, 1823, personally appears Richard Thompson before me, the subscriber, and makes oath, according to law, that the signature to the foregoing instrument of writing he believes to be the true signature of Edward Hall, brother of Joseph C. Hall, formerly of the firm of Joseph C. Hall & Co., of Washington. JAMES ORD, *J. P.*

JOHN W. RICH, *Witness.*

I hereby certify that the signature to this instrument, as witness, is the genuine signature of John W. Rich, as it purports to be.

WM. RICH, *Brother of John W. Rich.*

Washington, February 24, 1823.

B.

INDIAN OFFICE, GEORGETOWN, April 23, 1816.

SIR—You mentioned to me the other evening that your brother was then in Baltimore, and that he would be glad to attend to the purchase of any articles of merchandise I might want for this office. I respectfully avail myself of this tender of services, which you will be pleased to understand as being accepted *only* upon the condition that the articles I am about to name be, if purchased, *entirely acceptable in price and quality, and in such other respects as shall render them entirely proper for the purpose for which they are intended.* With this condition, you may write to your brother to procure and send on, with as little delay as possible, twenty pieces of dark purple and chocolate brown cloth, (that is to say, ten pieces of each,) to be three quarters of a yard wide, good quality, to cost *here* not more than seventy-five cents per yard; one hundred pieces of strouds, (about twenty yards in a piece.) Strouds are a blue cloth, six quarters wide, with a narrow cord about one inch from the selvage. For these I will allow (if good) one dollar and twenty-five cents per yard. Six pieces of green cloth (nearly grass-green,) six quarters wide, not to exceed in price one dollar and twenty-five cents per yard.

If these goods can be procured, and can be furnished to this office in fifteen or twenty days, (sooner would be desirable,) and under the conditions named, I will buy them. I am, &c. THOS. L. MCKENNEY, *S. I. T.*

Mr. EDWARD HALL, *Georgetown.*

NOTE.—Mr. Hall bought, also, a parcel of blankets, at his own risk, which, on arriving, were inspected; and, being then wanted were bought for the supplies then making up.

C.

OFFICE OF INDIAN TRADE, May 8, 1818.

SIR—I will thank you if you will take the trouble to make inquiries in your city after the following articles, and of the following descriptions: Northwest Company blankets—so called—three points, to measure six feet six inches long, and five feet six inches wide; to weigh, per pair, eight pounds and a half. Two and a half points, to measure six feet three inches long, and five feet two inches wide; to weigh, per pair, seven pounds and a half. Strouds, from six to seven quarters wide, to weigh, per yard, from one and half to one pound and three-quarters.

If these goods can be had, please inform me at what prices.

Respectfully, &c., THOS. L. MCKENNEY, *S. I. T.*

To J. L. DIAS, *New York.*

D.

Extract from so much of J. L. Dias's letter as relates to the call on him for information of prices, as per letter C.

As to the inquiries contained in your favor of the 8th, I regret to inform you that I have not been able to find out any blankets of the description therein stated, nor do I believe it possible to meet with any.

In 1813, I purchased, by order of General Mason, and forwarded to some of the factories, some two and a half and three point blankets, but I believe they were of the ordinary sizes and weights, for I remember that I had previously endeavored, in vain, to procure such ones as you describe.

Note by Colonel McKenney.—It will be recollected that both Mr. Dias and Mr. Simpson had the inducements of a commission for buying

E.

The same letter as that to Mr. Dias to Mr. H. Simpson, of Philadelphia.

F.

Copy of H. Simpson's letter.

PHILADELPHIA, May 11, 1818.

SIR—In reply to your favor of the 8th instant, I beg leave to state, that there are no blankets in this market of the precise quality and dimensions as those you ask for. For the particulars of the quality of mine, which are the best in the market, I refer you to my letter to you of the 14th March, &c. &c. H. SIMPSON.

THOS. L. MCKENNEY, Esq., *S. I. T.*

G.

Extract of a letter from General Cass to the Superintendent of Indian Trade.

I have been much gratified to find the goods sent here for the Indians are very well selected. Perfect justice has been done. I am informed, by persons in the Indian Department, that such a selection was never sent to this country. In fact, I cannot conceive that they could be better suited to the objects for which they are sent.

I refer to my letter-book D, page 348, to a letter of 24th June, 1817, in reply, in part, to one which I had received from J. W. Johnston, of Prairie du Chien. From the following paragraph, (although his letter to me is not at hand, but may be found by referring to the records of the Indian Office,) an inference may be made of the tenor of his letter to me from the following reply:

"It affords me pleasure (I say to him in reply) to learn that those goods are so very acceptable. It is surely a high commendation you bestow; and it is the more welcome, because you certainly know how to estimate an entire suitableness of the articles to the tastes of the Indians in your quarter. I notice with pleasure that you are attracting, by means of those goods, the attention of the Indians."

T. L. MCKENNEY, *S. I. T.*

H.

Letter to Colonel Cox.

OFFICE OF INDIAN TRADE, April 10, 1821.

SIR—Understanding that you are in Baltimore, I think proper to write to you on the subject of the merchandise conditionally purchased of you. The blankets, on being opened, turn out to be so inferior as to be almost unsuited to the trade. Besides the appearance and poorness of covering, which shows the twill on both sides, the wrong side almost uncovered, and having a black narrow stripe instead of an indigo-blue and wide one, the three points are charged to weigh eight pounds and a quarter, and weighs only seven pounds and a half. The smaller blankets are of a similar quality.

The strouding, charged as being the same with *the best* of last year's purchase, weighs four pounds less, and is narrower and thinner, of course.

It will be difficult to use these goods at all, and impossible to do so at the prices charged in the memorandum left by you. Nothing can authorize the admission of any part of them into the stock except a reduction of prices, governing the depreciation by the falling short of the weights.

I wish you to write me immediately, and say whether you are willing to let these articles be used at the rates embraced by the unlikeness of their quality to those that they have been called *equal* to in your invoice. If not, it is proper I should say, *they cannot be used at all.* I regret this the more, as there will be an interruption in the packing until I hear from you. Write *definitely* and *conclusively;* and this you can do, because I have no interest in misrepresenting these goods, and I wish to receive them only on fair terms.

Respectfully, &c. THOMAS L. MCKENNEY, *S. I. T.*

To Col. JOHN COX.

I.

GEORGETOWN, D. C., February 21, 1823.

DEAR BROTHER—I received, late this evening, your letter of yesterday, in which you request me to "embody the offer I had made me by a gentleman of New York, to engage with me in a mercantile establishment in Georgetown, stating the amount in cash which he proposed to furnish, the *chief object* of that proposition, and the conversation that passed between you and myself when I made it known to you."

In accordance with said request, I now make the following statement:

Not long after you had received the appointment of superintendent of Indian trade, a gentleman (Mr. William Floyd) from New York, then trading under the firm of Floyd, Smith & Co., proposed to me to engage with him in a large dry goods establishment in this town, which should have for *one of its objects*, or its principal object, a reference to sales to your office, and, of course, to keep the most abundant and suitable supplies of Indian goods. He proposed to furnish the means to carry it on *extensively.*

I communicated to you information of this offer, and stated its principal object, expressing my belief that we should be able to sell to you upon as good terms as any other merchants, and that the offer was one of importance to me. You instantly, with some degree of excitement, rejected the plan; and, as well as I can recollect, replied, "tell or write the gentleman that I can consider his proposition in no other light than an indirect attempt upon my honor and reputation." You further said, that no disbursing officer could, with every possible precaution, keep himself free from the suspicions of the evil-disposed, the disappointed and the malicious, deal with whomsoever he might; and that for me, however fair and honorable were my views, and would or might be your purchases, were you to make any, yet, as I was your brother, the public would never be satisfied but that corruptions and frauds were practised; that you had set out to avoid, as far as might be in your power, any just grounds of suspicion against any act of yours in the discharge of the trust which had been committed to you; and you never would, no matter how advantageous it might be to me, sanction the offer that had been made me, so far as it looked to your office to purchase goods of us. I recollect perfectly well that I endeavored to remonstrate with you, and begged you to consider that we never should ask you or expect you to buy a single article that should not be at a *fair price*, as low as it could be had elsewhere, and suitable to your wants, or the Indian trade; and that I could not see why it must follow, because I was your brother, and you made purchases of me, that therefore you must be corrupt. I assured you that it was not expected by Mr. Floyd, when he made me the offer, that you *should* or *would*, in *any instance*, depart from the *strict* line of your duty, for we would only expect you to purchase of us when our offers were good, and as cheap as others. You replied to me, with some sharpness: "Hush it. I never will sanction it. I am a better judge of this matter than you can be," or words to that import. Seeing me considerably hurt at your manner, and refusal of what I considered a perfectly fair and honorable offer, which might be of great advantage to me, you stated that it was your duty to *yourself* and *reputation* that forbade you to sanction the contemplated business between Mr. Floyd and myself, and that I knew you had the best and most affectionate feelings towards me; but, nevertheless, you reiterated your refusal, and declared most solemnly that you would not countenance the offer, nor buy of us, directly or indirectly, no matter how superior and cheap our goods might be. Not seeing the justice of your resolution, after I had repeatedly told you we could only expect or *desire* you to purchase when our goods were suitable to your wants, and *as cheap as they could be had elsewhere*, I made known to my brother Samuel what had passed, and requested him, as he thought you were fastidious, to call and see you on the subject. He did so, but without being able to change your views or purpose; and I abandoned the contemplated establishment.

Your affectionate brother, WM. MCKENNEY.

WASHINGTON COUNTY, *District of Columbia, ss:*

On the 22d day of February, 1823, came Wm. McKenney before me, the subscriber, a justice of the peace, in and for the said county, and made oath on the Holy Evangelists of Almighty God, that the foregoing statement is true, to the best of his knowledge. DANIEL BUSSARD.

J.

GEORGETOWN, February 22, 1823.

DEAR BROTHER—I received your letter of the 20th instant, in which you request me "to state, on oath, the conversation you had with me on the subject of the proposition which our brother William had made to him by a gentleman from New York."

I recollect that our brother William, I think in 1817 or 1818—I forget which—came to me, and represented that he thought you had taken a very unjustifiable stand in relation to an offer he had made to him by a gentleman of New York, of a considerable capital, to open a dry goods store in Georgetown, by refusing, if he did commence the business, to buy an article from him, at no matter what rates he might offer it. Thinking that you had not duly weighed the subject, and knowing that it was not necessary for a purchaser, because he dealt with his brother, to be a rogue, I went to your house, and found you in the fields. I represented my views to you, and urged you to think differently; and that, if William sold as cheap as any one else, and dealt in the right kind of goods, I could not see any reason why you should not deal with him. Your answer was, in substance, that you were a public officer; suspicion would attach to you, deal with him as fairly as you might, and that your reputation was worth more to you than any moneyed advantage, arising under his proposed establishment, would be to him. You rejected my entreaties, and with fervor declared you never would deal with him while you remained a public officer, thereby subjecting yourself to the slanders of the suspicious, which you might never have it in your power to put down. This I believe to be the substance of our conversation; and I am now constrained to acknowledge the propriety of your decision.

I remain your affectionate brother, SAML. MCKENNEY.

Mr. THOS. L. MCKENNEY.

DISTRICT OF COLUMBIA, *County of Washington, to wit:*

On this 22d day of February, 1823, before me, the subscriber, one of the justices of the peace in and for said county, personally appears Samuel McKenney, and makes oath on the Holy Evangelists of Almighty God, that the foregoing statement of the matters and things as therein mentioned is just and true to the best of his knowledge and belief. JAMES ORD.

GEORGETOWN, February 24, 1823.

We, the undersigned, having sold to Thomas L. McKenney, superintendent of Indian trade, on the 23d of March, 1820, two dozen single-bladed penknives, at $7 per dozen, and two dozen double-bladed penknives, at $5 50 per dozen, have no hesitation to say that they were charged *at the fair market price*, at that period; but have no recollection that the *one knife* furnished as a pattern is any part of the above sale. WHARTON & GRINDAGE.

We certify that we packed the above knives for Chicago factory in the year 1820.

JERE. W. BRONAUGH,
M. FITZHUGH.

(C.)

June 9th, 1819.—With delight we find in the few publications which reach us, that Christians of the different denominations are gradually approaching each other in a spirit of Christian love, tending to a closer union. Oh! that all those who feel themselves called to take an active part in the conversion of the heathen, would enjoin it on their missionaries to keep, as much as in them lieth, the heathen ignorant of the deplorable dissensions prevailing among Christians, and to live with laborers of other churches, whom they may find in the countries to which they are sent, or who may come after them, in such harmony, that the heathen of our day may be induced to repeat what those of the first ages of Christianity used to say: "See how these Christians love one another."

November 18th, 1819.—Upon our repeated request, the directors of our society at Salem, N. C., sent unto us the Rev. Abraham Steiner, late inspector of the young ladies' academy at that place, who actually, twenty years since, had gone out thence, as the first missionary to the Cherokees. He is a warm friend to the Indians, and in particular to the Cherokees, to whom this was his seventh visit. If I tell our esteemed friend, Colonel McKenney, that we expect much good to redound to the poor Cherokees from this visit, I know, from manifold proofs of his cordial interest in our undertaking, and great love to our dear people, he will kindly pardon our otherwise inexcusable silence. You kindly notice the state of my health. With thanks to our Almighty Benefactor, I can assure you, my dear sir, that since the cool weather has set in, I feel greatly revived. I own my constitutional weaknesses make me dread summer's return; yet, whenever a dreadful thought arises in my breast, I am reminded of our dear Saviour's prohibition, Matthew vi., 34. This sets my mind at ease; and I can truly enjoy the blessings of the present season, casting my cares for the future on Him who has with mercy upholden His poor weak child hitherto. Truly, no thought would to me be more grievous, than to be necessitated to bid farewell to the dear Cherokees, whose welfare is so very closely united with mine own; likewise, that for my weakness' sake, my good husband should be torn from his element—serving that dear people, according to their spiritual and bodily wants. We will trust in the Lord, and serve His cause with gladness here, while he affords strength. He can support us in our greatest weakness by his Almighty hand!

Of the marvellous manifestations of the power of our dear Lord, in the conversion of our people, and of the bright examples they give to others of a real change of heart, I will let your friend G. speak to you. Suffice it to say, for the present, that our hearts rejoice, and our eyes overflow with grateful tears! Yes, dear friend, you will yet see joy! You will hear true, good report, of your dear Indians! Thus will your unwearied faithful labors for their welfare be rewarded by Him, who alone is able to reward, and that most gloriously!

How sweet, how heart-melting are your sentiments, respecting our favorite bard! Truly, the sublime, the well-tried in the furnace of affliction, well-refined Cowper, had no thought, when he held forth the purest Gospel in his inimitable poems, that his spiritual songs would reach the poor heathen also—yea, even the North American Indians, and he be loved and admired by the Cherokees also! How would such an idea have gladdened his mind, and raised his drooping spirits; for he was the warm friend of all mankind! Some of his most expressive hymns are among our collection of hymns, used in our church, and frequently sung, even here, in our meetings of worship.

November 26th, 1819.—I will not intrude upon your valuable time, by a long apology for my too-long interrupted correspondence, but simply tell you, that now I snatch the first leisure moment, granted me by other multifarious avocations, for the self-gratification of conversing with you, and to paint on paper some expressions of gratefulness for your disinterested friendship, and its valuable effects. On the 14th of September we received three communications from your hand of the 17th July and 2d August, for which please to accept our warmest thanks. Since then, viz., on the 10th of November, I received from the General Post-Office an appointment, as postmaster at Spring Place, no doubt by your intercession. What can I render in return? My situation affords no probability that I shall ever be able to do anything for you. All I can do is, to draw on my faithful Banker above, to reward, in His divine way, your kind works of love. I have still another proof of your assiduous friendship, in a letter from the Hon. the Secretary of War, requesting me to report to his office the present state of our school, with the views and prospects for extending the plan, &c., &c., in order to come in for a share of the ten thousand dollars, which the President wishes to divide among those who are laboring for the instruction of our aborigines. The present year, 1819, will, in the eyes of posterity, form a memorable era in the annals of the Cherokee nation. Great things have been achieved for them, and deep and pure plans for their future felicity, have been laid. Memorable, also, will this year be in the annals of Spring Place. The number of souls gained to the banner of Christ, in this place, since the commencement of this year, though not great in itself, exceeds the number of those gained in the nineteen years preceding. It was in 1799, when the Cherokee chiefs granted permission to missionaries of our church to reside among them, which, therefore, is deemed the beginning of this mission. The first ten years produced no apparent fruit of the preaching of the Gospel; then the first person was by baptism engrafted in the Church of Christ. Two years later, a second person, and at the same time a white man, joined it. These three constituted our whole church, until the month of March last. But although the number was deplorably small, yet we have found the promise of Jesus truly verified: "Where two or three are gathered together, in my name, there will I be in the midst of them." In March, the mother of the renowned James Vaun was baptized, and shortly after her husband, a white man, joined the church. Since the beginning of September, William A. Hicks, brother to your friend, Charles R. Hicks, and his wife, and the wife of Major Ridge, whom you probably have seen, as he was formerly with a deputation at Washington, have been baptized into Christ's death. Perhaps, ere the year closes, another may be added to this number, as we know some who are earnestly seeking those things which the world cannot give. Do not these things, and many more, not here enumerated, warrant us to say: "The Lord hath done great things for us," &c. Our faith has, indeed, been much strengthened, and our hope enlivened, that we shall yet see the knowledge of our God and Redeemer fill this land, and the poor Cherokees walk in the light of His countenance. May He make us faithful in His service, diligent in the work assigned us, humble in ourselves, but confident in our reliance on Him. May He also be with you, our esteemed friend, and make your house His temple, wherein He dwelleth.

Spring Place, July 19th, 1820.—From this wilderness, we cannot, indeed, cheer your heart with the news that a nation is born, or converted in a day. The work of the Lord is progressing but slowly—still it is progressing; and for the smallness of the number of converts, we are amply compensated by the humble Christian walk of those who profess the religion of Jesus. Hitherto we have not had the painful experience to make use of church discipline, on account of deviations; how long we shall be favored to continue in this pleasing course, is known to Him only, before whose eyes the secrets of hearts are disclosed. May He grant us a long continuance of it; and whenever it shall be our lot to experience a reverse, may He endow us with wisdom from on high, to act according to the mind of Christ. On Sunday next, God willing, two more of the Cherokee tribe shall receive the seal of regeneration in holy baptism. May their names, and the names of their predecessors, be enrolled in the book of the Lamb, and there found unblotted in His great day! Our little flock will then, besides ourselves, consist of twelve persons.

(D.)

City of Washington, 25th January, 1827.

Sir—We beg leave to state, that in our opinion, much good would result to the various Indian tribes within our jurisdiction, and the humane objects of the government be greatly promoted, by sending some intelligent individual to visit those tribes upon whom it is deemed most important to make a favorable impression as to their settlement west of the river Mississippi.

Colonel McKenney is not only fully possessed with the views of the government, but, in our opinion, he possesses more the confidence of the Indians than any person in the United States, who could so easily be employed for this desirable object. He has perhaps, likewise, equal, if not a superior knowledge of the Indian character and disposition than any person who would likely undertake this work. We would, therefore, suggest the propriety and expediency of directing him under proper instructions to visit the Chickasaws, Choctaws, and other southern tribes, after he has completed his work to the north, with Governor Cass, this coming summer. The seat of that operation will be at Green Bay, we understand, from which point it would be easy and convenient for him to pass through the Western States to the tribes, and visit most, if not all, previous to the next session of Congress.

There is a peculiar propriety of devolving this duty upon the person who is at the head of the Bureau of Indian Affairs, and if he should fail in making as deep and favorable an impression, in a first visit, as may be anticipated or desired, yet the information which he would acquire, and bring back to the government, of the condition, feelings and disposition of those tribes, would be, in our opinion, exceedingly valuable; and the good resulting from such a tour, in this respect, would be worth the trouble and little expense attending such a work. With these impressions we recommend that such information be obtained, as to what are the real views and feelings of these tribes, and we respectfully recommend that Colonel McKenney be employed to ascertain and report them, and to execute such other trust as you may deem it proper to confide to him.

With great respect,

Your obedient servants,

Richard M. Johnson,
Thomas B. Reed,
William H. Harrison,
William Hendricks,
H. W. Conway,
J. S. Johnston,
H. W. Edwards,
E. F. Chambers,
T. P. Moore,
William McLean,
William Haile,
Joseph M. White.

(E.)

Chickasaw Nation, 10th October, 1827.

Sir—I have met the Chickasaw chiefs in council, and, in pursuance of your instructions, ascertained their views in regard to their removal west of the Mississippi. They consent to go, on the following basis:

First, that provision be made for three chiefs from each of their districts, (there are four of these,) three white men of their own choosing, and a physician, to be joined by three scientific men from Washington, or elsewhere, to be appointed by the government, to go with them and visit the country, and judge of its fitness in soil, climate, &c. They agree to go upon this business of examination on the first of May next.

Second.—If they approve the country, they consent to accept it, acre for acre, for theirs, provided it be cleared of every body, and guarantied to them for ever; and provided they be placed upon it, in such improvements as, on examination, they may be found to own here, in houses, mills, fences, orchards, stock, &c.; and provided the country be laid off into counties, and schools established in sufficient number for the education of their sons and daughters, and a government be established over them, upon the basis of that of the Michigan Territory; and provided that a suitable force be kept among them to secure them from harm, which they propose to augment by an organization of their people upon the plan of our militia; the whole to embrace, on their part, political privileges and civil advantages, as these are laid down in your report.

I need not tell you, that I found the subject one of extreme delicacy, and the way to it almost wholly barred by excited prejudices and a deep sense of wrongs long endured. Upon a full survey of the whole ground, from Saturday till yesterday, I concluded there was but one way of approach—this I attempted, and it succeeded as stated.

I will have the honor of forwarding, the moment I can find time to copy them, my address, with a minute of the proceedings of the council, and the answer of the chiefs. The council included all the chiefs of the nation except three, and these were prevented, by causes over which they had no control, from attending—but the nation will bear out those who have acted, and it now remains for the government to sanction and confirm the understanding, or to decline it.

I shall leave here in half an hour for the Choctaw Nation, having sent runners ahead to Colonel Ward, to assemble the chiefs to meet me. I wrote in haste, and in my tent, and upon my knee, not a little fatigued from the anxiety and toil of yesterday, and from being up till late concluding and signing the conditional understanding with these people.

The Rev. Messrs. Stuart and Bell, and Blair and Holmes, attended the council. It affords me sincere pleasure to state, that those gentlemen most heartily cooperate with the government on the subject of removing, to a permanent and suitable home, these long oppressed people. They agree that the salvation of these people can be secured in no other way. You may rely upon it that the Chickasaws are honest in their designs to fulfil every *tittle* of their obligations, if their terms are accepted. I believe it is the only ground on which they will listen to an exchange of country, and, I must add, we ought to ask of them to assume no other.

I have the honor to be,
With great respect,
Your most obedient servant,
THOMAS L. MCKENNEY.

To the Hon. JAMES BARBOUR, Secretary of War.

I omitted to add, that a condition is inserted providing for reservations for some of their people, not exceeding *twenty*. I could not do else, after so unexpectedly favorable a result, than make these chiefs, some of them aged and poor, and who had come from twenty to fifty miles to meet me, without knowing for what, (for I kept everything to myself till yesterday, except to tell them and to counsel them as their friend,) a present of $50 each, and the lesser chiefs $25, with a present of goods amounting to about $245, for their families, in all about $750, on bills to each one on Major Smith, with authority to him to draw on you for their respective amounts.

This is a cheap council. I have promised a medal to each chief in addition, and some three or four rifles to the young men. I have tried to give pleasure to all, and I believe have succeeded.

THOMAS L. MCKENNEY.

MAYHEW MISSION STATION,
Choctaw Country, October 10th, 1827.

Sir—I had the honor of writing to you yesterday from the Chickasaw Nation, thirty-five miles from this, that I had, the day before, concluded a conditional arrangement with the chiefs of that nation for an exchange of their country; the outlines of which arrangement I had the honor, in that letter, hastily to embody. I now enclose, herewith, copies of my address, their answer, and my reply, marked A. B. C.

It will be seen from my address, that I act, as well for the Indians as for the government; and from their answer, that the address was, in all things, fully responded to. It may, perhaps, be proper for me to explain why I assumed to act in this twofold character; and why the Indians were not left to propose their own terms. It might be sufficient for me to state, that I have never been able to separate the justice and honor of the government from the best interests of the Indians; and assuming this to be true, my duty, to say nothing of policy, embraced not only the province of a negotiator on the part of the government, *but under the existing state of things*, of moderator, and so far as I might esteem it essential to the great object in view, *guide* also. And it might be added, that no exception ought to be taken against the adoption of any means, that are in themselves moral and just, which may be used with the view of accomplishing a righteous end; and surely none, if those means result, as in the present case, in the accomplishment of such an end. But I prefer to be more particular.

Aware of the settled dislike of these people to anything in the shape of a direct proposition for their country, and that recent negotiations, though conducted by three distinguished citizens, chosen no less on account of their intelligence, than for their admitted knowledge of the Indian character, had totally failed; and that the large amount of means, which, by Congressional appropriation, had been placed at their disposal as an auxiliary aid, had been equally inoperative, it would have been presumptuous in me, when employed in the same service, and so immediately after the recent failure, and unsupported by a single dollar, to have occupied any one of the positions assumed by those commissioners; or to have approached the subject by any one of the avenues which had been trodden by them. There appeared to me to be one way, and *only* one way, left, and that was the way of my preference, and would have been under any circumstances. But although thus restricted by my views of the subject, I felt the greater enlargement, and more confirmed hopes of success. The way, in a word, was precisely that in which, from my heart, I preferred to approach these people. Accordingly, I gave out, on entering the nation, that my visit was a visit of friendship, that I had taken a long journey to see and shake hands with my brothers, the chiefs of the Chickasaw nation, and as they were scattered over the country, and my time was short, I hoped they would meet me at Levi Colbert's, where I would remain a few days to give them time to come in. And to make sure of their receiving this message, I sent runners, where I could do so, to deliver it to the chiefs, personally. On arriving at Colbert's, which was on the eighth day after my leaving Memphis, (visiting in my way, in pursuance of your instructions, the missionary establishments, which, together with my visits to the agencies on my entire route, also in pursuance of your instructions, will form the subject of a special communication,) I found I had been preceded by Major James Colbert, and the old interpreter, McGee, who, on receiving my message, had hastened to meet me. I was received by Levi Colbert, who is the counsellor of the nation, and by these two men, with every demonstration of gladness. I repeated the message that I had sent through their country, when Levi Colbert, in reply to the hope I expressed that I should not be disappointed, asked how long I could remain? I answered, until Monday. "If," said he, "you will tarry till Wednesday, I will try and have them all in, and if possible, by Tuesday, at twelve o'clock." I consented; when he immediately sent off runners from twenty to fifty miles round. Meanwhile the chiefs began to arrive, until by Monday night they had all come in except three, and two of these were sick, and one was absent; one of the former, however, sent an aid to represent him. Each chief met me with the utmost cordiality, and in terms of friendship and confidence that it would be tedious to state. I will, however, note the language of Levi Colbert. "It makes my heart glad, brother," said he, "to see you. I feel as if some good thing was to happen to us." Then grasping my hand, he continued: "Yes, and never since, about three years ago, when I left my son with you, have I gone to sleep without having you before my eyes. You are our friend, and we all look upon your visit as a great blessing, for we are in trouble."* I replied, that a regard for them, and a strong desire to see them, and to see them happy, had brought me into their country; that their troubles, of whatever sort they might be, should have my closest attention, and such as I could relieve on the spot, I would; and such as I could not, I would take home to their Great Father at Washington, who looked upon them as his children, and would listen attentively to their cries; and then added, that I knew of some of their troubles, and serious enough they were, and if they would meet me in council, in the morning, I would prove to them that I was their friend, by showing them the way to become a great and happy people, and by advice in other things, which, if they regarded their own happiness, and the happiness of their children, I hoped they would take. They greeted this language like a people would the return of milder and calmer seasons, after having been long buffeted by storms and tempests, and replied: "*We know you well.* We promise to meet you in council, and listen well to what you may say." I then prepared the address, as it now stands, giving none of them, meanwhile, the slightest conception of the nature of the advice to which I had referred, nor had they any idea of it until it was disclosed by the address itself, in council.

It may now be seen why I adopted the course I did. I found myself surrounded by a people who appeared to look up to me as their friend. I felt that I had their confidence, and knew well that the charm of this powerful influence would have been dissipated by the very first sentence that I might have delivered, bearing directly on the subject of an exchange of their country. All their hopes in my

* His reference was, as I found afterwards, to their domestic matters, but especially to their agency concerns.

friendship would have vanished, and the issue, I am confident, would have been *a total failure*, besides a loss of their confidence in the future.

Our council met the next day, (Tuesday,) at 10 o'clock. There had been the evening before a severe storm of thunder and lightning, and rain. The morning was bright, and calm, and beautiful. I told them I could not help thinking that the confusion and storm of last night, its restless and unsettled character, and the suffering which everything around appeared to endure, was an emblem of their own past lives. They had never been a composed and settled people, but were like the storm of yesterday, in constant excitement, and knew no rest. They answered, "*It is so.*" But this morning, I continued, is calm and beautiful; and I cannot help hoping that the Great Spirit has sent it as an emblem of what your future lives are to be. They said, "It did look a good deal like it." Four of the missionaries being present, having come that morning on my invitation to attend the council, I added—The business we are about to engage in being viewed by me of the greatest importance, and as the Great Spirit directs and governs all things, and takes pleasure in seeing his children happy, it is my wish, if you have no objection, that our aged father Bell, would ask the Great Spirit to smile upon our council, and direct our deliberations to a happy and prosperous issue; that in their Great Father's great council in Washington, a good man every morning spoke to the Great Spirit, and asked for direction in all things, and to bless their deliberations. They answered, "It will be very agreeable to us;" when this excellent, and useful, and venerable missionary, prayed accordingly. I then told them I had a great respect for the pipe: it was an emblem of peace and friendship: that I had brought a long and handsome one, made by their brothers on the other side of the Mississippi; which, if one of their young men would fill and light, we would smoke. They answered—"That is good—the pipe is the Indian's—we will be glad to smoke." It was lit, and smoked accordingly.

I then told them I was ready to hear them; and, as they had spoken of troubles, I would listen attentively to them, and promised to relieve them all I could. [These I will have the honor to hand to you on my return, with a statement of my reply, and what I did towards a relief of their grievances.]

Having heard all they had to say, and noted it all down, I told them I would now make good my word, by showing them that I was their friend, and give them advice which I doubted not they would follow; that to have all well understood, and that their interpreter might be able the better to interpret it, I had written it down, and would read it. They spoke and said, "We will be glad to hear you." I then delivered the address, and the council rose at about one o'clock. In the afternoon they assembled, by themselves, to deliberate; and in two hours sent me word they had agreed to all I had said, and asked for my paper, from which to make out their answer. By twelve o'clock at night the whole business was closed.

I hope I may be excused for including in this report the foregoing detail. It will no doubt be tedious, but I mean it to take the place of the usual accompaniment of a separate paper containing the proceedings of such councils.

I will now proceed to offer some remarks on the terms proposed for an exchange of country with those people, and which they are sincere in their desire to carry into effect; and upon the probable cost attending their execution.

The reasonableness of the liberty proposed to be granted to them first to examine the country, will not be disputed; nor will, it is presumed, the stipulation which provides that the cost of the examination shall be ours. The justice of both is too apparent to need illustration or justification. The proposition to emigrate comes from us, not from them. The cost of looking at the country to which they are invited to go, and which we propose to give them in exchange for theirs, it were time thrown away to attempt to prove, should be ours. And as little would it comport with justice, for us to ask them to leave their homes, and such comforts as they have here, without providing them with homes as good there, and comforts of at least equal extent. Their work-shops and their mills, though few in number, and common enough, are the labor of their own hands, and should not be asked of them without an equivalent, not in quantity only, but in kind—and even improved. They should not be left to toil again in their erection. A want of skill quadruples the labor, if performed by them, and the absence of science multiplies it even beyond that. The work should be done for them. As to their stock, it is their personal wealth; and not attaching to the soil here, and being indispensable to them anywhere, it should not be considered a burden to replace it for them, and at our cost, at their new homes. Theirs they could not get there; and it would not comport with our magnanimity, as a great nation, to ask them to sell, and give us the money wherewith to purchase more! When they shall sell, they will need the proceeds to pay off their debts, settle up their affairs here, and should any be left, it will be needed, wherewith to secure those little comforts which, as human beings, they may require in a new country; and for which there is no provision in the terms of exchange, not even the usual one of support for a year after they shall arrive at their new homes. This, then, will be the only item for which we do not receive at least a partial equivalent here, in the increased value which their houses and fences, &c., will add to the lands proposed to be left by them; unless, indeed, it be thought proper to count the cost of supporting the government of the territory proposed to be established over them, and of the county schools. These latter, we are bound, in common justice, to support anywhere, if we mean to maintain our character for an enlightened and humane and Christian people; and as to the former, or both, what, I ask, is their cost, compared with the proceeds of all this vast and fine country which they propose to abandon? Nor will it be thought unreasonable, that they should be made secure, in the new country to which they propose to go; because, here they lie down and rise up in the most perfect security—there their fears, at least, may be alarmed, if no more. It becomes us, therefore, to see to their security. Justice and humanity both demand it.

It is presumed that no exception will be taken to their having a government, or their being represented in the manner stipulated in the Congress. Both measures are right in themselves; and as to the privilege of sending a delegate to Congress, if the privilege of living under a government be ceded, it appears to follow as a consequence, and a consequence no less important to ourselves than to them. This connecting tie between the territorial government there, and the Congress here, it is presumed, would be esteemed indispensable. But if there be any exceptions taken to it, they can be those only arising out of prejudice; and this feeling it is easier to meet and overcome by precedent than argument. In compliment to it, therefore, I will refer to a similar privilege, guarantied in 1785, I think; and in the 12th article of the treaty of Hopewell. If I am not mistaken, the provision is in these words:—

"*That the Indians,* (meaning the Cherokees,) *may have full confidence in the justice of the United States, respecting their interests, they shall have the right to send a deputy, of* THEIR OWN CHOICE, *whenever they think fit, to Congress.*" This may suffice.

It may possibly be thought by some, that money should have been proposed, as an equivalent for the enumerated improvements which it is proposed to abandon, and on the grounds, that the government would be saved the trouble of building and putting up houses, and mills and fences, &c., in their new country. I could not in my conscience recommend this. All who know anything of the Indian character, know how improvident they are, and will admit that a moneyed consideration would be a fruitful source of evil to them, and would, doubtless, render the majority of them homeless and houseless for the rest of their lives. A recent illustration has been had, of the impoverishing effects of a money payment, in the Creeks. I believe them to be poorer, and to have suffered more, since they received the large amount secured to them under the treaty of Washington, than they have been for twenty years before. Besides, it will not be a task of such difficult accomplishment, nor will the cost be so enormous, as perhaps at first view it might appear; and this I proceed now to show.

In regard to the first, the whole undertaking should be upon contracts, in the usual form of public advertisement, and by bond and security for the faithful execution of the trust. There should be three contracts; one for building houses and mills; one for putting up fences and planting orchards; and one for supplying the stock, &c. Commissioners should be appointed, to examine and report the kind, and sizes, and numbers of houses, and the quantity of fences and orchards, &c., here. And now for the probable cost.

The population of the Chickasaw nation may be put down at four thousand, they having increased about four hundred within the last five or six years. I will suppose the families to average five souls each; which will give eight hundred houses. These houses, judging from what I have seen, and from inquiries made with a view to the estimate, may be built, with the addition of puncheon floors, for an average cost of one hundred and fifty dollars. This I think a *high estimate.* The most of them I have seen, are of rough logs, piled up in a square, with roofs of boards, confined down by pins and saplings, and daubed in, (such of them as are filled in at all,) with mud. The chimneys, those that have any, are generally of split or round sticks, put up in squares, and daubed with mud; and the houses are generally small and comfortless, and might, numbers of them, be put up for ten and twenty dollars. But there are some comfortable houses owned by the half and quarter breeds, some of which, and the best of them, (but they are few,) may have cost a thousand, and some, including their cribs and stables, &c., two thousand dollars. The estimate of one hundred and fifty dollars for each family, I think, will cover the cost of building, if the country they may select be a wooded country, and they will take care to select no other. This branch of the expenditure, then, may be put down at one hundred and twenty thousand dollars.

The number of their mills, it is believed, does not exceed ten. I estimate these to cost an average of five hundred dollars each, which is five thousand dollars.

Their work-shops, I do not think, exceed fifty—which, with their tools, may be estimated at fifty dollars each; or twenty-five hundred dollars for this item.

Their orchards are few, and limited in extent, and may be replaced for one thousand dollars.

Their fences may be estimated to cost fifty thousand dollars.

Their stock of all kinds, averaging two horses and two cows, and five hogs and a dozen of poultry to each; and the price of a horse at forty dollars, of a cow at ten, a hog at five, and a dozen of poultry at one dollar, will make a total of eighty-four thousand eight hundred dollars.

The probable cost of the visit to examine the country, I estimate at $10,000; and of their removal to it, at one hundred thousand dollars.

The total of cost, (except the annual estimate for the government, the schools, and the military,) is, according to the foregoing estimate, *three hundred and ninety-five thousand eight hundred dollars*—or, suppose a fourth be added, so as to show *the utmost* extent of cost, it will make the cost $494,750.

The annual expense, on account of the government, may be assumed to be the same as that of Florida or Michigan; for the support of schools annually, for twenty years, (where the limit may be fixed,) at $50,000,—and for the military, not more than it would require to support ten companies elsewhere; and I assume, that this force, if judiciously located or moved about, would be sufficient, in the present broken state of the Indian power; nor need this be retained but for a few years, as the proposed organization of their own people will doubtless, very soon, supersede the necessity for it.

In regard to the missionary establishments—these would, of course, be broken up here; but these excellent people would follow their present charge to their new homes. Whilst justice would demand that a remuneration of the amount expended by them in buildings and improvements, over and above that received from the government, should be made them, it would, from what I have seen, be fully realized in the extra price which the lands they stand on would bring; and which might be sold, owing to the high state of improvement in most of them, at a great advance. This sum, too, would form part of the fund for the civilization and improvement of the Indians, wherever they may settle, as it has been applied here.

I am aware that exceptions are taken by some to the policy of a removal, *even under such circumstances*, or, indeed, under any; but, whenever the time may come for a trial, it can be defended; and unless I am wholly deceived in the entire scheme, it can be demonstrated to be the *only policy* by which the Indians can be saved, and elevated to that rank of being which there can be doubt it is the pleasure of their Maker they should enjoy.

I shall leave here to-morrow for the Choctaw Agency, having sent an express with my greetings to the chiefs, and an invitation to meet me at the agency. I hope to conclude my interview with them by Tuesday next, when I shall pass on to the Cherokees, and thence to the Creeks. Should the Creeks not have concluded to cede that strip of land, I shall endeavor, under your special instructions, to secure it; and will, at the same time, ascertain their dispositions to unite in the plan adopted by the Chickasaws. I can form no opinion of the probable success which may attend my interviews with the remaining tribes, but hope for the best.

One thing, I think, may be assumed as certain; and that is, if the Chickasaws become once placed under the kind of government proposed to be given to them, the other three southern tribes will follow. It may require time, but they will all, in my opinion, with suitable management, eventually go.

I have the honor to be,

With great respect, your ob't serv't,

THOS. L. MCKENNEY.

Hon. JAMES BARBOUR, *Secretary of War.*

Talk delivered to the Council held with the Chiefs of the Chickasaw Nation, at Levi Colbert's, on Tuesday, October 9th, 1827, by Thomas L. McKenney.

FRIENDS AND BROTHERS: I have long wished to see and shake hands with the chiefs and head men of the Chickasaw nation. The Great Spirit has made my way clear, and I am come. My heart is glad.

Brothers: This visit, so long wished for on my part, I sincerely hope may not be without its use to you and your people. It is to show you my heart that I have come. I know there is nothing in it but friendship for you; and the more I can make my heart plain, the more will you see why I am come. I have nothing to conceal from you; you are my brothers. My great difficulty will be in making plain to you what I see, though I see it so clearly myself; and that is, *the path which is to lead you and your children's children to prosperity and happiness.* Is not this the path you all desire to walk in?

Brothers: Give me your ears, and, what is of equal importance, give me your confidence. If you think I am come to do you wrong, or give you bad counsels, you do me great injustice. I am not come but as your friend, and if there is a chief present who doubts this, let him speak, and I will not say another word.

Brothers: I know well who you are that I am addressing. I know you are not children, but men, and men of experience, and men of wisdom. I know, too, that the smoke of this council-fire comes not of ashes, but of living fire—it rises out of our hearts, for we are friends.

Brothers: You have long had your eyes open upon the past. You have seen much, and your hearts have suffered much.

Brothers: What have you seen? It pains me to call your attention to it—but I must be just to you; and if a review of what has gone by is painful, it may also be useful. Look to the rising sun! Was there not a time when the red man roamed free over all the hills, and reposed in all the valleys, even to where the sun comes up from behind the eastern mountains? But who occupies all that great country now? Not the red men! Purchase after purchase has been made until those who are left, and they are few, indeed; (like the few dying leaves that quiver on the trees, after the frost has come,) until those few, I say, have got back to this distant region; and now, though you were once a strong and mighty people, you are weak, and poor and helpless!

Brothers: This thought would not be painful to you, if, after all your difficulties, and the thinning of your people, those of you who remain were situated as men ought to be; if your present state were secure; if you felt easy on your lands; and if no more evils appear to await, or if you had hope to cheer you—a hope that would say something like this to you:

"It is true you have been a wandering and afflicted people; you have become diminished to a few; but see there! In the future you will rejoice and be glad; there you will find a firm footing. No people will ever move you more. Your children will flourish, and your children's children will be a happy and a great people."

Brothers: Behold that hope now: I am come to bring it to you. It was that you might hear this cheering voice, and see that lovely prospect, that I am come. I knew you were afflicted, and I was sorry for you—I knew you were in darkness, and I am come to bring you light. But listen yet longer to what is not so agreeable.

Brothers: Need I tell you, who know so well, what strife there is all around you? How your father, the President, is pressed to buy your lands? Need I tell you that it is because your country is surrounded, and pressed upon all sides by the whites, that he has so much trouble to keep you from being crushed by them? Need I tell you that your friends everywhere are full of anxiety about you? I am sure I need not. You know all this, and you feel it in your hearts, and it makes you sad!

Brothers: When you are asked to exchange your country, and leave it, and go to another, you remember the past, and think of your fathers. You say, "Here lie the bones of our fathers, and here has been the home of our infancy, and we love this country." This is honorable to you. It is proof that you have hearts, and that you are men. I think the more of a man who cherishes in his heart a sacred remembrance of his father and mother, and who loves the land which covers their bones.

Brothers: All that is noble: but then you are not to forget your children, and your children's children. Your fathers are no more—their spirits are gone up to the Great Spirit. What remains of them is but dust. They feel not, and care not, whether the foot of the red or the white man treads upon their graves. But your children live, and they feel, and they will feel, down to the latest generations.

Brothers: Whilst, then, you cherish a sacred remembrance for the bones of your fathers, forget not to provide for your children, and never stop a moment, but hasten with all speed to place them in a situation that will secure them against the evils that your fathers have endured, and from the sorrows that fill and afflict your own hearts. This, brothers, is wisdom. The past, I know, has been cloudy and dark enough; but, brothers, be not discouraged: the Great Spirit will yet open your way, and shine upon your path.

Brothers: Am I too long keeping you from a sight of that path? Be patient, and I will show it to you in good time.

Brothers: It was but the other day that you met commissioners who were sent to buy your country—you know what passed between you on that occasion. Now, brothers, I admit that no people ought to be asked to exchange their situation, without a certain prospect of realizing a better; but no people should be so unwise, if an offer is made that *will* better their condition, to reject it. That, you know, would be foolish, and men do not act so. Men always are seeking to do better. That is right; and it was to improve, and do better, that the Great Spirit put man on the earth.

Brothers: I am not for the Indian's taking the white man's word in an affair of bargain and sale, but I advise him always to examine for himself. As your friend, I tell you, now, always hear attentively, and then examine closely, and then decide; and when you convince yourselves that you can make a good bargain, make it, but be careful.

Brothers: I know I am your friend—I have even suffered for being so—yet I would not ask you to take my word in anything affecting your present or future welfare; but I would prefer that you should examine well into such momentous subjects for yourselves. All I feel free to do, is to shed light upon your destiny; and, as a brother, *advise;* and were I not to do this, I should not be worthy to be called your friend.

Brothers: I wish to counsel you as men, and not as children; and I am mistaken, if your wisdom will not lead you, by the light of this council-fire, to adopt my counsels, so far as these may go; and I shall take care that they shall go no farther than they ought. I will point out your path, and show you the way to honor and prosperity. It will be left to you to walk in it, or take another.

Brothers: It is said, since you did not agree to the proposals of the commissioners, that you are a self-willed and obstinate people. I do not believe it. But many people, who do not know you as well as I do, may incline to think this true. This, as far as it may be believed, will lessen the number of your friends; and these are few; *you have not to spare.* Now, I wish you to put it out of the power of anybody to say so. I wish you to take such steps as shall convince the world that you are a people who require no more, when an offer is made to you, than that your acceptance of it should improve your condition, and put you out of reach of the evils that have afflicted you in the past, and make sure your prosperity for the future. When, by your conduct, you do this, you strike a stroke that will break down the power of your enemies, and this will make your friends numerous and strong, and make sure your prosperity wherever you may be.

Brothers: Is not all this reasonable? Have I said a single word that is not exactly agreeable to your own views? Do you not feel in your hearts that what I say is the truth?

Brothers: I see the causes of your weakness and poverty—I see why it is that your fathers never maintained their ground, and the reason why you are as you are. I will tell you.

Brothers: Here you are on a piece of land surrounded by a great and powerful nation. In that nation you see a distribution of honors and appointments to office, in the state, in the army, and in the navy. You see the white man and his children flourish and prosper all round you, and made great; then you look round on yourselves, and on your children, and your hearts sink in you because you are shut out from all these, and are no people. You feel no emulation; you give up, and say, what's the use of it? An impassable mountain is between our people, and the honors and profits which the whites enjoy; they flourish and prosper, but we fade away, and decay, and die, like our fathers!

Brothers: THERE IS A CAUSE FOR THIS.

Now listen, and I will tell you what that cause is—Open wide your ears, and I will tell you how to break down that mountain, and then you will see the path with light shining upon it, for you and your children to walk in.

Brothers: When you were asked by the commissioners to exchange your country, *that was your time:* then you had an opportunity of making yourselves a great people, and in all respects like the whites. That was your time to have put your feet on strong ground that never would have slipped from under them more.

Brothers: Our country, you might have said, is good enough for us. We are contented, so far as that is concerned; but as you want it, you may have it, if you will agree to our terms. You ought to have told them, like all other people, we wish to better our condition. Show us how we are to do this, make it plain to us, prove it, and we will exchange. You might have asked if the country they offered you, is healthy? if it is rich? if the water is plenty and good? and if it is well wooded? If it is, point it out to us, and we will go directly and examine it; and then, you might have said, if we like it we will exchange, provided you will agree to make us a people, by your first marking it out to us, acre for acre, for ours, and then dividing it into counties: leaving a good piece in the centre for a seat of government; and provided you give us parchment for our farms, that we may choose within that country; you driving everybody from it, and provided you guarantee it to us *forever*, with the right to sell to our brothers,* by permission of our great father, the President of the United States; and provided you put us up there houses, and mills, and fences, and work-shops, as good as we have got here; and provided you will give us stock there as we have it here; and provided you establish schools in all the counties, sufficient for the education of our children, and to teach our girls how to spin, and manage household affairs; and provided you send a force there to protect us from danger; and organize our people into companies like your militia, to be commissioned by our great father, the President of the United States; and then establish a government over us, suited to our condition, with plain good laws, like one of your territories—and then give our people the right of suffrage, as they may be prepared by education to vote and take part in the government; and then allow us, after the territory is organized, to send a delegate to Congress, like your territories; and give us here a few reservations for people who may want them; and then we will exchange, if, after we look at the country, and examine it well, we like it—you paying the expense of our going to see it, and when we go, of our removal to it. Make us in this way, you might have said, a people, and part of yourselves—give us and our children the hope of rising above the sorrows and sufferings, and degradation of the past—secure to us our privileges as members of the great family of man—and then we will go.

Brothers: An answer like that, would have been the proper answer. You see in it the ground-work of your future greatness as a people. You see it includes everything.

Brothers: It is this I have been aiming at for you. This is your path, and the light of reason, of justice, and of Heaven, shines upon it.

Brothers: I will suppose the commissioners had rejected such terms—what then? why, you would have convinced the world that you are not a self-willed and obstinate people. You would have made your friends strong, because you would have asked nothing but what is just, and in doing so, you would have broken the power of your enemies.

Brothers: I now put my finger on a country†—will you not go and look at it? Should it turn out to be sickly, or poor, or not be sufficiently watered, and not well

* Meaning Indians.

† The map was open, and before me.

wooded—and should you be able to find no good country, why, then, who could ask you to leave your own? No good man would wish to impose it upon you to go to a country that you could not live in—and then, should that be the case, that there is no suitable country, why the next step would be to improve you all here as fast as possible, that the distinction which exists now, might exist no longer—for you know, as many of you can read, that one great reason urged against your improvement, is, that if you are improved, you will be less likely to part from your lands.

Brothers: Am I understood? Do you feel the force of my remarks? Have I opened the way for your eyes to see your future greatness? It is not yet too late. But perhaps you doubt whether anything so good could be granted? *That is precisely what I want you to authorize me to try.* I wish to carry home such an answer, as I have told you ought to have been given to the commissioners, to your great father. Let your terms be stated—say how you will treat for your lands—and thus decide the question.

Brothers: Say to me, for the sake of your children, and children's children, that you will go quick and look at the country—fix the day, and let it be the first of next May. Now, let me tell you, is your time. The time for such terms never came before, and it may never come again. Take hold of it, then—and if you think I know anything, and am your friend, put such a paper in my hands to take home with me. It may secure your future happiness, which is what I want, and your children's prosperity forever—and this will serve to make amends, in some way, for the sufferings of the past.

Brothers: If you do not, I shall still fear—for the storm about Indian's lands is terrible indeed! I wish to screen you from it.

Brothers: I have done—I pray the Great Spirit to direct you.

Answer of the Chickasaw Chiefs to Colonel McKenney's talk.

Council-Room, Chickasaw Nation,
October 9, 1827.

Brother: We have opened our ears wide to your talk; we have not lost a word of it. We came together to meet you, as an old friend, and to shake hands with you. We were happy, and our hearts grew big, when we heard you had come to our country. We have always thought of you as our friend; we have confidence in you; we have listened more close, because we think so much of you; we know well you would not deceive us, and we believe you know what is best for us, and for our children.

Brother: Do not you forsake us. Our friends, as you told us, are few, we have none to spare; we know that.

Brother: You think it will be better for us to take your advice. It has truly made deep impressions on our hearts. Without making a long talk, as you are to leave us in the morning, we will state our terms for an exchange of country. We have no objection to our country; if we could be let alone, we might do well; but we are great sufferers; everything seems against us, and we will agree to almost anything that can make our condition better. We believe, if the government of the United States is honest towards us, and wish us to be a people, and not outcasts always, that we may yet do better. We will now tell you what we will do.

Brother: You would not wish us to move away, and into a country where we could not live, and as well as we live here. Then, as you have pointed us out a country, on the north of the State of Missouri, and between the Missouri and Mississippi river, and speak well of it, we agree, first and foremost, to go and look at it, and any other country that we may choose; when twelve of our people, three from each district, have examined it, assisted by a scientific doctor, to see to our health; and by three good white men, to be selected by ourselves, and three of your men of science, from Washington or elsewhere; we say, when we have examined it, if we like it, if its soil is good, and well wooded; if water is plenty and good, we will agree to exchange acre for acre, provided you, on your part, will mark out the country, and divide it into counties, and leave a place in the centre for a seat of government; and then drive everybody off it, and guarantee it to us forever; and as soon as may be, divide it for us into farms, and give us a parchment for them to be recorded, with a right to sell to our brothers, with the consent of our father, the President of the United States. And provided, also, that in addition, you examine our houses, and mills, and fences, and our workshops here; also, our orchards, and build, and put up, and plant as good there, at such places, within the territory, as we may choose. Also, provided you count our stocks here, and put an equal number, of each kind, within their respective owners' limits there. Also, provided you establish schools in all the counties, sufficient for the education of our children, and to teach our girls how to spin and manage household affairs; and provided, also, you send a sufficient force there to insure our protection, and organize our people into companies, like your militia, to be commissioned by our father, the President of the United States; and provided that you establish a government over us, in all respects like one of your territories, (Michigan, for example,) and give the right of suffrage to our people, as they shall be prepared by education to vote and act; and allow us, after the territory is organized, a delegate, like your territories enjoy, in Congress; and provided there be allowed, to some of our people, reservations, not exceeding twenty, to be surveyed, and given to them on parchment, to sell, if they please, like the white man.

Brother: Grant us these terms; better our condition as a people; give us the privileges of men; and if the country you point us to, or any other we may find, turns out to be acceptable to us, we will treat for exchange upon the above basis. We ask, also, for a millwright, and three blacksmiths; they will be needed by us.

Brother: We are willing to go next May, in steamboats, from Memphis to St. Louis, and thence over the line, and examine the country thoroughly; and, on the following spring, then we shall know all the seasons, and how the climate is. Should you think proper to take us at our offer, provide the means, and let us know the time, (say by the first of April next;) the cost is to be yours, and everything; and each of our people, who may go, must have a fine rifle, and horn, and powder, and lead, and plenty of things for an outfit, in provisions, and tobacco, and blankets, and the like.

Brother: Should our offer not be accepted, then we are done. We hope to be let alone where we are, and that your people will be made to treat us like men and Christians, and not like dogs. We tell you now, we want to make our children men and women, and to raise them high as yours, in privileges: we will have inducements then to do so; now we have not.

Brother: Understand, nothing is done, unless the country we go to look at suits; and not then, unless all we require is agreed to on your part.

Brother: We shall shake hands with you, and our hearts go with you.

Tish-a Mingo, his + mark.
William M'Gilvery, his + mark.
Levi Colbert, his + mark.
Committee of the Nation.
Stimo-luct, his + mark.
Pus-ta-la-tubbee, his + mark.
Ma-taash-to, his + mark.

Witness:

Pitman Colbert, *Secretary.*

To Col. Thomas L. McKenney.

Col. McKenney's reply to the Chickasaw Chiefs.

Council-Room, Chickasaw Nation,
October 9th, 1827.

Friends and Brothers:—I have received, and read your answer to my talk to you of this morning. Having no power to conclude an agreement with you, I have to state in answer, that I will lose no time in laying before your father, the President of the United States, the terms on which you propose a compliance with his wish to see you a happy people on lands west of the Mississippi. So soon as he makes your views known to his great council, he will direct an answer to be made to you.

In return for the confidence you have expressed in me, and for the promise that your hearts will go with me, I have to assure you that your confidence is not misplaced. In me you have always had a friend, and I hope always to remain so. I will never advise you but for your good.

I will bear in mind that the hearts of the Chickasaw chiefs go with me: and this will make my journey home the more agreeable; for the hearts that go with me are the same that have stood by my country in the hour of danger, and often fearlessly entered the battle-field in defence of American rights and liberty. It is not possible but that I should wish you and your posterity every possible prosperity and happiness.

I shake hands with you, and pray the Great Spirit to preserve and bless you.

Your friend and brother,
[Signed] Thomas L. McKenney.

To Tish-a Mingo, Levi Colbert, and other Chiefs of the Chickasaw Nation.

(F.)

Department of War,
Office of Indian Affairs, May 1, 1829.

Dear Sir—Whatever relates to our Indians will, I know, be interesting to you. Indeed, the subject is one which takes hold not only of your feelings and the feelings of your Board, but of other associations similarly organized, and also of the feelings of the good citizens of our republic, generally. All unite in the wish to see those people rescued, and elevated into a participation of the blessings of the civilized and Christian state. The question is, how can this be best accomplished? Now, we know, men often agree in regard to various matters as to the *end*, but often differ as to the means for its accomplishment. This is precisely the case with this Indian subject. All desire to save the remnants of this once mighty race, but the means have not, I humbly conceive, been as yet exactly hit upon—at least they have not been carried out fully. If I am not mistaken, I will be able, in the course of this letter, to lay bare to you the cause, to a great extent, of the present degraded state of this people. To make manifest the evil, will make manifest also the remedy. I do not mean to be general in my remarks, but apply them chiefly to one great point—and that relates to their landed possessions within our States and organized Territories; and the necessary, but fatal connection of the Indians, arising out of that relation.

For myself, I have always viewed the subject of our Indian landed possessions, and the relation which these bear to our States and Territories, as full of interest, and pregnant with difficulty. All that I have felt of hope for the preservation and improvement of our Indians, has been clouded with fear, that the time would arrive, when, between them and the States, and the General Government, the issue would have at last to be tried. It cannot have escaped the observation of those who have paid attention to this subject, that the right of the Indians to the lands held by them, is but a *possessory* right; and that whatever guarantees may exist, as they do in our treaties, these cover no more than a right of this sort. *It could not have been otherwise.* To interpret these guarantees by any other rule, would be to decide that sovereignty should be set up against sovereignty—the sovereignty of the Indians against the sovereignty of the States. It never was so meant. Whenever, then, with a view to the cultivation of their local resources, or for an extension of power, the States should feel their Indian population to be burdensome, it was most clear that this feeling would, in some way, manifest itself. At first, it was natural to suppose it would be disclosed in acts of the legislatures, extending over the Indians, as one attribute of sovereignty, their respective laws. This, in two of the States, Georgia and Alabama, has been actually done. The laws of the latter are now in full operation; those of the former are prospectively enacted, and are to take effect in 1830. In this state of things, it was natural to suppose the Indians would look, *under their mistaken conception of the nature of the guarantee*, spoken of in treaties with them, for protection, from the operation of those laws, to the Federal Government; nor was it less natural that they should be, whensoever the question should be raised, undeceived in regard to this matter—since it could never have been contemplated that the General Government would bare its arm, and go forth with an array of power to contend against the exercise of any one attribute of sovereignty of any one of the States. The States having made no grant, expressed or implied, to the Federal Union of the kind, it was not to be expected that the General Government would *assume* the power.

I have never before, I believe, attempted to place this subject before you in this light, but looking more to the *issue* of the question, I have, from time to time, urged upon you, and the friends of Indian improvement, generally, the importance of so enlightening the Indians as to show them clearly the very delicate, nay, hazardous, relation in which they stand to the States, within whose bosom they are. I never doubted, nor do I now doubt, that if they were made to see the peril of this relation, they would seek to establish a better one upon a different basis than that which secures their lands to them, as *possessory tenants*, *only;* and this would lead them west of our States and Territories, where *every sort of guarantee* could, and I doubt not *would,* be given to them; and every protection and blessing within the power of the General Government to confer, extended to their race. Upon such a basis, only, can they expect to be preserved, and improve themselves, or be improved by others. Need I stop to demonstrate how utterly impracticable it is to remodel the Indian character, and fashion it after the civilized form, situated as are those tribes who are within our States? Where is the example of a single transformation in a tribe of this sort? I know of not one. But I know of many in which, even amidst efforts the most untiring, the Indians have (although individuals have profited) disappeared, until now many of our States, that once swarmed with an Indian population, contain not a vestige of one! Whence comes this decay, and final disappearing of the red before the white man? It comes not of the color, nor of physical or moral malformation; nor of destiny—but from causes the most natural, which a change in our relations to each other would work, even upon us. The elements may all be found to lie in the *intellectual, moral, political* and *social* relations which exist between them and us. It would require a volume to descant upon these. I will merely touch each, and pass on.

Who does not see the effect of intellectual superiority, even among our own citizens? And where we see one absolutely superior, and another absolutely inferior, does not the consciousness of that inferiority, in the person feeling it, depress his energies, and paralyze his efforts? Do we not see this daily? Now, why should a different result of the same cause be looked for in the Indian? But the relations between the white man and the Indian stop not here. The latter finds himself *always* the victim of that intellectual superiority, and feels that he *must* always remain so. Bereaved in the past, by superior tact, he feels that he is no less so in the present; and what he sees of the future is even more hopeless still. The existence of this relation alone, did it stop here, would, in time, work his overthrow—but there are others. The moral energies which will sustain, to a degree, even conscious inferiority, are not felt by the Indian. To these, he is almost a stranger. And where does he derive anything but depression and despair, when he sees the political distinctions enjoyed by the white man by his side; the high honors to which he is elevated; the privileges which these confer, and the freedom they entail? Is there anything in this view calculated to inspire him with the spirit of emulation?—to rouse him to action, and to the performance of deeds of virtue, or of renown? Far from it. If he be human—and that he is, none will deny—what must he feel when even his *oath* is not deemed worthy to be taken? Can a human heart beat free when oppressed by such degradation? Must it not sink into despair? And what then? We all know. But the Indian has to endure one more thought. It is the total impracticability of his ever participating in those refinements of the social state, which are the necessary result of the white man's superiority over him, in intellectual, moral, and political advantages. If there had been any light left to shine, although but dimly, on his prospects, this would obscure it, and shroud his prospect in the deepest gloom. Well, then, this is the relation in which the red man stands to his more cultivated white brother.

This, however, is but one side of the question. There is another: the action of the white man *upon him.* The first is the worm within, eating out his vitals—the last the storm that crushes the shell which the worm may not have devoured. This comes of the same elements. The Indian is seen to be degraded; and unfortunately for man, it is too true, there is the disposition in his nature to exercise upon such, cruelty, injustice and revenge. Will any one suppose it possible that thus situated, the Indians can exist? much less, rise into that high state, as to take station alongside of our citizens? If they could, then would they demonstrate themselves to be *more than human.*

I assume it, then, that the Indians cannot be saved and elevated in their condition, without a change in existing relations. But to return.

I did certainly look to the period when the issue between the States and their Indian population would be tried. I have for some time past seen the elements forming, out of which the question would arise. I supposed it highly probable the next Congress would be applied to; and that it would have been then decided. The Cherokees, I supposed, would bring it up. They have presented it. It has been accelerated by the very efforts of some of their best informed, to improve their own condition, and that of their people, in the constitution and laws they have framed and adopted. *Sovereignty* was here sought after, and the States, it was to be expected, would meet the attempt at its exercise. Hence the State of Georgia extends her laws over them, as an intimation of where the sovereign power does lie. "If," as Georgia no doubt reasoned, "these people are competent to self-government, they can receive and act under our own laws." The Indians, alarmed at this act of Georgia, have appealed to the President of the United States, to interfere and save them from the consequence of the operation of those laws. The appeal has been promptly met, and the matter decided. The Secretary of War, in the name of the President, tells them what they wish cannot be done—the government of the United States will not resist Georgia in this exercise of her sovereignty. *The die, therefore, is cast!*

The grounds on which the question is met by the Secretary, are the following:—

1st. These people, the Cherokees, were arrayed against us, and in league with Great Britain, in the war of the Revolution.

2d. With the fall of the British power, fell their power; and with the extinguishment of the British rights, was extinguished their rights.

3d. By the treaty of peace with Great Britain, sovereignty was acknowledged to be in the United States, over all the territory over which the British crown had previously exercised it; no reservation is made in favor of those Indians, vesting in them any attribute to sovereignty;—but

4th. The United States gave peace, three years after the pacification with Great Britain, to the Cherokees, and *took them under the protection of the Union, and into favor.* Limits were allotted to them, within which, (as *possessory occupants,*) they were permitted to live and hunt, and a guarantee given.

5th. Subsequently to the pacification, and between 1785 and 1791, those same Indians waged war upon our border population. This was a treaty of peace and of limits; and in this treaty the Cherokees were again taken under the protection of the Government of the Union, and their limits guarantied to them, as possessory occupants, however, *and of course,* for the reasons which I have hastily glanced at.

6th. Those limits, embracing in part certain portions of the jurisdictional limits of Georgia, it became necessary for an understanding to be had between the United States and Georgia, on the subject, which resulted in a compact, (in 1802,) in which the United States pledged to possess Georgia of her territory, as soon as it could be done upon peaceable and reasonable terms. Thus it appears that so far back as 1802, it was fixed (as the compact fully implies,) that not the Indians, but Georgia, held the right of sovereignty; and the Indians retained the soil, only as *possessory occupants.*

Under those several heads the Secretary of War has, with great force and clearness, and in a spirit of frankness, surpassed only by its kindness, demonstrated the true state of the question. He tells the Cherokees that whilst the General Government can never oppose Georgia in the exercise of her right of sovereignty, it will protect them in the full enjoyment of all their possessory rights.

He then presents to them two alternatives—one is, to come under the laws of the State, the other to emigrate; and advises them to adopt the latter. He then adverts to the power of the General Government, to establish them upon a different basis, on the lands west of our States and Territories, west of the Mississippi; and expresses a readiness on the part of the General Government to protect them there, and invest them with *such rights and privileges as will preserve and elevate them as a people.*

Now this is precisely the end at which every friend to the Indians should aim. It is worse than useless to take other ground. It is unkind, nay, unmerciful to the Indians, to do it. That they cannot exist in their present relations to us, I think has been shown; to flatter them with the belief to the contrary, would be fatal. The past proves it, and the present teems with admonition. Nothing could be more kind to these people, than the frank and firm answer which has been given to them. It requires, however, to make it effectual, that the bodies of citizens who have associated to meliorate and reform the condition of these people, as also all who really wish well to them, should heartily co-operate in convincing them of the destroying effects of their existing relations, and of their necessary, and final, and fatal issue, and of the vast benefits which would flow to them from a change.

I glanced rapidly, in a previous part of this letter, at the elements of those causes which are working the destruction of those Indians who reside within our States and organized Territories. You may, perhaps, expect me to say something upon the subject of those preserving influences, which would operate to save them, were they to withdraw from within their present limits; and also of a plan of operations for their advancement, and reformation, and prosperity as a people.

Three of the four southern tribes who are more immediately concerned in this question, to wit: the Choctaws, Cherokees, and Creeks, have now, west and north of Arkansas, and west of Missouri, a country which, on recent examination, is represented to be in soil, climate and salubrity, unexceptionable. The Chickasaws and the Choctaws, being neighbors in their present possessions, and the Chickasaws numbering only about four thousand souls, would, there is no doubt of it, be received gladly by their Choctaw brothers; and the Government would doubtless compensate the latter for this accommodation. The Creeks have already expressed their willingness to receive the Seminoles of Florida. Here, then, is a home for all those southern Indians, unexceptionable in all respects, and even desirable.

In the occupancy of this country, those Indians would be at once relieved from the direct action of those elements, which, as I have shown, beat so destructively upon them in the States. This negative result would prepare them at once for an action of another sort, and what this ought to be, I will now briefly state.

They should hold those possessions in the west by a tenure as durable as time; and the guarantee of the Union ought so to secure them in such right. Their lands should be divided and parcelled out among all the families. The frame-work, at least, of a government, ought to be immediately placed over them, for their protection and improvement. In the administration of this government they should participate. Their relation to the Union should be that of one of our Territories; and the entire scheme should look to their elevation to the enjoyment of all the privileges of American citizens, civil, political, and religious. They should be assisted in their agriculture, and encouraged to cultivate the ground. Schools should be distributed over all their country. The children should be taken into these, and instructed, in addition to the usual branches, reading, writing and arithmetic, in mechanics and the arts; and the girls in all the business of the domestic duties. They should have the Gospel; and be enlightened as they could bear its rays at this great source of light and blessedness. In a word, the work of their preservation and improvement, and happiness, ought to be undertaken in earnest, persevered in with diligence, and followed out in all those departments which govern *us* in our rights, and privileges, and advancements.

For their property here, they should be justly paid;—but in money to those only who would husband it to improve their western homes. Others less enlightened, and less provident, should have it applied for them in building their houses, fencing their fields, buying them cattle, hogs, poultry, &c., &c., implements of husbandry, and articles for domestic use.

Now can any one doubt, who knows the present unhappy and depressed condition of our Indians, that this removal, and this system, would not lift them in a single generation to a level with ourselves? But suppose any should doubt the happy issue of such experiment? To such, I would put the questions: Does not the present wretched condition of these people demand the adoption of *some* effort to save them? And if something is not attempted, is it not plain that while we are reasoning in the forum, the enemy, having scaled the walls, is within the city, devastating and whelming it in ruins? My own opinion is, and I speak from a personal knowledge of the condition of most of our Indians, that the crisis has arrived in which they are to be *saved or lost!* The call of humanity is loud in their behalf. Justice also demands for them a last resting-place for the soles of their feet; and the Union, in dread of the final and fatal issue, demands that the stain of permitting these people longer to suffer, and finally to *perish*, may be not found on its ermine, to be regretted and deplored by posterity.

But the questions may be asked, will all this be recognized by the Government? Will the Congress sanction such a provision? and will the Indians accept it? To the first I answer, *I have not a doubt of it.* To the second, it is my sincere belief that it will; and to the third, all that can be done by their friends, is to labor to induce them to do so. If they shall persist in refusing to accept terms like those I have glanced at, and which, perhaps, may be made still more inviting, then the reproach of being idle, and letting the Aborigines of North America perish, will be wiped off; and posterity will recur with gratification to the honest efforts of their forefathers to arrest so great a calamity. All that can be required of any individual in a righteous cause is to exert his best efforts—if these fail, then he is blameless. So with nations; and although history may often overlook the honest efforts of individuals, in the cause of humanity and justice, her eye is wide open to national acts, and these she will be sure to record, and to convey to posterity. Our country is deeply concerned in the question of saving our Indians, or permitting their destruction. I believe it has the power to accomplish the one, and avert the other. Dreadful will be the responsibility if it shall not act!

If the answer of the Secretary of War to the Cherokees, which conveys to them the decision of the President, shall awaken these people to a sense of their real situation, and induce a wish in them to change it, much will have been done towards the accomplishment of the end which we all have in view: viz. the *preservation*, *improvement*, and *happiness* of our Indians.

I am, dear Sir,
With great respect and regard,
Your friend,
THOMAS L. MCKENNEY.

(G.)

T. L. McKenney to the Secretary of War.

CHOCTAW AGENCY, October 17, 1827.

Sir—I had the honor of writing to you, by the last mail, from this place, that I expected to hold a council with the Choctaw chiefs to-day. The arrival of Colonel Leflore, at an earlier hour of the afternoon of yesterday than I expected, enabled me to convene the council a little before sun-down, which I was the more anxious to do, from the peculiar slow movements of Indians; the tedious process of passing through the mouth of the interpreter what may be to be said; and above all, from my increasing anxiety to get home.

I was aware that I should have some obstacles to contend with, of a new and imposing character, and such as it was doubtful whether *any* thing could move. I knew that two chiefs, *Mushulatubbee* and *Cole*, had been displaced to make way for Colonels Folsom and Leflore, and on the express grounds that they were to resist *any and every proposition* that might be made to the nation, for a sale or exchange of territory. Then, again, I saw difficulties in the plan of inviting them to another country, other than that which they already claim in Arkansas; and difficulties, (on the ground of the objections of that territory to Indians forming part of its population,) in pointing them to their lands there; for to do this would destroy the harmony of the plan of uniting them under one head, in a territory, on the plan as approved by the Chickasaws. I concluded, finally, that all things should give way to the proposition as made to the Chickasaws, hoping that their acceptance of it might act as an encouragement, and produce, *if not a prompt acceptance*, at least a willingness to break ground under cover of some pretext, so as to co-operate, actually, in the plan accepted by the Chickasaws, though by *seeming* to reject it. I thought I saw this much, in my first interview. It was afterwards confirmed. The chiefs were bound, I discovered, to reject, *openly*, any proposition of the sort, or bring upon themselves the charge of inconsistency, and possibly the rebuke, if not chastisement, of the nation. I, nevertheless, resolved to try; and I accordingly addressed them, in the main, upon the same ground as stated in the copy of my talk to the Chickasaws, adding some reasons derived from the question of State sovereignty and State rights, and of their operation upon them, and in the simplest forms. It made a deep impression. ——— came to my room, and conversed with me till twelve o'clock at night, palliating his intended objections to the propositions, and yet manifestly approving them. He is an intelligent man, and withal ambitious, though honorably so, and felt the influence of the prospect which a government, and the proposed provisions, held out for his people, as, indeed, did ———, who is also a man of vigorous intellect. But I anticipated the answer which I should receive from them *in council*, and meanwhile prepared to elude its force. Indeed, one of the ——— told me, in plain terms, it was not possible for the chiefs even to *seem* to approve it, as, before another day, the opposition (meaning the party who had been *unchiefed* by them,) would declare they had *sold* their country, which, if it did not result in shooting them by the way-side, or cutting their throats, would lose them their influence, and *put it out of their power, after the country should be examined and approved, to lead their people to it, as proposed.* He added, it would be much easier to have persons go under any other form, get their report, *and treat afterwards.*

On receiving their verbal answer in counsel, (which I have the honor herewith to enclose in writing, marked A,) I made a reply pretty much in substance like the answer herewith enclosed, marked B, in which I concluded by the proposition to them to send two men from each of their districts, (six persons in number,) to accompany their elder brothers, the Chickasaws; when they might return by the way of Arkansas, and see their country and their friends there. I told them, I made the offer on the grounds that their great father would approve of it, and purely to oblige them; but that I could not promise anything until it should be sanctioned at Washington. You will see their answer on this head in the paper marked A.

I am decidedly of opinion, from all I can gather, and I have literally sifted these people, that nothing but the recent change in the chiefs, or rather their pledges to the nation, kept the council from adopting openly, and fully, and cheerfully, and *unanimously*, the proposition submitted. This plan of a government, and of civil and political privileges, is very agreeable to them, and they think of it with pleasure; yet each feels the possible peril in which a *declaration* might involve him.

They speak much of the failures in the propositions of former times, and doubt the promises made to them. And, whilst upon this head, Leflore went so far in council, (as you may see in the written answer to me,) as to say, in substance, that, "*if the guarantees were with me, from their confidence in my friendship for them, and had not to pass into other hands, the answer might have been different.*"

The way I consider to be fairly open; it will depend wholly upon those who may go with those Indians in search of a country, whether what has been thus favorably commenced, be carried to a successful issue, or shall stop short of it. Upon this part of the subject, I will have the honor to converse with you at large on my return, and to give, at large, in conversation, my reasons for the belief that the Choctaws, as a people, are even now willing to adopt the offer made to them.

The plan of opening the way, and fixing depots, with suitable inducements in accommodations in the Indian territory, and comforts by the way, should *be at once* adopted, and be made ready against the return of those who go to look at the country. There is no difficulty in regard to the country. Of this I will satisfy you.

I shall leave here in the morning, early, rain or shine, and lose no time in seeing the other two tribes, if I can, *but certainly the Creeks.*

I have the honor to be, with great respect, &c.,

[Signed] THOMAS L. MCKENNEY.

Hon. JAMES BARBOUR, *Secretary of War.*

Answer of the Choctaw Chiefs to Colonel McKenney.

CHOCTAW AGENCY, *October 17th,* 1827.

BELOVED BROTHER—We rejoice to have taken you by the hand, and that the Great Spirit above has given you health and strength to perform a long and tedious road. Our hearts are proud—we have attentively listened to your talk; and, after much thinking and consultation, we are sorry we cannot agree to your proposition of yesterday. It was the talk of a friend. We are thankful for your advice—but more than sorry, that we have been unanimous in declining to accept it. It always gives us pain to disagree to a friend's talk—we are poor and blind people, and need much advice and indulgence—you gave us much good advice. If you had the power to do everything, and it had not to go into other hands, it might be different. We have confidence in you—we hope to part friends, as we met friends; and although we do not agree to your proposition for an exchange of country, we would have no objection, if our great father would permit, although not with any view to exchange our country, to let six of our people go with our older brothers, the Chickasaws, and return home by the way of the Arkansas. We make this proposal, because you suggested it in council.

We now wish you a plain and straight path home, and that health and happiness may attend you.

Your friends and brothers,

WA SHA SHI MAS TUBBE, his + mark.
HOOP PA YA SKIT TA NA, his + mark.
RED DOG, his + mark.
DAVID FOLSOM,
TAPENA HOMMA, his + mark.
GREENWOOD LEFLORE,
} *Principal Chiefs.*

E, YAH, HO TUBBEE, his + mark.
AH CHE LU LUH, his + mark.
MITLOKACHU, his + mark.
WILLIAM HAY, his + mark.
JERH FOLSOM, his + mark.
HOLUHBEE, his + mark.
HOK LOON TUBBEE, his + mark.
HOOSH SHI HOOM MA, his + mark.
JAMES PICKENS, his + mark.
OOK CHAUH YAH, his + mark.
P. P. PITCHLYNN, *Secretary pro tem.*
M. FOSTER, Jr., *National Secretary.*

To Colonel T. L. MCKENNEY.

Colonel McKenney's Reply to the Choctaw Chiefs.

CHOCTAW AGENCY, October 17th, 1827.

FRIENDS AND BROTHERS—I have received your answer to my talk, declining to accept the conditional arrangement I proposed to enter into with you in council yesterday. I am sorry for it, because it contained the elements of your greatness, and which, if complied with, would have made you, at no distant day, a great and prosperous people. I do not yet despair of your *asking* for these privileges. This hope comforts my heart. I told you I had come to counsel with you as men, not as children; and to mark out a path for you, and then leave you to walk in it, or take another. Your declining to walk in my path has not changed my feelings towards one of you—but rather increases my anxiety for your happiness.

I thank you for the kindness with which you have received me, and for your good wishes, as expressed for my safety home, over a plain, straight path.

Brothers: I cannot but feel troubled for you—I wish you may escape the thickets, I think I see you may be entangled in—and the dark mountains, in which I tremble to think you must be lost, if you do not rise up and look around you. Let my voice keep sounding in your ears—think of me, and of my counsels; and if you get into trouble, send me word, and, if I can, I will help you. Do not fear—we will part friends. I never will forsake you. I am the red man's friend, and shall always be so.

Brothers: I have no presents with me, but have put means in the hands of your agent to get a few things for your wives and children. They will be few—but they will be marks of my good-will for you, and so I hope you will receive them.

Brothers: You spoke in your talk in council, about your blood having been mingled with our blood in wars, and of your friendship for the American government. I felt that—I know it well—and that is one reason why I want you to be a great people. You deserve to be great, and to enjoy rewards and honors, like our great men. I tell you, I yet have hope. I do not think you will long hold back, but soon (taking my advice,) I shall see you smile over your children, rejoicing to think they are born to the enjoyment of the rights and privileges of our free and happy republic.

Brothers: I will ask your great father to let six of your people, and an interpreter, go with your elder brothers, the Chickasaws; and, on their way home, to visit their friends in Arkansas. I hope he may grant the request.

I shake hands with you, and pray the Great Spirit to preserve and bless you.

Your friend and brother,

[Signed] THOMAS L. MCKENNEY.

To Colonel DAVID FOLSOM, Colonel GREENWOOD LEFLORE, TUP-PE-NA-HOMO, and others.

(H.)

Colonel McKenney to the Secretary of War.

MILLEDGEVILLE, GEORGIA, November 17, 1827.

Sir—I am happy in having it in my power to inform you, that articles of agreement and cession were, on the morning of the 15th inst., entered into, at the Creek agency, with the Creeks, and which were concluded at the moment of the arrival of the stage, which left me no time to announce it from there, which secure to the United States *all the lands owned or claimed by them, within the chartered limits of Georgia.* This agreement is signed by the Little Prince, the head of the nation, and five of his principal men, and is to be binding, when approved and ratified by the President and Senate, on the one hand, and sanctioned on the other by a council of the Creeks, which, it is stipulated in the articles, shall be immediately convened for the purpose. This sanctioning, in council, is required by one of their laws.

I left the articles with the agent, who will attend to the council, and superadd the usual certificate in such cases. The agent having been previously enjoined to prosecute this subject, if possible, to a favorable issue, is joined in the instrument with me. It is due to him that he should be so associated, no less on account of the powers with which I found him vested, than to the zeal with which I discovered he had endeavored to fulfil your instructions with regard to this matter.

I have time only to add, that the condition-money for the land is forty-two thousand five hundred and ninety-one dollars.

I derive an additional gratification in making this communication, from my knowledge of the deep anxiety which you have so long felt to have this controversy settled.

I will make you, as soon after my return as possible, a detailed report of my proceedings under this, as also other branches of your instructions of 28th March last, and 10th April; and submit, also, views of policy in regard to our Indian relations, especially those of the four southern tribes, which have been suggested by a personal inspection of the condition of three of them.

I have the honor to be,
Very respectfully,
Your obedient servant,

THOMAS L. MCKENNEY.

Hon. JAMES BARBOUR, *Secretary of War.*

